STAR TREK.
30 YEARS

RadioTime

D0247400

OFFICIAL COLLECTOR'S EDITION

Contents

2 *Star Trek* **- 30 Years:** It morphed into a pop culture phenomenon – and stayed that way for three decades. A longtime fan examines why *Star Trek* remains so compelling on the big and small screen.

I: THE RODDENBERRY LEGACY

4 **Generation After Generation:** Guest columnist Leonard Nimoy looks back on his early years with *Star Trek* and ponders the effect of Gene Roddenberry's vision on the world.

8 **In the Beginning:** *Star Trek*'s turbulent on-again, off-again voyage to present-day TV admiralty.

12 **The Great Bird of the Galaxy:** Majel Barrett sets the record straight on the myths and misconceptions surrounding her late husband, *Star Trek* creator Gene Roddenberry.

16 **Star Wars No More:** *Federation* alliances have long mirrored the real space race, where competition and paranoia between former enemies have been replaced by co-operation and joint space efforts.

20 **Keeping the Flame:** Rick Berman is the designated torch-bearer, carrying forward the Roddenberry dream.

24 **Haven't We Met in a Parallel Universe?** Some *Star Trek* phenomena are just so good they keep repeating themselves, giving the viewer a constant feeling of déjà vu: alien abductions, return from the dead...

II: BEHIND THE SCENES

28 **100 Influential People in the *Star Trek* Universe:** An annotated who's who in *Star Trek*, listing 100 influential writers, directors, actors, producers, composers, illustrators, set and costume designers, special effects masters, make-up artists and, of course, the fans who have made *Star Trek* endure.

42 **Make It So:** From script to final wrap, our writer follows the making of a *Star Trek* episode from casting and story-idea meetings to props, special effects and photography – with bonus tips for wannabe *Star Trek* writers.

54 **Clothes Encounters:** The evolution of *Star Trek* uniforms, alien costumes and make-up. So long to miniskirts!

58 **Back to the Future:** The gadgets of the 23rd century are appearing everywhere as cell phones and other household devices, forcing *Star Trek* innovators back to the drawing board to stay one step ahead of the future.

64 **The Okuda Files:** Michael Okuda is responsible for all *Star Trek* props, graphics and set pieces, but that doesn't stop him from working in the occasional hidden wisecrack – though you'll have to look closely to catch them all!

66 **Let's Talk *Klingon*:** Linguist Marc Okrand explains the roots of the *Klingon* language, and offers ten *Klingon* expressions written just for *Radio Times* readers. Plus tips on speaking the alien tongue.

III: THE FAN UNIVERSE

70 **Caught in the Act:** Surprise encounters with fans are often more meaningful to the *Star Trek* stars themselves.

74 **Famous Players:** Celebrities reveal how *Star Trek* has changed their lives.

78 **Galaxy-Class Collectibles:** *Star Trek* memorabilia collector Kevin Stevens displays his prize possessions.

IV: EPISODE LOG

81 Your launch point to every *Star Trek* series episode and movie produced to date.

Plus an Exclusive Pull-out Colour Map of Space in the 24th Century!

Star Trek
A vision for the future

Thirty years later and
Gene Roddenberry's hopeful
world view still beams
from the set with no signs
of phasing out

BY **DAVID PEMBERTON**

WHAT PRECISELY IS IT THAT MAKES GENE Roddenberry's still-expanding, fictional television universe so compelling after 30 years on screen?

Hundreds of TV shows have come and gone, even dozens of spacebound shows, yet none has triggered the seismic pop culture tremors caused by *Star Trek*. Witness its phenomenal spinoffs: four series, eight movies, conventions, countless books, T-shirts and software programs... There's something in the shows which instils an almost religious devotion among a great many viewers, and to understand the causes of that rapture is to begin to come to terms with the unprecedented pop cultural event that is *Star Trek*.

Don't forget that when Roddenberry, a former bomber pilot and police officer turned TV writer, was pitching his space opera to the networks in the mid-1960s, he was up against a lot of industry indifference bordering on outright rejection. At the time, science fiction on TV was infantile (witness *Lost in Space*), so there wasn't much early enthusiasm for a show that promised intelligent grownup drama set on a spaceship. Not only was the notion suspiciously unusual, all the network executives could see was the potential cost of the venture – they saw a sea of red.

It was largely at this point, when Roddenberry knew the survival of his vision depended on mollifying the network beancounters at the tepidly-interested National Broadcasting Company (NBC), that some of the defining and most enduring characteristics of *Star Trek* were born. For example, initially Roddenberry imagined a program in which farflung planets were routinely visited, a concept he soon realized would be costly. That's how he arrived at the idea of the spaceship as a largely self-contained dramatic universe and the transporter concept – he had to get his characters on and off the ship somehow. A masterstroke as it turned out: Not only did the transporter process look cool, it was original and it cost a heckuva lot less to replicate than a space shuttle.

Roddenberry also forged the unusual – for a mid-'60s TV sci-fi show – dramatic emphasis on ideas over action. In the absence of hairpin space chases and elaborate extraterrestrials, Roddenberry drew on his training as a writer in American TV's late-'50s Golden Age: He created compelling human drama based on concepts and conflict. And then he conceived the long-enduring, so-called "class-M planet theory."

Faced with the difficult question of how to credibly dramatize contact between the *U.S.S. Enterprise* crew members and extraterrestrials, Roddenberry had two conundrums to settle: how to land on other planets that aren't really required to look like other planets – which could be shot on back lots or nearby locations – and how to account for creatures who, for budgetary reasons, would always have to look at least vaguely humanoid. The "class-M planet" theory also paved the way for what is perhaps the key dramatic element of the entire *Star Trek* universe: the moral investigation of the meaning and limits of human experience.

It goes like this: According to Federation regulation, class-M planets are those which have an atmosphere like Earth. An atmosphere, in other words, where one could breathe. Federation starships could therefore visit and explore class-M planets, thus accounting for the fact that Kirk and company could leave the ship in their Starfleet uniforms and that many of the alien beings they encountered were humanlike.

This too proved dramatically fertile, as it facilitated the driving motor of the entire fictional universe: the interaction of humanoid races as an excuse to conduct the philosophical investigation of the nature of humanity itself. The class-M theory also established the emphasis on verbal and intellectual conflict which made *Star Trek* perhaps the ultimate expression of science fiction for television. Roddenberry was free to steer the program in the direction of chin-to-chin conflict which is the essence of enduring television drama.

That's why it's strange that, apart perhaps from *Star Trek*, *Doctor Who*, *The Prisoner* and currently *The X-Files*, science fiction has so rarely tapped into the narrative potential which is distinct to episodic TV: the potential to develop characters and histories – indeed, universes – as vast and deep as space itself. Roddenberry understood this, and from the beginning *Star Trek* was scrupulous in its attention to dramatic consistency and expansion. With each episode one learned a little more about the nuts and bolts of Roddenberry's fictional future, and the cumulative effect was more like epic fantasy fiction than episodic television. This, of course, was what made the ensuing *Star Trek* cult possible.

To watch this show was to be drawn into a world of such richness and detail it was the TV equivalent of books like the "Oz" and "Narnia" series, or "Dune" and "The Lord of the Rings." The more you watched the more you learned and the more at stake you had in the fiction. It is no wonder that people began to respond to *Star Trek* more intensely than just about any series in network history. Roddenberry in fact created two virtual communities with *Star Trek*: the fictional community of the dramatized future, and the community of viewers – who, like any self-respecting cult, shared their own specialized knowledge and language – who became as dependent on *Star Trek* as it was on them.

To account for the enduring attraction of *Star Trek*, we must look at the world view which developed within this dramatic framework, the *Star Trek* philosophy. But even this can not be discussed without a flashback to its conception, for even today, in the expanded universe that now sprawls across four series and so much else, *Star Trek* still bears the marks of its birth.

First aired in September 1966, *Star Trek* was unveiled during a time of profound uncertainty and conflict: America was by then over its head in Southeast Asia, racial tensions and campus unrest were building daily, and the apocalyptic implications of the Cold War had by then seeped permanently into the public imagination – one button could obliterate the whole kit and caboodle and everybody knew it. In this context, Roddenberry's Kennedy-esque liberalism, with its emphasis on negotiation, diplomacy, racial harmony and interplanetary cooperation was irresistible. By emphasizing the triumph of human decency at a time of epidemic depravity, *Star Trek* reflected

positively on all the hell breaking loose in the here and now. Surely if it was possible for the Federation to negotiate with Klingons – a potent metaphoric combination of the Russians and also, to some, the Viet Cong, the Black Panthers and hippie radicals – it was possible to make peace in the real world. Or so *Star Trek* permitted one to dream.

Besides, Roddenberry's vision was inspirational by definition, for quite simply it implied there was a future. Moreover, a future where all earthly conflict had been resolved, thus freeing humankind to embark on the greatest mythical adventure of them all: the exploration of infinite space. Fittingly, the principles which made this future possible were dramatically put to the test on each show: Would Kirk abandon diplomacy for violence if pushed far enough? Were there times when peace wasn't possible? Could the quality of mercy be strained?

The fact was, it could not, and Kirk and crew – as subsequent Starfleet captains and crews would – passed the test every time. And as they passed these tests of basic human tolerance and decency, so did we, which lent hope to the present and a sense of infinite possibility for the future.

Of *Star Trek*'s distinct pop cultural status only one thing remains to be said, though it may be the most crucial component of its enduring allure of them all. By now, the mythology of fandom in *Star Trek* is as potent as the imaginary future itself, for the *Star Trek* universe as we know it would not exist without its fervent fan base. It was fan pressure which convinced NBC to keep the original series on a third season, fan enthusiasm which turned the syndicated reruns into an unprecedented TV phenomenon, and fan support which begat the movies, *Star Trek: The Next Generation*, *Star Trek: Deep Space Nine* and now *Star Trek: Voyager*. Therefore, simply to watch a *Star Trek* program is to be reminded of the bottom-line democracy of pop culture, the power of viewers to make things possible, to virtually raise the dead. In a way, this is just as reassuring as the vision of a tolerant future itself, for in a world where powerlessness and isolation prevail, *Star Trek* gives us a sense of influence and belonging. ✧

Generation after Generation

Leonard Nimoy ponders *Star Trek*'s enduring appeal and the reasons it has been able to live long and prosper for three decades

BY LEONARD NIMOY

ENE RODDENBERRY'S VISION CAN be described in any number of ways: Idealistic, optimistic, a belief that mankind is endlessly improvable – any of those is applicable. I think the most important element was that Gene could not abide worship of anything but mankind.

For example, Gene and I were talking about the tremendous success of "Chariots of the Gods?" by Erich Von Daniken. The whole idea was that Earth had been visited by ancients from another civilization, and they had created various artifacts that remain on the planet today. Gene was outraged by the concept because, he said, it diminishes the accomplishments of mankind. It suggests that some beings more powerful than man attained certain triumphs that mankind couldn't. And if you believed that, you would never understand how interesting and powerful man is.

He was also very much involved with the idea that man continues to search for God and doesn't find him. In fact, the first *Star Trek* motion picture was dealing with that issue in a way. It was also the subject of a pilot Gene did in 1973 [*The Questor Tapes*], about a robot created by a group of scientists, who, when it is about to be finished and has become conscious in this laboratory, realizes there is terrible dissension among the scientists. They're fighting about who should have control of this robot and its power. Knowing that only one of these scientists is truly his friend, the robot escapes, finishes creating itself, and then goes in search of its friend.

The concept of this character searching for its creator is also true of V'ger in *"Star Trek: The Motion Picture."* Its mission was to collect information and return to its creator.

So Roddenberry was often preoccupied with this issue of man's fundamental quest: Who made me? Who is the higher power? Where is he or she?

Gene was also a marketer, no question about it, and we cer-

tainly had our differences, but the differences were never about these issues. I think he sincerely believed in the timeless principles and values that *Star Trek* portrayed. The central issue, in my opinion, is to discover what mankind is capable of, and to aspire to the best of what we can achieve. *"To boldly go"* – that's what boldly going means to me.

I always saw *Star Trek* as a story about a family, a group of people, Kirk, Spock, McCoy, Scotty and the rest, who set out to seek out ideas and help solve problems, and to report back with information that would be useful to mankind. And in that way, the stories could illuminate people's lives, and through interaction of the characters, show how they treated each other with dignity and professionalism, which is terribly important.

I enjoyed making *"Star Trek III: The Search for Spock"* because it was about loyalty to the family. These people would risk their lives in a dangerous mission because they felt there was a chance – a chance – they could help their friend.

The whole experience of *Star Trek* has been absolutely fascinating. I knew while we were doing the show that it had great merit. There was no way to predict it would go on like this. Admittedly, there were also times when I was very uncomfortable about certain scripts, days when I thought it was awful. We had done better. We did our share of trash, but by and large we had some wonderful moments, great stuff.

Within the Roddenberry universe, it was always possible, perhaps inevitable, that we drew from contemporary world events. When I created the story for *"Star Trek VI: The Undiscovered Country"* for example, it was at the time the Soviet Union was crumbling, and the Berlin Wall had come down. The Klingons had always been a metaphor for the Communist bloc, and I went to Frank Mancuso, who was running Paramount at the time, with the idea of Klingons reaching out to the Federation because they were troubled. They'd

had their own version of Chernobyl, and now they wanted to talk, despite having their own group of hard-liners who were opposed to any contact. While we were shooting the story, in which the Klingon president who has contacted us is assassinated, Gorbachev was placed under arrest during an attempted coup. It was life imitating art, imitating life.

What's interesting to me is the fact that in the Klingons, Gene gave us an adversary just like the Indians and the cavalry in old westerns. They were fierce, great warriors, but unreasonable, macho, territorial, paranoid, hostile – the way Indians were depicted in the 1930s, '40s and '50s in America.

So Gene gave us that adversary, but I think in *"The Undiscovered Country"* I designed the last of the Klingon-as-enemy stories. After someone in the Klingon Empire had reached out, there had to be a shift, and a new approach to Klingon mythology.

There may also be a particularly American attitude in that approach. I had the most shocking experience along those lines in Japan. I was promoting *"Star Trek III: The Search for Spock"* and everything was going well. I was having a good time. I seemed to be well received. One day I was taken to a bookstore for an autographing session and a man was seated in the car with me. He was the translator of the *Star Trek* novels in Japan. He began telling me that the *Star Trek* universe "doesn't work for Japan." In the translations, he had to shift the sociology of *Star Trek* to make it "more acceptable for Japanese readers – *Star Trek* is too democratic!" he said. "Japanese people don't like this! Can't have people discussing with the captain what is right and what is wrong. Captain tells people what to think, how to act, how to function."

Then he said: "Character of Spock is like Samurai warrior. Samurai only use power to extent necessary in given situations. He has discipline, self-control, but you are not correct actor to play this role. Should be Japanese."

I said, "Well, we do have a Japanese actor, George Takei." And he responded, "George Takei not Japanese," meaning he was an assimilated American. I thought, George would be interested in hearing that – he spent time in an internment camp because he was Japanese.

I was outraged – I thought the very essence of *Star Trek* is democracy in the military.

The saddest thing for me in the whole *Star Trek* experience was that Gene Roddenberry could never say to me, "well done." He knew that I had made two *Star Trek* films, and in fact he sat in the screening room to watch *"Star Trek IV: The Voyage Home,"* the most successful of the *Star Trek* movies. It received four Academy Award nominations. But you could never get him to say it. He just couldn't.

Is the world getting any better, as Roddenberry would have us think? Do you remember the poem "Desiderata"? "Whether or not it is clear to you, no doubt the universe is unfolding as it should..." That's what I believe. I look at life now in a most bemused and interested way.

I see the cruelties, I see the pain, the suffering. It's incredible to me that some people are destined to lives of hard labour, deprivation, death, illness. And others are blessed. I'm saddened by it, but I can't pretend it's possible to make everybody's life be what you want it to be. It just doesn't work that way.

You can enlighten, you can improve and be charitable, but there will always be people whose need it is to try and eliminate hunger and suffering, and I think there will always be people who are hungry. I've been asked if playing Spock made me a better person. I hope so. It goes to the issue of why I chose to act in the first place, which coincides with the nature of the *Star Trek* series and the nature of the Spock character in a successful way.

I always go back to a quote by Arthur Miller, who wrote "Death of a Salesman." He said, and I'm paraphrasing, that all plays that we consider important, let alone those we consider great, are concerned with one major theme, and that is: How can a man make the outside world a home?

To me, it's all about the struggles a human being has to go through, to find a way to live in dignity, some sense of self-worth, some sense of fulfilment, some sense of contribution to society.

A producer I've known for many years recently met with the Dalai Lama. And he asked the obligatory question: What is the secret to life and happiness? And the Dalai Lama answered, "A serene heart." And I believe that covers everything. I think I have today the most serene heart I've ever had. At times in my life I've been supremely happy and had moments of loving my work. But each day is special these days, working or not working.

I don't have to be working to have that sense of connection. When I came out here, I was 19 years old, and desperately wanted to be part of this world of acting. And I had 15 years of infrequent work. I used to drive a taxi in the neighbourhood I now live in. I knew no one. I got off the train in Pasadena and walked down the street carrying my suitcase, like an alien.

That's going to leave a lasting mark. Finally, 46 years after getting off that train, I'm OK. I don't have that monkey on my back anymore. ✧

Alien encounters

They're frequently bizarre and always captivating: They're the *Star Trek* aliens. Though light-years from us in appearance, their conflicts with the *Federation* reflect current issues facing mankind. In fact, their histories are often strangely human. —CHRISTOPHER BLAND

The Klingons Proud warriors, with a long-standing military tradition, the Klingons of classic *Star Trek* were drawn as a crude analogy for the Communist bloc – obvious stand-ins for the Union of Soviet Socialist Republics. When John Colicos appeared as the first Klingon, in 1967's original-series episode "Errand of Mercy," the tension between the United States and the Soviet Union was acute, as the threat of nuclear holocaust loomed high on the horizon. The fear and mistrust that long existed between the Klingon Empire and the *United Federation of Planets* mirrored the superpowers' decades-old history of posturing and fear. And Colicos (pictured), with his sinister goatee and dark simmering disposition, was the face at the button of a nuclear missile. In the 29 years since, this war-loving race has emerged as a highly-complex, honour-bound society, and the Klingon storylines – uneasy détente with the *Federation*, attempted coups d'état by the Duras family, and the more threatening return to hard-liner politics in recent *Star Trek: Deep Space Nine* episodes – continue to neatly mirror events in the former Soviet Union.

The Borg Defining maxim: assimilation – the loss of the individual's identity in the face of the all-important collective. The Borg's mission to assimilate civilizations into their one "brain" touched on a pervasive fear of becoming nothing more than a component in a world that was, and is, becoming more computer-ized and – to some degree – dehumanizing (witnessed in such classic episodes as "The Ultimate Computer" and "The Changeling"). The relentless incursion of the Borg didn't address the question of whether or not technology was going to come, but rather *when* it would arrive and how much damage it would inflict on the human condition. In Picard's case, here was a man who would always strive to maintain a sense of individuality and self-worth amid the tendrils of assimilation. *Star Trek* advanced that notion by introducing the very same possibility to the Borg itself, through Hugh, the injured Borg who gained a sense of self (and a name) while convalescing among humans aboard *Starship Enterprise-D*.

The Cardassians and Bajorans Having squandered the resources of their once archeologically-rich civilization, the Cardassians (in photo) pursued military might as a means of conquering other worlds, Bajor among them. Riddled with labor camps, mass exterminations and cultural cleansing, the history of the Cardassian-Bajoran conflict is an all-too-familiar echo of 20th-century Earth, from Nazi terrors to present-day Bosnia. As freedom fighters, the devout Bajorans would call upon their faith to sustain them through the more than 40 years of Cardassian occupation.

The Ferengi Their 285 governing Rules of Acquisition leave few doubts about the Ferengi's latinum-coated pursuit of capitalism. Alas, greed isn't the only human blight on their race; it seems the Ferengi are unapologetic in their discrimination toward women. While females are equals in *Federation* society, the Ferengi (for whom the hammer is a symbol of sexual prowess) view non-Ferengi females strictly in terms of sexual opportunity, and do not allow their own females to wear clothing or aspire to anything more than a domestic role. Among primitive restrictions placed on the other half: Ferengi women may not leave the house, make a profit or learn to read.

Shape-shifters Fluid beings who can transform themselves into anything – animate or inanimate. Shape-shifters were rare in *Star Trek* (though a female shape-shifter did trap Kirk and McCoy in "*Star Trek VI: The Undiscovered Country*") and in *ST:TNG*, but in the fast-paced '90s, shape-shifters (now known as Changelings) are emerging as *DS9*'s paranoia-inducing foe, who can manipulate the usually-tolerant *Federation* to the point where blood-screening is considered mandatory, and bring *Starfleet* to the brink of insurrection within the *Federation*. It's only shape-shifter Odo, the diligent security officer, who provides reassurance and teaches us to trust amid the great uncertainty. ✧

In the beginning

Its launch was uncertain and the original flight path unsteady, but *Star Trek* stayed its course and rose to the zenith of TV history

BY CHRISTOPHER BLAND

THE *STAR TREK* SERIES, SEEMINGLY destined for galactic obscurity after its initial NBC network run was cancelled in 1969, proved to be an amazing success story, on the big and small screen. Its amazing voyage home has been one of near-death experiences and astounding come-backs. Herewith are some of the milestones from the *Star Trek* 30-year log-book.

THE CONCEPT: Gene Roddenberry, bomber pilot-turned-police officer-turned-TV writer, unveils the genesis for the first *Star Trek* on 11 March 1964. Roddenberry (whose credits included episodes of *Dragnet* and *Highway Patrol,* two very successful police dramas in the United States) completed his 16-page outline for a sci-fi series – described as "a *Wagon Train* to the stars" (referring to American TV's popular western series of the '50 and '60s) when NBC cancelled his Marine Corps drama, *The Lieutenant* (where he met Leonard Nimoy, Nichelle Nichols and Walter Koenig). One of the first people to read the outline was D.C. Fontana, Roddenberry's secretary, who'd become a *Star Trek* writer. The seminal sketch placed the U.S.S. *Yorktown* "somewhere in the future," propelled by an adventurous crew: Capt. Robert T. April; a female executive officer, Number One (a role intended for Majel Barrett); and a first lieutenant named Mr. Spock (who was described as a "half-Martian").

THE FIRST PILOT: NBC greenlights $630,000 (£415,000) in September 1964 for the first *Star Trek* pilot, "The Cage." Stepping aboard are Jeffrey Hunter as Capt. Pike, Leonard Nimoy as Spock, and Majel Barrett as Number One. In "The

Cage," Roddenberry renamed the ship the *U.S.S. Enterprise,* and gave Matt Jefferies the task of designing the first vessel, thus establishing the basic look of all of the *Enterprises* to come.

THE SECOND PILOT: In an unprecedented move, NBC opts for a second pilot: "Where No Man Has Gone Before" goes into production 15 July 1965. The network had rejected the first pilot, "The Cage," finding it "too cerebral" and called for major character changes – including the elimination of Spock and the dismissal of Barrett as Number One, which was the second-in-command seat after the captain. Roddenberry won his fight to keep Spock, maintaining the Vulcan role was too important, but the network couldn't accept a female as the second-ranking officer on the bridge (no woman would be first officer in a series until Major Kira stepped onto the deck in *Star Trek: Deep Space Nine*). Jeffrey Hunter bows out, paving the way for Canadian-born William Shatner. James Doohan (also from Canada) signs on as Scotty, while George Takei takes the role of the ship's physicist, Sulu. Among the post-production casting changes, DeForest Kelley is signed aboard as Dr. Leonard "Bones" McCoy, Sulu is made a helmsman, and Nichelle Nichols takes the bridge as Lieut. Uhura – a role that would inspire many fans (including Dr. Mae Jemison, who would be one of the astronauts on the shuttle *Endeavour* in September 1992 – and later guest-star in *Star Trek: The Next Generation*'s "Second Chances" episode). And Spock is given a facial in promotional photographs! Still nervous about the Vulcan's appearance,

NBC publicists doctor photos in a press release giving Spock less conspicuous eyebrows and human ears.

DISAPPOINTMENT JUST BEFORE TAKE-OFF: The *Star Trek* team excitedly awaits the series' 8 Sept. 1966 debut. Disappointment hits. NBC airs "The Man Trap" episode at 8:30 p.m., pitting it against such popular sitcoms – ratings heavyweights – as *Bewitched* and *My Three Sons*. *Star Trek* loses out in the ratings.

FIRST NEAR-DEATH EXPERIENCE: NBC almost cancels the series in December 1966 because of disappointing ratings. To cut their losses, the network considers turning *Star Trek* into a children's show, but a letter-writing campaign (initiated by Harlan Ellison, Frank Herbert and other sci-fi authors) convinces NBC to keep the series on the air.

Problems, unfortunately, continue into late season. In March 1967 – despite major TV award nominations – the network bumps *Star Trek* to a poor Friday-night time slot to make

ORIGINAL STAR TREK *SERIES CAST MEMBERS, WITH* GENE RODDENBERRY, *AT THE SEPTEMBER 1976 NASA ROLL-OUT OF THE SPACE SHUTTLE NAMED THE* ENTERPRISE

room for *Ironside*, a police drama. Rival series, the sitcom *The Andy Griffith Show* and Dean Martin's comedy-variety show, continue to rate higher than *Star Trek*.

ANOTHER THREAT OF EXTERMINATION: Once again NBC considers zapping *Star Trek* after the start of its second season on 15 Sept. 1967 – also remembered as Walter Koenig's first appearance as the Russian Ensign Chekov (it was thought that a young, handsome male with a Monkees haircut would attract more viewers). Fans Bjo and John Trimble, however, stave off cancellation in December by organizing a massive letter-writing campaign that floods NBC offices with hundreds of thousands of responses. The rescue mission works. NBC decides to produce the *Star Trek* series for another year, but chops the budget.

INCOMPLETE ASSIGNMENT: While struggling to keep *Star Trek* on air in 1967, Roddenberry co-writes a pilot script for a new TV series called *Assignment: Earth*, about a space traveller who is determined to save Earth from destruction. He's accompanied by his shape-shifting cat, Isis, and is assisted by a flighty assistant (Teri Garr). NBC rejects the series option; the pilot airs instead as a *Star Trek* episode in March 1968.

MISSION ABORTED: The season première, "Spock's Brain," airs at 10 p.m. on 20 Sept. 1968 – it had originally been slat-

ed for the more attractive 7:30 p.m. time-slot. Poor ratings dog the show, which is bumped four times throughout the season. Despite an outpouring of fan support, NBC cancels *Star Trek*. The final episode, "Turnabout Intruder," airs 3 June 1969. The *U.S.S. Enterprise*'s mission is cut short.

STAR TREK BREATHES AGAIN: Paramount syndicates the classic series (selling it to various networks who broadcast the show simultaneously) in the summer of 1969 after the world watched Neil Armstrong's first lunar walk. Taking the show into syndication, the execs commit themselves to produce the best TV possible. There was also a surge in fans' demand for *Star Trek* memorabilia and magazines. In June 1971, sci-fi devotees Elyse Pines and Devra Langsam convene a gathering of fans in a New Jersey library. Dubbed "The Committee," the group organizes a meeting several months later in Brooklyn College's Gershwin Auditorium – which can barely house the turn-out. New York City hosts the first large *Star Trek* convention in January 1972. Promoters expect 1,800 people; more than 3,000 show up.

A DIFFERENT LIFE FORM: Exactly seven years after *Star Trek*'s first show, the little-known animated version begins its two-season NBC run on 8 Sept. 1973. Garnering an Emmy as the Best Children's Entertainment Series for the 1974-75 season, the show features the voices of all but one of the original cast (Walter Koenig wasn't part of the voice team, but he did write one of the episodes).

THE SERIES THAT ALMOST MADE IT: With *Star Trek* popularity still growing, Paramount lays the groundwork in 1977 for a *Star Trek II* TV series based on the adventures of Capt. Kirk, and signs every original-series cast member except Leonard Nimoy. Paramount had earlier considered either a feature film or a made-for-TV movie that could be produced on a modest budget, but scuttled the idea in 1977 when George Lucas stormed the box office with his special effects show-stopper "Star Wars." Twelve episodes of *Star Trek II* are written, but none is filmed. There is fierce competition from rival U.S. networks, CBS and ABC among them, for limited advertising dollars. Anticipating poor ad revenues, Paramount shelves the idea. Also in this period, Trekkers Bjo and John Trimble – the couple who staved off *Star Trek*'s cancellation in 1968 – initiate another letter-writing campaign, and convince NASA to name the first space shuttle after the *U.S.S. Enterprise*.

STAR TREK **HITS THE BIG SCREEN:** The entire original-series cast is beamed to the big screen with "Star Trek: The Motion Picture" during the week of 7 Dec. 1979. Paramount, wanting to capitalize on the movie success enjoyed by Steven Spielberg's box-office hit "Close Encounters of the Third Kind," had adapted the *Star Trek II* script "In Thy Image." By the end of 1996, seven more *Star Trek* movies will be produced.

LIFE AFTER DEATH: The financial success of the movies – over $800 million gross (£528 million) in box office sales and video rentals by 1995 – convinces Paramount to return *Star Trek* to the small screen, and in 1986 the company announces a new series, *Star Trek: The Next Generation*. Leonard Nimoy must decline a producer's position, so Roddenberry takes the executive producer's chair. Ratings climb steadily after the two-hour première of "Encounter at Farpoint" during the week of 28 Sept. 1987. *ST:TNG* quickly attracts a loyal following as Patrick Stewart and cast endear themselves to fans over the seven-season run. The series perseveres even in the face of the 1988 Writers Guild Strike, during which two unused *Star Trek II* scripts are hauled out – one revamped for the series' second-season opener, "The Child." During the week of 29 Oct. 1990, *The Next Generation* surpasses the original series' total of 79 episodes with the première of the 80th episode, "Legacy."

25TH ANNIVERSARY COUPLED WITH TRAGIC LOSS: The *Star Trek* creator dies on 24 Oct. 1991– *Star Trek* 's 25th anniversary. Gene Roddenberry's death is mourned all over the world. On 28 June 1992, William Shatner and Leonard Nimoy commemorate The Great Bird of the Galaxy at Southern California's Anaheim Convention Centre. Also in 1992, the Smithsonian's National Air and Space Museum, in Washington, D.C., hosts *Star Trek: The Exhibition.*

A NEW LIFE: *Star Trek: Deep Space Nine* debuts during the week of 2 Jan. 1993, with the two-hour "Emissary." Created by executive producers Rick Berman and Michael Piller, the show (a sort of space western) gets mixed reviews at first. But fans, fiercely loyal to *ST:TNG*, gradually embrace the *DS9* universe and the remote space station inhabited by Capt. Benjamin Sisko and his diverse crew. Intended to be grittier than *ST:TNG*, *DS9* offers a curious mix of characters (such as Odo the shapeshifter and the dreaded Jem'Hadar) and transforms the Ferengi race from hostile traders to charming schemers.

LONGTIME FAN BJO TRIMBLE APPEARS IN "STAR TREK: THE MOTION PICTURE" WITH WILLIAM SHATNER AS CAPTAIN KIRK

A NEW FLAGSHIP: Paramount launches the United Paramount Network in January 1995 with the *Star Trek: Voyager* series as the flagship. But not without a few scary moments. French-Canadian actor Geneviève Bujold, cast as *Star Trek*'s first female captain of a series, walks off the set after two days. In the mad scramble, Kate Mulgrew steps in as Capt. Janeway. The two-hour opener, "Caretaker," features a gutsy crew tossed into the Delta Quadrant, some 75 years from home. Much like the *ST:TNG* and *DS9* series, *Voyager* initially gets a mixed welcome but soon takes off, partially due to Ethan Phillips as the lovable Talaxian Neelix, and Robert Picardo as the holographic Doctor.

THE CONTINUING VOYAGE: In January 1996, Paramount Studios announces the November release of "Star Trek: First Contact." The film, a follow-up to "Star Trek Generations," will reportedly star *Star Trek: The Next Generation*'s Patrick Stewart, Jonathan Frakes, Brent Spiner, LeVar Burton, Michael Dorn, Gates McFadden and Marina Sirtis – aboard the *Federation*'s newest flagship the *U.S.S. Enterprise-E*, which will *"boldly go"* forth to save Earth from the assimilating Borg. Jonathan Frakes is slated to direct, and Data will further his exploration of human emotions.

ONE MORE CROWNING ACHIEVEMENT: On 24 Feb. 1996, the casts of *Star Trek: The Next Generation, Star Trek: Deep Space Nine* and *Star Trek: Voyager* assemble on stage during a live broadcast of the Screen Actors Guild Awards. Rick Berman accepts, on behalf of the *Star Trek* team, the Guild's Outstanding Portrayal of the American Scene Award for 30 years of diversity in casting, including a balanced representation of seniors, performers of colour, women and people with disabilities. Gene Roddenberry's vision lives on. ✧

The great bird
of the
galaxy

Majel Barrett dispels some
of the myths orbiting her
late husband, *Star Trek*
creator Gene Roddenberry

BY MICHAEL LOGAN

AS ONE OF THE ENTERTAINMENT WORLD'S few true visionaries, *Star Trek* creator Gene Roddenberry soared so high that he was affectionately known as The Great Bird of the Galaxy. But, as with all legends, there are those who want to knock him off his perch. "The myths about him have been written and rewritten and he's been done wrongly so many times," says his widow, actor Majel Barrett. "People get jealous. But there are many people who knew him who think of him reverentially, as do most of the fans, and those are the people who count." Still, she is bothered, in particular, by some of the former Roddenberry associates who co-operated in the writing of *Gene Roddenberry: The Myth and the Man Behind Star Trek*, Joel Engel's 1994 tell-all biography which often paints the maestro in an unflattering light.

"But, you know what?" says Barrett. "Gene never would have gotten mad at the naysayers. He never reacted strongly to anything. He probably would have said, 'Let 'em go ahead and say what they want.' Of course, were he alive, he would be able to get back at them with his own statements. But, then, most of the inaccuracies would never have been written or said because no

MAJEL BARRETT IS REVERED OF THE FAITH FOR HER LATE HUSBAND, GENE RODDENBERRY

one would have ever done it to his face. They all waited to attack until he was gone. I'm sure Gene would have said, 'Consider the source.'"

Dan Madsen, a longtime Roddenberry chronicler and president of the Official *Star Trek* Fan Club, says: "Gene once told me that he wanted the truth to be told about him, as he put it, 'warts and all.' He believed people were not all good or all bad and that's what he created and promoted within the *Star Trek* universe."

Star Trek scenic art supervisor Michael Okuda concurs. "Gene was a man. He did some wonderful, heroic things but he had shortcomings like the rest of us. I think it's inappropriate to lionize him as a hero," says Okuda, who worked closely with Roddenberry on the development of *Star Trek: The Next Generation*. "People are let down when they hear that he had limitations, that he made enemies, that he made mistakes. If you put him – or any other media figure – on a pedestal, you're going to be disappointed." He then adds, "I'm sure Gene enjoyed the notoriety but he didn't set out to be a guru."

However, many of his friends and co-workers consider him to be just that. Actor Leonard Nimoy says he is still astounded by Roddenberry's unflappable belief in his own vision.

"Gene's ongoing battles with the NBC network over the original series remain a classic example of courage in our business – especially so where Spock was concerned," Nimoy recalls. "There was pressure from the network to eliminate or, at the very least, homogenize my character. They could not understand, in their formulaic thinking, how an American family could relate to him. At the time, the thinking was that a show must have a father for the fathers, a mother for the moth-

ers, a couple of teenagers for the teenagers and a pet – and that was your cast. The fact that Gene won that war is a testament to his imagination and theatricality and bravery."

But, notes Dan Madsen, "Gene also won that war because he knew how to pick his battles. At the time of the Spock furore, he had also wanted a female first officer, to be played by Majel Barrett. He agreed to let that idea go by the wayside in order to keep Spock on the show. People forget that one of his greatest talents was his willingness and ability to negotiate."

Many describe him as a real straight-shooter. Actor Michael Dorn, who plays Worf, says: "Gene was the kind of person you could always go to if you needed an answer about your character – and the answer always made sense. There was never any B.S. After he was gone, it was harder to get those answers. *Star Trek* became a conglom-erate." Says Majel Barrett with a laugh: "Gene didn't pull any punches. He didn't necessarily always happen to be right – but at least he'd give you an answer." Roddenberry's longtime crony A.C. Lyles, who was Para-mount's highly-respected publicity chief, remembers that the *Star Trek* creator was accessible to everyone – from the stars to the studio janitors. "Just as he was one among a few, he was also one among equals," says Lyles. "We don't develop a Gene Rod-denberry too often, the same way we don't develop a substitute for gold."

Dan Madsen says Roddenberry "never seemed awed that *Star Trek* had come so far but he was pleased. One time he told me, 'Thank God I have created something that was positive and had morals and stood for something. If I'd created a show where the characters had a 'Hey, man, screw you, get-yours-while-you-can' kind of attitude, I'd feel really bad. If I'd cre-ated something negative that exploded into a phenomenon, I couldn't live with myself.'" Adds Majel Barrett: "There was nothing negative about this man. He was positive to the point of being annoying. To his dying day, he would avoid con-frontation. In doing so, he would leave all sorts of little mess-es behind him, and we would all be running around picking up those messes. Then he'd say, 'See, my way works!'"

In discussing the creation of *Star Trek: Deep Space Nine*, Rick Berman (creator and executive producer of *DS9* and *Star Trek: Voyager* often comments on not seeing eye-to-eye with Roddenberry regarding conflict among core characters (see "Keeping the Flame," page 20). Barrett sees it differently:

> "The myths about Gene have been written and rewritten and he's been done wrongly so many times," says Majel Barrett. "People get jealous. I'm sure Gene would only have said, 'Consider the source.'"

"There was never any real differ-ence of opinion between them. Toward the end of his life, Gene did not want any more of *Star Trek*. He had done enough. He had taught Berman and Michael Piller [*DS9* creator and executive producer] so well that he could sit back and let them do what they wanted." If he would have had any squabbles with *DS9*, they would have been about the space station itself. Says Barrett: "Gene believed that when the people think of space, they think of travel-ling through it, not sitting on a little rock somewhere." For that reason, she says he would have loved *Star Trek: Voyager*. "When I went to the screening of the première episode, I sat there thinking, 'Gee...this looks familiar.' Then I started piecing it together and realized it was an absolute total, almost word-for-word [re-make] of Gene's original pilot 'The Cage.' Afterward, I walked up to Piller and said, 'Michael...!' He said, 'Well...it worked once.'"

In a way, says his widow, Rodden-berry felt trapped by the space suc-cess that came with the whole *Star Trek* creation: "There was a time when Gene would say that he didn't want to go to his grave with his tomb-stone marked, 'Here lies the creator of *Star Trek*.' But that's where his success was; that's where his money was made. So eventually he said, 'Hey, if this is what I do well, then why don't I just keep doing it?'" She says he "revelled in police stories and westerns and would have loved to have moved on to those genres, yet, at the same time, his phi-losophy was, 'As long as I tell a good story, what does it matter what the characters are wearing?'"

As bull-headed as he was about his vision, he also had his insecurities.

"He wouldn't be human if he didn't," says Barrett. "Of course he had his private moments of doubt. Of course he had his worries. He wanted his work – especially *Star Trek: The Next Generation* – to be accepted."

John de Lancie, who plays Q, recalls the climate on the set during the making of the two-hour *ST:TNG* pilot: "It was not a time where everyone worked with supreme confidence – and it was certainly not a cakewalk for Roddenberry. My sense was that he really didn't know what he was about to create. In fact, he was very concerned not about taking this big new step forward but about how he could jump-start what he'd had with the original. Every day, a young Rick

GENE RODDENBERRY DIRECTS MAJEL BARRETT – AS NUMBER ONE – IN THE 1964 STAR TREK PILOT "THE CAGE." THIS WAS TO BE A SHORT-LIVED ASSIGNMENT FOR BARRETT, WHO LOST HER PLACE ON THE BRIDGE DURING THE SECOND PILOT. SENIOR TV EXECS WEREN'T READY FOR A WOMAN AS SECOND-IN-COMMAND.

Berman would walk around with Roddenberry and the two would be conferencing, as near as I could tell, on almost every decision that had to be made."

Lyles believes that Roddenberry's passing of the mantle to Berman was indicative of his extraordinary and all-too-rare foresight. After all, what other Hollywood visionary – from Walt Disney on down – actually found and nurtured his own replacement? Says Lyles: "Gene had strong desire and a dedication to his vision but he had the same desire and dedication to see that it was going to continue long after he left. He was a mother hen. He was Uncle Mame. He was happy about his success but even more happy that those who worked for him would have careers that would extend over a long period of time. He was very generous. He wanted to see that everybody connected with *Star Trek* was recognized and rewarded and

known. Roddenberry was very unselfish in sharing accolades."

Though Roddenberry and Lyles are two of the few non-actors to have buildings currently named after them on the Paramount lot, Lyles remembers Roddenberry's office as almost spartan. "It was a working office," he says. "It was not tremendous in size. No expensive furnishings. Very unpretentious. Gene was a very low-key fellow. He didn't try to create a high profile. I never heard him say, 'Let's publicize such-and-such.' Unlike some in the business, he did not concentrate on building an image."

And therein lies the irony. As Lyles notes: "Gene Roddenberry's image is even bigger today than when he was alive. Like Elvis Presley and Marilyn Monroe and 'Casablanca' and 'Citizen Kane,' he just gains more momentum as time goes on." ✧

RADIO TIMES OFFICIAL COLLECTOR'S EDITION

Star wars no more

Federation alliances in *Star Trek* mirror today's space industry where former enemies now join forces to seek out strange new worlds

BY NICK OLIVARI

THE FORCES THAT FUELLED THE *STAR Trek* phenomenon were in motion as early as 1960 – six years before the first television episode – as the world woke from the nuclear nightmare of the 1950s Cold War to a dawn brimming with promise and new beginning. And these were the prevailing sentiments that fed Gene Roddenberry's dream, as embodied in Capt. James T. Kirk's solemn overture, "Space, the final frontier."

In his 1960 nomination speech, youthful White House contender John F. Kennedy breathed fire into the American imagination with his pronouncement, "We stand today, on the edge of a new frontier..." And with those words, three years into a space race which had seen United States' prestige plummet, the American public was quite ready *to boldly go where no man has gone before.*

Remember, the Soviet Union had beaten America twice already. The Soviet space team succeeded in launching the first unmanned satellite, *Sputnik* 1, in orbit around the Earth on Oct. 4, 1957 – four months before the United States launched the *Explorer* 1 satellite. And then on April 12, 1961, Russian scientists launched *Vostok* 1, sending cosmonaut Yury A. Gagarin in a single orbit around the Earth – one month before Alan B. Shepard completed his much shorter 15-minute flight in America's *Mercury* capsule on May 5. It was also in 1961 that the newly-minted President Kennedy declared to the world that the United States would put a man on the moon before the end of the decade: "In a very real sense it will not be one man going to the moon...it will be an entire nation."

So, on a wave of public enthusiasm, Roddenberry boldly launched the *U.S.S. Enterprise* in 1966. Set against the backdrop of the real race, Roddenberry thrust his starship deep into outer space. And it was a very different space he brought to the screen.

A decade earlier, Hollywood science-fiction writers were still conjuring up images of mankind waging a defensive war against space aliens intent on dominating and enslaving our planet. Roddenberry challenged this portrayal of life in outer space. *Star Trek* viewers encountered a starship crew that roamed the galaxy in search of strange new worlds and confronted the unknown on its own turf. Exploration and discovery replaced fear and conquest as central themes of this sci-fi universe. *Star Trek* veteran Bob Justman, who was an associate producer on the classic series, recalls that *Star Trek* did as any ordinary or out-of-the-ordinary series did then and now: "It dealt with what is important in contemporary society."

Roddenberry once referred to *Star Trek* as the "*Wagon Train* to the stars," likening the show to a space version of the popular American western series about pioneers courageously journeying across the wild continent in their search for a new home. But *Star Trek* would shed this action-adventure veneer and transform itself almost immediately into something much more insightful and thought-provoking. The starship *Enterprise*'s journey through the galaxy reflected the human interest in unknown worlds, evoking a thirst for exploration. To Justman and many others there was an obvious

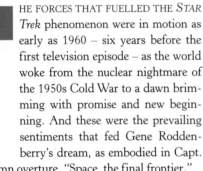

RIGHT: SPUTNIK I SATELLITE NEXT PAGE: BUZZ ALDRIN'S MOON WALK. INSETS, CLOCKWISE FROM TOP LEFT: EDWARD WHITE IN AMERICA'S FIRST SPACE WALK; THE LAUNCH OF A SATURN ROCKET; SOVIET COSMONAUT VALENTINA TERESHKOVA, THE FIRST WOMAN IN SPACE; SOVIET YURI GAGARIN, FIRST MAN IN SPACE

analogy: The Federation was an embodiment of the United States and the United Nations. "You could find parallels to the [U.S.A. versus U.S.S.R.] space race between the Federation (who are the good guys in *Star Trek*) and the Romulans or the Klingons."

Star Trek epitomized the Utopian vision of the 1960s. In the 23rd century, hunger, poverty and racial intolerance become memories of a bygone era, with mankind – for the most part – living harmoniously with the civilizations (aliens included) of other planets. The

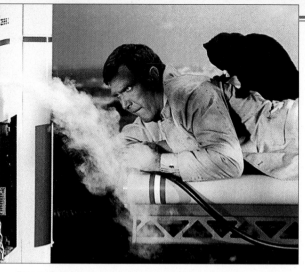

ROBERT LANSING AS A BENEVOLENT SPACE TRAVELLER WHO WANTS TO SAVE THE PLANET IN THE CLASSIC EPISODE "ASSIGNMENT: EARTH"

bridge of the *Enterprise* embodied the ultimate wish of every peace-loving human being: a workplace staffed by a mini United Nations, including in the *Star Trek* scenario a Russian, a Scot, an African, a Japanese and a Vulcan, all working together for the common good.

Parallels of this peaceful co-existence are found among the various space programs, such as the British National Space Centre (BSNC), the United States' National Aeronautics and Space Administration (NASA) and the European Space Agency (ESA). Just think of the various astronauts from different nations (the U.K. native Michael Foale among them)

who have boarded NASA shuttles at Cape Canaveral in the United States. And Americans and Russians, ideological foes in the 1960s, now orbit the earth elbow-to-elbow in one space vessel.

Roddenberry's space explorers transcended the paranoia that clouded the world during the Cold War. There was an all-pervasive fear attached to the space race. Who would have envisaged that Britons, Russians and Americans would one day co-operate on space expeditions? When chemist Helen Sharman became the first Briton in space, she did so aboard the Soviet *Soyuz* TM-12 – which carried her to the Soviet space station *Mir*. Hearken back to post-Second World War, when the Soviet Union and the United States competed for German scientists who were experts in rocket technology. Now shoot forward to *Star Trek*'s 24th century: It's peace between the Klingons and the Federation that enables Worf to stand on the bridge of the *U.S.S. Enterprise* as a senior officer. Such transformations in international relations and diplomacy do not, of course, appear magically overnight. Nor is a change of this magnitude the result of just one body politic. Consider the period of enhanced

Britons and space:
The U.K. contribution

The author and the astronaut. Two different callings, born 40 years apart, both mesmerized by space, eliciting two very different responses to their first explorations of the galaxy. World-renowned British science-fiction writer Arthur C. Clarke (born in Minehead, Somerset, 1917) was much belittled when, as early as 1945, he described in uncanny detail a future world of astronauts, space stations and satellites in an article titled "Extra-Terrestrial Relays" for the journal "Wireless World." Then fortysome years later, we have NASA's first British astronaut, Cambridge astrophysics graduate Michael Foale (birthplace: Louth, Lincolnshire, 1957), making his country proud as he successfully explores space not once but three times. The general public's perception of space exploration has indeed made a galactic leap.

Foale, having participated now in three space shuttle missions, has logged more than 630 hours in space, and is

BRITISH-BORN, SPACE-BOUND: ASTRONAUT MICHAEL FOALE

currently stationed at the Cosmonaut Training Centre, Star City, Russia, preparing for a long flight on the Russian space station *Mir* in 1997. During his most recent mission on the shuttle *Discovery* (February 1995), Foale and fellow astronaut Bernard A. Harris (from America) completed a space walk that lasted four hours and 39 minutes. Their goal was to test new devices designed to warm their space suits (in the brutal cold of space) and also to determine how well they could manipulate the 2,600-pound *Spartan*-204 satellite – a concept Britons balked at when Clarke suggested in the '40s that there would one day be astronauts in space – as well as satellites that could relay radio and TV signals all over the world. (It wasn't long before naysayers had their come-uppance, though: Just 12 years after these notions were criticized as ludicrous, the Soviet *Sputnik* 1 satellite was launched.) The widely-published sci-fi writer Clarke, who collaborated with Stanley Kubrick on the 1968 hit film "2001: A Space Odyssey," was cooperation that followed on the heels of the election of American President Jimmy Carter in 1976. It translated into a global warming of politics – with Russians and Americans soon docking in space together – and was built on over time.

It's international co-operation that equips each space shuttle with the Canadian-made Canadarm, one of the most advanced robotic devices employed in space. Witness also the 1983 launch of the unmanned Infrared Astronomy Satellite (IRAS), which was a collaborative effort of the United States, United Kingdom and The Netherlands. And the up-coming *Cassini-Huygens* mission (scheduled for an October 1997 launch) – which will eventually penetrate the atmosphere around Saturn's moon, Titan – is a joint effort of NASA, the ESA and the Italian Space Agency. Does all of this noble-sounding parlance suggest that Roddenberry meant to punch out a morality message week after week? According to Justman, no. *Star Trek* was never "intended to be preachment, it was intended to be a show that was entertaining

THE CANADARM: NOW EMPLOYED IN EVERY NASA SPACE SHUTTLE MISSION

and gripping." He describes the script writers "as thinking beings, concerned with the state of what our society was then and whether or not we were doing the right thing."

Like Gene Roddenberry, the cast and crew behind the current *Star Trek* TV series and films exert their own influence, firing our collective imagination, seeking to bring us closer to a 24th-century world of co-operation and exploration in space. – WITH FILES FROM DOUG O'NEILL AND JANET ROWE ✧

celebrated last year in the "British National Space Centre News" as "The Godfather of the Space Race." He also received the Space Achievement Medal from the British Interplanetary Society.

The satellites that Clarke wrote about and astronaut Foale tested during his third shuttle mission have figured prominently in Britain's space efforts, many of which are launched through the British National Space Centre's (BNSC) partnership with the European Space Agency (ESA). And Britons understand the high risks affiliated with such projects. As recently as March 1996, Space Minister Ian Taylor committed £2.8 million to ill-fated *Ariane*-5 launcher programme, whose first payload, the four-satellite science mission *Cluster,* was destroyed in the 4 June 1996 explosion. Britain is also involved in *Cluster's* twin project, *SOHO,* which successfully photographed the comet Hyakutake's encounter with the sun.

Another project benefitting from U.K. technology has been the Hubble Space Telescope mission (1990), which relies on the U.K.-designed Faint Object Camera to capture images of the sun, distant stars, nebulas and other bodies. Britain is also working with the ESA in planning the Horizon 2000+ project, which, commencing in 2006, will involve a visit to Mercury. Back on the Earth's surface, the universities of Kent and Oxford will be on the receiving end when the *Cassini-Huygens* mission to Saturn's moon, Titan, transmits data back to earth in 2004. And transported on Russia's 1998 *Spectrum-X* mission will be Jet-X, the U.K.'s large X-ray telescope. – DOUG O'NEILL

Keeping the flame

Rick Berman heads up the creative team devoted to continuing the vision of *Star Trek* creator Gene Roddenberry, and sometimes that means bending the rules a little

BY **MICHAEL LOGAN**

RICK BERMAN CARRIES THE SWORD FOR the late, great *Star Trek* creator Gene Roddenberry – and it is a double-edged sword indeed.

"*Star Trek* is not my vision of the future, it's Gene's – and it is my responsibility to keep it that way," says Berman, whose desk on the Paramount Pictures lot is crowned with a porcelain bust of Rodden-berry. A bright red bandanna covers Roddenberry's eyes, not because Berman – the co-creator and executive producer of the *Star Trek: Deep Space Nine* and *Star Trek: Voyager* series – and his team of writers and techno-wizards are doing anything the maestro would object to but because, Berman says, "We do bend his rules a little. If we didn't we'd have some very dull shows. In fact, *Deep Space Nine* would probably not exist – nor, maybe, would *Voyager*. But we try not to bend them too far. And we never break them."

Trekkers simply won't allow it. "We walk a very interesting tightrope," says Michael Okuda, scenic art supervisor and technical consultant for *Star Trek: The Next Generation, Star Trek: Deep Space Nine* and *Star Trek: Voyager*. "These shows are both blessed and cursed with loyal, intelligent and extremely observant fans. They do not hesitate to let us know when we mess up. It's particularly difficult on Rick. It's his responsibili-ty to keep *Star Trek* lore as consistent as possible in all the series spinoffs and motion pictures – but also fresh and exciting. I wouldn't want the job."

There are times Berman doesn't want it either. "Sometimes I'd give anything to be working on a show set in the 1990s, with grime and cops and squad cars," he admits, "but then I snap out of it

and realize I'm the luckiest guy on earth. The *Star Trek* franchise is unlike anything the entertainment industry has ever seen – or probably will ever see – and we never forget that our good fortune is only possible because of Gene. He is with us every step of the way."

Sometimes eerily so. Michael Piller, who co-created *Deep Space Nine* (with Berman) and is co-creator and executive producer on *Voyager* (with Berman and Jeri Taylor), recalls a meeting between the *Star Trek* execs and Paramount at the end of *Voyager*'s first season:

"The people from the studio said, 'We think *Voyager* is good but there aren't enough aliens on this show.' Now the first instinct of a producer when somebody starts telling him how to write his show is to get defensive and say, 'Go jump in the lake.' Well, not exactly in that language, but some-thing a little stronger. But in this particular case, I had to reflect back on the first day I came to work on *ST:TNG*. The very first words I heard out of the mouth of Gene Roddenberry were, 'There aren't enough aliens on this show.' So, you see, Gene continues to speak to us in some very unusual ways. He reminds us what these *Star Trek* shows are really about."

Both Piller and Berman admit their dark, gritty concept for *Deep Space Nine* got only a qualified blessing from Roddenberry.

LEFT: DEEP SPACE NINE *CO-CREATOR MICHAEL PILLER AND EXECUTIVE PRODUCER JERI TAYLOR. RIGHT PHOTO: RICK BERMAN, CHIEF TORCH-BEARER*

PHILIP SALTONSTALL/OUTLINE PRESS (2) GEORGE LANGE/OUTLINE PRESS

"Gene was very much against setting a *Star Trek* show in a place where there was conflict among the [core] characters," Berman remembers. "But Michael and I felt it was a necessary element of good drama. So we compromised by not having conflict among the *Starfleet* characters. That's why we created a first officer, Major Kira Nerys [played by Nana Visitor],

Roddenberry in the 1960s. "Gene continues to speak to us in some very unusual ways," confesses executive producer Michael Piller

Well, not quite everybody. Honouring Roddenberry's vision of a positive future where the strong morals of mankind prevail has proven crippling to some writers who venture into *Star Trek* territory. "And those writers have not lasted long," says Piller. "You cannot fight this vision. You must embrace it. Melinda Snodgrass, a second- and third-season writer on

who is a Bajoran, and populated the cast with a Trill, a shape-shifter and a Ferengi, and put them all in a sometimes very inhospitable environment filled with everything from bar drunks to temple priests. The combustible mixture allows for conflict but the solidarity of the *Starfleet* officers is always maintained. So everybody was happy."

ST:TNG, went off and wrote [about her experiences] what a ridiculous vision this is and how nobody could write to it and that [*ST:TNG*] would never work. Well, guess what? That vision happens to be the reason the *Star Trek* shows do work. This is something other science-fiction series have not always kept in mind in their quest for the *Star Trek* audience. They always manage to find a way to do the vision inside out – almost all their shows are about war or annihilation. They make the future dark whereas Gene wanted it to be light. He wanted Earth to be a paradise. As far as I'm concerned, the commitment to honour his vision also forces us to be more creative, to find new ways to tell stories."

But sometimes it seems as if these *Star Trek* experts are paying more homage than they actually are. Case in point: The addition of the *U.S.S. Defiant* during the third season of *Deep Space Nine*. "When we created the ship, everyone said, 'Oh, they're trying to do what Roddenberry did on *ST:TNG*' – but that wasn't the case at all," insists *Deep Space Nine* executive producer Ira Steven Behr. "We had to add the *U.S.S. Defiant* because we'd built up the Dominion as this huge enemy. How were we going to face it with three little runabouts? Copying *ST:TNG* – or, for that matter, the original *Star Trek* – was the furthest thing from our minds. A series, as it develops, reveals its own unique needs. It should constantly be evolving if it is to survive – and no one knew that better than Gene."

Kate Mulgrew – the first woman to helm a *Star Trek* series – believes her character, *Voyager*'s Capt. Kathryn Janeway, "would not have been acceptable to audiences in Roddenberry's day but he was smart enough to start planting the seeds by placing women – including an African-American woman – in important positions [on the *U.S.S. Enterprise*]. He knew we would someday be ready for this. Though I never had the honour of meeting him, I think Gene Roddenberry would have been very proud of Janeway, as I'm sure he would have been just as proud of [African-American] Avery Brooks playing a captain."

While creating the original *Star Trek* series in the mid-1960s, Roddenberry made a serious effort to portray the various intergalactic cultures as significantly different from *Starfleet* – both physically and philosophically. This too is another tradition carried on in each *Star Trek* episode today by Berman and his creative team.

"Gene also made sure that each alien group was unique unto itself – right down to colours," says Rick Sternbach, senior illustrator for both the currently-running *Voyager* and *Deep Space Nine* series. "The *Starfleet* ships are robin's egg blue, Klingon ships are dark, dirty greens, Cardassian ships sort of a desert yellow and they are all architecturally unique. Each also has dis-

Kate Mulgrew plays *Voyager*'s Kathryn Janeway, the first woman to captain a series starship: "I think Roddenberry would have been very proud of Janeway. He knew we would someday be ready for this."

tinct technological capabilities. Gene knew the audience would enjoy and appreciate the ability to instantly recognize each culture. This concept, which started with Matt Jefferies' design work in the original series (he created the look of the original *Enterprise),* picked up where it left off in *"Star Trek: The Motion Picture"* and continued on in the three spinoffs."

Wherever possible, a tangible remnant of Roddenberry's legacy is recycled. *Deep Space Nine* production designer Herman Zimmerman, who is also designing *"Star Trek Generations II"* (scheduled for late 1996) says: "We reuse set pieces as often as possible, not only because it's financially wise but because it feels wonderful to have the continuity with Gene. The next film will use the only existent pieces of the original bridge from '*Star Trek: The Motion Picture*' – the turbolifts and turbolift doors." Zimmerman's favourite *Deep Space Nine* episode – "Explorers," in which then-commander Benjamin Sisko builds an ancient spaceship with solar sails – was created with a special nod to the sea-loving Roddenberry. "Gene based the idea for the structure of Starfleet on nautical concepts – specifically the Horatio Hornblower series [by C.S. Forester] – so we love to make Navy allusions and we do it frequently." That extends to the dedication plaque on *Deep Space Nine*'s *Defiant* – a quote from the beloved poem "Sea Fever," by John Masefield: "And all I ask is a tall ship and a star to steer her by."

But for all the homage still paid to original *Star Trek* creator Roddenberry, Rick Berman notes: "It is important to remember that we are not sworn to do things exactly the way Gene would. We would all go crazy if we sat around saying to ourselves, 'Now what would Gene do here in this instance?' or 'Would Gene really approve of such-and-such?' even though there is a portion of our audience that believes we ought to. Instead, we remember that Gene was the biggest rule-bender of all. When he decided on Patrick Stewart to play Capt. Jean-Luc Picard, he got a lot of opposition from some industry people who wanted more of a standard heartthrob type – but Gene really stuck to his vision. People said to him, 'How can you have a bald captain? It makes absolutely no sense! Baldness will be cured by the 24th century!'" But Gene didn't see it that way. His attitude was, 'Whether there is still baldness or not in the 24th century does not matter. The point is that mankind will not care.'" ✧

Haven't we met in a parallel universe?

Some *Star Trek* phenomena are just too good to happen only once, and fans sometimes get the impression they've been there already!

BY **CHRISTOPHER BLAND**

EJA VU SEEMS TO BE ONE OF the most common experiences for *Star Trek*-watchers. Certain themes – running the gamut of alien abductions and broken-hearted lovers to time travel and body snatching – are always cropping up in the *Star Trek* universe, prompting committed viewers to ask themselves: Where have we seen that one before? Here's a roundup of some of *Star Trek*'s most popular, recurring trademark themes.

DIDN'T I SEE YOU IN A PARALLEL UNIVERSE?

Parallel – or alternative – worlds have become a regular ingredient in the *Star Trek* experience. In fact, it wouldn't be a bad idea to drill all new Starfleet Academy cadets on this topic – every starship trooper seems destined to cross the mirror to the other side sooner or later. *U.S.S. Voyager*'s encounter with a co-operative parallel universe crew (Janeway meets Janeway, Kes meets Kes...) in "Deadlock" was a picnic compared to the hostile twin crew that Kirk and his party stumbled upon in the classic episode "Mirror, Mirror." The latter introduced an alternate *Federation* with an unforgettable mirror version of Spock. Sisko and crew visited the "Mirror, Mirror" world in two *Star Trek: Deep Space Nine* shows: "Crossover" and "Through the Looking Glass" (where Sisko saves the life of his "mirror" wife, something he couldn't do in his universe).

LET'S DO THE TIME WARP AGAIN: TIME TRAVEL

Many *Star Trek* characters have wrenched the cosmic clockworks travelling back in time. Kirk almost altered Earth's history after the *U.S.S. Enterprise* was tossed back to the 20th century in the original-series episode "Tomorrow is Yesterday." Sisko took a bullet when he went back in time and lived through a violent chapter of 21st-century Earth history in *DS9*'s two-part "Past Tense" (with O'Brien and Kira dropping in and out of the past in their search for Sisko, Bashir and Dax). And Kirk travelled back to the 20th century where he was faced with a terrifying decision: save the woman he loves, which would have changed the timeline (meaning the Nazis would have ruled the world), or allow his beloved to die and maintain history as it was ("The City on the Edge of Forever"). And Tasha Yar? Though killed by Armus in "Skin of Evil," she reappeared in "Yesterday's Enterprise" and went back in time to fight a battle to restore the 24th-century timeline.

WALK LIKE A ROMULAN: CREW MEMBERS POSING AS ALIENS FOR COVERT OPERATIONS

When *Starfleet* personnel don the cloak and dagger, chances are that pointed ears are part of the disguise. Humans, it seems, pass easily for Romulans. Kirk, with little more than pointy ear tips and upturned eyebrows, tricked the Romulans in the original-series episode "The Enterprise Incident." Picard and Data also assumed Romulan disguises in the two-part "Unification." It's little wonder the Romulans themselves abducted Deanna Troi to pass as one of their own in *Star Trek: The Next Generation*'s "Face of the Enemy."

A FAMILY TREE GROWS IN STARFLEET

Unexpected family members continually sprout up in the *Starfleet* clan. Worf was introduced to his half-human, half-Klingon son, Alexander, during a reunion with his Klingon lover, K'Ehleyr, in *ST:TNG*'s "Reunion," and he also met Kurn, the brother he never knew existed, in "Sins of the Father." Data's family also expanded. He discovered his

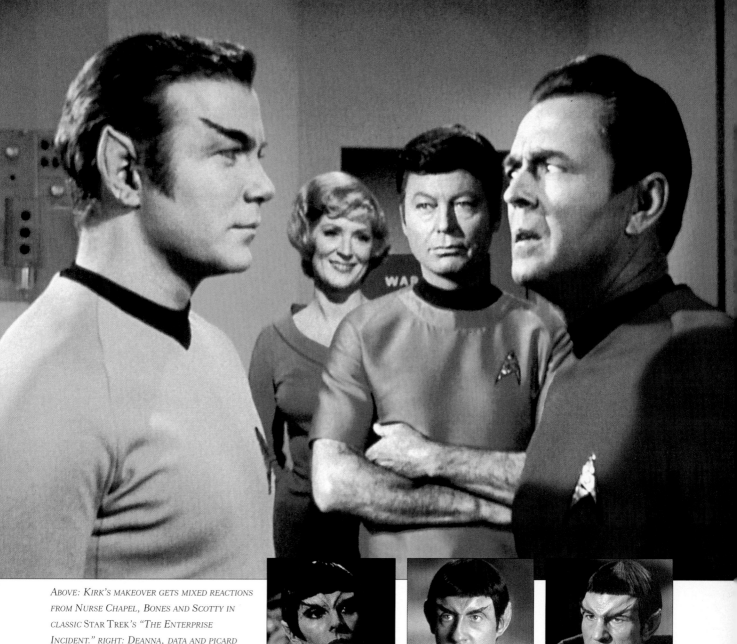

ABOVE: KIRK'S MAKEOVER GETS MIXED REACTIONS FROM NURSE CHAPEL, BONES AND SCOTTY IN CLASSIC STAR TREK'S "THE ENTERPRISE INCIDENT." RIGHT: DEANNA, DATA AND PICARD TAKE TURNS GOING UNDERCOVER AS ROMULANS

android "brother," Lore, in "Datalore" and later his father-creator, Dr. Noonian Soong, in "Brothers." Deanna Troi's discovery, however, was one of the darkest. In exploring the roots of her mother's emotional trauma (while in a coma) during *ST:TNG*'s "Dark Page," Deanna learned of a previously unknown sister, Kestra, who drowned as a child. Lwaxana had blocked the memory for years.

THE STARSHIP LOVELESS

Cupid's arrows rarely stick in the *Star Trek* universe. Scotty was a trooper in "Who Mourns for Adonais?" as he competed with Apollo for the affections of Lieut. Carolyn Palamas – but ultimately lost. Ditto for Dr. Beverly Crusher, who fell in love with the Trill mediator Odan in "The Host" – only to discover that her amour was actually a symbiotic creature. Paris, too, has been luckless in the relationship department, and the Doctor (played by Robert Picardo) has lost out not once but

twice. The first time, he fell for the shield-maiden Freya, who was then tragically killed at the hands of Unferth in "Heroes and Demons." In "Lifesigns," the Doctor loved a Vidiian, but again, a long-standing romance was not to be his – the Vidiian was a holographic creation who couldn't survive. Yet the Doctor can count himself lucky. After all, 'tis better to have loved and lost, than never to have been a hologram at all.

THOSE OMNIPOTENT, PLAYFUL BEINGS

For many *Star Trek* creatures, *Starfleet* personnel are little more than playing pieces in a galactic game, and the game is not always friendly. The extra-dimensional Nagilum (*ST:TNG*'s "Where Silence Has Lease"), for example, threatened to kill almost half of the *Enterprise* crew in his gamble to understand humans' reactions to death. However, other beings are more prone to mischief than malice. The petulant Q is one of the biggest gamesmen, having toyed with the crews of the *Enterprise*, *DS9* and *Voyager*. Just as eager for a jolly good game with humans was astro-adolescent Trelane ("The Squire of Gothos"), who – in exchange for not blowing up the *Enterprise* – got to scamper after Kirk in a fox hunt through the Gothos woods.

MURDER ON THE STARFLEET EXPRESS

Starfleet officers charged with murder: Riker was accused of murdering Dr. Nel Apgar in "A Matter of Perspective"; Paris was fingered for killing Baneal physicist Tolen Ren in *Voyager*'s "Ex Post Facto"; and Scotty was accused of doing in the Argelian dancer Kara in "Wolf in the Fold." Any good defence lawyers in the galaxy?

THE BODY SNATCHERS

B'Elanna Torres' abduction by a robot in "Prototype" placed her on a long list of crew carted off by aliens, which began with Capt. Pike in the original pilot "The Cage." In *ST:TNG*'s creepy "Schisms" episode, crew were victims of hideous experiments (arms cut off and crudely sewn back on) by Solanagen-based aliens. Geordi had a knack for getting abducted, first by the Pakleds ("Samaritan Snare") and later by the Romulans ("The Mind's Eye"). In one of *ST:TNG*'s funniest scenes ("Allegiance"), a Picard imposter (after the real one is abducted) leads the crew in a boisterous song-fest.

OOPS, WE THOUGHT YOU WERE DEAD!

Everyone wants their own Lazarus experience. Spock died saving his mates in *Star Trek II* but was regenerated by the effects of the Genesis planet in *Star Trek III.* Similarly, Paris died after testing Infinite Velocity in *Voyager*'s "Threshold," but recovered through genetic acceleration.

SPOCK, MEET SPOCK! LEONARD NIMOY IN THE ORIGINAL SERIES EPISODE "MIRROR, MIRROR," A TALE OF PARALLEL UNIVERSES

Harry Kim, it seems, is on a virtual death roll: He died and was resurrected in *Voyager*'s first-season episode "Emanations," then died again in "Deadlock" after being sucked through a hull breach – but returned when a parallel universe ship happened along. As for Tasha Yar? Her reincarnations are just too many to mention.

RULES ARE MEANT TO BE
BROKEN: THE PRIME DIRECTIVE

In *Star Trek*, it's verboten to mess with the *Federation*'s Prime Directive of noninterference in alien civilizations, but there's

Just the facts

Like many pop culture phenomena, *Star Trek* has given birth to a Milky Way of myths that many Trekkers firmly hold to be true. We thought we'd set the record straight on some of the heresy floating about the *Star Trek* universe:

To beam or not to beam
Kirk never said "Beam me up, Scotty" in the classic series or in any of the *Star Trek* movies. The actual command "Beam *us* up, Scotty" is from the 1970s *Star Trek* cartoon series.

Mighty Morphing Spot
Data's pet Spot was a *male* Somali cat in early *ST:TNG* episodes "Data's Day" and "Phantasms." But by season seven's "Genesis," the feline is female – and pregnant. The cause of Spot's gender switch is unknown.

Romulan and Juliet
Contrary to myth, Kirk didn't romance every female alien in the galaxy. In the original-series episode "That Which

Survives," he actually refused the advances of Losira. Nor was there an official (or unofficial) "Kirk make-out theme" in *Star Trek*'s music.

Both Picard manoeuvres
The original "Picard Manoeuvre" was the fighting tactic employed by the captain during the Battle of Maxia (*ST:TNG*'s "The Battle"). By accelerating the *Stargazer* to warp speed, Picard outwits his opponent's light-speed sensors and briefly appears in two places at once, allowing him to destroy a Ferengi ship. The "other" manoeuvre refers to Picard's habit of tugging his tunic during confrontations. Riker was a serious practitioner of the tunic tug, but other crew members (particularly Dr. Crusher and Wesley) also snuck in the occasional tug – as did one of the dreaded Jem'Hadar in *DS9*'s third-season opener, "The Search."

Chekov's check-in?
Pavel Chekov didn't appear in the first season of the original

mounting evidence that captains have in fact broken that commandment from time to time. When Wesley Crusher strayed into a "forbidden zone" on Rubicun III and was subsequently sentenced to death ("Justice"), Picard interfered and forced the planet's inhabitants to release the lad. Kirk also ignored the Prime Directive in "A Private Little War," giving flintlock rifles to the hill people of Tyree (it seems Kirk felt the firepower was skewed in favour of the opposing villagers and he intervened to correct the balance – a definite no-no).

THANKS, BUT I LIKE MY JOB
Turning down promotions – Riker dominates this category. He rejected every opportunity to command his own starship (the *U.S.S. Drake*, *U.S.S. Aries* and *U.S.S. Melbourne* were among the many offers). The message: Career advancement isn't everything in *Star Trek* space. Capt. Kirk would quickly agree – he was bored as an admiral. The captain was promoted to the lofty post prior to his first big-screen adventure, but jumped right back into the familiar captain's chair for *"Star Trek: The Motion Picture."* In *"Star Trek Generations"* Kirk advised Picard, *"Don't* let them promote you" – which spoke of the thrill and excitement of captaining a starship. Picard had already learned that himself, having turned down a promotion to admiral in "Coming of Age."

POSSESSED BY ALIENS
Aliens regularly take over the minds and bodies of *Starfleet* personnel. Troi, O'Brien and Data, when possessed by aliens in "Power Play," tried to take control of the *U.S.S. Enterprise*. In "Dramatis Personae," the *DS9* crew split into warring factions when telepathic energy from ancient Saltah'na spheres caused them to re-enact an age-old war. But alien possession wasn't always dangerous. Picard, affected by a Kataan probe in the Hugo Award-win-

ner "The Inner Light," relived the life of Kamin, the Kataan iron weaver who knew of his planet's pending doom and was powerless to stop it. By possessing Picard, Kamin ensured the Kataan history would not be forgotten.

THE GHOSTS OF GALAXIES PAST
Picard was induced by Q to revisit his past in the emotionally intense episode "Tapestry." Jean-Luc, regretting the brashness of his youth and a heated scuffle with a Nausicaan (who stabbed him in the heart), saw the route his life would have taken had he avoided the Nausicaan. In "Second Chances," Riker meets his double, Thomas, and gradually regrets his past decision to place his career over his relationship with Deanna Troi. His regret only intensifies when Thomas pursues and wins the affections of Deanna.

WE HAVE FEELINGS TOO
Starfleet seems to constantly redefine sentience. In "Evolution," Picard decided the Nanite microscopic robots were sentient when they escaped into the ship's computer core and developed self-awareness. Picard's greatest challenge, however, presented itself in "The Measure of a Man," when Cmdr. Maddox wanted Data disassembled. Picard had to prove that Data was indeed a sentient being – entitled to freedom from human rights violations, including "death."

DIDN'T YOU JUST LEAVE THE ROOM? DISTORTIONS IN THE TIME-SPACE CONTINUUM
Picard encountered his double – who actually existed six hours into the future – in "Time Squared." As for the starships, the *Enterprise* was repeatedly destroyed in "Cause and Effect" when it was trapped in a time loop for 17 days, and *Voyager* responded to a distress call in "Parallax" – only to find another *Voyager*! ✧

GALACTICAL BARFLY MORN, PLAYED BY MARK ALLEN SHEPHERD IN DS9

series despite Khan's insistence in *"Star Trek II: The Wrath of Khan"* that he remembered the Russian ensign from the classic series' first-season episode "Space Seed." Chekov's first appearance was in the second-season opener, "Amok Time."
Trouble tracking the Tribbles
The affectionate fur balls from the classic episode "The Trouble with Tribbles" did not depart for good after their first appearance. One was displayed to McCoy in *"Star Trek III: The Search for Spock."* They were also seen in the animated-series episode "More Tribbles, More Troubles."
For whom the red shirt tolls
Star Trek's original-series extras in the red shirts were usually the first ones to bite the bullet – or phaser beam. Kirk would typically assemble a landing party consisting of Spock, McCoy and a character unknown to viewers. The new guy would then beam down to a planet, eager to per-

form well on his first landing party assignment, and then he'd become a tall drink for an energy vampire or get pegged off before drawing his phaser. It was never a pretty sight. Moral of the story: Dress for survival.
M-o-o-o-r-n!
DS9 creators did *not* intend barfly Morn (Mark Allen Shepherd) to be a duplicate copy of George Wendt's immortal Norm Peterson character from *Cheers*. Insiders say the *DS9* production crew simply noted the similarities in demeanour between the two characters after the series had already gone into production, and suggested Morn (a spin on Norm) when the character needed a name for the "Progress" episode. Perhaps the most beloved of *DS9*'s background characters, Morn – who *still* hasn't spoken a line! – has his own fan club: Morn Watchers, c/o Tina Jafari, P.O. Box 630175, Houston, Texas USA 77263-0175.

100
INFLUENTIAL PEOPLE IN *STAR TREK*

GENE RODDENBERRY
The Great Bird of the Galaxy

Roddenberry was the original creator and producer of *Star Trek*. He was the visionary whose imagination spawned the *Star Trek* universe, established its guiding principles and shaped the formula that would lead to four television series, an animated TV version and, by the end of 1996, eight *Star Trek* movies. His talents were legion: Roddenberry's writing credits span *Star Trek* and *Star Trek: The Next Generation* (for which he co-wrote the opener, "Encounter at Farpoint"). And when Paramount launched *ST:TNG*, he also took the job of executive producer. The Great Bird would see the development of *Star Trek: Deep Space Nine* before his death in October 1991, whereupon his vision would be carried on by co-executive producers Rick Berman and Michael Piller. Roddenberry had been a mentor to many aspiring directors and producers.

Roddenberry's vision transcended the immediate arena of *Star Trek*. To many, it was largely the efforts of this one man that allowed sci-fi to flourish on TV (the Great Bird was involved in other sci-fi ventures, such as *The Questor Tapes*). But most importantly, Gene Roddenberry provided a vision of hope and a future that promised great things, and in doing so he touched the lives of many. "The number of people who have been positively affected by the show is staggering," reflects Leonard Nimoy. "It has helped change people's attitudes towards themselves and the world."

We decided to honour here the talented individuals who have made *Star Trek* "happen." Few of us realize how much goes into the creation of a *Star Trek* series (or movie), so we went behind the cameras – going back 30 years – and sought out 100 of the people who have made *Star Trek* endure and flourish. In addition to the actors, creators and visionaries (many of whom are well-known to you already), our honour roll includes writers, make-up artists, costume designers, producers, directors, illustrators, composers and special effects masters. These are just some of the people who have allowed *Star Trek* to live long and prosper.

BY CHRISTOPHER BLAND, WITH FILES FROM MICHAEL LOGAN AND ERIN McLAUGHLIN

RICK BERMAN
Creator/Executive Producer

ST:TNG's executive producer for seven seasons, Berman – the Second Great Bird of the Galaxy – co-created and is now executive producer of *Deep Space Nine* and *Star Trek: Voyager*, and co-developed the stories for both series' openers. Keeping *Star Trek* alive on the big screen, he produced the movies "Star Trek Generations" and "Star Trek: First Contact." By experimenting with Roddenberry's vision, Berman has discovered other strange new worlds. (See "Keeping the Flame," page 20.)

GENE L. COON
Writer/Producer

A line producer during the early days of the classic series, Coon (who died in 1974) had an innate understanding of what made a good *Star Trek* story, and a knack for veiling social commentary with science fiction. He penned many great episodes for *Star Trek*, including "Space Seed" (which introduced the charismatic Khan Noonien Singh), "Errand of Mercy" (which ushered in the Klingons) and "A Taste of Armageddon" (a powerful analogy of the Vietnam War). Coon helped set the tone of the *Star Trek* universe by standardiz-

ing the style of many early scripts, creating the notion of the noble Prime Directive, and focussing the show on Kirk, Spock and McCoy and the interplay between the characters.

MICHAEL PILLER
Creator/Executive Producer

Joining Rick Berman and Gene Roddenberry as a *ST:TNG* executive producer at the start of the series' fourth season, Piller co-created and was an executive producer for *DS9*. In addition to writing *DS9*'s opener, "Emissary" (based on a story he developed with Rick Berman), and the two-part "The Best of Both Worlds" (where he cast Picard into the Borg collective), Piller also co-created and was executive producer for the fourth *Star Trek* series, *Voyager*, and co-wrote its opener, "Caretaker."

D.C. FONTANA
Writer/Assoc. Producer

Gene Roddenberry's secretary when the classic *Star Trek* series was in its infancy, Fontana went on to become a series script consultant and key writer.

Her original-series, *ST:TNG* and *DS9* credits include "Charlie X," "The Ultimate Computer," "That Which Survives" (under the name Michael Richards), "Encounter at Farpoint," "The Naked Now" (as J. Michael Bingham) and "Dax." Fontana was associate producer on *Star Trek: The Animated Series*, and is credited with the suggestion that Picard's first name be changed from Julien to Jean-Luc.

JERI TAYLOR
Creator/Executive Producer

As *Star Trek* has expanded, so too has Taylor's role in the *Star Trek* world: She has been supervising producer, co-producer, executive producer and co-creator (*Voyager*). She wrote the teleplay for *Voyager*'s "Eye of the Needle" episode (capturing the crew's painful longing for home) and co-wrote the series' opener, "Caretaker." Taylor promoted strong roles for women, as in Sharon Lawrence's portrayal of the heroic Amelia Earhart in *Voyager*'s "The 37's."

WRITER/PRODUCER GENE COON

MATT JEFFERIES
Art Director/Production Designer

The first starship *U.S.S. Enterprise* as it appeared on TV screens in 1966 was largely the work of Jefferies, who was an art director with Desilu Studios when he was asked to join Gene Roddenberry on the original *Star Trek* series. His achievements as art director and production designer include many other firsts, such as the original shuttle, the original Klingon battle cruiser and the first hand

MATT JEFFERIES

phasers. The Jefferies Tube (an original-series *Enterprise* service conduit that became part of *ST:TNG* and *Voyager*) was named in his honour.

MIKE MINOR
Artist/Designer

The original-series artist/designer created the Melkot puppet for "Spectre of the Gun," artwork for the walls of the original *Enterprise*, and the "*Star Trek II: The Wrath of Khan*" warp core installation (which became the basis for the *U.S.S. Enterprise-D*'s warp core installation). He also designed sets and created matte paintings for "*Star Trek: The Motion Picture*" and "*Star Trek II: The Wrath of Khan.*"

WAH CHANG
Production Designer

Chang's mask designs gave form to the Gorn race and the *M-113* salt vampire. As production designer with the original series, Chang also developed the first communicator and tricorder, and designed the laser pistols that were used briefly in "The Cage" before they were replaced by phasers.

FRED PHILLIPS
Make-up Artist

The original-series make-up artist (he stayed with the show as it struggled through its initial three-year run) created his 2,000th Spock ear during the production of "*Star Trek: The Motion Picture.*" Phillips (who used hair from the belly of a yak for Spock's eyebrows)

also created the look of the original-series Romulans and created a new image for the Klingons in "*Star Trek: The Motion Picture*." The new Klingon look remained for *The Next Generation*. Batlh Daqawlu'taH! (Translated from the Klingon language: You will be remembered with honour.)

LEONARD NIMOY
Spock

Nimoy, who claimed "I Am Not Spock" in a 1975 autobiography and followed up with "I Am Spock" in 1995, starred in the original *Star Trek* series, participated in the animated version, appeared in the first six *Star Trek* films and also drew huge ratings for *ST:TNG* when he returned for the two-part "Unification." He also directed "*Star Trek III: The Search for Spock*" and "*Star Trek IV: The Voyage Home*" and assumed the job of executive producer of "*Star Trek VI: The Undiscovered Country.*" But it's his role as Spock, the epitome of logic and reason, for which he's most remembered. And, of course, his signature split-finger sign of long life and prosperity will leave its imprint forever.

WILLIAM SHATNER
Capt. James T. Kirk

Shatner was the consummate adventurer as Captain James T. Kirk – the original-series captain whose presence as a cowboy diplomat and bold strategist made

WRITER/PRODUCER BRANNON BRAGA

him a formidable force until his big-screen demise in "*Star Trek Generations.*" (Kirk was later resurrected in April '96 in William Shatner's book "*Star Trek*: The Return.")

Of his part in the original series, Shatner recalls: "We never thought of it as this great creative act. It's like making a painting. All you worry about is where you put the brush strokes. When you're done, someone says, 'Hey, that's the best thing I've ever seen.'"

The French-Canadian actor starred in the first seven *Star Trek* movies, including "*Star Trek V: The Final Frontier*" (which he also co-wrote and directed), and is the author of several books about his *Star Trek* days, as well as a successful series of "TekWar" novels, which have enjoyed a television spinoff.

HARLAN ELLISON
Writer

"My contributions to *Star Trek* are probably small, but I would suspect that they're at least germinal," says the renowned science-fiction author who wrote the multiple-award-winning episode "The City on the Edge of Forever" (in which Kirk must allow the death of the woman he loves to preserve the timeline). The only *Star Trek* teleplay Ellison authored is considered by many to be the best episode ever written (though, in the original script, Kirk ignored the consequences and tried to save Edith Keeler). Ellison attributes the episode's continuing appeal to its "attempt at true dramatic tragedy. That's what it is. It is the dealing with a serious, actual confrontation by a normal human being with an unsolvable, crushing life situation. It's a love story; my attempt to do serious drama within the framework of space opera."

Ellison also spearheaded the 1966 letter-writing campaign that kept *Star Trek* on the air after its threatened cancellation. The original version of "City" has been published as a book.

DAVID GERROLD
Writer

Gerrold is probably best remembered for his first script, "The Trouble with Tribbles," which proved that *Star Trek* principals could deliver comedy while remaining true to their characters, thus setting a lighter tone for many follow-up episodes. He also drew on social commentary, evident when he co-wrote "The Cloud Minders," which explored the notion of class structure. And, when Data was introduced in *ST:TNG*, it was Gerrold who recommended the android's skin be golden .

BRANNON BRAGA
Writer/Producer

A writer of breadth: Braga explored the reality-versus-fantasy theme in *ST:TNG*'s "Frame of Mind," co-wrote the movies "*Star Trek Generations*" and "*Star Trek: First Contact*," and is credited with writing *ST:TNG*'s western romp "A Fistful of Datas." He was also a producer with *ST:TNG* before becoming a *Voyager* producer.

RONALD D. MOORE
Writer/Producer

Moore wrote the teleplay for *ST:TNG*'s haunting two-part "Chain of Command," which offered an unflinching look at torture and the strength of the human spirit. A *ST:TNG* producer then a *DS9* supervising producer (he wrote many episodes for both), Moore also co-wrote "*Star Trek Generations*" and "*Star Trek: First Contact*."

RENÉ ECHEVARRIA
Writer/Producer

A key *ST:TNG* and *DS9* writer, Echevarria worked a virtual miracle when he wrote "I, Borg" and humanized the cold, mechanistic heart of the Borg collective. Indeed, Echevarria excelled at scripts involving emotional struggles, including *ST:TNG*'s "The Offspring," in which the android Data creates – and then loses – a daughter.

PATRICK STEWART
Capt. Jean-Luc Picard

His on-screen snippets of Shakespeare were reminders of his training in classical theatre. Stewart accomplished the impossible when he took the helm as *ST:TNG*'s captain and established a commanding presence distinct from William Shatner, becoming the benchmark for future captains. He starred in "*Star Trek Generations*" and is also cast in "*Star Trek: First Contact*." Stewart directed five *ST:TNG* episodes, includ-

HARLAN ELLISON WROTE THE AWARD-WINNING EPISODE "THE CITY ON THE EDGE OF FOREVER"

ing "Phantasms" and "A Fistful of Datas." Says Stewart: "Picard's qualities are admirable. He is open, generous and unwavering in his belief that mankind is good." Stewart says his only regret is that "Picard rarely got to be a little silly."

BRENT SPINER
Data

Spiner has had many fine turns – often comedic – as the ever-curious Data, who forever tries to comprehend and display human emotions. In *ST:TNG*, Spiner played Data, as well as the android's creator, Dr. Noonian Soong, and his "brother," Lore. Data is also known as

Ol' Yellow Eyes (a nod to Frank Sinatra), and Spiner (who was a Broadway singer earlier in his entertainment career) used that nickname on his album, "Ol' Yellow Eyes is Back," where he sang with backup from Patrick Stewart, Jonathan Frakes, LeVar Burton and Michael Dorn (calling themselves the Sunspots). Spiner returns as Data in the upcoming "*Star Trek: First Contact*."

MAJEL BARRETT
Lwaxana Troi/Nurse Chapel

Barrett, widow of Gene Roddenberry, was involved with *Star Trek* from the very beginning. She was originally cast as the aloof Number One in the first *Star Trek* pilot, "The Cage," but was cut from the cast – the network wasn't ready for a female second-in-command. Barrett then dyed her hair blond and won the role of Nurse Christine Chapel in the original series. Nurse Chapel then became Dr. Chapel – who was promoted to Commander Chapel during the *Star Trek* movies. Barrett was the computer voice in the original series and *ST:TNG*, and is still heard as a computer voice in *DS9*, *Voyager* and on the CD "*Star Trek*: Omnipedia." Her most memorable role, though, was *The Next Generation's* Lwaxana Troi, the sexually-charged empath and mother of Deanna Troi. Her shenanigans and adventures were always entertaining. A keeper of the flame in her own right, Barrett (who developed the *Deep Space Nine* story "The Muse") has long been a fan icon.

JAMES DOOHAN
Montgomery Scott

Canadian Doohan played Montgomery "Scotty" Scott as the quintessential engineer, able to work technical miracles in a universe where the technobabble alone could squash mere mortals. With appearances in several *Star Trek* movies, Doohan (a master of accents and voices) returned to the *Star Trek* universe in *ST:TNG's* "Relics." Memorable line: Scotty to holodeck computer, "N-C-C-1-7-0-1. No bloody A, B, C or D." Doohan's autobiography, "Beam Me Up, Scotty," will be released in October 1996.

DEFOREST KELLEY
Dr. Leonard H. McCoy

"Damn it, Jim" perfectly captured the spirited and cantankerous don't-call-me-a-bricklayer "Bones" McCoy. Kelley was cast in the *Star Trek II* series (that didn't fly), then lent his voice to the animated series before appearing in the first six *Star Trek* movies. He also reappeared as 137-year-old Admiral McCoy in *ST:TNG's* "Encounter at Farpoint."

JOHN DE LANCIE
Q

"Growl for me. Let me know you still care." The arrogant Q delivered many such memorable lines throughout *ST:TNG*. Fans, however, wouldn't have

been able to enjoy Q's humour had *ST:TNG's* opening episode "Encounter at Farpoint" gone ahead in its original form: a shorter, 90-minute show that didn't include Q. Only after Paramount requested a rewrite for a two-hour pilot did Q appear, and de Lancie perfectly fit the part as the bad boy of the galaxy. Embracing a role that could have died in the hands of lesser actors, de Lancie succeeded in creating a fan favourite (and a recurring act) through the wit and dramatic power the gifted actor brought to Q, whose humour ranks among *ST:TNG's* best. De Lancie reprised Q in *DS9* and *Voyager*.

ALEXANDER COURAGE
Composer

ALEXANDER COURAGE

Courage wrote the theme music for *Star Trek*, later used by composer Dennis McCarthy to highlight the first appearance of *U.S.S. Enterprise-B* in "*Star Trek Generations.*" It was this original composition created by Courage that fans first associated with *Star Trek*.

MICHAEL WESTMORE
Make-up Supervisor

The multiple-award-winning make-up supervisor for *ST:TNG*, *DS9*, *Voyager* and "*Star Trek Generations*" vir-

WILLIAM THEISS: PROVOCATIVE COSTUMES

tually created the look of every alien introduced over the course of the three series. Although he's proud of his designs for the Cardassians, Westmore – whose mother was a hairdresser on the original *Star Trek* series – gives Number 1 ranking to the featureless, silvery robot make-up used in *ST:TNG's* "Angel One" and reused for another android in *ST:TNG's* "The Offspring." Westmore won an Oscar for his work in the 1985 film "Mask."

HERMAN ZIMMERMAN
Production Designer

Let the credits roll: Zimmerman designed the overall look of *ST:TNG*, *DS9* and several *Star Trek* movies; created the design of the *Enterprise-D* in "*Star Trek Generations*," including the ship's breathtaking three-storey Stellar Cartography set; and designed numerous other on-board creations. It was Zimmerman who decided that the Cardassians would prefer dark colours and triad design concepts, thus accounting for *DS9's* three concentric rings, the three upper and lower docking pylons, and the triangular nature of the station's interior architecture.

ROBERT BLACKMAN
Costume Designer

ST:TNG's costume designer for seasons three to seven, Blackman (who also designs for *DS9* and *Voyager*) earned Emmy nominations for his work in "Devil's Due," "Time's Arrow, Part II" and "All Good Things..." Memorable creations: The feminine-yet-frightening outfits of the Duras sisters; the Cardassian uniforms; Worf's R'usstai cloak; and *ST:TNG's* third-season two-piece captain's uniform, which led to Patrick Stewart's tunic tugging (the Picard Manoeuvre). Blackman also designed for "*Star Trek Generations*." (See "Clothes Encounters," page 54.)

WILLIAM WARE THEISS
Costume Designer

Theiss often opted for less. Provocative female outfits became the trademark of the original-series costume designer, who also created the first *ST:TNG* uniforms (including Picard's formal frock coat) and won an Emmy Award for his costume designs in the *ST:TNG* episode "The Big Goodbye." (See "Clothes Encounters, page 54.)

MICHAEL DORN
Worf

A snarl is worth a thousand words! As chief of security in *ST:TNG*, Dorn's character, Worf, elevated the perception of Klingons from bloodthirsty warriors to complex beings instilled with honour and spiritual values. Dorn also played Worf's grandfather and Kirk's defence attorney in "*Star Trek VI*," as well as his regular Worf character on *DS9*. He appeared as Worf in the seventh movie "*Star Trek Generations*" and will be in "*Star Trek: First Contact*." Dorn narrated the "Conversational Klingon" companion cassette to linguist Marc Okrand's "The Klingon Dictionary."

JONATHAN FRAKES
William T. Riker

Riker has spent countless episodes boldly going where few men have gone before – namely alien romances. In addition to his starring role in *ST:TNG*, Frakes has taken the director's seat for numerous *ST:TNG* episodes, including "The Offspring" and "Sub Rosa." Post-*ST:TNG*: director's chair in various *DS9* and *Voyager* episodes, as well as "*Star Trek: First Contact*."

BJO & JOHN TRIMBLE
Enterprising Fans

These two ardent *Star Trek* fans leaped to the fore in late 1967 and early 1968 and saved the original show from cancellation by organizing a massive letter-writing campaign. In 1968, Bjo Trimble authored the original "*Star Trek* Concordance" (the original series cast and episode descriptions), with a revision in 1995, plus a book of fan memoirs titled "On the Good Ship Enterprise, My 15 Years with *Star Trek*."

PETER LAURITSON
Supervising Producer

An associate producer when he began with *ST:TNG*, Lauritson helped develop the videotape-layering technology that achieved the crisp, realistic visual effects of *ST:TNG*, *DS9* and *Voyager*,

and helped develop episode soundtracks with a level of detail comparable to feature films. Currently the supervising producer for the on-going *DS9* and *Voyager*, Lauritson (who co-produced "*Star Trek Generations*") is co-producer of "*Star Trek: First Contact*." Trade secret: For the squeaking sound made by the *Enterprise-D*'s automatic doors, Lauritson incorporated a mixed recording of tennis shoe squeaks.

WINRICH KOLBE
Director

Kolbe directed numerous *ST:TNG*, *DS9* and *Voyager* episodes, including the fan favourite "All Good Things..." which was the final *ST:TNG* episode. The latter was no small feat. But Kolbe

proved himself a master at complex scripts. Even with Capt. Picard shifting through three different timelines, and despite the numerous set and make-up changes, the final product had a big-screen tone and remarkable continuity.

LES LANDAU
Director

ST:TNG's "Sarek" (which dwelt on the Vulcan ambassador losing his grasp of logic and control) and "Future Imperfect" (which blurred the lines between fantasy and reality) are just two of Landau's many *ST:TNG*, *DS9* and *Voyager* credits. As a *Star Trek* director,

JOHN AND BJO TRIMBLE: THE COUPLE'S 1968 LETTER-WRITING CAMPAIGN SAVED STAR TREK

RICHARD STERNBACH, MICHAEL OKUDA: THE VITAL ROLE OF DESIGN AND TECHNOLOGY IN STAR TREK

Generation Technical Manual," he also designed the exterior of the Intrepid-class *U.S.S. Voyager*, the Cardassian hand weapon and the storyboards for *Voyager*'s spectacular opening credit scenes. Sternbach also produced the *"Star Trek: The Next Generation U.S.S. Enterprise NCC-1701-D* Blueprints."

JIM MARTIN
Illustrator

Martin created the first concept drawings of *Voyager*'s bridge using the production designs of Richard James. He also illustrated (for *DS9*) the *U.S.S. Defiant* and the Bajoran militia rifle.

ROBERT FLETCHER
Costume Designer

He redesigned uniforms for the Klingons (after the originals were irreversibly altered during a *Mork and Mindy* shoot), created robes for Spock's Vulcan superiors ("*Star Trek III*") and altered *Starfleet* dress uniforms. Fletcher has also contributed to "*Star Trek: The Motion Picture*" (featuring his new engineering safety suits), "*Star Trek II*" and "*Star Trek IV*."

MARC OKRAND
Linguist/Author

If you have "qay'be'" (no problem) speaking the Klingon language, then you have Mr. Okrand to thank. The linguist was first hired to create Vulcan dialect for "*Star Trek II: The Wrath of Khan*," and subsequently developed a full working language for the Klingons (presented on Simon & Schuster's 1992 "Conversational Klingon" cassette). Okrand says that Klingon, as a fictional language, has inspired a general "awareness of language, in the sense of how languages are different from each other, and also how they're similar to each other, and how they play a role in defining a culture."

The author of "The Klingon Dictionary," Okrand derived Klingon from American Indian dialects, Chinese and Southeast Asian languages. Due out in spring 1996 is Okrand's "The Klingon Way: A Warrior's Guide," a collection of Klingon proverbs. Also in the works: Simon & Schuster's instructional Klingon language CD featuring Robert O'Reilly as Gowron.

he was particularly successful in managing the difficulties of location shooting. In "Ensign Ro," Landau cinematically captured the Bajorans' suffering inflicted by the Cardassian oppressors, and created a dark, coarse look for the Bajoran refugee camp scenes.

MICHAEL OKUDA
Scenic Art Supervisor/Technical Consultant

A highly-valued contributor to the *ST:TNG*, *DS9* and *Voyager* series and "*Star Trek Generations*," Okuda (whose wife, Denise, is a *Star Trek* graphic artist) has created countless control and electronics panels, various alien scripts and trademark "Okudagrams." (See story page 64.) Okuda also co-authored "*Star Trek* Chronology," "The *Star Trek* Encyclopedia" and "*Star Trek: The Next Generation* Technical Manual."

RICK STERNBACH
Senior Illustrator/Technical Consultant

Geordi's VISOR – largely made from a plastic barrette – is just one of Sternbach's achievements as senior illustrator and technical consultant for *ST:TNG*, *DS9* and *Voyager*. The co-author of "*Star Trek: The Next*

DAN CURRY
Visual Effects Producer

The inventive Curry once created a sun's corona for *Star Trek* by bouncing a laser beam off a beer can onto a white piece of cardboard. Considering the extent of his creative ability, it's no wonder that he went from visual effects co-ordinator for *ST:TNG* to become the visual effects producer for both *DS9* and *Voyager*. He also devised the opening title sequences of *Voyager*, the concept drawings for the *Array* in "Caretaker" and the initial drawings for the Kazon vessels.

RICARDO DELGADO
Illustrator

As illustrator for *DS9*, Delgado co-created the series' opening title sequence as well as the overall look of *Voyager*. His other contributions include an updated version of *ST:TNG*'s replicators and the initial sketch for *DS9*'s Promenade.

ANDREW PROBERT
Consulting Senior Illustrator

Stepping aboard *ST:TNG* to work alongside technical consultant Rick Sternbach, Probert created the first *Enterprise-D* bridge concept drawings (emphasizing comfort and function) and redesigned the overall look of the Romulan Warbird in *ST:TNG*.

MAURICE HURLEY
Writer

Hurley scripted wonderfully-entertaining Q episodes, including "Hide & Q" (under the pseudonym C.J. Holland) and "Q Who" (under his own name). Hurley illuminated Worf's past when he wrote the teleplay for "Heart of Glory." He co-wrote "Datalore."

IRA STEVEN BEHR
Executive Producer

Producer of *ST:TNG*'s popular "Sarek" episode, Behr became executive producer and a key writer for *DS9*. Behr is credited with developing the Ferengi Rules of Acquisition, which Pocket Books subsequently published as "The Ferengi Rules of Acquisition." Some nuggets of advice: "More is good... all is better," "Treat people in your debt like family... exploit them" and "No good deed ever goes unpunished."

ROBERT LEWIN
Writer

Lewin worked with writer Maurice Hurley on "Datalore," which introduced *ST:TNG* fans to Data's "brother," Lore, who would reappear in the sixth season's two-part "Descent," one of the best cliffhangers of the series.

IRA STEVEN BEHR: FERENGI ACQUISITION RULES

LEVAR BURTON
Geordi LaForge

There's more than a talented engineer behind that VISOR. Burton drew on his dry wit to inject a dose of humour into *ST:TNG*, and portrayed a visually impaired crew member with confidence. Burton moved into the director's chair for *ST:TNG* episodes "Second Chances" and "The Pegasus," and his *Voyager* directorial credits include "Ex Post Facto" and "Dreadnought." He appears as Geordi in the films "*Star Trek Generations*" and "*Star Trek: First Contact*."

WHOOPI GOLDBERG
Guinan

Goldberg played the mysterious Guinan, who tended bar in Ten-Forward, listened compassionately to everyone's problems, doled out bits of wisdom – and flaunted some of the biggest head-

gear in *Starfleet*. She once described her character as a blend of Yoda, Andrei Sakharov and herself (she had the perfect smile and laugh). Goldberg (who also appeared in "*Star Trek Generations*") says she is "more grateful for *Star Trek* now as a mother and grandmother. We all need to believe there is a good, positive future for us."

JEFFREY HUNTER
Capt. Christopher Pike

Hunter was cast as Capt. Pike in the first *Star Trek* attempt, "The Cage," but left the bridge after NBC rejected that pilot episode. His one powerful performance, however, had a dramatic impact. Some longtime fans still think of charismatic Hunter as a powerful *Star Trek* captain. "The Cage" was later reworked and called "The Menagerie."

ROBERT BUTLER
Director

Butler contributed to *Star Trek* in the very beginning when he directed "The Cage." Although NBC initially rejected the overall "idea" of *Star Trek*, the network remained interested in the series, which some Trekkers have attributed to Butler's effort to focus attention on the human drama of "The Cage" when *Star Trek*'s technology alone wasn't going to carry the show.

WALTER KOENIG
Ensign Pavel A. Chekov

Koenig, coiffed like a Monkee but definitely not sounding like one, signed on at the start of *Star Trek*'s second season. His presence, a Russian ensign on the *Enterprise*, acknowledged the role of the Soviets in the space race. Koenig also appeared in the first seven *Star Trek* movies.

MARC OKRAND: KLINGON TALK

GATES McFADDEN
Dr. Beverly Crusher

McFadden exuded an air of medical professionalism that sent a clear message: Crusher was a healer to be taken seriously.

Yet the actor tempered her *ST:TNG* character, remaining feminine and approachable – in sharp contrast to Diana Muldaur's brief second-season stint as Crusher's replacement, Dr. Kate Pulaski, who treated Data little better than a food replicator before warming to the android and learning to appreciate him. McFadden directed one *ST:TNG* episode: "Genesis." Movie appearances: *"Star Trek Generations"* and the upcoming *"Star Trek: First Contact."*

MARINA SIRTIS
Deanna Troi

As *ST:TNG*'s empathic Betazoid counsellor Deanna Troi, Sirtis didn't require a lot of dialogue or screen time to prove her acting abilities. Case in point: Helping Picard through the grief of tragically losing family members in a fatal fire in *"Star Trek Generations,"* Sirtis – by facial expressions alone – powerfully conveyed how deeply Deanna was affected by Picard's tragedy. And when she did land front and centre she positively shone, as in "Face of the Enemy," where she was tough and gritty as an unwilling Romulan. She was also perfect playing the exasperated daughter to the brash and impossible Lwaxana.

MARK LENARD
Sarek

Lenard's Sarek, who was Spock's father and the venerable Vulcan ambassador to the *Federation*, appeared in the original

RICARDO MONTALBAN AS THE RUTHLESS KHAN

series, *ST:TNG*, *"Star Trek III: The Search for Spock"* and *"Star Trek IV."* In his very first *Star Trek* appearance, however, Lenard was a Romulan (in the classic episode "Balance of Terror"); in *"Star Trek: The Motion Picture,"* he was a Klingon.

NICHELLE NICHOLS
Lieut. Uhura

Nichols had a visible role as the original series' communications officer Lieut. Uhura, and was an inspiration for many young black women in the 1960s, including Whoopi Goldberg (who'd later find her place on *ST:TNG* as Guinan) and Dr. Mae Jemison (who actually became an astronaut and made a guest appearance in *ST:TNG*'s "Second Chances"). Nichols almost quit the show after the first season, but was convinced by Dr. Martin Luther King Jr. of the vital message of hope she was providing for other African-Americans. Appearing in the first six *Star Trek* films, Nichols also lent her voice talents to the animated *Star Trek* series of the '70s, and engaged in TV's first on-screen interracial kiss with William Shatner in the classic episode "Plato's Stepchildren."

GEORGE TAKEI
Hikaru Sulu

Takei was originally cast as the ship's physicist in *Star Trek*'s second pilot, "Where No Man Has Gone Before," and shortly after became the helmsman for the duration of *Star Trek*'s three seasons. He appeared in the first six *Star Trek* films, and also lent his voice talent to the animated *Star Trek* series.

DENISE CROSBY
Tasha Yar

Bing Crosby's granddaughter originally read for the role of Deanna Troi but wasn't chosen. Then she found her niche in *ST:TNG*'s "Encounter at Farpoint," as Tasha Yar, the *Enterprise-D*'s chief of security. A powerful performer, Crosby let viewers know that Yar could be trusted to keep ship and crew safe when conflict erupted. Killed off as a cast regular in "Skin of Evil," Crosby returned as Yar in the third season fan favourite "Yesterday's Enterprise." She also appeared as Sela, Yar's half-Romulan

daughter in *ST:TNG*'s fifth-season two-part nail-biter "Unification." Most unforgettable scene: Yar seducing the "fully functional" Data in "The Naked Now."

RICARDO MONTALBAN
Khan Noonien Singh

The Klingon proverb "Revenge is a dish best served cold" is chillingly suited to sum up the ruthless Khan, played by Montalban in the original-series episode "Space Seed" and its big-screen sequel, *Star Trek II: The Wrath of Khan."*

RENÉ AUBERJONOIS
Odo

Before morphing into *DS9* as the shape-shifting security chief Odo, Auberjonois (who directed *DS9*'s humourous third-season episode "Family Business") was cast as Colonel West in *"Star Trek VI: The Undiscovered Country."* He plays Odo with reserve and dignity, a role that has much in common with Spock and Data, who also existed on the margins of human experience. Odo is able to offer his objective opinions of humanity while determined to fit in.

ARMIN SHIMERMAN
Quark

Making his first *ST:TNG* appearance as the vicious Ferengi Letek in "The Last Outpost," actor Shimerman (who once described the early Ferengi as "angry gerbils") appeared again as a Ferengi in "Peak Performance." His third Ferengi character was – and continues to be – his triumph: *DS9*'s Quark. Shimerman plays the character with the right blend of humour and deviousness, helping to distinguish the Ferengi from other militant races in the *Star Trek* universe. He has transformed them from war-loving creatures into strangely honourable, entertaining wags.

KATE MULGREW
Capt. Kathryn Janeway

Mulgrew was not the original choice for the role of Kathryn Janeway: Geneviève Bujold, from Quebec, Canada, was first cast as the captain, but stormed off the set after only two days of shooting. Enter stage right: Kate Mulgrew – who had a very difficult job in the beginning as *Star Trek*'s first female starship captain in a regular series. As Janeway, she has had to display a Kirk-like toughness, balancing the *Federation* rule book in one hand and a phaser in the other, all the while under the sharp scrutiny of *Star Trek* devotees. Mulgrew admirably met the challenge of space (and studio) by summoning up the power necessary to lend a commanding edge to *Voyager*. Mulgrew's previous credits included the starring role in *Mrs. Columbo*.

COLM MEANEY
Miles O'Brien

Sheer charisma and determination transformed Meaney into fan favourite Chief Miles O'Brien – many light-years from his first role as the *ST:TNG* ensign with no name. The O'Brien appeal grew steadily after he transferred to *Deep Space Nine*. Apart from *Voyager*'s Tuvok, he is *Star Trek*'s only other regular series character who is married.

ROBERT PICARDO
The Doctor

The Doctor, *Voyager*'s irritable holographic medical guy, is reminiscent of the original series' Dr. Leonard McCoy. Picardo provides much comic relief – and endless perspectives on the human equation – as *Voyager* roams the Delta Quadrant. Despite his importance to Janeway and crew, the Doctor still has no name!

ETHAN PHILLIPS
Neelix

Phillips first played opposite René Auberjonois (Odo in *DS9*) in the series *Benson* and appeared as a Ferengi in *ST:TNG*'s "Ménage à Troi" before boarding *Voyager* as Neelix, the Talaxian and Delta Quadrant guide whose ongoing schemes as the morale officer-cum-cook are original and humourous.

JENNIFER LIEN
Kes

One-time cast member of the long-running American daytime soap *Another World*, the 21-year-old Lien jumped ship and joined *Voyager* as Kes. Able to project both strength and vulnerability, Lien was realistic in her portrayal of the alien youth who bucked Ocampan tradition by leaving her underground home, becoming the Doctor's assistant, and developing her telekinetic powers.

BEFORE AND AFTER: ARMIN SHIMERMAN TRANSFORMED INTO QUARK

MICHELLE FORBES
Ensign Ro Laren

The sharp-edged Bajoran Ensign Ro Laren was created to stir up some trouble among the *ST:TNG* crew. And Forbes fit the part. She was a cutting individual, disrespectful and defiant of authority. The product of Cardassian atrocities, Ro quickly won the hearts of fans for her candor, and remained a recurring character with *ST:TNG* until the seventh season's "Pre-emptive Strike," when Ro joined the Maquis to fight the Cardassians. Ro's background, drawing on the Bajoran-Cardassian conflict, set the groundwork for much of *DS9*, and the determined ensign was slated to be the station's second-in-command. Forbes, however, chose to pursue

other film projects; her departure allowed for the new role of Major Kira Nerys, played by Nana Visitor.

DWIGHT SCHULTZ
Lieut. Reginald Barclay

The *Enterprise* crew bestowed upon Barclay the nickname "Broccoli," a well-suited moniker for Schultz's *ST:TNG* character. His aversion to stressful situations was completely human. Schultz became a champion for the average viewer as he fumbled his way from one adventure to another.

NANA VISITOR
Major Kira Nerys

Major Kira exudes fire and grace as *DS9*'s second-in-command. Visitor, passionate in her portrayal of a woman haunted by Cardassian horrors – and driven to right them – reveals the subtle force of her acting skill as *DS9*'s writers explore Major Kira's romantic and spiritual side as the series progresses.

ROBERT DUNCAN McNEILL
Tom Paris

McNeill first appeared as the rule-breaking Acadamy cadet Nicholas Locarno in *ST:TNG*'s "The First Duty"; in *Voyager*, he continues to break the rules as the rebellious Lieut. Paris. McNeill also directed *Voyager*'s "Sacred Ground" (for season three).

ROGER C. CARMEL
Harcourt Fenton Mudd

The original-series actor was unforgettable as the womanizing cad Harry Mudd in "Mudd's Women" and "I, Mudd." Carmel was also the voice of Mudd in the animated *Star Trek* series.

JONATHAN DEL ARCO
Hugh Borg (Third of Five)

Arco was the first to provide an in-depth glimpse into the Borg psyche. In "I, Borg," viewers expected a soulless assimilation machine; instead, they encountered the Borg as a frightened being on the road to self-awareness. Borg emotions swung the full pendulum in *ST:TNG*'s two-part "Descent."

TERI GARR IN "ASSIGNMENT: EARTH"

ROGER C. CARMEL IS MUDD

JOHN COLICOS
Commander Kor

The first actor to portray a Klingon (in the original-series episode "Errand of Mercy"), Colicos, a Canadian who used to act with the Old Vic Company, reprised his Kor character in two *DS9* episodes: "Blood Oath" and later "The Sword of Kahless."

BARBARA MARCH and GWYNYTH WALSH
Lursa and B'Etor, the Duras sisters

Where Klingon females in past *Star Trek* outings tended to function as humble counterparts to Klingon males, the Duras sisters were equal to any ten Klingon warriors, thanks to fiery and powerful performances by March and Walsh. The two Canadian actors – March (Lursa) and Walsh (B'Etor) – inspired the term "Klingon kleavage." They were mean and alluring. Marching into *ST:TNG* in the two-parter "Redemption," the pair reappeared in *ST:TNG*'s "Firstborn" and *DS9*'s "Past Prologue" and then met their doom in *"Star Trek Generations."*

JOAN COLLINS
Edith Keeler

Playing Kirk's love interest in the classic episode "The City on the Edge of Forever," Collins reflected humanity's uni-

PRODUCER/WRITER HARVE BENNETT

versal thread of hope for a better world in her role as Edith Keeler, who dared to dream and gaze upon the stars.

AVERY BROOKS
Capt. Benjamin Sisko

Comparisons to Patrick Stewart were inevitable as Brooks took command of *DS9* in the series' opener, "Emissary." Picard was a tough act to follow. In an effort to woo viewers, producers would promote Sisko to captain and redo his image (on Brooks' suggestion). This creative effort paid off with Brooks developing a loyal fan following. He directed many *DS9* episodes, including the controversial "Rejoined" in which two female Trills passionately kiss.

TERI GARR
Roberta Lincoln

Garr was captivating and charming in "Assignment: Earth" as Gary Seven's dizzy secretary, Roberta Lincoln, who valiantly tried to understand the comings and goings of her strange employer and the *Enterprise* crew. Shades of her performance would later surface in her role as a confused homemaker in "Close Encounters of the Third Kind."

WALLACE SHAWN
The Grand Nagus

"The fire dims. I'm just not as greedy as I used to be." Shawn's role as the Grand Nagus in "The Nagus" *(DS9)* epitomized the odd charm of the Ferengi race. Loud and flamboyant as the cantankerous Ferengi leader (whose appetite for Quark's holosuites appeared bottomless), Shawn made The Grand N's lamentations humourously entertaining. He was just as hilarious as a self-proclaimed genius in "The Princess Bride".

WILLIAM CAMPBELL
Trelane, Squire of Gothos

Delightfully dangerous as "The Squire of Gothos" in his first *Star Trek* role (a virtual precursor to Q), Campbell resurfaced as the Klingon Captain Koloth in "The Trouble with Tribbles" before reprising the same character 27 years later in *DS9*'s "Blood Oath," which also revived classic Klingon characters Kang (Michael Ansara) from "Day of the Dove" and Kor (John Colicos) from "Errand of Mercy."

Director Nicholas Meyer on the set of "Star Trek VI: The Undiscovered Country"

CHRISTOPHER PLUMMER
General Chang

Plummer instilled a sense of honour in his role as the Klingon General Chang in "*Star Trek VI.*" Reminiscent of Khan, the character (a far cry from Plummer's leading role in "The Sound of Music") was given a bald head at the actor's request – he refused the designated head-piece. You have to respect a Klingon who doesn't mind having an eye patch bolted to his head.

JERRY GOLDSMITH
Composer

Goldsmith composed *Voyager*'s Emmy-winning opening theme, the music of "*Star Trek: The Motion Picture*," and "*Star Trek V: The Final Frontier*" on his own, and *ST:TNG*'s opening theme with Alexander Courage.

DENNIS McCARTHY
Composer

Garnering Emmy awards for *ST:TNG*'s "Unification" and *DS9*'s main title theme, McCarthy also got an Emmy nomination for the dramatic underscore of *ST:TNG*'s "Yesterday's Enterprise." He wrote the music for "*Star Trek Generations,*" and stitched together the themes from the motion picture and the original series to create the *ST:TNG* theme music.

JAY CHATTAWAY
Composer

Composed much of the incidental music for *ST:TNG*. Among his most memo-rable underscores: "Relics," with touch-ing notes from the original series; and the haunting strains of "Sub Rosa."

JAMES HORNER
Composer

The tension and musical surprises woven throughout the battle scenes greatly explain why "*Star Trek II: The Wrath of Khan*" remains such a grip-ping thriller. Horner also composed the music for "*Star Trek III,*" recording the film's soundtrack in just one week!

HARVE BENNETT
Producer/Writer

The executive producer of "*Star Trek II,*" Bennett wrote and produced "*Star Trek III*" and produced and co-wrote "*Star Trek IV*" and "*Star Trek V.*"

NICHOLAS MEYER
Director

A No Smoking sign on the bridge in *"Star Trek II"* and the appearance of pots and pans in the *Enterprise* kitchen in *"Star Trek VI"* are just a couple of Meyer's unconventional directorial touches. His film philosophy – design for the future with an eye to the past – influenced the work of Herman Zimmerman, production designer for *ST:TNG* and *DS9*.

RALPH WINTER
Producer

Good producers have a yen for detail. Winter, for example, can recall that 325 lunches were served every day during the filming of the Khitomer conference scenes shot in a university synagogue for *"Star Trek VI: The Undiscovered Country."* Winter was also post-production co-ordinator for *"Star Trek II,"* associate producer for *"Star Trek III"* and had the role of executive producer for both *"Star Trek IV"* and *"Star Trek V."*

DAVID CARSON
Director

Co-creators Rick Berman and Michael Piller wanted a sombre tone for *DS9*, and that's exactly what Carson delivered when he directed the series' opener, "Emissary." The episode's low-level lighting and often-hectic sequences quickly let viewers know that *DS9* was far from the comfortable, orderly confines of *Starfleet* Command. Carson also directed *"Star Trek Generations."*

THEODORE STURGEON
Writer

Sturgeon wrote the classic episode "Amok Time," in which Spock first delivered the immortal line "Live long and prosper." The author was also part of Harlan Ellison's letter-writing campaign that saved the classic *Star Trek* from cancellation in 1966, and he wrote the original-series episode "Shore Leave," which fleshed out much of Kirk's romantic and professional past.

TRACY TORMÉ
Writer

Tormé is the award-winning writer of *ST:TNG*'s "The Big Goodbye," in which Picard introduced fans to private detective Dixon Hill. Tormé also wrote "The Schizoid Man" (which gave Brent Spiner an early opportunity to portray Data's emotional side) and scripted several other episodes under the pseudonyms Terry Devereaux and Keith Mills.

VINCE McEVEETY
Director

McEveety reached for a hypnotic effect for the dramatic showdown in "Spectre of the Gun" by calling for unusual camera angles and extended use of close-ups. Other original-series directing credits: "Miri," "Dagger of the Mind" and "Balance of Terror."

STEPHEN KANDEL
Writer

Kandel wrote the original-series episode "Mudd's Women," then resurrected the roguish Harry Mudd when he co-wrote "I, Mudd," which contained unforgettable scenes of the crew play-acting in order to deactivate Mudd's androids.

JOE MENOSKY
Writer

Menosky's "Darmok" planted Picard in a situation in which the universal translator finally proved incompatible with another language, and the captain had to struggle to communicate with a new species. Menosky also wrote *DS9*'s gripping episode "Dramatis Personae" and *ST:TNG*'s "Hero Worship."

CLIFF BOLE
Director

The Cliffs of Bole (*DS9*'s "Invasive Procedures") were a tribute to the director of numerous *ST:TNG*, *DS9* and *Voyager* episodes. Credits have included *ST:TNG*'s fast-paced "The Best of Both Worlds" (which thrust Picard into the Borg collective) and the *DS9* nail-biter "Dramatis Personae."

BILL GEORGE
Art Director

George designed the *"Star Trek III"* vessel *U.S.S. Excelsior*, which was later modified to become the ill-fated *U.S.S. Enterprise-B* in the movie *"Star Trek Generations."* George was the visual effects art director on the latter.

OSCAR KATZ
Vice-President, Desilu Studios

Katz bet on *Star Trek* in 1964 when Roddenberry first failed to sell the series. In charge of new show development for Desilu Studios (the American production group that first produced

DIRECTOR DAVID CARSON AND PATRICK STEWART ON THE MOVIE SET OF "STAR TREK GENERATIONS"

THEY'RE TROUBLE, THEY'RE TRIBBLES: CAPTAIN KIRK IS BESIEGED WITH THE FUZZY LITTLE FUR BALLS IN "THE TROUBLE WITH TRIBBLES"

Star Trek), Katz helped convince NBC to finance the pilots "The Cage" and "Where No Man Has Gone Before."

RICHARD JAMES
Production Designer

James (a six-season veteran of *ST:TNG*) re-created the classic series' *Enterprise* bridge for *ST:TNG*'s "Relics" by mixing a partial reconstruction of the original set with footage from the classic episode "This Side of Paradise." He also designed the interior look of *Voyager* and the functional appearance of its bridge.

DAN MADSEN
Official *Star Trek* Fan Club Founder

"When I started [the club], I was a kid sitting in front of a little typewriter in my bedroom," recalls Madsen. Today, his organization is the official *Star Trek* club, with some 150,000 members world-wide. Write to: *Star Trek: The Official Fan Club*, P.O. Box 111000

Aurora, Colorado, USA 80042. The club offers an official magazine: *Star Trek Communicator*. Closer to home, Titan Books Ltd. publishes *Star Trek: The Official Monthly Magazine*. Write to: 42-44 Dalben St., London, SE1 0UP.

PETER ALLAN FIELDS
Producer/Writer

A *DS9* producer and writer, Fields wrote "The Circle" and "Necessary Evil," creating a level of conflict among the regular characters rarely encountered in the harmonious *ST:TNG* crowd. Fields also wrote "Duet," which uncovered the true horror of the Cardassians' occupation of Bajor.

WIL WHEATON
Wesley Crusher

Playing the whiz-kid son of Dr. Crusher, Wheaton was *The Next Generation*'s youngest regular cast member but was always treated as an equal by the other cast. "I never felt like an outsider," he says.

LOLITA FATJO
Pre-production/Script Co-ordinator

Fatjo reads and catalogues all scripts submitted for *Star Trek*. She's a dedicated participant at the *Star Trek* writing seminars and workshops, and has helped discover many great episode concepts.

THE STAR TREK WELCOMMITTEE

The volunteer body (est. in 1972) operates in seven countries and answers questions on any aspect of *Star Trek*. Write to: *Star Trek* Welcommittee, Box 12, Saranac, Michigan, USA 48881.

TRIBBLES
Fur Balls of Trouble

We couldn't resist adding these non-human fur balls to our list, bringing our total to 101. The Tribbles first appeared in the original series' "The Trouble with Tribbles," and – except for the Klingons – *everybody* loves them. ✧

Make it so

Music, lights, action!
An insider look at the making
of an entire *Star Trek*
episode from script to screen

BY MICHAEL LOGAN

LARGE PHOTO: DIRECTOR CLIFF BOLE PUTS KATE MULGREW (CAPT. JANEWAY) ON HER MARK DURING SHOOTING OF VOYAGER'S "TUVIX." INSETS, CLOCKWISE FROM LEFT: DIRECTOR JIM CONWAY AND FIRST ASSISTANT DIRECTOR B.C. CAMERON ON SET FOR DS9'S "SHATTERED MIRROR"; A CLOSE-UP OF MICHAEL DORN (WORF) AS ANDREW ROBINSON (GARAK) DELIVERS LINES OFF-CAMERA; LAST-MINUTE HAIRSTYLING FOR VOYAGER'S JENNIFER LIEN AND KATE MULGREW; AVERY BROOKS (CAPT. SISKO), PHOTOGRAPHY DIRECTOR JONATHAN WEST AND DIRECTOR JIM CONWAY DURING A DS9 REHEARSAL; CLOSE-UP OF VOYAGER SLATE; SET COSTUMER MATT HOFFMAN ADJUSTS ROBERT PICARDO'S COLLAR JUST SECONDS BEFORE SHOOTING A VOYAGER SCENE

VERY SINGLE EPISODE IN THE HISTORY OF *Star Trek* has sprung from the same source: a blank piece of paper.

"And that piece of paper is getting harder and harder to fill," says Jeri Taylor, co-creator and one of the executive producers of *Star Trek: Voyager.* "Fresh ideas are golden – especially when we're talking about a phenomenon that has had four series incarnations and eight movies [by end of 1996]. We have a very open policy where the story is concerned. We take pitches from anyone."

Once Taylor and her team decide to buy that story concept, it is assigned to a teleplay writer (he or she could be an established freelancer or someone on the *Star Trek* writing staff). "Then, we set up a story meeting where we all kick around the idea to make sure it has a dramatic spine and character arcs, as well as a beginning, middle and end," explains Taylor. "The writer is sent off to do a six- or seven-page treatment of what we discussed so that we have something down on paper. That version is signed off by [executive producer] Rick Berman, who otherwise does not get involved with the day-to-day writing details."

Then comes the most crucial part of the creative process – the 'storybreak meeting' – which is attended, in the case of a typical *Star Trek: Deep Space Nine* episode, by the teleplay writer, executive producer Ira Steven Behr, such longtime staff scribes as producer René Echevarria, and supervising producer Ronald D. Moore.

"At this stage," says Moore, "we go through the teaser and the five acts beat-by-beat, scene-by-scene and really hash it

STAR TREK "VOYAGER"

SCENE 41C TAKE 1

DIRECTOR ALEX SINGER
CAMERA MARVIN RUSH A.S.C.
DATE 2-21-96   PROD# 40840-141

out in detail. We make sure we know where the conflict is, where each character is at emotionally, and when the teleplay writer leaves he has a very good blueprint for what the script needs to be." The writer is usually given two weeks for the first draft. "But like any show we can get into a real time bind," says Jeri Taylor. "We've been in situations where we've had to turn around a first draft in four days – which is insane. Sometimes things are so crunched, we have had to split up the show and give different acts to different writers and hope it all magically melds together – but this situation is hardly desirable."

When the first draft is handed in, Taylor gets tough. "We really attack the problems head-on," she says. "We ask ourselves, 'Is this script rich and deep enough for the *Star Trek* audience? Are the characters textured and layered enough? Are we being too obvious? Is it shallow and sophomoric?' All these things can be true in a first draft – and if the teleplay writer is from the outside, the staff will often take over the script at this point." While this may hardly seem fair to the writer in question, Taylor insists that it is necessary in the interest of time. "We *must* stay on schedule," she says. "I think of *Star Trek* as a giant maw that just gobbles up scripts and is constantly saying, 'Fee-oooood meeeeeeeee.' We start shooting a new *Star Trek* episode every seven to eight days and the next script absolutely

DEEP SPACE NINE STORY MEETING: L - R: WRITING INTERN CHUCK GORDON JOTS DOWN IDEAS WHILE RENÉ ECHEVARRIA, RONALD D. MOORE, FREELANCE WRITER NAREN SHANKAR, HANS BEIMLER, ROBERT WOLFE AND IRA STEVEN BEHR DISCUSS POSSIBLE STAR TREK STORY LINES

must be ready or the maw is going to be snapping at us."

While the second draft is being completed, a beat sheet is prepared, briefly describing each scene. This allows the producer – Merri Howard, in the case of *Star Trek: Voyager* – to get a head start on pre-production. She books the cast members and any necessary locations and ensures there is adequate prep time to build new sets or props. Seven days before the start of principal photography, the writer, producers, director and department heads merge for a one- to three-hour pre-production meeting.

VOYAGER DIRECTOR CLIFF BOLE CONFERS WITH MERRI HOWARD (PRODUCER UNIT)

"And that," says Howard, who started with *Star Trek* as a first assistant director during the second season of *Star Trek: The Next Generation*, "is where it's my job to get out my red pencil and say, 'Guys, let's be realistic. Think about the budget.' I'm now the official company spoil-sport. The script may say 'Six Kazon ships go by at warp speed,' but that shot could end up costing [the equivalent of £25,000] and send the episode over budget. I will say to Rick Berman or Jeri Taylor or Michael Piller, 'The idea is great – but let's talk about other ways we can do it. Will four Kazon ships work?' They may still want to spend the extra money because it's a swell story point or they may say, 'We've got some expensive ratings shows coming up, so let's cut back on this episode.' We call the less expensive shows the 'get well' or 'make-up' shows. As long as the bottom line is zero at the end of the season, Paramount really doesn't care how we spend the budget money."

Inevitably, the first departments to be hit with cutback requests are sets and opticals (the latter includes any visual or special effects – from a simple phaser beam to the creation of an entire planet). Says Howard: "The writer might envision two scenes on an alien ship which require two full sets. We may ask him to compromise by using one set and maybe a little corridor. This is a real collaborative effort. It's OK to have your vision but you also have a responsibility to the production." During the prep period, casting directors Junie Lowry-Johnson and Ron Surma have a pre-casting meeting with the writer, director and producers. During the course of this meeting, Howard explains, "The writer might say, 'I envision the guest-star character to be 20 years old and sort of a Tom Cruise type.'" Casting commences immediately so that the wardrobe, make-up and hair departments have ample time.

One or two days before filming begins, costume designer Robert Blackman and make-up supervisor Michael Westmore give the executive producers a show 'n' tell preview. Execs will also take a "stage walk" – also attended by the director, production designer, art director, construction coordinator, property master and director of photography. "Everybody must be in agreement on the vision," says Howard. "There can be no surprises when shooting starts." A production meeting is held two days before principal photography, primarily to deal with any changes in script, which, in Howard's experience, have sometimes proven to be surprisingly extensive. "The entire concept of an episode has been known to change during prep. Entire sets may be dropped, major scenes may be cut. Sometimes Jeri Taylor and I will have to talk 15 times a day about changes." As filming proceeds, the executive producer will view "rushes" (Americans call them "dailies") not only to stay abreast of the action but to prevent a crisis later down the line. Says Jeri Taylor: "There have been cases where we do not feel a scene has been shot well enough. We may ask for a reshoot or – if we're not sure whether we really got what we want – we will ask the editor to drop everything and edit the scene immediately to see if anything needs to be reshot. Going back to reshoot after we've moved on to the next episode can be disastrous to the budget."

So can an episode that ends up running too short or too long. One of Star Trek's six rotating film editors (three on Voyager, three on Deep Space Nine) will cut an episode to the pace and length he sees fit. The director steps in for three to four days to do his version – the "director's cut" – and, finally, J.P. Farrell, who serves as supervising film editor for both series, will make further adjustments based on Rick Berman's tastes. "The editor and the director cut the gem and I polish it," says Farrell, who considers himself

Cast calls

Junie Lowry-Johnson and Ron Surma – casting directors

A bit of advice for all wannabe Star Trek stars: Know your techno-babble. "The single biggest problem for actors auditioning for Star Trek is the technical language – more often than not it's what keeps them from getting the part," says Junie Lowry-Johnson, who casts DS9 and Voyager with partner Ron Surma. "The trick is to do it simply – which is hard." According to Surma, "The tendency is to try to make too much of the techno-babble, to over-emphasize rather than to say it with calm conviction. The formality of Star Trek is also difficult. Starfleet officers have supposedly had at least four years of training, but very few actors today can relate to a military-school background." And don't try to fib your way through an audition. Lowry-Johnson is adamant on this point. "We'll have people come in to read for a Klingon role who have never seen our shows. We'll say, 'Do you know what a Klingon is?' and they'll go, 'Uh...er...yeah...sure,' and proceed to blow their audition out of ignorance." Lowry-Johnson (who started in the business by casting extras for Roger Corman "B" films) and Surma (a Chicago stage actor) rely heavily on theatre-trained talent because the language of Star Trek borders on the classical. "Some actors are just too contemporary, too '90s to be convincing in the 24th

century," says Surma. "And some actors are so classical they're cartoonish. We look for the happy medium." And a pretty good bod – at least where Starfleet characters are concerned. "Aliens can come in all shapes and sizes," says Lowry-Johnson, "but you've gotta be in shape to wear that Starfleet uniform."

Trade secrets

Herman Zimmerman – production designer

His job is a big one – in fact, he is responsible for the overall visual concept for everything you see on *Deep Space Nine*. Herman Zimmerman weaves much of his magic with tiny, often secret detail. "The casual viewer probably doesn't realize the space station is based on the Cardassian love for the number three," says Zimmerman. "We made up an entire set of Cardassian design rules – they like circles and trapezoids and they don't like squares. If you look down on the station, you'll see what vaguely resembles a Mercedes emblem. There's a 120-degree division in a circle, three concentric rings, three arms that join the rings to each other and three docking arms above and below the station. On top of this basic wire-frame structure, we laid a set of alien-like scales and equipment pods which mirror the Cardassians' own crustacean-like outer skeletons." It's a far cry from the original concept for *Deep Space Nine* – a Tower of Babel-ish rust bucket in space that was built by four or five different cultures living in different time periods and speaking different languages. "You could walk from one part of the station to another and it would look completely different," says Zimmerman. "We spent a month and a half making stacks and stacks of drawings and constructing models. It was a neat idea but it turned out to be a visual hodgepodge. In fact, it was quite a mess. Nobody liked it." But those drawings – if they ever surfaced at a *Star Trek* convention – could be worth zillions.

Alan Sims – property master

The *Star Trek* writers don't give Alan Sims much help. "The script may simply say, 'Chakotay is building a shelter,' but the rest is left up to me," says the *Voyager* property master. "I have to decide what kind of tools he'd use and what they'd look like. It's the 24th century, so he wouldn't use hammer and nails – so maybe I would suggest to the producers some sort of laser instrument that fuses materials together. But they don't always want to go futuristic. I've never felt our characters should still be eating with a knife and fork 400 years in the future – but I keep losing that battle." His favourite kind of prop? "Alien food," replies Sims. "It's giggly, it's gaggly, it'll bite you if you look at it. I love it." Surprisingly, live animals even fall under his domain. When the script for a recent *Voyager* episode called for an alien primate, Sims found a spider monkey which, on command, could walk on its hind legs

with its tail erect. "At first, Rick Berman just laughed. He couldn't believe that a spider monkey – which you could find in any zoo – would look convincingly alien. But when I showed him photographs of what the monkey could do, he said, 'That looks alien enough to me. Book him!'" Other animal acts have not gone as smoothly. Sims recently hired a trained hawk (for *Voyager*'s "Tattoo") that was supposed to swoop down and attack Neelix (Ethan Phillips). "Instead," he gasps, "the hawk spotted a crow and went off after it in the opposite direction. It took hours to find him. The delay was a nightmare." How does he select such special guest stars? "Just as with actors, you have to hold auditions. And who knows," muses Sims, "one of these days, I may hold a real cattle call."

Keeping up appearances

Robert Blackman – costume designer

Don't ask Robert Blackman to pick his favourite *Star Trek* outfit. "They're like my children – I couldn't possibly choose one over the other." This from the designer who has created costumes for all three series spinoffs (he has also designed the new Starfleet uniforms in the upcoming "*Star Trek Generations II*"). "Besides, if I assign such importance to something that's behind me, I'll feel like I'm just resting. I must keep looking to the future – and when you're working in space that's the best thing to do." Costuming two *Star Trek* shows simultaneously can be tricky, and Blackman says he breathes easier when an episode comes along that just features the regulars. "We refer to them as 'ship shows' or 'bottle shows' – meaning they're in the bottle – but they can really fool us. We're so used to trouble-shooting and looking over our shoulders all the time on the complicated shows that we sometimes take it too easy on the simpler

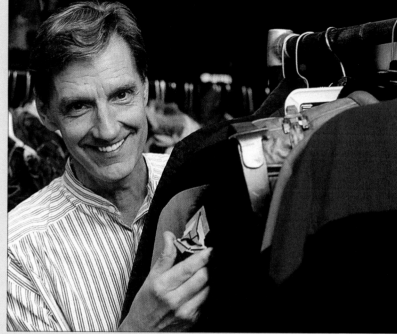

ones. In one episode, I failed to notice a tiny scene in the script where an alien came on board – we were all suddenly running around like crazy people trying to make an alien costume in three minutes! That's when you really want to bite yourself in the butt big time."

Michael Westmore – make-up supervisor

One quick look at a script and Michael Westmore knows exactly how much time he needs to prepare the make-up. "A full alien mask takes a week, a humanoid takes three days and a Vulcan? I've got plenty of ears in stock," says Westmore, a third-generation Hollywood legend, who takes his job very seriously. (Note the intricate make-up work in the accompanying photo – each "work of art" of this sort is signed and dated.) He won an Oscar for the movie "Mask" but it was his work in the "Genesis" episode of *The Next Generation* (which got him an Emmy nomination) that proved his greatest challenge. "Everybody mutated – Riker became a Neanderthal, Troi an aquatic animal, Barclay a spider," he recalls. "We never would have been ready if the episode hadn't miraculously fallen right after Christmas. We worked through the holiday." Westmore is always playing beat-the-clock, but technological advances have made things less stressful. "Gone are the days when you sat for six hours with plastic straws up your nose while we made a plaster cast of your face. Now it takes 20 minutes." Still, some players get claustrophobic under Westmore's prosthetics. "It's never the women," he says. "It's the macho-man types. They lose all control."

Berman's proxy producer. "I started editing *Star Trek* with the first hour instalment of *The Next Generation* and have been with Rick ever since. At this point, I'm pretty much inside his brain. I know what he likes and what makes him twitch." If an episode runs overtime, Farrell will ask the appropriate executive producer – either Taylor or Ira Steven Behr – to make cuts. That means some very expensive footage ends up on the cutting-room floor. A show that runs too short can cause even bigger headaches. According to Farrell, "Directors get nervous if their shows end up too long because they will have to be clipped – so they're very aware of directing their scripts at a very brisk pace. However, sometimes they can be too brisk and an episode will come in so short that we have to write and shoot new material." Jeri Taylor knows what that's like: "We recently had an episode of *Voyager* that came in a full eight minutes short – which had to be some sort of *Star Trek* record. We had to shoot an additional day-and-a-half's worth of footage. It turned out to be good stuff – with all the urgency and energy of the rest of the episode – but it was very expensive." Taylor says some of *Voyager*'s very best scenes were never in the original script. "When we are padding for time, we have no obligation to serve the plot, so we can wind up with some wonderful character scenes that are funny or droll or insightful – whatever the case may be. But we've had episodes that were really hurt by padding. If a scene has no point, it can slow the show to a crawl."

Farrell takes two or three passes at an episode, and then views it with Rick Berman on a 32-inch monitor in the exec's private screening room. "At this point, we're viewing for pace, rhythm and content rather than picture and sound quality. Rick may say, 'Tighten up that character's exit' or 'The scene just sort of lays there – let's liven it up with some off-camera wild lines of dialogue.'" With optical effects still to come, Berman uses his imagination. As Farrell explains, "A card will flash on the screen saying 'Closeup: Hands Punching Computer Buttons' or 'Klingon Ship Decloaks.' The effects are put in later." Many times, such effects – which fall under the banner of second unit photography – are still being created just days before an episode airs. Visual effects producer Dan Curry says this stage can be very complex and time-consuming: "An episode with a couple of phasers and a transporter is one thing. An episode with a slime monster who comes out of a wall and engulfs everybody is quite another."

Of course, there is considerable guesswork involved. If the script calls for a shot of a starship entering and quickly exiting the frame, the editor and director will leave, say, a five-second hole and trust Curry and his crew will be able to make the ship (actually a miniature) complete the action in that amount of time. A scene with a character in an unusual location – an alien planet, for example – will be created by having the actor play the scene against a blue-screen backdrop. Farrell has relied on this technique many times: "The planet will be created either electronically on the MacIntosh or with that traditional 15th-century technology, the matte oil painting, and is photographed on film. That film is then transferred to digital video and composited with the film of the actor so it appears the character is actually standing on the planet."

The last remaining production elements – music, sound

Prime directives

Three directors and a space show

Robert Duncan McNeill owes his directing break to Jonathan Frakes, which is telling in itself. Frakes was one of the first in a long line of series actors to try their hand at directing – and with some it has become a second calling. "Frakes was scheduled to direct an episode of *Voyager* and backed out in order to direct "*Star Trek: First Contact*" – so they gave his slot to me," says McNeill. His assignment: "Sacred Ground," an episode to air early in season three which he describes as "an extremely spiritual show about Capt. Janeway having to let go of logic, take a leap of faith and consider the magical, mysterious, godlike elements of the world. As a scientist, this is not easy for her to do." As an actor, this wasn't easy for McNeill, either. "It's the cliché in Hollywood to say, 'What I really want to do is direct.' I really needed to prove to Rick Berman that I was serious. I first put the bug in his ear in March of 1995. He said, 'Go to

school for a year,' meaning study *Star Trek,* hang out, observe, soak it all up," McNeill says. Even on days when he wasn't playing *Voyager* skirt-chaser Tom Paris, McNeill would show up on the Paramount lot to watch editing sessions and second-unit photography. "I sat with the producers when they screened episodes. I studied their likes and dislikes. I followed the directors around. I was a pest." Almost a year to the day of his first discussion with Berman, McNeill got a phone call. "I was out of town doing a *Star Trek* convention and got an urgent message, 'Phone Rick at home this weekend.' My wife called all weepy and said, 'I just know that you're fired.' But I had a feeling it was good news." So it was. Call it director's instinct.

Avery Brooks was chosen to helm one of the most controversial episodes in *Star Trek* history – the romance between two female Trills on *Deep Space Nine* – but he refused to be influenced by executive

BOTTOM LEFT: DIRECTOR ROBERT DUNCAN
MCNEILL. TOP: SUPERVISING FILM EDITOR J. P.
FARRELL WITH FILM EDITOR DAVID RAMIREZ.
RIGHT: RAMIREZ EDITS A DS9 EPISODE

worries. "The producers and the studio had their set of concerns about the story – but I could not make them mine," says Brooks, who plays *DS9*'s Capt. Sisko. "My responsibility was to get inside the story and present it in a way that was honest and true, to make it something we could all be proud of." Guiding co-star Terry Farrell (Dax) through the notorious kissing scene – which she was openly uncomfortable with – was a real challenge. "But," enthuses Brooks, "the advantage of actors directing actors is that we communicate in an emotional shorthand. We understand what the other is up against because we've all been there – and that creates a potential for greater and deeper trust."

René Auberjonois, *Deep Space Nine*'s Odo, says of his first time directing: "Everybody bent over backwards to make sure I was comfortable. The actors, in particular, were very sympathetic to my situation. The second time, everyone was still supportive but the actors started to have some very strong opinions about their characters. You're constantly aware of the time pressure, yet you want to give everybody their say – so you wind up being drawn into lengthy conversations that you're not really listening to. You see the actor's mouth moving but all you really hear is 'Tick...tick...tick.' The third time I directed, all bets were off. They were terrible to me." Auberjonois gets no argument from co-star Alexander Siddig (Bashir). "Colm Meaney and I gave René a bad time by being recalcitrant and unbelievably impossible and never showing up on time," laughs Siddig. "He thought we were from hell. He really hated us. We both had to apologize."

effects, voice-overs (like Majel Barrett's *Federation* computer voice) and looped dialogue (crowd sounds and other lines recorded in a sound studio) – are fused, along with all visual effects, into a master edit of the episode. It is approved by Berman and only Berman. Copies are presented to all key personnel four to five days before the episode hits the air. Some pop it into their office videos and watch it immediately. But Taylor takes hers home. "It's a little tradition. I purposely get away from the craziness of the studio and watch it quietly and privately with my husband [retired writer-producer] David Moessinger. It is my first opportunity to see the episode with all of the effects and the music score, which can make a dramatic difference. It's like a whole new experience. No matter how well I know an episode, it still has the magic and the power to stir me."

So, that's how the creative team at Paramount puts together a *Star Trek* show. But what about you, the fans? Got a fabulous idea for a *Star Trek* episode? Well, here's some encouraging news:

"Anyone can write a spec script for *Star Trek: Voyager* or *Star Trek: Deep Space Nine* and submit it for consideration," says Jeri Taylor, *Voyager*'s executive producer and co-creator.

Majel Barrett does her Federation *computer voice-overs for* Deep Space Nine *and* Voyager

"It *will* be read. We openly turn to the fans for help with story ideas. Even if a script is not up to snuff, we might spark to the idea and buy it."

Now, for the reality check: "Our standards are extremely high," Taylor cautions. "We keep them that way because we have an enlightened audience and we don't want to become complacent. We must provide a number of things with each *Star Trek* story: a wonderful sci-fi element, something magical, wondrous, intriguing and thought-provoking. We need to have some kind of jeopardy that creates tension in our characters. And at the core of all our episodes, I firmly believe, there must be a deeply felt personal story."

"But we don't like to tell personal stories that make obvious points about relationships or the human condition. We like to investigate humanity from a fresh slant, an oblique angle. We like to turn it on its ear and look at it from another perspective. We want to provide new insight. Contemporary series can tell a story in a very straightforward way – but we feel that if we settle for that, we are not utilizing the *Star Trek* franchise to its greatest advantage."

"However, story ideas that really stand up to all these crite-

Music notes

Score keepers – composing for *Star Trek*

The final stage in creating a *Star Trek* episode is the music: The emotional sweetener on top of the action. And it's added by the two main composers, **Dennis McCarthy** and **Jay Chattaway**, who alternate in writing the scores for *Deep Space Nine* and *Voyager* in a process that can take anywhere from one to two weeks, depending on the show. An average action-packed *Voyager* show requires about 25 minutes of music; DS9 usually calls for 20. To begin, McCarthy or Chattaway works with a video of the final cut, and spends three to seven days composing the score on a piano in their home studios. "It's written out with pencil and paper and copyists – like it was 100 years ago," explains Chattaway. The melodies are honed until the Thursday before airing, when the battle sequences and special effects have been added. Then the composer writes the last-minute themes for the battles, which, because of tight timelines and the volume of music, are the most challenging ("They're the ones that make you old," McCarthy sighs). By the next day, the composer takes the finished score into the studio with as many as 50 musicians (both DS9 and *Voyager* rely on orchestral instruments, only using synthesizers for other-worldly music and sounds). The conductor faces the musicians – and a huge screen showing the episode – and they spend the next four to seven hours recording music for a one-hour episode. Although there are no music themes for individual characters (the legendary "Kirk make-out music" was just a rumour, says McCarthy), the composers choose from a different "palette" depending on the type of episode. Sometimes DS9 music "has to help sell a little bit of the claustrophobic feel," says Chattaway, relying on the lower strings and mournful French horns "to capture the feeling these people [are] in a place they [aren't] exactly thrilled to be." Since the introduction of the *U.S.S. Defiant*, the scores have added more triumphant brass to underscore the high-adventure theme. *Voyager*'s scores frequently rely on the brass and horns found in ST:TNG and the original series. Both composers say the holodeck sequences are the most fun: *Voyager*'s French café set allowed for off-beat accordion music, and ST:TNG's "A Fistful of Datas" boasted a western-influenced score. So how does an earth-bound 20th-century composer create music for the 24th? McCarthy, without skipping a beat: "I start out with a blank piece of paper." –ANDREW MEESON

ria are not easy to come by," Taylor cautions. "People pitch us ideas that may be too similar to things that we've done or are in the process of doing. And, frankly, they sometimes get a little hokey. Some are obvious retreads of stories from the original series. Our production budget can also kill a fabulous idea. We can't do visits to planets that require a great deal of set building. The same goes for stories about aliens who look extremely unlike humanoids. We don't have the resources and time to turn a bunch of actors into reptile people. When you put these restrictions together, it's amazing how many story ideas fall by the wayside."

Are you still up to the challenge? The *Star Trek* production office will gladly provide wannabe *Star Trek* writers complete submission guidelines, including a Paramount Television release form. Fans may call the *Star Trek* Hotline at 001-213-956-8301, or send a self-addressed 9-by-12 manila envelope with 55 cents in U.S. postage to Lolita Fatjo, Paramount Pictures, 5555 Melrose Avenue, Hart Building 105, Los Angeles CA USA 90038. Be careful not to send cheques or money orders in lieu of stamps (British requests may include international reply coupons instead of U.S. postage). The submission guidelines will answer all of your questions regarding policies and procedures. The production office currently accepts scripts for both the *Deep Space Nine* and *Voyager* series. The office does not handle telephone inquiries or return long-distance phone calls, nor provide sample scripts. Please allow four to six weeks for delivery. ✧

Picture perfect

Jonathan West
- director of photography

Eagle-eyed Trekkers noticed a big difference in the look of *Deep Space Nine* when it entered its third season – and it was largely due to the hiring of *The Next Generation* director of photography, Jonathan West. "Whereas [*The Next Generation*] needed a soft, pleasing, easy-on-the-eye look, I thought of *Deep Space Nine* as a film noir crime-drama in space," says West. "I incorporated many elements of the expressionistic films of the '30s and '40s – low light, heavy shadow, lots of form, texture and contrast. It's all about darkness and light, not colour. When I watch *Deep Space Nine* dailies [rushes], I turn off the colour. If the drama holds true in shades of grey, then I know it works." The original look for *DS9* also emphasized character over environment with the frequent use of telephoto lenses which West says "isolate the actors and blur out the background. You didn't really get a sense of how huge and full of colour, movement and activity the station is or how it related to the characters. By using wide-angle lenses, we get a real feel for the background, too. We now see the big picture."

Just for effect

Of beer tins and models and other great things - *Star Trek*'s special effects

Bouncing a laser beam off a beer can to create the sun's corona is just one of **Dan Curry**'s many tricks. As visual effects producer for *Voyager* and *Deep Space Nine,* Curry oversees an entire team of special effects innovators. This page: (top left) motion-control rigger Dennis Hoerter prepares to mount the Bajoran freighter onto a model-mover; (top right) *Magellan* shuttle from the first movie. Bottom: Dan Curry inspects a 1.5-m model of *Voyager,* while motion control operator Jim Rider moves ship and camera into position. Next page (from top to bottom): a model of the shuttle *Sacajawea* is shot against an orange-screen matte; special effects team prepares the Klingon *Bird of Prey* for filming; visual effects co-ordinator David Takemura, motion control operator Josh Cushner and visual effects supervisor Glen Neufeld program a ship's movements on computer screen.

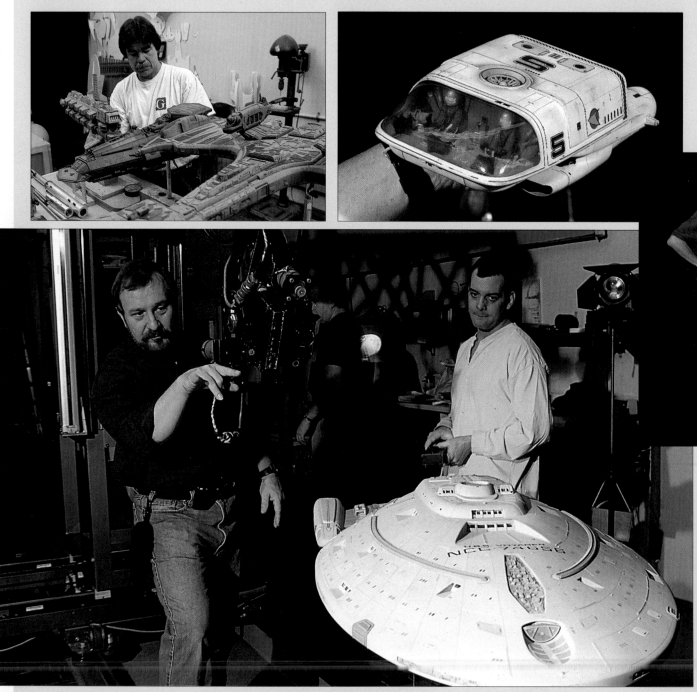

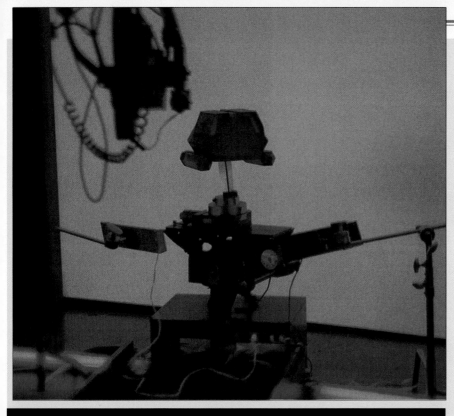

A STARSHIP IS BORN

*PHOTOGRAPHING U.S.S. VOYAGER:
(1) THE "BEAUTY PASS" IS A VITAL SHOT,
USED FOR OVERALL LIGHTING AND EXPOSURE;
(2) THE MODEL'S SILHOUETTE IS SHOT AGAINST
A BLUE SCREEN, WHICH ALLOWS THE VESSEL TO
BE DROPPED INTO A SCENE LATER ON. THE
INTERIOR LIGHTS (3), THE DEFLECTOR DISH (4)
AND THE RUNNING LIGHTS (5) ARE DONE
SEPARATELY TO ACHIEVE THE PROPER
EXPOSURE. THE FINAL COMPOSITE (6)
SHOWS ALL OF THE PASSES TOGETHER.*

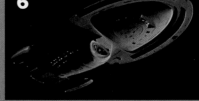

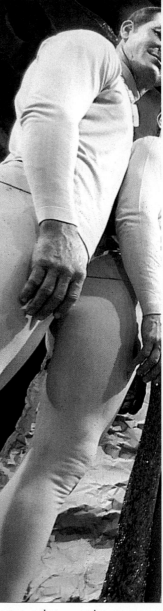

Clothes encounters

Whether tight-fitting nylon uniforms or loose flowing robes, the clothes definitely make the man and the woman in *Star Trek*

BY ERIN McLAUGHLIN

SHE'S DRESSED TO THE GALACtic nines. Electric-blue and silver lace-cut dress, heavily kohled eyelids, an astral explosion of flaming red curls – and are those fingernails metallic green? If we didn't know it was Majel Barrett in costume as Lwaxana Troi on the set of *Star Trek: Deep Space Nine,* we could easily imagine ourselves warped to a scene backstage at a chic designer fashion show.

Throughout *Star Trek,* the costumes of the future have had an uncanny resemblance to the fashions of the day. It's no accident. When William Theiss was recruited to design for *Star Trek,* he brought years of costuming experience for *General Hospital* and *The Dick Van Dyke Show,* where the wardrobes were modern. For *Star Trek,* Theiss was given the mandate of designing clothes that were literally out of this world.

There was one catch: Just as all *Star Trek* aliens would be "human-like," the clothes also had to be connected to current fashions so viewers could relate.

Surprisingly, it wasn't really that difficult to conjure up a wardrobe for human-looking aliens. Theiss's scantily clad aliens became a fixture for '60s viewers, and mirrored haute couture designers Paco Rabanne and Pierre Cardin (think green-tinted Orion slave woman wrapped in a tiny piece of glittery fabric in "The Cage") and waif model Twiggy and "James Bond" starlet Ursula Andress. Many Theiss

fashions, such as the seductive armour and knee-high boots, were reflected in what young women were wearing at the time and in films. (Remember Jane Fonda as the saucy Barbarella?)

Theiss also promoted a new sensuality for women. By designing costumes that would expose parts of the human anatomy that weren't typically considered sexy – the hipbone, for instance – Theiss revolutionized erogenous zones. The colourful, sequinned females (production insiders called them "space hookers") in "Mudd's Women," and Lieut. Palamas, in her beehive and shiny, navel-baring pink toga in "Who Mourns for Adonais?" were perfect examples of Theiss's unique costuming. But it was Shahna, the drill thrall, in belted, silver lamé bikini and gloves in "The Gamesters of Triskelion" (far right inset) who fully captures Theiss's mastery of titillation.

As for the men, it was easier for Theiss to make them more accessible. The Monkees-inspired Ensign Chekov's bowler cut, and men wore simple tunics and tight, dark pants. Theiss's novel colour-coding also helped viewers predict who would die first (those in red tunics) and who would rule the universe (those in body-hugging blue or yellow tops). The early aliens, Romulans and Klingons for example, generally wore heavier tunics with coarsely woven fabric to give the illusion they were somehow less civilized than the mod-looking, velour-wrapped Starfleet boys – hitting on the notion that rougher fabrics are equated with more primitive folk.

The *Star Trek* costumes of 1996 are obviously less campy than the 1966 outfits, but it isn't because Robert Blackman,

Opposite page: Jane Fonda as Barbarella. Above: original cast on set of "Mudd's Women." Insets from left: 1960s icon Twiggy; revealing high-booted, miniskirted '60s fashion (centre) also seen in Star Trek (right)

who beamed aboard as costume designer in 1989 during the third season of *Star Trek: The Next Generation*, has a bigger budget or is more concerned about dressing women in politically correct utilitarian uniforms. In fact, Blackman attributes the early look of *Star Trek* entirely to Theiss's taste – not to a small budget. "Even when Bill started doing *ST:TNG* in the first season," he claims, "there were episodes still [with] that sense of flimsy bare exposed clothing that I think is more a trademark of him than just that there was no money. In the 1960s that was his deal. Today it's obviously harder because everything is exposed.

But then, if you saw that the navel or the breast was covered but all of a sudden the back was bare and there was just a small patch of fabric, that was fairly revolutionary."

"It's 1996 – not 1966," exclaims Terry Farrell, when asked if the women's costumes in the current series are designed with a nod to the politically correct. "With more women in the military than in the '60s, it's appropriate for them to be dressed equal to men. I think that fashion was more about fantasy back then, I mean, all right, what's with the spray-painted hair?" Other than a slightly snugger fit, Jadzia Dax's utility uniform is identical to that worn by male crew.

And, of course, you can't get away from marketing when it comes to the women's costumes, says Blackman. The costuming of Betazoid counsellor Deanna Troi, played by Marina Sirtis, and Major Kira Nerys, played by Nana Visitor, are good examples of "selling" *Star Trek*.

"Each person has to represent something that one viewer wants to see," Blackman believes. "It's usually about keeping the 18-to-34 males interested, I'm sad to say, but it's true. That's what controls to some degree the look of those two women. When Kira was created, she was so strict and abrasive in a way. In the fourth season, they wanted her to soften. And guess what, the ratings have gone up. So if that's what works, that's what works."

In the first season of *ST:TNG*, Troi's dark, curly hair was pulled severely off her face in a tight bun and her pantsuit was an unflattering grey burlaplike fabric. Before season two began, Troi's appearance got a major overhaul. Her hair hung loose, framing and softening her once-sharp features, and a form-fitting uniform replaced her frumpy duds. A simple costuming change transformed Troi from a *Star Trek* wallflower to the object of much fan attention.

While Major Kira's costume didn't change significantly from year to year, her manner did. Instead of the humourless Kira from the first season, she is now sexy and approachable. Her stiff bobbed hair has softened to a short, saucy cut, and she does not shy away from shedding her uniform to play dress-up on the holodeck with Dax.

Appearances aren't solely market-driven, though; actors often contribute to their on-camera appearance. Avery Brooks was among those wanting a new image (see next page) and, according to Blackman, Marina Sirtis had a lot to do with softening Troi. "That bun and that miniskirt," he laughs. "I mean give me a break!"

Blackman says he's not working against Theiss when he overhauls *Star Trek* costumes; he's just changing with the times. "Things were more eccentric [back] then," he insists. "Psychedelic patterns, go-go boots, miniskirts and all kinds of polyester fabric, all current at the end of the '60s. We tend to stay away from those more spectacular parts of our modern fashion world. Not that I don't try to use some of them, but there's no Christian Lacroix or Versace, there's no blast of showiness. But there are lots of Japanese designers and amazing tailored looks that I draw upon. It's about trying to make things look as alien as possible without making it impossible to relate to the aliens."

One *Star Trek* character whose clothing verges on showy in the 24th century is Ethan Phillip's Neelix. His image is one of *Star Trek* makeup supervisor Michael Westmore's favourite designs, and that character's clothes are about as garish as they get

Star Trek **women are no longer wrapped in gauze, but dress in comfortable, functional uniforms just like their male deck-mates**

on *Star Trek: Voyager*. With the ship's crew as a backdrop, Neelix's blousy costumes are bold and unapologetic. Phillips, who was trained for the stage, laughs: "There's a certain flamboyance to Neelix. Even in the pilot episode, you see him wearing a huge fur. The guy's into flashiness. I always kid the costume guys by saying that they must have raided every upholstery shop in Los Angeles."

Never underestimate boredom as an impetus for a change in fashion. Many stars complain bitterly about wearing the same uniform show after show, perpetuating the identical look. But then there are other actors for whom a particular costume becomes familiar and comfortable. And how do you suggest a change in those situations? Blackman recoils, "Oh my lord, you might as well be pulling your finger nails out!"

As for future fashions, Blackman won't comment on possible changes – "I just don't think in those terms." But with high-fashion designers like Gianni Versace and Pucci bringing psychedelic patterns and micro-minis back to the runways, could they ever return to *Star Trek*? "Oh no," he says, dismissing the possibility. "What is most noticeably different about style on *Star Trek* these days is that content is more important than glamour. There will be short skirts but never miniskirts. Except for the James Bond episode ["Our Man Bashir"] where there were go-go boots, but that's it."

In the 1990s, *Star Trek* style does have some influence on contemporary fashion. Spied recently in a packed elevator in a posh hotel was an elegeant businesswoman wearing a striking chain-link ear-ring. "Bajoran?" the reporter asked. "Oh," she eagerly confirms. "I'm a huge fan!" Yes, a genuine Trekker – dressed in a grey banker's suit and sporting a conservative haircut.

Bajoran earrings have now gone mainstream. The unconventional accessories, usually purchased by fans at conventions, lend a bit of the same glamour and sexiness that worked its magic on the once-stiff Major Kira. The earrings were originally designed by Blackman and his staff for all Bajorans. "Then," says the costume designer, "when we were shooting the pilot, Michael [Westmore] and Rick [Berman] got very nervous [the Bajorans looked too similar], so we took 40 per cent of them off. Now we're pretty much 80 per cent wearing them. I always think of them like a cross or prayer beads. It's a spiritual thing. It's also about their caste system."

As for the make-up, there have been many sophisticated advances in special-effect polymers since the 1960s, but, says Ethan Phillips, who spends nearly two and a half hours in the chair for his role on *Voyager* every day, "They did an extraordi-

The morphing of Klingons

Y ou'd think repeated make-up sessions over successive *Star Trek* seasons would mean less time in the chair for the Klingon characters. But, says make-up supervisor Michael Westmore, it actually takes longer now than in the original series, when Klingon features were achieved simply with a deep tan colour, a fuzz of black hair and pencil-thin moustaches. When they were transported to the big screen, a ridged forehead was added to make Klingons more ominous. Shortly after Westmore came on board *The Next Generation*, the ridges were intensified because the "subtlety of the original ridges did not translate onto television." (Currently, about 35 different ridge designs represent the various Klingon houses.)

As for Michael Dorn's rumoured griping about the havoc wreaked on his skin by Klingon make-up, it turns out that it wasn't the weight of Worf's make-up, but the glue that caused so much grief. This has now been remedied. "The forehead weighs less than an ounce," says Westmore, "but he's only glued around the edges now, which could also mean more touch-ups." Now that there is less glue, Dorn is an expert in moving his facial muscles so the prosthetics don't fall off. "People would be surprised to know the make-up only takes 20 minutes," he says. "It's the gluing of the hair that takes most of the time. When we can speed that up, I'll be a happy man." –WITH FILES FROM MICHAEL LOGAN

nary job with what they had." And what they had was minimal. Simple effects like full-body paint gave the alien illusion to many characters, including the blue Andorians and the nut-brown-tinted Klingons, while make-up artist Fred Phillips, who breathed Spock to life, had to crop Leonard Nimoy's hair short and give him perfectly straight bangs. All that was required for Nimoy to transform was spirit gum, foam-rubber ear tips, a razor to shave the outside halves of his eyebrows, and yak-belly hair to blend in with his own brows. A final touch of base and contour make-up left Nimoy pale and brooding, yet still very human-like.

Now, in the 1990s, effects are more realistic, but still require a lot of time and methodical application. Westmore has painted Trill spots on Terry Farrell more than 360 times (he says it takes about 20 minutes), while Phillips has to wear contacts as well as prosthetics that mask his face and head. "The only thing that's mine is my chin."

Next to Neelix, Westmore's other favourite alien outfit was also his most challenging – and it was used twice. To design a costume for the silvery android character in "Angel One" (*ST:TNG*), Westmore built a head for dancer Leonard John Crowfoot that prohibited him from breathing, eating or hearing. Crowfoot wore silverized contact lenses, submitted to a rubber chest and

wore a diaper (once in costume, this fellow wasn't going *anywhere!*). "It took about three to four hours to glue him into it, and then he would work 12 hours or more each day," recalls Westmore. "Leonard could breathe by putting his finger in the alien's mouth, which was down where the chin was. He was very co-operative. We couldn't do a lot of what we do if the actor doesn't want to." Unfortunately for Crowfoot, he was treated to that makeover a second time – same costume, different android character – for the "The Offspring" episode.

Evolution of technology and social attitudes in *Star Trek* parallels the changes in costuming and make-up. Women are no longer wrapped in gauze, but wear comfortable, functional uniforms like their male colleagues. The influence now is on tailored and sophisticated designs, which allow characters to exude their sex appeal through a commanding attitude (Major Kira) or a didactic personality (Dr. Bashir). Make-up designs are now lighter, less restricting, requiring less time in the chair for more realistic appearing aliens.

As *Star Trek* moves further into the 24th century, one concept remains: No Starfleet member will be anything less than humanoid. "Two eyes, two ears," says Ethan Phillips, reminding us that in adhering to "Roddenberry's edict that *Star Trek* characters aren't far from human, *anything* is possible." ✧

THE MAKING OF A MAN: AVERY BROOKS WAS INSTRUMENTAL IN THE EVOLUTION OF CAPT. SISKO. THE GOATEE AND LATER THE CHROME DOME REINFORCED HIS COMMANDING PRESENCE

Back to the future

High-tech gadgetry of the 23rd century is appearing as everyday appliances in the 20th, forcing *Star Trek* creators to reinvent the future to stay ahead of the present

BY NICK OLIVARI

T WAS A GALACTIC LEAP FORWARD. WHAT TRANSPIRED in a Geneva laboratory near the France-Switzerland border in September 1995 was something *Star Trek* techno-enthusiasts had only dreamed of: the creation of antimatter in atom form. German professor Walter Oelert and his team of scientists were able to produce – for a minute fraction of a second – the essential ingredient that powers warp speed. It signalled yet another classic *Star Trek* concept made a reality. Could warp drives and the ability to boldly go where no man has gone before follow closely behind?

Well, not quite. The nine anti-hydrogen atoms created by Oelert survived only 40 billionths of a second. Even in science fiction, that's not enough time to get through a wormhole and back. (To create an ounce of antimatter would take over 20 billion years.) But the Geneva success legitimized (yet again) Gene Roddenberry's use of antimatter to propel the *U.S.S. Enterprise* starship through the galaxy. Opting for antimatter as a transport of choice was not far-fetched; it was rooted in scientific knowledge. To echo Leonard Nimoy: "Science fiction becomes science fact."

Entrenched in the *Star Trek* credo – and one of the reasons for its popularity among science buffs – is that its technological precepts are grounded in reality whenever possible. Part of Roddenberry's notion was that the devices used in the 23rd century would be determined by the science and technology of the present. What humanity accomplishes by the 23rd century would spring from today's scientific knowledge. Likewise, with *Star Trek*'s use of antimatter.

Star Trek science consultant Andre Bormanis explains that the first antiparticles were created in the 1950s (though not in atom form), so it wasn't unrealistic for Roddenberry (in the 1960s) to power the engines of the *Enterprise* with fictional antimatter fuel.

Many-worlds theory, skin regenerators, phasers, androids and communicators... Obviously, not all *Star Trek* inventions are rooted in scientific fact; some are products of Roddenberry's rich imagination, dramatic devices injecting the show with tension and intrigue. The transporter was a Roddenberry stroke of genius. The ability to break a person down into matter and energy, then beam them elsewhere was an unabashed work of pure imagination. Roddenberry would have been right out of his orbit had he tried pointing to science to explain that one. The transporter conveniently solved the problem of landing an interstellar spaceship each week – never mind the production costs involved. And as for the existence of the human soul and its whereabouts during transportation? None of the science consultants would touch that one with a ten-foot Klingon painstik. Interestingly, the look of the transporter – itself a device existing only in fiction – has evolved because of the digital effects

OPPOSITE PAGE: ORIGINAL STAR TREK COMMUNICATOR WITH FLIP-UP ANTENNA GRID. NOTE STRIKING SIMILARITY BETWEEN THE COMMUNICATOR CAPT. KIRK USES IN THE CLASSIC STAR TREK PERIOD (ABOVE) WITH THE CURRENT PORTABLE CELLULAR PHONE (RIGHT)

technology currently at the disposal of TV and film crews. The real special effects technology has made this fictional device much more exciting and sophisticated.

As the *Star Trek* contrivances predicted 30 years ago in the classic series have materialized in our daily lives, the series' technical wizards have been forced to add new technologies and reinvent others. Consider the flip-open communicator. It was originally based on the lowly two-way radio with dials and buttons. (Remember Dick Tracy talking into his wrist?) Well, your everyday portable Motorola cellular phone took its form from that early *Star Trek* communicator. Again, existing technology catches up to the 23rd century, sending *Star Trek* innovators back to the drawing board. And implanting the personal communicator in the Starfleet emblem put the *Star Trek* device one step ahead of industrial designers. "It certainly was a natural development for these communication devices to get smaller, sleeker and have enough battery power to communicate from afar," explains Rick Sternbach, senior illustrator for *Star Trek*. "Ever since science fiction invented distant communications devices, I think that everybody has wanted to get into this."

The ever-changing science of computers is another obvious area that has challenged the *Star Trek* team. Desktops and laptops purchased over the counter at your local computer shop make the 23rd-century *Star Trek* hardware look antiquated. There were no PCs and hand-held calculators in the late 1960s. Today, speech dictation systems on PCs are emerging in popularity: Your home computer not only types what you say, but reads back what you've just typed. So where does that leave *Star Trek*'s futuristic computers? Bormanis anticipates that the *U.S.S. Voyager*'s computers will probably become a reality within a 20- to 30-year time span. However, he is adamant that in the interests of drama, *Star Trek* computers will never become smarter than humans.

So with science fact forever on the verge of overtaking science fiction, *Star Trek* technocrats have got their gravity boots firmly planted in the 24th century. The creators are modifying the *Star Trek: The Next Generation* gadgetry for the *Star Trek: Voyager* and *Star Trek: Deep Space Nine* series, and have invented an entire holodeck technology. Encountered in *The Next Generation*, the holographic imagery offers – through shaped force beams – three-dimensional images of objects which appear to be solid. And the system can also create life-like humanoids and other life forms, allowing, for example, Data to play poker with Albert Einstein, Isaac Newton and real-life physicist Stephen Hawking. Escapism at its very best. Bormanis says it's merely the final example of today's virtual reality – without the goggles and sensor suit.

In a more earthly sense, what does holographic and virtual reality technology represent for us as flat-wall TV screens (forerunners to the holodeck, says Bormanis) take root in society? The possibilities are endless. Even NASA has

Accessories before the facts:
Post-23rd century *Star Trek* gadgets

The Communicator

With clones of the 1960s classic *Star Trek* communicator materializing everywhere in the form of cellular phones, its appearance in the *Star Trek* universe has had to undergo several evolutions to stay one league ahead of the real world. The communicator of the original series was a practical hand-held unit with flip-up antenna grid. In the *Star Trek* movies it was condensed into a convenient, less intrusive wrist band; and for 23rd-century users, the device is hidden in the Starfleet insignia on the crew's uniforms with access restricted by dermal sensors (Roga Danar, pursued by security aboard the *Enterprise-D* in "The Hunted," outsmarted this restriction by using the finger of an unconscious officer!). The science behind the communicator, however, has remained constant: It relies on the same sub-space radio technology developed by Roddenberry, enabling a crew on the planet surface to communicate with each other on the ground and with orbiting spacecraft.

Andre Bormanis, science consultant, is not surprised by the communicator's development. In his view, it's merely become smaller and better. "It's just the evolution of technology," he says. No further revisions are planned for the device in the TV series, but senior illustrator Rick Sternbach hints the communicator in the upcoming "*Star Trek: First Contact*" movie could take a different form.

The Universal Translator

Star Trek creators foresaw potential language barriers when they created a multilingual universe. Solution: The Universal Translator, whose basic function is two-way translation of spoken languages. It was the Universal Translator that allowed Kirk to communicate with the Companion in "Metamorphosis" (the original series), and made dialogue possible with the Nanites in *The Next Generation*'s "Evolution."

The Universal Translator is now integrated with the central computer and runs in conjunction with the communicator worn on the Starfleet uniforms. In *Deep Space Nine*, where there are more breeds of aliens, the translator is sometimes implanted. "It allows those (on or off the station) to communicate with other alien species – directly into the brain," explains Bormanis. They can translate any language that is accessible to the translator. Bormanis says more beings (alien and human) could be fitted with implants to interact with the various humans on the station in *Deep Space Nine*.

THE HAND-HELD UNIVERSAL TRANSLATOR FROM ORIGINAL STAR TREK *SERIES*

already developed its own virtual reality system for research purposes. Sternbach, however, insists there's little to change on the technologically innovative holodeck. The *Star Trek* illustrator believes the holodeck functions best as dramatic effect, "a place where people can go and let off steam in a relatively safe environment" – without leaving the ship.

It's the weaving of current scientific theory with a plausible storyline that renders *Star Trek* both believable and entertaining. Witness the medical advances of the 23rd and 24th centuries. *Star Trek* medical consultant Dr. John E. Glassco suggests that "Most of these things have seeds of reality but it is 23rd-century medicine and you can extrapolate as much as you want." There are developments in modern medical

technology that closely parallel *Star Trek* predictions.

One of Dr. Crusher's quick-healing devices is hypospray, which allows the *Enterprise* physician to infuse medicine by applying the gadget to the body – no injection or piercing of the flesh. But wait, this device isn't merely restricted to Sick Bay. "You now have these types of things in the army," says Bormanis, "where they line you up and shoot through the skin without needles [via jets of air]."

Physiostimulators and magnetic resonance imaging? Which of these medical wonders allowed Capt. Picard a quick recovery after his artificial heart problems in the "Tapestry" episode? The procedure that so quickly healed the demobilized Picard was the physiostimulator, a hand-held medical

The Holodeck

U.S.S. ENTERPRISE-D
*WITH SEPARATING
SAUCER SECTION*

Although the holodeck was used in *Star Trek*'s 1970s animated series, it wasn't fully developed and appreciated until it appeared in the first episode of *The Next Generation*. Also used on *Voyager*, with smaller versions (holosuites) appearing in *Deep Space Nine*, the holodeck remains the critical let's-keep-'em-happy device for prolonged voyages. To Bormanis, the holodeck is the ultimate virtual reality technology. Holographic imagery systems create three-dimensional environments through force-beams – which give objects the illusion of being real – instantly allowing one the pleasure, say, of a street-side French café ("We'll Always Have Paris"). Rick Sternbach can't fathom what's in store for the holodeck as real virtual reality technology develops. "The world is quickly creeping up on us and we are still scratching our heads on how to make this stuff better." He admits they can create smaller and faster devices but "once you have a holodeck that works perfectly, it isn't really necessary to take it any further. I think the holodeck, at least for us in the foreseeable future, is going to remain the place where people can go and let off steam, doing some interesting exploration without going very far."

The *U.S.S. Enterprise*

Star Trek's principal vessel shares its name with a real nuclear-powered aircraft carrier of the 20th century, and throughout *Star Trek*'s history there have been five starships bearing that name – the sixth is on its way ("*Star Trek: First Contact*" in November 1996).

The *U.S.S. Enterprise NCC-1701-D* commanded by Picard differed visually from the ship in the classic series, but Sternbach says the differences were mainly in size and mandate. "With all the families on board, it was not just a warship. There were more diplomatic missions, more scientific experiments going on, so it was really more a floating city than a single battleship going out protecting the Federation." To Andre Bormanis, the *Enterprise* underwent significant improvements as opposed to outright changes, citing the increased range of the transporters, and the introduction of technologies such as the holodecks and the replicators. Improvements also extended to size and speed of the craft. "The *Enterprise-D* crew is 1,012 (the original crew numbered 400 people), so it is a much larger ship and can travel at higher velocities."

As for the next starship, *Enterprise-E*? Only time and technology will tell. – NICK OLIVARI

The tricorder: More than a gadget

When inventors David Sweetnam and Tim Richardson were teaching a group of Canadian school students how to use an electromagnetic field sensor just over a year ago, they never imagined that within months they would be warping into the 24th century with an authentic tricorder. (In *Star Trek*, it's the tricorder that takes environmental measurements then computes, stores and communicates the data to other computers.) "The kids were measuring how strong the fields were from the PA system, the computer screens and then, when they ran out of things to scan, they began scanning one another," Sweetnam recalls. "And I asked, 'What are you doing?' and one kid said to me, 'It's a tricorder!'"

Inspired by this group of youngsters, Sweetnam and Richardson, who have conducted scientific measurements for the National Aeronautics and Space Administration (NASA) and Canada's federal environment ministry, considered the possibility of building a functional tricorder. They were *Star Trek* enthusiasts, though not "rabid" fans, and appreciated the importance of being the first to construct a real tricorder. After all, says Sweetnam, "every scientist [we've met] knows what *Star Trek* is."

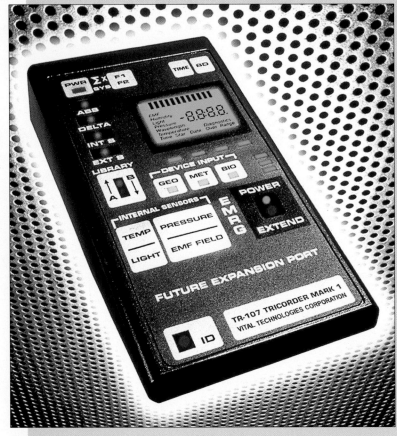

Sitting in Sweetnam's office in the small Ontario town of Bolton, it's hard to imagine that his modest company, Vital Technologies Corp., has secured the worldwide copyright to the real tricorder. Tall and clean-cut, Sweetnam looks like he might be more comfortable on the golf links than hawking his product at a crowded *Star Trek* convention. But as soon as he begins to discuss the genesis of the tricorder, it's clear why he embraced the project. "*Star Trek* is proven to be one of the best tools for teaching science," he says, gesturing to the stack of tricorders on his desk. "It's great to be able to teach."

According to Sweetnam, the tricorder he has developed with Richardson is the only multifunction measurement instrument currently in existence. "There's no single tool that you can get that does temperature readings, barometric pressure, electromagnetic radiation, incident light intensity, colour scanning...you can't buy it. You can buy other tools [that will cost between £400

device that initiates the healing process within a few minutes, a magic wand working without incisions or chemicals. Magnetic resonance imaging (commonly known as MRI), on the other hand, is actually a real technique available worldwide, employing magnetic fields to see inside the human body, relatively non-invasive – just like the physiostimulator. Glassco says there are currently ways of stimulating tissue growth by electrical means and scientists are working on chemical stimulation. Again, scholarly links between the science of 23rd-century *Star Trek* and today's medical knowledge. The functions of the physiostimulator, however, are various: It's an imaginative device when put into practice on screen, thus enabling *Star Trek* technology to be more advanced, but more importantly in terms of logistics, it also allows the show's pace to continue unabated. Would Capt. Picard have ever regained the helm of the *U.S.S. Enterprise* had a six-month convalescence in Sick Bay been proscribed after his routine heart replacement?

So where will *Star Trek* technology advance next as the 20th century moves further and further into the reality forecast by each *Star Trek* series? Bormanis says they have "not thought that through in terms of the show itself and how long *Star Trek* is on the air. The chances are we won't see significant upgrades in the technologies."

But with a wormhole to explore and another starship lost on the edge of the galaxy, fans can expect the show's science consultants to keep ahead of industrial designers and incorporate each scientific discovery as the universe unfolds before us. ✧

and £900] but they won't be digital and they won't store the information either."

After a brainstorming session, the two scientists began to realize it was possible to bring Gene Roddenberry's 23rd-century reality to the 1990s. Their next task was to convince Paramount that they could do it. As a dare, Richardson told Sweetnam, "You get the licence [to use the name "tricorder"] and I'll build the unit."

"I called the licensing department at Paramount...and they said 'C'mon!' I guess they get a lot of requests from people who want to build the *Enterprise* out of plywood in their backyard," laughs Sweetnam, "but part of Roddenberry's contract with Paramount was that if anyone came through the door to make the technology real, then Paramount...would have to support them. And we were the first." After the initial discussions, Sweetnam braced himself for the "interminable" legal negotiations. "I was naive to think it would happen quickly."

With the paperwork eventually out of the way, the invention process itself took almost eight months. "It seemed endless," recalls Richardson, who says there were many long nights tinkering and developing the instrumentation that could make accurate environmental measurements. They succeeded.

The tricorder *Mark 1* (*Mark 7* is the model used on *Star Trek: The*

Next Generation) produced by Sweetnam and Richardson is easy to use, weighs 10 ounces and is held comfortably in one hand, making the user feel like a member of Starfleet. When switched on, the *Mark 1* lights up and flashes, a sound chip emitting the beep of a working tricorder. It's applications are impressive: This tricorder can detect electromagnetic radiation from power lines and computer screens; monitor light and colour intensities; record temperatures; and measure barometric pressures. Vital Technologies Corp. is refining the device so that it can make additional environmental measurements.

As for potential markets, the two inventors aren't relying solely on *Star Trek* fans to buy the *Mark* 1. Both Sweetnam and Richardson are promoting the use of the tricorder to help students conduct science and physics experiments, and they're also discussing with major agricultural groups the potential use of the *Mark* 1 to measure chlorophyll or nitrogen in leaves through colourimetry. And are many farmers *Star Trek* fans? "Are you kidding?" says Sweetnam. "I turned off the flashing lights and the sound one time when I took the tricorder out to show one farmer because I didn't want him to think that it was a toy, and he looked at me with disappointment when I turned the device on and exclaimed, 'Hey, I thought it was a tricorder!'" —Erin McLaughlin

---

Cyberspace: The next frontier

Feeling lost in Cyberspace amid the myriad of Websites devoted to *Star Trek: Voyager* and *Star Trek: Deep Space Nine*? Then set a course for **Paramount Pictures Home Page** (*http://www.paramount.com*), a Cyberdock with an entire array of sights and sources of information to satisfy Trekkers' requests.

The adventure begins at a 1920s image of Paramount's Hollywood movie-lot gates and its three main menus: Now Playing in the Paramount Theater; Available on Paramount Home Video; and Paramount Television Presents – which functions as a launch point to *DS9* and *Star Trek: Voyager*, and also introduces The Official Star Trek Site (presented by *paramount.digital.entertainment*) forthcoming on The Microsoft Network.

To bypass the main menu for direct access to *Voyager*, key in *http://www.paramount.com/VoyagerIntro.html*. Capt. Kathryn Janeway, via the voice of Kate Mulgrew,

greets users in an audio clip. First-time visitors are asked to report to Sickbay where Robert Picardo, the Doctor, extends his welcome and offers tips on how to use the on-screen PADD (personal access display device) for navigating the site. Visitors may choose either the full graphics mode or graphics-lite, which dramatically reduces the time it takes to fully display images for users with modems at 9600 baud or less. Site content includes character pictures and profiles (did you know Tom Paris's aunt was an admiral?), cast bios (detailing such bits as the role of Roxann Biggs-Dawson – B'Elanna Torres – in the sci-fi film "Darkman II"), and descriptions of every *Voyager* episode aired to date in America, plus a place for fans' comments.

Paramount's *Deep Space Nine* site (direct access: *http://www.paramount.com/DS9Home.html*) provides information specific to whatever show (first-run or repeat) current to the American broadcast schedules. ✦

The Okuda files

Michael Okuda is the conjurer of the *Star Trek* props, graphics and set pieces, not to mention the occasional hidden wisecrack

BY MICHAEL LOGAN

MICHAEL OKUDA PLAYS A vital role in the *Star Trek* universe: He is in charge of the nuts and bolts of *Star Trek* lore – literally. As scenic art supervisor and technical consultant, he either creates or passes inspection on every single technical prop, graphic and set piece used in the television series and films. The buck also stops with Okuda and his associate, senior illustrator and technical consultant Rick Sternbach, whenever there is a question about what is – and is not – scientifically possible in the fictional universe created by Gene Roddenberry.

But they are not spoil-sports. Says Okuda: "We do not see our roles as people who tell the *Star Trek* writers, 'That idea you have makes no scientific sense.' Instead, we say, 'OK, let's see…well, if you really want that to happen in the script, then here's a way you could tell the story so that will work.' We never forget something Gene once said: "The real mission of the *U.S.S. Enterprise* is to serve as a vehicle for drama.'"

But there's also room for a few wisecracks. Some of Okuda's best graphics – nicknamed "Okudagrams" by *Star Trek: The Next Generation* set decorator John Dwyer – have had cast and crew in stitches. The "We'll Always Have Paris" episode of *ST:TNG* featured – unbeknownst to viewers – an Okuda-scripted menu offering such delicacies as "Croissants Dilithium," "Tribbles dans les Blankettes" and "L'antimatter Flambé." One of the *Enterprise* panel identification labels on

ST:TNG captured part of the well-known theme song for *Gilligan's Island,* a long-running American comedy about a miscellany of characters marooned on a deserted island after a shipwreck: *Just sit right back and you'll hear a tale, a tale of a fateful trip, that started from this tropic port, aboard this tiny ship…* Another one teased: *In space, no one can hear you scream.*

"If we have an opportunity to throw in a joke, or a movie reference or some bit of fun information on a computer readout, it's usually for our own enjoyment," explains Sternbach. "The viewers usually never see them – they just go by in a blur – though I'm sure a few fans have burned out their videos by single-framing through a scene just to catch something [secretive]." Such messages merely enhance the mystique.

Okuda, who joined the *Star Trek* team in 1986 during the making of "Star Trek IV: The Voyage Home," has co-written several reference books, including "Star Trek Chronology," "Star Trek: The Next Generation Technical Manual" and "Star Trek Encyclopedia," as well as the latter's CD-ROM version, "Star Trek Omnipedia."

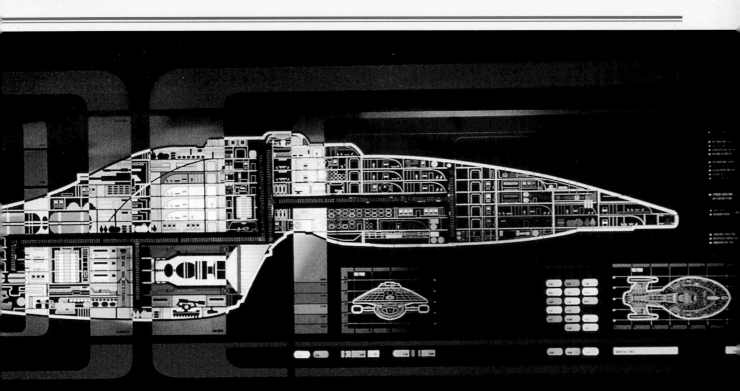

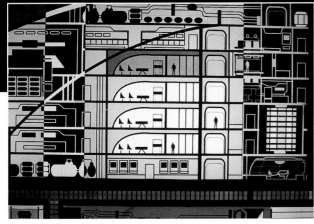

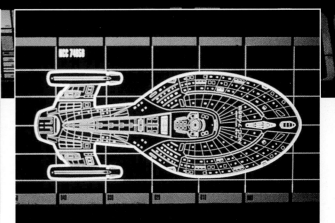

"And even I have to refer to them," he admits. "Sometimes one of the writers will call to check out a certain historic or technical fact and I'll say, 'I don't remember, but I'll look it up for you.' It's a little embarrassing. People think we know this stuff because we wrote the books – but, in actual fact, we wrote the books so we'd know where to look things up."

Sternbach readily confesses: "And when we can't find it, we just make it up. But even when something is bogus, we make every effort to keep it consistently bogus."

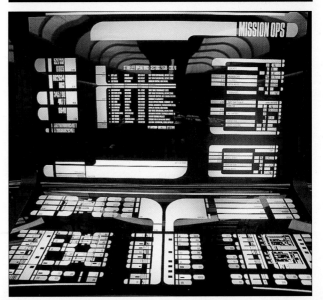

LARGE PHOTOGRAPH ABOVE: LAYOUT OF ENGINEERING PANEL ON THE MAIN BRIDGE OF U.S.S VOYAGER. *FAR LEFT INSETS:* MICHAEL OKUDA, *WHIMSICAL OKUDAGRAM AND DUCK PANEL FROM* THE NEXT GENERATION. *ABOVE AND TOP RIGHT INSETS: HIGHLIGHTED SECTIONS OF PANELS FROM BRIDGE STATION SHOWN ABOVE. IMMEDIATE RIGHT: MISSION OPS BOARD FROM* THE NEXT GENERATION.

Let's talk Klingon

Devoted Trekkers are relearning their ABC's (and uHq's) just so they can jatlh in Klingon

BY **CHRISTOPHER BLAND**

T HREE YEARS AGO, ON 15 AUG. 1993, Trekkers converged on Red Lake Falls, Minnesota, USA, for what was billed as the first Klingon language camp – two weeks of bingo (using Klingon numbers, naturally), Klingon language classes, and softball games in which players were never "safe" or "out," but rather were ruled "alive" or "dead." In 1994, American translators tackled the Bible and now The Gospel According to Mark can be read in Klingon. (The Klingon vocabulary, however, lacked many necessary words for a complete translation so the translators opted for substitutions in places, replacing, for example, "loaves" and "fishes" with "grain food" and "water animals.") Even Hamlet gets to bemoan his woeful life in Klingon. Early in 1996, the Klingon Language Institute, based in Flourtown, Pennsylvania, USA (with more than 1,000 members throughout 30 countries, including the United Kingdom, Canada, Brazil and Australia) turned out 1,000 hard-bound Klingon versions of the Shakespearean tragedy.

So what touched off this language-learning explosion? Why have *Star Trek* fans endeavoured to study and develop a language which outwardly has no application in the real world?

On the simplest level, an understanding of Klingon permits fans to enjoy the *Star Trek* movies and series at an intimate, exclusive level similar to the experience enjoyed by fans who study starship technical drawings and operations manuals. The attraction of privileged membership to some secret club in this case promotes the desire to learn.

On a more complex level, learning to understand and speak Klingon is to *become* Klingon, and Marc Okrand (in photo), lauded as the inventor of the Klingon language, clearly understands the allure of pretending to be one of the warrior race.

"When you're [pretending to be a Klingon], you can do things that you can't do if you're a human," says Okrand, the expert linguist who began his association with the *Star Trek* universe when he was asked to write some Vulcan dialogue for the movie "*Star Trek II: The Wrath of Khan.*" "You can get away with being demanding and bossy and just saying what you want" – something which "polite society prevents you from doing. You can step back from that."

Indeed, rare are the social engagements, outside of a Klingon fan gathering, in which a guest is perfectly welcome – even encouraged – to converse in a manner "guttural and grunty." Not only that, but "you can spit and make funny noises and stuff like that, and it fits right in with this character of the Klingons."

Ironically, the very man credited as the inventor of the Klingon language (developed for "*Star Trek III: The Search for Spock*") has yet to master the ability to speak and understand the language as proficiently as many devoted fans.

"I don't speak it in the sense that I don't carry on conversations with anybody," says Okrand, now applying his communication skills at America's National Captioning Institute in Vienna, Virginia. "But when I'm working with the language, I'm comfortable doing it, and if someone writes me a letter or something, I know what they're talking about…but there are other people

THIS PAGE: PHOTO BY M.J WARDALE. FACING PAGE: ©1996 PARAMOUNT PICTURES. ALL RIGHTS RESERVED. PHOTOS BY ROBBIE ROBINSON, JOHN SHAJMON, GREGORY SCHWARTZ, ELLIOT MARKS. COURTESY EVERETT COLLECTION (2).

OPPOSITE: MARC OKRAND. THIS PAGE, TOP: JOHN LARROQUETTE (MALTZ), CHRISTOPHER LLOYD (KRUGE), STEPHEN LISKA (TORG) FROM "STAR TREK III: THE SEARCH FOR SPOCK." BOTTOM, LEFT TO RIGHT: CHRISTOPHER PLUMMER (CHANG), BARBARA MARCH (LURSA) AND ROBERT O'REILLY (GOWRON)

who carry on great discussions in [Klingon], and can carry on casual conversations and stuff like that. They do that all the time. Someone once likened my role to that of a football coach who says, 'Don't do what I do. Do what I say.'"

The foundation of what Klingon character actors and fans say – and *how* they speak Klingon – is rooted, however, not in Okrand's linguistic inventions but in those of James Doohan. The original-series actor, who landed the role of Scotty partly because of his ability to master accents, actually created the first lines of Klingon for the 1979 film *"Star Trek: The Motion Picture."* "[Doohan] wanted to create [Klingon] language [for the movie] because he's really into accents and dialects," recalls Okrand. Doohan thought it would be fun to create a dialogue which "sounded weird and otherworldly," and tape-recorded his work. The tape was later given to actor Mark Lenard (whose best-known *Star Trek* role as Sarek spans the classic series, *Star Trek: The Next Generation* and most of the films). Lenard phonetically transcribed Doohan's "otherworldly" dialogue for his role as a Klingon in the opening scenes of *"Star Trek: The Motion Picture."* Miraculously, Lenard still had those transcripts a few years later when he was asked to play Sarek in *"Star Trek III,"* for which Okrand was asked to create a true, working Klingon language.

Okrand wasn't aware of actor Doohan's involvement in the Klingon language for the first *Star Trek* film. The linguist (who has studied Spanish, Chinese, and Indian languages of the American southwest) had simply watched the film, then had made his own phonetic transcriptions as the basis for his *"Star Trek III"* assignment. The resulting language, which today is known as *tlhIngan Hol* (or "official Klingon" among fans), was derived from the influences of American Indian, Chinese and Southeast Asian languages. It was only after Okrand sent his Klingon dialogue to Hollywood that he encountered Lenard on the *"Star Trek III"* set and was shown the actor's first set of transcripts. The two found that their interpretations of Doohan's words were very similar.

Despite subtitles which provided English translations of the Klingon dialogue spoken in *"Star Trek: The Motion Picture"* and *"Star Trek III,"* the language largely remained a mystery to the public until 1985, when Okrand's work resulted in *"The Klingon Dictionary"* (Simon & Schuster). An instant hit with fans, the book (later revised and re-released in 1992) offered Klingon word definitions, pronunciation rules, syntax guidelines and a helpful list of Klingon expressions. Fans no longer had to remain in the dark. They could suddenly shout *"jIyaj!"* ("I understand"). Insight into the formerly secret world of the Klingons was *"qay'be'"* ("no problem"). One could even ask the burning question: *"nuqDaq waqwIj vIlam-Ha'choHmoH?"* ("Where can I get my shoes cleaned?")

Oddly, *Star Trek: The Next Generation* writers didn't adopt *"The Klingon Dictionary"* as a guide until after the first-season episode "Heart of Glory." Okrand doesn't know what the Klingon language in that show is all about, but defends the writing team: "I don't know if, at the time, the writers were even aware that the book [the dictionary] was available."

Two instructional audiotapes followed: the 1992 cassette "Conversational Klingon" (the companion to "The Klingon Dictionary" narrated by Michael Dorn) and "Power Klingon" (in 1993). Okrand created more *tlhIngan Hol* (official Klingon) for *"Star Trek V: The Final Frontier"* and *"Star Trek VI: The*

Speaking Klingon

Ten Klingon Phrases Created Exclusively for U.K. Trekkers! You won't find these phrases in "The Klingon Dictionary" or in any of the *Star Trek* films or episodes. We asked the inventor himself, Marc Okrand, to translate these phrases specifically for *Radio Times* readers. He has also provided the literal translations. *tIv!* (Enjoy!)

1. We are U.K. Klingons! .... wo' tay' tlhInganpu' maH!
2. Come along then. .... Ha'.
3. Give us a kiss, love. .... HIchop, bang.
4. Spot of tea? .... Dargh DaneH'a'?
5. Beam me up, mate .... HIjol, jup.
6. Not bloody likely! .... ghaytanHa' jay'!
7. Be quick about it. .... tugh.
8. Cricket, please. .... DaH ghew yIQuj.
9. Let's go to the pub. .... tach vI'el. HItlhej.
10. What has Lady Di done now? .... DaH nuq ta'pu' Day joH?

(**Literal translations:** 1. We are together Empire Klingons!; 2. Let's go; 3. Bite me, love; 4. Do you want tea?; 5. Beam me up, friend; 6. Not &*@%# likely!; 7. Hurry up; 8. Play bug now (Klingon has no word for cricket the game; "ghew" can mean "bug," "cootie" or "insect"); 9. I am going into the bar. Accompany me; 10. What has Lord/Lady Di accomplished now? (The title *joH*, meaning "Lord," is also used for a woman, ie., "Lady.")

Warrior talk: "They're all difficult," Michael Dorn says of the words which make up *tlhIngan Hol*. Playing the stolid Klingon Worf, Dorn has spoken Klingon dialogue through seven seasons of *Star Trek: The Next Generation* and one season of *Star Trek: Deep Space Nine.* He also narrated Marc Okrand's first instructional cassette, "Conversational Klingon." One could suppose that the actor's ease with Klingon comes from experience and, to a degree, that's correct. Yet Dorn admits he still relies on phonetic pronunciation guidelines to keep his Klingon dialogue on target. "As far as I know, [observant fans] haven't called us on [any mispronunciation]. Not that I've heard," he says. "[The *Star Trek* writers] stick pretty much to Okrand's book, 'The Klingon Dictionary.'" If Dorn could persuade *Star Trek*'s writers and producers to bend the rules on anything, he says he would "like to see subtitles, not with just the Klingons, but with all alien characters." ✦

MICHAEL DORN IN HIS SIGNATURE KLINGON ROLE AS WORF

Undiscovered Country" while *Star Trek* series writers continued developing Klingon for *ST:TNG* and *Star Trek: Deep Space Nine*. And somewhere along the line, Klingon started to affect fans in unexpected ways.

Okrand recalls one particular teenage student who was doing very well in physics and math but struggling with French. "Then he got into the Klingon stuff…and by trying to learn the Klingon, became very interested in the way languages work, and suddenly his French studies were getting better." The student was so motivated he went on to learn Chinese.

Okrand remembers another teenage boy who accompanied his mother to a Klingon language camp. The boy wasn't particularly interested in Klingon, but he accompanied his mother and taught classes in martial arts. That brief camp experience was enough to change him: Learning to speak just a bit of Klingon, the inspired teen then enrolled in a junior college and started taking Russian.

After 1985, a new fan-driven Klingon language developed with its own followers and practitioners: *klingonaase*. It's based on smatterings of the Klingon tongue created by author John Ford in his *Star Trek* novel "The Final Reflection," and Okrand has nothing but praise for the fans who developed the alternative Klingon speech. "One of the things that even the *Star Trek* writers seem to, if not ignore, at least gloss over, is the fact that the Klingon Empire is an empire. And…that means it's made up of a bunch of different units of some kind…and there's no reason to assume that all those different units are exactly the same as each other. They're going to be different from each other in some ways, and one of the ways is going to be linguistically."

In *klingonaase*, for example, the Klingon homeworld is called *Klinzhai*, whereas in *tlhIngan Hol* the planet is *Qo'noS*. And the *United Federation of Planets* in *tlhIngan Hol* is *yuQjIjDIvI'* – a real tongue-twister compared to *federazhon*, its *klingonaase* equivalent. The differences, with their varying degrees of difficulty in pro-nunciation, make a lot of story sense to Okrand. "Not only would [the Klingon homeworld have] different dialects, meaning slightly different pronunciations and different vocabulary choices, but there'd also be other languages altogether. So that's fine to have [*tlhIngan Hol*] and *klingonaase* coexist."

Whether or not *klingonaase* can survive is another matter. In the *Star Trek* universe, where *tlhIngan Hol* rules, "Survival must be earned," according to Marc Okrand's new book, "*Star Trek:* The Klingon Way – A Warrior's Guide" (published by Simon & Schuster). The work includes Klingon proverbs from all four TV series and the films – with some entirely new phrases included – and is loaded with conversation-stoppers such as

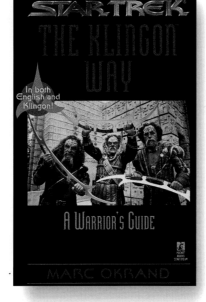

"Drinking fake ale is better than drinking water" and other pithy Klingon proverbs from linguist Marc Okrand

"Four thousand throats may be cut in one night by a running man" and "Drinking fake ale is better than drinking water" (expressions are in Klingon and English). The book isn't about learning to speak Klingon. It's a glimpse into the psyche of the warrior race.

Fans seeking to expand their knowledge of Klingon language will fare better with the new three-CD adventure "*Star Trek:* Klingon" (Simon & Schuster Interactive). The set is a Klingon role-playing game and offers an instructional language component by Okrand. On the Language Lab CD, the user selects one of a variety of word categories, including curses which, according to "The Klingon Way," is a fine art among Klingons. Words in each category are displayed in English and phonetic Klingon for easy pronunciation. Robert O'Reilly (who plays the Klingon character Gowron) appears on the CD set demonstrating how to speak various Klingon words. Okrand narrates part of the Language Lab (which can run in a standard audio compact-disc player). With the appropriate hardware, you can use the voice-recognition software to learn correct Klingon pronunciation. The three-CD set, which is directed by Jonathan Frakes (William T. Riker on *Star Trek: The Next Generation*) also contains samples of two other *Star Trek* products: "*Star Trek:* Omnipedia" and "*Star Trek* Technical Manual." And Okrand says Paramount has plans in the works for an Internet site which will include a Klingon-instruction component with his voice.

Despite the great success of his Klingon endeavours, the 48-year-old linguist is modest about his contribution to *Star Trek*. When he talks about the show, he's surprisingly boyish and simply can't say enough about the enthusiastic fans who, in learning to speak Klingon, demonstrate that fun and learning go together.

"It's fulfilling," Okrand says of his work with Klingon. "I was concerned, when I first started doing all this Klingon stuff, about what the linguistics community would think." He didn't want to appear as one who had sullied the profession, and he never did. "All the people I've met and talked to… think it's terrific," and he knows why. Thinking back to the book that started it all, "The Klingon Dictionary," Okrand reminds himself of the volume's most important lesson: The *process* of learning Klingon is of the greatest value. "What you're *really* learning is English, or whatever language you speak first, because in order to translate into Klingon you have to first think about what it means in English… so you learn about how your own language works, you learn about different ways of thinking, which helps you think about how other languages work," which, in the end, reflects the kind of universal understanding and communication that is *Star Trek*. ✦

THE FAN UNIVERSE

Caught in the act

Surprise encounters with the fans are part of the job when you're a *Star Trek* cast member, but it's often the actors who are left starstruck

BY **MICHAEL LOGAN**

IFE AS A *STAR TREK* STAR IS ALMOST always unpredictable. Legions of Trekkers positively worship their favourite stars, heaping upon them great praise. Sometimes they're just curious, but who isn't? Often, fans want to tell a Stewart or a Koenig how a certain character portrayal or episode has touched them in some special way. But once in a while, it's the cast who are affected by the fans. Be it a brief moment on the street or a meaningful exchange at a convention, these fan encounters invariably leave their mark on the *Star Trek* stars.

PATRICK STEWART (Capt. Jean-Luc Picard, *Star Trek: The Next Generation*)

"A few years ago, I was working with a film company in Croatia, and one night my girlfriend and I went to a restaurant recommended to me in the old town of Zagreb. We were ushered in by a very dignified and formal maitre d', shown to a table and given menus. Neither of us could speak one word of Croatian so we had to order everything by pointing. And when our salads arrived, sitting in the centre of each – beautifully carved out of cucumber and green and red peppers – was a perfect little replica of the *U.S.S. Enterprise!*

LEFT: NICHELLE NICHOLS. RIGHT: ROBERT PICARDO, ALL PREPPED FOR THE AFTERLIFE

The other courses were served, and there was no change of any kind in this man's demeanour; we paid our bill and left – without any other comment being made. It was the classiest bit of recognition I have ever experienced."

ROBERT PICARDO (The Doctor, *Star Trek: Voyager*)

"A while back I went through this very actorish, angst-filled period where I was faced with the gripping realization – because of the popularity of *Voyager* and all the merchandising and the whatnot – that this might be the last role of my career. So I go to this convention where this nice man, Gary Parker from Georgia, presents me with a large marble tombstone with the likeness of the Doctor carved on it. The guy made tombstones for a living and it was a really sweet, incredibly thoughtful gesture – he had no idea he was playing right into my neurosis. But it was a very nice tombstone. I planted it in the flower bed."

NICHELLE NICHOLS (Lieut. Uhura, classic *Star Trek*)

"The most marvellous thing happened when '*Star Trek V: The Final Frontier*' and *The Next Generation* were both shooting on the Paramount lot. I had a couple of days off from the film and when I returned, everybody was saying, 'Hey, Nichelle, Whoopi Goldberg came over here looking for you.' I said, 'Yeah, right, guys,' because we had become masters at playing practical jokes on each other. They insisted it was true, but I just knew they were pranking me and that they'd get me all excited and then yell, 'Whoopee!' Then somebody from Gene Roddenberry's office called and said, 'Nichelle, you'd really do us a big favour if you'd meet with Whoopi Goldberg,' and I'm saying, 'Oh, c'mon, guys, not you too!' But it turned out to be

ROBERT
PICARDO
AS
DOC ZIMMERMAN
ART & CARVING
BY
GARY PARKER
203 SHELBY ST

KATE MULGREW (CAPT. KATHRYN JANEWAY): ONE WOMAN'S PASSION

helping non-ethnic people see us as we are supposed to be seen. The quality, the dignity with which you've created this character makes it imperative that she be there to belie the myths. Please stay.' What do you do? Of course I said, 'Yes, sir.' On the following Monday, I told Gene Roddenberry that I'd stay. Dr. King became my mentor and good friend."

KATE MULGREW
(Capt. Kathryn Janeway, *Voyager*)

"Kathryn Janeway is an ardent scientist and this confounded me [when getting the role] because Kate Mulgrew is not a scientist. I am extremely right-brained. How do I understand nebula and plasma? I struggled for some time and then a marvelous thing happened: About two months into the run of *Voyager,* I was invited to the White House to attend an international conference honouring women scientists. I thought, 'Well, this is great, I'm going to go and meet the First Lady and I'm going to steal something from every one of those female scientists and [then be able to] stitch Janeway together. I'll come in like a thief from the cold!'

It turned out to be a seminal day in my life. I was introduced to 20 teenaged girls who were studying science. I shook their hands, and each [spoke briefly] with me. But one of them said, 'Ms. Mulgrew, may I speak with you privately for just a minute?' She pulled me aside, looked at me, alive and aglow with promise, and said, 'All my life I have loved science fiction and I have adored science. And I told my parents early on this was my journey, my dream, and they said, 'No, no, no honey, it's not gonna work.' I'm from a small town in Pennsylvania and they wanted me to stay and marry a nice guy. My father was adamantly opposed! On the night of the *Voyager* première, I pulled them into the living room, sat between them on the couch, and we watched in complete silence. And when it was over, my mother turned to my father and she said, 'Bill, I think we just lost the battle, but this girl's gonna win the war.'

And then this young student said to me, 'I have won a scholarship to study and one day I will be a physicist.'

I looked at that beautiful face and thought to myself, 'Katie Mulgrew, no more theft. You are going to go back to that sound stage on Monday and you are going to understand the difference between nebula and plasma and you are going to endow this role with the same passion and power this young woman just imparted to you.'"

ARMIN SHIMERMAN
(Quark, *Star Trek: Deep Space Nine*)

"I was at a convention in Pennsylvania when a group of people raised their hands and said they were from a *Star Trek* chapter in my home town of Lakewood, New Jersey – a small farming community about 60 miles away. They had a presentation to make, so I invited them on stage and they gave me a proclamation from the mayor of

true! One day I'm on the set waiting to go on for a scene and there's a tap on my shoulder – I turn around and look right into the beautiful face of Whoopi Goldberg. We just hugged. To learn that I had some small part in influencing her was an honour – and it always will be.

After the first year of *Star Trek,* I went in to Gene Roddenberry and told him I intended to leave the show, and he was upset. That weekend I was at a fund-raiser and someone came up to me and said, 'Ms. Nichols, there's someone who wants to meet you. He's a great fan of yours.' Instead of some young person, there stood Dr. Martin Luther King Jr.! 'Yes, I'm a big fan of yours. As a matter of fact, my entire family never misses the show,' he said. I thanked him and explained that I was planning to leave the show, to which he immediately responded, 'You can *not!*' I was stunned. 'I beg your pardon?' I said. I'll never forget his words: 'You cannot leave. Don't you know what you are? Don't you know you're part of history? You're opening up a door that simply must not be allowed to close. Your being on the starship *Enterprise,* going in peaceful exploration, is changing the face of television forever. You're not just important to black people but to everyone. You are

Lakewood stating that very day was 'Armin Shimerman Day.' Every person, no matter what they do in life or what they achieve, has a daydream of being recognized by their own community. We all want to amount to something, to show the people you grew up with that you've made a difference in the world. I've always had that daydream – and when mine came true, I was moved to tears."

LEONARD NIMOY (Spock, classic *Star Trek*)

"In a very interesting way, one of the first and most memorable *Star Trek* fans was also one of the most influential – American TV GUIDE columnist Cleveland Amory. The original series was on the air at the same time as two other sci-fi series, *Voyage to the Bottom of the Sea* and *The Time Tunnel*. Cleveland assessed the three in various articles and – though he gave thumbs down to *The Time Tunnel* – he heaped praised on *Voyage to the Bottom of the Sea*. *Star Trek,* he judged, was more suitable for children than adults. But then Amory revisited the series in a column two months later titled 'Second Thoughts,' in which he not only admitted 'the show most over-criticized was *Star Trek*' but acknowledged the series had begun to fulfil its promise and potential! That was a very proud moment for us – we were beginning to be understood."

MARINA SIRTIS (Deanna Troi, *The Next Generation*)

"I will always be indebted to one *ST:TNG* fan whose name I will never know: I attended a convention in the earlier years of the series and during the question-and-answer section, a fan said, 'You're really funny and lively. We think Troi's really dull but you're great!' And that really took me aback. I thought, 'Troi's *dull*? Well that's not good. She should be cerebral – but never be dull.' I was really rather hurt, but I went away and thought about it and, from that point on, I injected more and more of Marina into Troi. That fan had done me a great favour."

JOHN de LANCIE (Q, *The Next Generation, Deep Space Nine, Voyager*)

"Most clubs in life are exclusive, but the *Star Trek* fan club is the most inclusive club in the world. Everyone is welcome, everyone is allowed – literally. I remember walking down a very empty street in New York City one night when I saw this big, very scary looking guy walking toward me. I gradually gravitated toward the left side of the sidewalk. He gravitated in the same direction. I gradually gravitated to the right of the sidewalk. He gravitated in the same direction. Finally, we came face to face and he stared me down. I'm thinking, 'OK, that's it, I'm dead. Or, at the very least, mugged.' But the guy said, 'Are you Q?' I sort of gulped and said, 'Uh...yeah.' He said, 'Can you make people come back from the dead?' For some reason, I said, 'Only people I like.' And then he walked off.

The questions at the conventions never cease to amaze me – especially when you need to wrap it up. One time, I said, 'OK, one last question!' and somebody asked, 'Have you taken Jesus as your personal saviour?' I'm going, 'Um...er...uh..OK, never mind that one. One more ques-

tion!' Then somebody asked, 'Do you read the Bible?' I'm going, 'Ahem...er...OK, one more question!' Then somebody said, 'Mr. de Lancie, I am praying for you.' I said, 'No thanks, just send cheques.' And I got off.

Some fan encounters aren't as strange as they first seem. I had a guy come up to me at 6 a.m. at Los Angeles Airport: He said, 'I want to thank you for many hours of pleasure.' Then he hands me his card , 'If you ever want to see the real thing, give me a call.' I'm thinking, 'Here's another intergalactic weirdo.' I look at the card and it turns out he's the head of [National Aeronautics and Space Administration] mission control at Vandenberg Air Base."

WALTER KOENIG (Chekov, classic *Star Trek*)

"I was having dinner in a restaurant last year with a bunch of actor friends who didn't want to talk about *Star Trek*. A young woman approached our table, hands shaking, and asked if I was who she thought I was. I said, 'I guess so.' She got all excited and flustered and asked if I would win a bet for her by going over to her table to prove my identity to her friend. I said, 'OK, sure, why not.' And as I was rising out of my chair, she turned to me and said, 'Oh, and by the way, could you please sing, 'Hey, hey, we're the Monkees?' One time in England, I was even mistaken for Woody Allen. On another occasion, I

WALTER KOENIG: MONKEE BUSINESS

had this group of four guys come up and tell me they thought I was Tattoo from television's *Fantasy Island*. Why is it these people never think I'm Tom Cruise?"

JENNIFER LIEN (Kes, *Voyager*)

"It was the day before my 21st birthday and the Make-A-Wish Foundation was visiting the set. The crew and cast showed them around and explained what was going on. There was one boy in particular who had a pretty tragic condition – let's just say he wasn't in top physical health. But he had the most incredible optimism. He just had so much fun and didn't let anything bother him. I had a birthday cake and he asked if he could have some, so I sat down and we shared it with his brother and his mum. Months later, his mother wrote and thanked us for letting her son spend time with us. It was one of the most memorable times of his life. It was the realization of a dream for him. It was cool that you could share that happiness with someone. It's just, you know, you tend to get caught up in a lot of stupid things that don't matter, so for me it was one of the best gifts I got last year." **–with files from Erin McLaughlin and David Rensin** ✧

Famous players

An author, an astronaut and a cast of other celebs reveal their private dreams and experiences of *Star Trek*

BY **MICHAEL LOGAN**

O NE IS A PRINCE AND ONE is a pig. Several are actors; at least one is a comic. There's an author, an astronaut and a soap star. One has already travelled in outer space; another is an officer in the Middle East. A handful have had their acting moments in *Star Trek*; a few became stars in other shows. And they're all famous: Camille Paglia, Joan Collins, former astronaut Dr. Mae Jemison, Miss Piggy, Prince Abdullah of Jordan... They're celebrity fans of *Star Trek*, famous people who have been touched by the *Star Trek* dream. Their testimonies – warm and witty, reverent and raucous – reflect the range of experiences within the *Star Trek* universe.

RICARDO MONTALBAN

"It's amazing how faithful Trekkies are," says Ricardo Montalban, who is still getting fan mail for his performances as Khan in classic *Star Trek*'s "Space Seed" episode and the 1982 motion picture "Star Trek II: The Wrath of Khan." The actor especially treasured the opportunity to take the villain onto the big screen. "Khan was a very interesting, very telling character," says Montalban. "I loved Khan's fire and his enormous passion. I have always had difficulty finding wonderful roles because Hollywood just doesn't write for Latins – and certainly not Latins of my age – so I was very grateful. Khan was particularly attractive to me after play-

ing Mr. Roarke for so many years on *Fantasy Island*, where I was the perfect host, never emotionally involved with the other characters, always cool, always in control." Still, he almost didn't accept the part. Recalls Montalban: "We were just days away from finishing the fourth season on *Fantasy Island* when they sent me the script for the film. I read it and thought, 'I don't know...maybe this part is not big enough for my return to movies.' But Arthur Rowe, one of the producers of *Fantasy Island*, read the script and said, 'But, Ricardo, when your character is not on the screen, they are always talking about you.' So, of course, I did it and it was a wonderful success. That taught me a great lesson: An actor should never count pages."

MISS PIGGY

She's bold, she's brassy and – she'll be the very first to tell you – she's absolutely b-e-a-u-t-i-f-u-l! She's our buxom barnyard babe, Miss Piggy, the preening porcine princess with a nose for high drama and adventure. She did, after all, hoof it through the galaxy in *The Muppet Show*'s "Pigs in Space," so it's no surprise she's a devoted fan of *Star Trek*. "Of course," squealed the four-legged femme fatale. "Moi am far too young to remember *Star Trek* when it first aired, but moi became a devoted fan watching it in reruns." Miss Piggy

MISS PIGGY:
BOSOM BUDDY

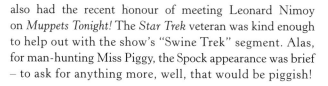

BEFORE SHE BECAME DYNASTY'S *NASTY, BACK-STABBING* ALEXIS CARRINGTON COLBY, JOAN COLLINS *WAS KIND-HEARTED SOCIAL WORKER EDITH KEELER IN CLASSIC* STAR TREK'S *"*THE CITY ON THE EDGE OF FOREVER*"*

also had the recent honour of meeting Leonard Nimoy on *Muppets Tonight!* The *Star Trek* veteran was kind enough to help out with the show's "Swine Trek" segment. Alas, for man-hunting Miss Piggy, the Spock appearance was brief – to ask for anything more, well, that would be piggish!

JOAN COLLINS

Long before she played the sexy, back-stabbing Alexis Carrington Colby on the popular night-time soap *Dynasty*, actor Joan Collins guest-starred in one of the most famous episodes of the original *Star Trek*: "The City on the Edge of Forever." "To this day, people still want to talk about that episode – some remember me for that more than anything else I've done," says Collins, who played Edith Keeler, the Depression-era social worker whom the time-travelling Capt. Kirk (William Shatner) falls in love with. "I am amazed at the enduring popularity of *Star Trek* and particularly of that episode," says Collins. "At the time none of us would

have predicted this kind of longevity for the show. I couldn't be more pleased – or more honoured – to be a part of *Star Trek* history."

DAVE THOMAS

Though Dave Thomas often skewered the original *Star Trek* when he was a regular on the North American comedy show *SCTV* (he once played "Bones" McCoy as a hostile waiter in an intergalactic greasy spoon), the comedian is reverent when it comes to *Star Trek: The Next Generation*. "Emotionally, I fall for it hook, line and sinker. No other entertainment moves me like that," says Thomas, co-star of the sitcom *Grace Under Fire*. "The writing was stellar, particularly the episode where Picard falls unconscious, is beamed – in his mind – to another planet, lives an entire life, dies, and regains consciousness. All in a few minutes! You don't see that on TV very often. The casting was also brilliant. When I first saw Patrick Stewart, I

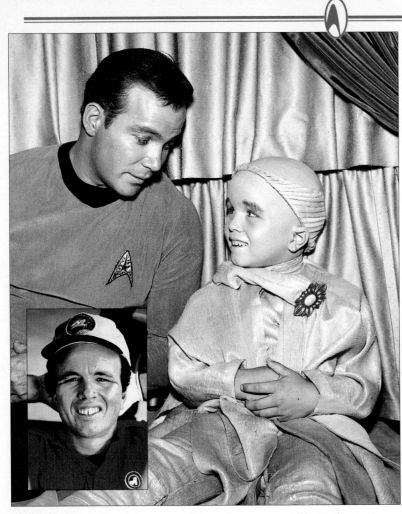

SEVEN-YEAR-OLD CLINT HOWARD – PRE-GENTLE BEN DAYS – WITH WILLIAM SHATNER (CAPTAIN KIRK) IN "THE CORBOMITE MANEUVER." INSET: HOWARD TODAY

CLINT HOWARD

As a kid actor, Clint Howard – who had yet to star in *Gentle Ben* (a popular show in North America about a young boy and his bear) – won the guest-star lead in "The Corbomite Maneuver," the first *Star Trek* episode to be produced after Gene Roddenberry's second pilot got the go-ahead from the NBC network (it actually aired as an original-series episode). "When I went in for the interview, they asked if I would shave my head," recalls Howard. "Even at that age I remember thinking, 'I'm an actor but I'm not an idiot.' I was seven years old and going to school. There was no way they were going to shave my head!" Roddenberry wanted Howard in the cast so badly, though, that the make-up department had to settle on a skull-cap. "I don't remember much about the filming," Howard admits, "but I do know it was a big enough deal that I made my father bring the Polaroid camera and take a picture of me in Kirk's chair." Years later, Howard auditioned twice for *ST:TNG* and, last year, was cast in an episode of *DS9*. But the casting execs, he says, "had no idea I was in the original series – and I was a little afraid to tell them. I didn't want it to affect their decision one way or the other." But he just loved being recognized by director George Lucas. "A few years ago, I went to see him on an audition and I was very nervous. But the moment I walked into his office, he said, 'Corbomite Maneuver, Commander Balok!' and it completely broke the ice. I was absolutely stunned. Here was a major movie director, a cinema legend, and he turns out to be a Trekkie! I just shook my head and said, 'Wow.' I think it was the very first time I really felt the full impact of *Star Trek*."

DR. MAE JEMISON

Like Whoopi Goldberg, former NASA astronaut Dr. Mae Jemison – the first African-American woman in space – was greatly inspired in her youth by actor Nichelle Nichols. And, like Whoopi Goldberg, Jemison wound up on the *Starship Enterprise*. "My love for *Star Trek* only grew greater when I actually put on a Starfleet uniform," says Jemison, who played Ensign Palmer, a transporter crew member in the "Second Chances" episode of *The Next Generation*. "It's exciting to see creator Gene Roddenberry's vision continue with new series and new movies. They say that at any given time, there is a *Star Trek* show airing somewhere in the world. That's a wonderful thing to think about.

DR. MAE JEMISON

thought, 'A bald guy as captain?' Two shows later, he and the rest of the cast were making the old series look camp. I guess the first one is pretty cheesy. That's why we parodied it on *SCTV*. But I still loved it – I was never trying to disgrace *Star Trek*." Thomas has never been asked to guest-star, though he'd jump at the chance – "as long as I don't have to wear a lot of latex like Andrea Martin did when she played a Ferengi. I once tried to get on but they didn't want to hear from me."

MICHAEL McKEAN

Michael McKean – of "Spinal Tap" and Lenny and Squiggy fame (odd-ball characters from *Laverne & Shirley*) – recently played a demonic circus clown in "The Thaw" episode of *Star Trek: Voyager*. But he didn't clown around when Paramount sent him the script: "It was one of those offers you know you're going to accept before you read the script, because you'll always be able to say, 'I did a *Star Trek*.' These shows are part of our culture." Last season on the evening variety show *Saturday Night Live,* he did a sketch in which he played Patrick Stewart filling in for William Shatner as the host of *Rescue 911.* "Everybody on the show was a devoted watcher of *ST:TNG* except me – I had to borrow tapes to bone up." McKean admits he is more of a classic Trekker. "I was 10 when the original series came on and I watched it every Friday night. I *think* it was Friday night. I was in college, so every night was Friday night."

I only hope it will continue to inspire young people to pursue their dreams, as it did with me. *Star Trek* tells us that anything and everything is possible."

PRINCE ABDULLAH OF JORDAN

The eldest son of Jordan's King Hussein, 34-year-old Prince Abdullah Bin-Al Hussein received his education in England and the United States and was raised on reruns of the original *Star Trek*. As chief of the Private Guards in the Jordanian Forces, he says, "I admire Captain Kirk and his way of taking command in a crisis. He never loses his temper; he inspires confidence in his men. Roddenberry wrote with a very good understanding of the military." A *Star Trek* memorabilia collector (he owns an original Kirk uniform autographed by Shatner), Abdullah also has a complete set of *Star Trek* on video. "I was stuck in the desert for a year and a half when I was in the army. I watched *Star Trek* every night to remind myself of civilization," says the prince, who recently made a cameo appearance on *Star Trek: Voyager* ("Investigations"). "The younger generations find *Star Trek* very appealing. It has no borders. It has a good message, a *Federation* policy of non-interference. It shows a time when the world comes together. It is good to escape once in a while into the world of *Star Trek*."

LOUISE SOREL

Her performance as madcap murderer Vivian Alamain on America's *Days of Our Lives* has made her a legend in the soap world, but actor Louise Sorel is a bit of an icon with the *Star Trek* crowd, too: She played Rayna Kapec, the "perfect woman" android created by the 6,000-year-old Flint (James Daly) in the 1969 episode "Requiem for Methuselah." Sorel remembers the episode as "really very sweet. I loved working with Shatner. We had played lovers once before. In the story, Flint forgot to give Rayna the tools to survive emotionally, and – when he and Kirk started fighting over her – she couldn't bear the pain. It was really very touching." But Sorel – a theatre actor – did not take *Star Trek* all that seriously. "They put me in this funny costume – I stood still and they just wrapped fabric around me – and I had an Annette Funicello bouffant and Dusty Springfield eye make-up. James Daly and I thought of ourselves as these two very serious theatre actors and we kept looking at each other, 'Why on earth are we doing this?' Eventually, we just started saying, 'Christmas money, Christmas money, Christmas money.'"

CAMILLE PAGLIA

The rebel of the feminist movement and best-selling author of "Sexual Personae" is also a devout follower of the classic series and *ST:TNG*. "They are the great educational tools," says Paglia. "They get us to think about the possibilities of politics in an intergalactic era." In her book of essays, "Vamps and Tramps," Paglia praised *Star Trek* for its racial subtext. "But not because these shows are all about tolerance as people think. They do not say everyone is beautiful and all that rainbow stuff which I loathe. *Star Trek* offers a very unsentimental treatment of racial differences. It says that different races can be repulsive to each other but can still cohabit. It is about cos-

mic law. It is about justice." Adds Paglia: "I am an Aries. I am a warrior. These shows are about evolved warrior cultures, where issues of ethics are intricately involved with issues of military prowess, strategy and battle."

JOHN COLICOS

A big favourite with sci-fi fans, John Colicos appeared in the movie "War of the Worlds," tried to freeze the planet as mad scientist Mikkos Cassadine on the North American soap

ABOVE: LOUISE SOREL AS THE "PERFECT WOMAN" IN THE 1969 EPISODE "REQUIEM FOR METHUSELAH." INSET: SOREL TODAY

General Hospital, and menaced *Battlestar Galactica* as the evil Count Baltar – but he will forever be remembered as Cmdr. Kor, *Star Trek*'s very first Klingon. "Some think of *Star Trek*'s optimism as being Pollyanna-ish but I don't," says Colicos. "This positive vision is so much more imaginative than the apocalyptic future so many producers put out. I am bothered by the concept of aliens as being out to destroy Earth. It's a lack of imagination to assume anything alien is dangerous. In 'War of the Worlds,' I was half-human, half-alien, part of a race who, because our sun was dying, wanted to kill off everybody on Earth so we could populate the planet. Well, this is a pile of crap. Why would we assume that any extraterrestrials with the technology to come from another universe would want to destroy us? It is the height of human ego." Colicos enjoys watching the evolution of *Star Trek* in the two current series – but he is confused about one thing: "When I did the original series, nobody knew what a Klingon was supposed to look like, so when I reported for work I said, 'Make me a futuristic Genghis Khan. Spray my hair black. Give me a Fu Manchu beard, green Mongolian make-up.'" But when he returned as Kor on *DS9*, "Klingons had sprouted armadillo bumps on their foreheads. I can only assume we had some sort of Chernobyl-type accident on our planet." ✧

Galaxy-class collectibles

Kevin Stevens' cache of collectibles says a lot about fan passion, as well as the art and science of collecting *Star Trek* memorabilia

BY CHRISTOPHER BLAND

KEVIN STEVENS STARTED COLLECT-ing *Star Trek* memorabilia when he was eight years old. Now the 31-year-old Los Angeles author has enough *Star Trek* collectibles to fill a basement – as well as a book: "Artifacts from the Future: A History of *Star Trek* Memorabilia," by Simon & Schuster, will beam into bookshops next year.

1 ONE-SHEET POSTER FOR CLASSIC EPISODES ON VIDEOCASSETTE – Posters of Kirk, Spock, McCoy and other *Star Trek* icons that have been rolled up and sent out as promotionals are generally worth more than posters folded and mailed to movie houses and video shops. Creases mar the image and make it almost impossible to lay the poster flat in a frame.

2 *STAR TREK: THE ANIMATED SERIES* ORIGINAL ANIMATION CEL – The cel of Spock is an origi-nal sequential drawing from the short-lived animated series of the 1970s. It's valued between £200 and £400 (please be aware that import tariffs may apply). Cels on film, actually used in production, are worth double the value of cels on acetate, produced specifically for collectors.

3 FRANKLIN MINT THREE-DIMENSIONAL CHESS SET – A replica of the game introduced in the classic episode "Where No Man Has Gone Before," Stevens' Franklin Mint set (worth about £165) has a bonus feature: It's fully functional and is accompanied by complete playing instructions.

4 MR. SPOCK PORCELAIN DOLL – A finely-crafted figure of Stevens' favourite *Star Trek* character. The 12-inch doll, sporting a fabric uniform, is valued at approximately £200.

5 PFALTZGRAFF *STAR TREK* CHINA – The Pfaltzgraff compa-ny was commissioned to produce fine china for some of the *Star Trek* movies, and then created a limited quantity of *Star Trek* china for sale to the public. One place-setting shown in photograph originally sold for about £25 and are now estimated in the £100 range.

6 FRANKLIN MINT 25TH ANNIVERSARY *U.S.S. Enterprise* – Stevens feels this commemorative die-cast starship, which is still available for about £200, is the most faithful reproduction of the original *Enterprise*. Some of the model's features: The saucer section of this *Enterprise* model lifts away to reveal the bridge and instrument pan-els, and a removable aft section conceals a shuttle.

COLLECTOR KEVIN STEVENS

7 *STAR TREK: THE NEXT GENERATION* PRESS KIT – Press kits are generally valued for their limited-run artwork, photos and gimmicks, and can range in price from £100 to £130 – or higher. The 1986 *The Next Generation* 20th-anniversary kit with a Patrick Stewart voice chip is valued at approximately £100. A *Star Trek: Deep Space Nine*-etched metal advance brochure can be purchased for between £130 and £165.

Beginner's tip

You don't have to spend a fortune to begin your *Star Trek* collection. There are many companies licensed to sell *Star Trek* items throughout the United Kingdom, and a quick flip through the pages of "Starlog" or "*Star Trek*: The Official Monthly Magazine" will probably steer you in the right direction. The UK *Star Trek* Fan Club (01923-227-691) may also know of a *Star Trek* convention that's coming to your city. With respect to guidebooks, "The Official Price Guide: *Star Trek* and Star Wars Collectibles" (by Sue Cornwell and Mike Kott, 1991) is currently *the* definitive shopping list of *Star Trek* memorabilia. The publisher, Random House, can be reached in London at 0171-973-9000. The book's ISBN number is 0-876-37831-9. *Star Trek* items featured in the book are listed values in American dollars. Stock availability, of course, varies according to demand.

between £13 and £20 when they were first released in the mid-1980s, original-series plates now typically fetch between £100 and £130. The *Star Trek* series plates were often – but not always – issued with certificates of authenticity.

12 HALLMARK'S 1991 *U.S.S. ENTERPRISE* CHRISTMAS TREE ORNAMENT – Hallmark underestimated demand in 1991 and only produced a small quantity of the ornament in commemoration of the 25th anniversary of *Star Trek*. The original retail price in the United States (the only country where the ornaments were released) was approximately £15. Price is now around £165, but reach as much as £265 at Christmas-time when collectors try to complete their sets.

13, 14, 15 PLAYMATES PROP REPRODUCTIONS – Play-mates' classic phasers, communicators and tricorders can sometimes be hard to find, which makes them uniquely collectible. Most toy shops in the U.K. order the items on an on-demand basis, so stock usually doesn't remain on the shelf for long. Each unit features working lights and sounds.

16 GOLD KEY COMICS *STAR TREK* #1 – The photo cover of this 1967 comic is a rarity. A mint condition copy can fetch £200; it originally sold for the equivalent of 8p.

8 MEGO *STAR TREK* ACTION FIGURES AND *U.S.S. ENTERPRISE* PLAYSET – Mego Corp's 8-inch tall *Star Trek* figures, issued in 1975 (four years before "Star Trek: The Motion Picture" made its debut), are indicative of the show's lasting appeal, six years after its cancellation by the National Broadcasting Company in 1969. The figures are worth more if they're still in the original blister packaging and have original hand equipment, such as phasers or tricorders. The figure carrying case (which doubles as a playset) features a series of cardboard slides to change the viewing screen.

9 NORTH AMERICAN BEAR COMPANY MR. SPOCK TEDDY BEAR – One of a series modelled after pop culture icons. The Mr. Spock Teddy Bear – now available only through collectors – has his own Starfleet uniform and tricorder.

10 AMT 1ST EDITION *U.S.S. ENTERPRISE* MODEL KIT – There are only two appreciable differences between the original AMT *Enterprise* kits and those currently available from ERTL, which purchased AMT and uses its molds. The original AMT *Enterprise* came with working lights and packaging far more colourful than present ERTL items.

11 *STAR TREK* ORIGINAL SERIES COLLECTOR'S PLATE – Hamilton/Ernst has issued various series of plates, with production runs so far drawing on the original series and *The Next Generation*. All of the plates are numbered and some are signed by the artist, Susie Morton. Worth

COLLECTOR'S TIP:
Don't remove a Star Trek *collector's item from its package. It's worth much more when preserved in the original wrapping. Collectors with small children, however, may wish to consider buying two action figures: one for the collection, the other for your eager child.*

17 PLAYMATES *STAR TREK: THE NEXT GENERATION* FIGURES AND *ENTERPRISE-D* PLAYSET – Some items quickly escalate in value as soon as they hit the market. Playmates' small plastic *Star Trek* figures, issued five years ago when *ST:TNG* was in first-run syndication (aired on multiple networks simultaneously), cost about £2 – now they're valued between £25 and £35 – and sometimes go up to £50. Stevens' advice: Purchase those *DS9* and *Star Trek: Voyager* action figures before the shows complete their runs, and don't assume figures of Sisko or Janeway will be the most sought-after. Alien figures, because of their bizarre appearance and the small production runs, climb higher in value. Mego's small Betelgeusian figures from "Star Trek: The Motion Picture" are worth £115 to £165, while a Kirk figure fetches £15 to £35. ✧

Episode Log

I f you were to sit down and watch every episode of *Star Trek* ever produced, you would be glued to your television set for almost 17 days non-stop. Over the past 30 years, the crews of *Star Trek, Star Trek: The Next Generation, Star Trek: Deep Space Nine* and *Star Trek: Voyager* have logged close to 400 hours in TV time. We've compiled a complete log – organized by series and season in order of air date – of all four series. (Note: American fans of *DS9* and *Star Trek: Voyager* are probably a season or two ahead of U.K. viewers.) Episode descriptions include title, stardate, the date of the show's world première, episode number, details on casts, directing and writing credits and a plot summary. For noteworthy shows – ones that introduced new characters, explained *Star Trek* milestones or featured prominent guest stars – we've inserted our own commentary. At the beginning of each season you'll find an overview of the significant developments in *Star Trek* for that season, with cast changes, character development and key story-lines, highlighted by our team of expert Trekkers.

EPISODE LOG CONTENTS

STAR TREK — THE ORIGINAL SERIES	82
— THE FEATURE FILMS	98
STAR TREK: THE NEXT GENERATION	100
STAR TREK: DEEP SPACE NINE	138
STAR TREK: VOYAGER	158

We've also chosen – from the approximately 400 *Star Trek* episodes – our all-time 100 favourites: 25 from the classic *Star Trek* television series, 50 from *Star Trek: The Next Generation*, 20 from *Star Trek: Deep Space Nine* and five from *Star Trek: Voyager*. These are indicated throughout by a 24th-century communicator badge (which is illustrated above).

STARDATES

Few *Star Trek* topics generate as much heated debate as the stardate system, the time calculation used by the *United Federation of Planets* which was introduced to the classic series by Gene Roddenberry, who borrowed the notion from the Julian date currently used by astronomers. Developed by Joseph Justus Scaliger (who named his dating system after his father, Julius Caesar Scaliger), the Julian time calculation measures the number of days elapsed since 1 Jan. 4713 BC, the date derived by Joseph Justus. In the case of the 30th anniversary of the air date for the original series (8 Sept. 1996), that's 2,450,335 days. To make it easier, astronomers only use the last five digits – making 50335 the Julian date for the *Star Trek* anniversary. For *Star Trek*, Roddenberry added a single digit after the decimal point (50335.2, for example) to represent one of 10 time increments in a 24-hour period.

• **Original *Star Trek*:** Roddenberry borrowed the five-digit Julian date, shortening it to four digits and renaming it "stardate." Not a precise measurement of each episode's time frame, the stardate was simply a reminder that the series was set in the future. Readers should note that stardates sometimes appear inconsistent because the episodes did not always air in the order they were filmed. The six films based on the classic-series characters maintain the four-digit pattern.

• ***Star Trek: The Next Generation*:** To distinguish *ST:TNG*'s 24th-century stardates from those of the 23rd century, Roddenberry introduced a fifth digit. While still not a precise measurement of each episode's time frame, attentive viewers will notice a pattern (see diagram, right) marking the series' episode order.

• ***Star Trek: Deep Space Nine* and S**
the third and fourth *Star Trek* series as well
Generations," were set in the same 24th-century time frame as *ST:TNG*, their stardates were correlated, which helps establish continuity in the *Star Trek* universe. Thus, *DS9*'s debut episode was assigned stardate 46379.1, since the third series première was during *ST:TNG*'s sixth season. Similarly, *Star Trek: Voyager*'s opener is dated 48315.6, as its debut was in the eighth season after *ST:TNG*'s initial launch.

4 2 523 . 7

• first digit (4) to indicate the 24th century	• second digit to indicate the season	• three digits, from 000 to 999, progressing unevenly through the season	• digit following the decimal to indicate one-tenth of a 24-hour period

Star Trek
The Original Series

Star Trek's daring first series transformed the world of science fiction forever in just three seasons

FIRST SEASON

THE 8TH SEPT. 1966 WAS A WATERSHED FOR SCI-FI FANS. IT WAS ON THIS DAY THAT AMERICA'S NATIONAL Broadcasting Co. aired the first episode of a strange and wonderful new series called *Star Trek*. And it had a prime-time slot, competing against such popular American series as *Bewitched* on ABC, plus *My Three Sons* and the Friday-night movie on CBS.

Star Trek's survival in that inaugural season was not immediately guaranteed. Less than three months after its debut, NBC hinted that it might pull the plug because of low ratings. Fans – spurred to action by a group of science-fiction writers – flooded NBC offices with thousands and thousands of letters, and saved the show.

Star Trek writers chartered a slightly different course in sci-fi TV, giving birth to stories that would focus on the human drama of the crews' lives as much as the new worlds and alien creatures they encountered. In retrospect, the first season's plots were unlike anything seen before on TV, ranging from frivolous ("Shore Leave") and frightening ("The Corbomite Maneuver") to touching ("Miri") and philosophical ("A Taste of Armageddon"). Creator Gene Roddenberry had thus established the *Star Trek* trademark: In space, anything can and often does happen.

THE MAN TRAP: *A SHAPE-CHANGING SALT VAMPIRE SETS HER SIGHTS ON THE ENTERPRISE CREW IN THE DEBUT EPISODE.*

THE MAN TRAP
8 Sept. 1966, No. 6
Directed By: Marc Daniels
Written by: George Clayton Johnson
STARDATE: 1513.1
A *U.S.S. Enterprise* landing party, delivering medical supplies to M-113, encounters a shape-changing "vampire" that completely drains bodies of their salt. **Professor Crater:** Alfred Ryder. **Nancy Crater:** Jeanne Bal. **Darnell:** Michael Zaslow. **M-113 salt creature:** Francine Pyne.

✦ *The debut episode established the tone for the series. Revealing Dr. Leonard McCoy's abysmal track record in matters of romance would signal a trend for the series: Scripts would delve into the personal lives of the crew – in addition to exploring strange new worlds outside the starship. Note the original phaser weapons (which would later be modified), the sound effects for the ship's turbolifts, and McCoy's curious medical instruments.*

SHOW WATCH: *Dr. McCoy would not be the last Starfleet officer to fire on the "woman" he loved: Riker would face the same tough decision in* Star Trek: The Next Generation's *"The Vengeance Factor."*

Shades of the M-113 salt "vampire" and its lethal hunger would reappear years later in Star Trek: Deep Space Nine's *fourth season episode "The Muse," in which the mysterious Onaya would draw life-sustaining energy from Jake Sisko's brain. And the notion of a shape-shifter, which resurfaced in ST:TNG's "The Dauphin" and "Aquiel," and in "Star Trek VI: The Undiscovered Country," would return to take a more enduring form in the character of shape-shifting Odo on DS9.*

CHARLIE X
15 Sept. 1966, No. 8
Directed by: Lawrence Dobkin
Written by: D.C. Fontana
Story by: Gene Roddenberry
STARDATE: 1533.6
A space orphan (Robert Walker Jr.) wreaks havoc on the *Starship Enterprise*, using his telekinetic powers to make people disappear. **Thasian:** Abraham Sofaer. **Tina:** Patricia McNulty. **Capt. Ramart:** Charles J. Stewart. **Tom Nellis:** Dallas Mitchell.

✦ *The wide-eyed performance by Robert Walker Jr. heightens the dramatic tension, and special effects are put to good use in a couple of horrifying segments as Charlie "removes" the face of a crew member he believes is laughing at him.*

STAR WATCH: *The talented Abraham Sofaer, who plays Thasian, was a British stage actor in the 1930s and '40s before moving to Hollywood. He also starred in "Quo Vadis?"*

SHOW WATCH: *The notion of a space orphan exposed to alien influences would return in the ST:TNG episode "Suddenly Human."*

STAR TREK'S *SECOND-SEASON CAST (FROM LEFT TO RIGHT):* James Doohan, DeForest Kelley, Walter Koenig, Majel Barrett, William Shatner, Nichelle Nicholls, Leonard Nimoy, and George Takei. Inset: Grace Lee Whitney appeared *in the first season in the recurring role of Yeoman Janice Rand.*

WHERE NO MAN HAS GONE BEFORE

22 Sept. 1966, No. 2
Directed by: James Goldstone
Written by: Samuel A. Peeples
STARDATE: 1312.4

The *Enterprise* encounters a force field that transforms a crewman into an all-powerful creature seething with energy. **Gary Mitchell:** Gary Lockwood. **Dr. Elizabeth Dehner:** Sally Kellerman. **Dr. Mark Piper:** Paul Fix. **Lieut. Lee Kelso:** Paul Carr. **Yeoman Smith:** Andrea Dromm.

✦ *This episode was originally filmed as the second pilot. Man's desire for immortality is brought to light as Lt.-Cmdr. Gary Mitchell – Kirk's Academy classmate and best friend – begins to change into a being whose superior mental powers put the ship and crew at risk. Shatner has some of his best moments struggling with the realization that he must kill his friend in order to save his crewmates.*

STAR WATCH: *Gary Lockwood would return to the stars as one of the astronauts in Stanley Kubrick's "2001: A Space Odyssey." Sally Kellerman played brashy*

Hotlips Hoolihan in the movie version of M*A*S*H.

SHOW WATCH: *Spock's eyebrows have a sharper upward angle in this episode, one of those originally shot as a pilot. The eyebrow style was toned down for the series itself. Viewers would note that Spock's eyebrows are less striking in later shows.*

THE NAKED TIME

29 Sept. 1966, No. 7
Directed by: Marc Daniels
Written by: John D.F. Black
STARDATE: 1704.2

While transporting a group of scientists, the *Enterprise* landing party is infected by a disease that causes the ship's crew to lose all inhibitions. **Lieut. Riley:** Bruce Hyde. **Joe Tormolen:** Stewart Moss. **Laughing Crewman:** John Bellah.

✦ *This episode has great comic overtones, but also exposes the innermost thoughts and feelings of the crew, and establishes the character traits of the show's main players: Kirk as the taciturn, heroic type; Spock as someone torn over his desire to submit to his human emotions; and the beleaguered McCoy, as the erstwhile man*

of science exasperated in his pursuit of a cure. Watch for the first appearance of Lieut. Kevin Riley (Bruce Hyde), an early fan favourite who commandeers the ship and entertains with Irish tunes from the old country. Also in this episode: the first glimpse of the Jefferies tube, named after classic series art director Matt Jefferies. The behaviour-altering disease would return to infect Picard's Enterprise-D crew in "The Naked Now."

BEST MOMENT: *The look on Kirk's face as Riley sings, one more time, "I'll Take You Home Again, Kathleen."*

SHOW WATCH: *Majel Barrett has her first scene-stealing moments as Nurse Chapel reveals her devotion to the emotionally distant Spock.*

THE ENEMY WITHIN

6 Oct. 1966, No. 5
Directed by: Leo Penn
Written by: Richard Matheson
STARDATE: 1672.1

A bizarre transporter malfunction splits Kirk into two beings – one good, one evil – who battle for control of the *Enterprise*. **Lieut. John Farrell:** Jim Goodwin.

Technician Fisher: Edward Madden.

✦ *Richard Matheson's script provides great opportunity for Shatner's acting skills. The notion of two Kirks would be reintroduced in "What Are Little Girls Made Of?" later in the season. Because of a similar transporter mishap, Cmdr. Riker would be called upon to confront his other self ("Second Chances").*

SHOW WATCH: *Spock's first use of the Vulcan nerve pinch.*

MUDD'S WOMEN
13 Oct. 1966, No. 4
Directed by: Harvey Hart
Written by: Stephen Kandel
Story by: Gene Roddenberry
STARDATE: 1329.1
Interplanetary hustler Harry Mudd transports aboard with three gorgeous women, who become pawns when the *Enterprise* has to obtain dilithium crystals. **Harry Mudd:** Roger C. Carmel. **Eve:** Karen Steele. **Magda:** Susan Denberg. **Ruth:** Maggie Thrett. **Lieut. John Farrell:** Jim Goodwin.

✦ *In the first of two show-stealing appearances, Roger C. Carmel delights in the persona of Harcourt Fenton Mudd, 23rd-century con artist.*

WHAT ARE LITTLE GIRLS MADE OF?
20 Oct. 1966, No. 10
Directed by: James Goldstone
Written by: Robert Bloch
STARDATE: 2712.4
While on the planet Exo III, Kirk discovers a scientist who has learned to create android duplicates – including one of Kirk himself. **Nurse Chapel:** Majel Barrett. **Dr. Korby:** Michael Strong. **Andrea:** Sherry Jackson. **Ruk:** Ted Cassidy.

✦ *Returning once again to the notion of a duplicate Kirk – this time as an android – the episode affords a rare glimpse into the private past of Nurse Chapel, who was once engaged to Dr. Roger Korby. First mention of Kirk's brother, George Samuel Kirk, whose dead body (played by Shatner) we will see in the first-season episode "Operation - Annihilate!"*

STAR WATCH: *Ted Cassidy (Lurch in the American television series* The Addams Family*) appears as the android Ruk. Cassidy was later cast in Roddenberry's unsold 1973 TV series pilot "Genesis II."*

MIRI
27 Oct. 1966, No. 12
Directed by: Vincent McEveety
Written by: Adrian Spies
STARDATE: 2713.5
An *Enterprise* landing party beams down to a planet that appears to be inhabited by children, but who in fact turn out to be more than 300 years old. **Miri:** Kim Darby. **Jahn:** Michael J. Pollard. **Lieut. John Farrell:** Jim Goodwin.

✦ *This haunting script is a spin on the Peter Pan fable about children who never grow old. In one frightening moment, Kirk is attacked by children, a scene intercut with a small girl's smiling face.*

STAR WATCH: *Kim Darby ("True Grit") and Micheal J. Pollard ("Bonnie and Clyde").*

SHOW WATCH: *The young girl Kirk carries to safety is actually Shatner's daughter.*

DAGGER OF THE MIND
3 Nov. 1966, No. 11
Directed by: Vincent McEveety
Written by: S. Bar-David
STARDATE: 2715.1
While delivering supplies to a penal colony on Tantalus V, Kirk is shocked to discover the colony's director is using a deadly device to control the prisoners. **Dr. Adams:** James Gregory. **Dr. Van Gelder:** Morgan Woodward. **Dr. Helen Noel:** Marianna Hill. **Lethe:** Susanne Wasson.

✦ *Truly disturbing moments as Van Gelder tortures Kirk with the neural neutralizer. These scenes would be echoed in ST:TNG's "Chain of Command" as Picard faces his Cardassian Torturer.*

STAR WATCH: *Morgan Woodward returned as Capt. Tracey in "The Omega Glory."*

SHOW WATCH: *The first incidence of the Vulcan mind-meld.*

THE CORBOMITE MANEUVER
10 Nov. 1966, No. 3
Directed by: Joseph Sargent
Written by: Jerry Sohl
STARDATE: 1512.2
The *Enterprise* is locked in a tractor beam by a vessel whose commander is seen as a fearsome alien on the starship's viewscreen. **Balok:** Clint Howard. **Dave Bailey:** Anthony Hall.

✦ *A great script with a simple moral: Appearances can be deceiving. The tension is heightened by the periodic image of the scary alien Balok on the ship's viewscreen.*

STAR WATCH: *Clint Howard (the brother of "Apollo 13" director Ron Howard) would return to* Star Trek *as a homeless man in DS9's "Past Tense, Part II" (See page 76).*

THE MENAGERIE, Parts I, II
17 Nov. and 24 Nov. 1966, No. 16
Directed by: Marc Daniels
Written by: Gene Roddenberry
STARDATE: 3012.4
The *Enterprise's* original commander, Capt. Pike (Jeffrey Hunter), is transported aboard the *Enterprise*, and Spock commandeers the ship and steers it to Talos IV, a planet outside *Federation* jurisdiction. **Capt. Pike:** Jeffrey Hunter. **The injured Capt. Pike:** Sean Kenney. **Jose Mendes:** Malachi Throne. **Vina:** Susan Oliver. **Miss Piper:** Julie Parrish. **Lieut. Hansen:** Hagan Beggs. **Dr. Phillip Boyce:** John Hoyt.

✦ *An award-winning episode remembered for its dramatic presentation. This rare two-parter makes use of scenes originally shot for "The Cage," the rejected pilot for the series filmed two years earlier. Note*

THE MENAGERIE: JEFFREY HUNTER PLAYED CAPT. CHRISTOPHER PIKE, THE VERY FIRST ENTERPRISE CAPTAIN, IN THE ORIGINAL PILOT EPISODE OF STAR TREK.

Spock's arched eyebrows and the appearance of Majel Barrett as Number One, the Enterprise's *original first officer. Spock becomes the first Starfleet officer in the original series to be court-martialled.*

BEST SCENE: *Kirk defends Spock's character – which is questioned by Dr. McCoy – and is stunned when he realizes his own life and career have been jeopardized by the Vulcan's inexplicable behaviour.*

SHOW WATCH: *The scarred and injured Pike is played by Sean Kenney, who also* appeared in "The Arena" and "A Taste of Armageddon." Malachi Throne would return as Romulan Senator Pardek in ST:TNG's two-part "Unification."

THE CONSCIENCE OF THE KING

8 Dec. 1966, No. 13
Directed by: Gerd Oswald
Written by: Barry Trivers
STARDATE: 2817.6

An interstellar Shakespearean troupe is to be transported to its next engagement by the *Enterprise*, although Kirk is convinced the leader is a notorious political figure. **Anton Karidian:** Arnold Moss. **Lenore:** Barbara Anderson. **Lieut. Kevin Riley:** Bruce Hyde.

◆ *Revenge for war crimes and mass murder fuels Kirk's obsession with uncovering the real identity of troupe leader Anton Karidian. The clever juxtaposition of Shakespearean themes, incorporating passages from "Hamlet" and "Macbeth," makes this drama a standout.*

SHOW WATCH: *The final TV appearance of Bruce Hyde as Lieut. Riley.*

BALANCE OF TERROR

13 Dec. 1966, No. 9
Directed by: Vincent McEveety
Written by: Paul Schneider
STARDATE: 1709.1

Conflict between the Romulans and the *Federation* turns into a galactic cat-and-mouse game after the Romulans attack Outpost 4, which guards the neutral zone between the two territories. **Romulan Commander:** Mark Lenard. **Lieut. Andrew Stiles:** Paul Comi. **Angela Martine:** Barbara Baldavin. **Robert Tomlinson:** Stephen Mines.

◆ *First appearances of the Romulans (whose features are surprisingly close to those of the Vulcans), the Romulan Bird-of-Prey and its cunning cloaking device. Leonard Nimoy has some fine moments as Spock confronts the distrust and open hostility of Lieut. Stiles, whose family had fought the Romulans. Kirk becomes the first captain to perform a shipboard wedding, a duty that Picard would later perform for Miles O'Brien and his bride, Keiko, in ST:TNG.*

SHOW WATCH: *The first appearance of Mark Lenard as the Romulan commander. He'd later become better known as Spock's Vulcan father, Sarek, first encountered in "Journey to Babel."*

SHORE LEAVE

29 Dec. 1966, No. 17
Directed by: Robert Sparr
Written by: Theodore Sturgeon
STARDATE: 3025.3

While on shore leave on an idyllic, Earth-like planet, Kirk and the *Enterprise* crew discover that having your every wish come true can have disastrous consequences. **Tonia:** Emily Banks. **Finnegan:** Bruce Mars. **Caretaker:** Oliver McGowan. **Lieut. Rodriguez:** Perry Lopez.

◆ *An Alice in Wonderland fantasy episode with a mix of humourous hits (such as Kirk being hounded by his rowdy old class-mate, Finnegan) and well-timed shocks (such as the scene in which McCoy is mortally wounded by a lance-wielding knight on horseback). McCoy becomes the first regular crew-member to be resurrected from the dead.*

SHOW WATCH: *In the 24th century, Picard would sojourn on the fantasy planet Risa in "Captain's Holiday," while he and his crew would accidentally encounter a region in space where thought becomes reality in "Where No One Has Gone Before." In the later Star Trek series, the holodeck would provide settings for fantasies of all kinds.*

THE GALILEO SEVEN

5 Jan. 1967, No. 14
Directed by: Robert Gist
Written by: Oliver Crawford and S. Bar-David
STARDATE: 2821.5

Spock and a landing party have to fend for themselves after crash-landing the shuttle on the planet Taurus II – just when they lose all contact with the *Enterprise*. **Lieut. Boma:** Don Marshall. **Lieut. Gaetano:** Peter Marko. **Latimer:** Reese Vaughn. **Lt.-Cmdr. Kelowitz:** Grant Woods. **Mears:** Phyllis Douglas. **High Commissioner Ferris:** John Crawford.

◆ *When Spock's ability to command the same respect as the captain comes into question, the first officer abandons his Vulcan logic and makes an emotional decision that saves the lives of his shipmates, changing the crew's perception of him from that of a cold-blooded scientist to a capable leader. Excellent confrontation scenes between Spock and McCoy. First use of the* Enterprise *shuttlecraft.*

THE SQUIRE OF GOTHOS

12 Jan. 1967, No. 18
Directed by: Don McDougall
Written by: Paul Schneider
STARDATE: 2124.5

A foppish man named Trelane captures the *Enterprise* and then transports Kirk and three others to his own world for his personal amusement. **Trelane:** William Campbell. **Lieut. Karl Jaeger:** Richard Carlyle. **Lieut. De Salle:** Michael Barrier. **Yeoman Ross:** Venita Wolf.

◆ *Another whimsical episode, revisiting the notion of a powerful, childlike alien, first encountered in "The Corbomite Maneuver." Trelane, who briefly puts Kirk on trial for treason, would become an entertaining 23rd-century precursor to Q, chief mischief-maker of the 24th century.*

STAR WATCH: *The voices of Trelane's parents are supplied by James Doohan and Barbara Babcock, who later appeared in the episodes "A Taste of Armageddon" and "Plato's Stepchildren."*

SHOW WATCH: *William Campbell would reappear in "The Trouble with Tribbles" as the Klingon captain Koloth, a role he would re-create 26 years later in* Star Trek: Deep Space Nine's *"Blood Oath."*

ARENA

19 Jan. 1967, No. 19
Directed by: Joseph Pevney
Written by: Gene L. Coon
Story by: Fredric Brown
STARDATE: 3045.6

An unseen entity transports both Kirk and the commander of the lizard-like Gorns to a barren world where they are forced into battle using makeshift weapons. **Metron:** Carole Shelyne. **O'Herlihy:** Jerry Ayers. **Lt.-Cmdr. Kelowitz:** Grant Woods. **Lieut. Harold:** Tom Troupe. **Lieut. Lang:** James Farley.

◆ *The desert setting of Vasquez Rocks, California (the location used for "Friday's Child") lends a stark element to this episode. Alone, Kirk is forced to use his own deductive reasoning to resolve the battle with the Gorn.*

TOMORROW IS YESTERDAY

26 Jan. 1967, No. 21
Directed by: Michael O'Herlihy
Written by: D.C. Fontana
STARDATE: 3113.2

After being hurled back to Earth's orbit,

circa 1960s, the *Enterprise* is identified as a UFO by an Air Force pilot, forcing Kirk and Sulu to beam down to Earth to retrieve the photographic evidence. **Capt. Christopher:** Roger Perry. **Colonel Fellini:** Ed Peck. **Air Police Sergeant:** Hal Lynch. **Technician Webb:** Richard Merrifield.

◆ *The episode is the first to place the Star Trek characters in a modern-day Earth setting – and with comedic results, particularly the scene in which an Air Force security man, beamed aboard the* Enterprise, *is astounded by the bowl of chicken soup created by the replicator.*

SHOW WATCH: *The classic crew would have numerous encounters with 20th-century Earth – notably in "The City on the Edge of Forever," "Assignment: Earth," and the feature film "Star Trek IV: The Voyage Home" – while DS9's Quark, Rom and Nog would be arrested as extraterrestials in "Little Green Men."*

COURT MARTIAL
2 Feb. 1967, No. 15
Directed by: Marc Daniels
Written by: Don M. Mankiewicz
and Steven Carabatsos
STARDATE: 2947.3
Kirk is charged with negligence for the accidental death of crewman Finney. **Benjamin Finney:** Richard Webb. **Samuel T. Cogley:** Elisha Cook Jr. **Lieut. Areel Shaw:** Joan Marshall. **Commodore Stone:** Percy Rodriguez. **Jamie Finney:** Alice Rawlings.

◆ *Kirk is the second officer, after Spock, to face court-martial. Shatner shines in an episode that places Kirk under intense personal scrutiny as he defends his record to salvage his career. Great insight into the senior officers' unswerving loyalty to Kirk. Not surprisingly, Spock's unwavering Vulcan logic saves the day and frees Kirk of the wrongful charges, much to the surprise of the exasperated McCoy.*

BEST DIALOGUE: *McCoy to Spock: "Mr. Spock, you're the most cold-blooded man I've ever known." Spock replies: "Why, thank you, doctor."*

STAR WATCH: *Elisha Cook Jr., who appears as Kirk's defence attorney, is best remembered for his role in the 1941 classic film "The Maltese Falcon."*

SHOW WATCH: *Both Kirk and McCoy would subsequently be tried (wrongfully) for murder, namely in the death of Klingon*

Chancellor Gorkon, in the movie "Star Trek VI: The Undiscovered Country."

THE RETURN OF THE ARCHONS
9 Feb. 1967, No. 22
Directed by: Joseph Pevney
Written by: Boris Sobelman
Story by: Gene Roddenberry
STARDATE: 3156.2
Kirk, Spock and Dr. McCoy beam down to Beta III, where they find an 1890s western-style town inhabited by placid Betans, living under the control of the dictatorial Landru – actually a computer – who has eradicated individual thought. **Landru:** Charles Macaulay.

◆ *In a universe driven by technology and the need for order, we observe in this episode a society that's computer-controlled and totally devoid of creativity and individualism. The citizens of Beta III are incapable of thinking for themselves, and emotional expression is restricted.*

SHOW WATCH: *Western motifs will crop up occasionally in* Star Trek, *as in* The Next Generation's "A Fistful of Datas."

🖖 SPACE SEED
16 Feb. 1967, No. 24
Directed by: Marc Daniels
Written by: Gene L. Coon
and Carey Wilbur
STARDATE: 3141.9
After the discovery of the sleeper ship S.S. Botany Bay, it's discovered that its crew – who are still on-board in suspended animation – are super-smart, super-strong individuals from the late 20th century, the products of genetic engineering. **Khan:** Ricardo Montalban. **Marla McGivers:** Madlyn Rhue. **Helmsman Spinelli:** Blaisdell Makee. **Joaquin:** Mark Tobin.

◆ *Star Trek was ahead of its time with this episode about genetic manipulation coupled with cryogenics – the freezing of human tissue – which introduced one of the classic series' most formidable antiheroes, Khan Noonien Singh.*

SHOW WATCH: *Montalban powerfully reprised his mythic role 15 years later in "Star Trek II: The Wrath of Khan," with Khan seeking to avenge the death of his wife (the Marla McGivers character). The topic of cryogenics would arise in later episodes of ST:TNG ("The Neutral Zone," "The Emissary") and Star Trek: Voyager ("The 37s," "The Thaw"). The*

SPACE SEED: *A MEMORABLE TURN BY RICARDO MONTALBAN IN HIS FIRST-SEASON APPEARANCE AS GENETICALLY-ENGINEERED KHAN NOONIEN SINGH.*

S.S. Botany Bay model was altered to later appear as a freighter in "The Ultimate Computer."

A TASTE OF ARMAGEDDON
23 Feb. 1967, No. 23
Directed by: Joseph Pevney
Written by: Robert Hamner
and Gene L. Coon
STARDATE: 3192.1
Kirk and a landing party discover a strange world on the planet Eminiar VII: two societies are at war, but instead of engaging in physical battle, each commands thousands of its citizens to voluntarily go to their deaths. **Ambassador Robert Fox:** Gene Lyons. **Anan 7:** David Opatoshu. **Sar 6:** Robert Sampson. **Mea 3:** Barbara Babcock.

◆ *Interesting take on the futility of war in one of Star Trek's most unsettling stories. Citizens of Eminiar VII willingly embrace death at the behest of their leaders.*

SHOW WATCH: *Barbara Babcock (Hill Street Blues) who provided the voice of Trelane's mother on "The Squire of Gothos," returns in person as one of the citizens slated for elimination, and would return in the third season's "Plato's Stepchildren."*

🖖 THIS SIDE OF PARADISE
2 March 1967, No. 25
Directed by: Ralph Senensky
Written by: D.C. Fontana
Story by: Nathan Butler
and D.C. Fontana
STARDATE: 3417.3
The *Enterprise* investigates a group of *Federation* colonists long presumed

dead. Instead, they find the colonists in perfect health, courtesy of spores on the planet that strip away negative emotions and leave people in a state of bliss. **Leila:** Jill Ireland. **Elias Sandoval:** Frank Overton.

◆ This is Spock's show, as the Vulcan gives in to human pleasure for the first time. The love scenes between Spock and Leila are very touching. Nimoy's performance attracts scores of new admirers.

STAR WATCH: Leila is tenderly played by the late Jill Ireland, who, before marrying Charles Bronson, was the wife of British actor David McCallum.

THE DEVIL IN THE DARK
9 March 1967, No. 26
Directed by: Joseph Pevney
Written by: Gene L. Coon
STARDATE: 3196.1
The chief engineer of a mining planet demands that Kirk and Spock dispose of the rock-like creature that is systematically killing the miners. **Chief Engineer Vanderberg:** Ken Lynch. **Lt.-Cmdr. Giotto:** Barry Russo. **Ed Appel:** Brad Weston. **Schmitter:** Biff Elliot. **Horta:** Janos Prohaska.

◆ This thought-provoking episode emphasizes Kirk's overwhelming compassion and respect for life. In the tunnel, when Spock begs him to kill the Horta, Kirk's humanity prohibits him from destroying what he cannot yet understand. Spock has his own moment of truth when he learns (through a Vulcan mindmeld) of the Horta's pain and suffering.

BEST LINE: Pressed into service to assist the injured rock creature, McCoy barks: "I'm a doctor, not a bricklayer!"

ERRAND OF MERCY
23 March 1967, No. 27
Directed by: John Newland
Written by: Gene L. Coon
STARDATE: 3198.4
An *Enterprise* away team and a Klingon contingent land on the complacent planet Organia at the same time. **Kor:** John Colicos. **Ayelborne:** Jon Abbott. **Claymare:** Peter Brocco. **Klingon:** Victor Lundin. **Trefayne:** David Hillary Hughes.

◆ The first episode to reveal the warlike nature of the Klingon Empire. The Federation, as represented by the Enterprise crew, is equally aggressive in their attempts to coerce the Organians from their peaceful pursuits. As it turns out, both are misplaced in their efforts.

BEST DIALOGUE: Kirk to his Klingon adversary: "The Organians aren't going to let us fight." Kor: "For shame, captain. It would have been glorious."

STAR WATCH: Stage and TV veteran John Colicos made a marvellous Cmdr. Kor, the first Klingon. He would re-create the role of Kor 27 years later on DS9's "Blood Oath" (See page 78).

THE ALTERNATIVE FACTOR
30 March 1967, No. 20
Directed by: Gerd Oswald
Written by: Don Ingalls
STARDATE: 3087.6
Kirk meets two versions of the same alien (Robert Brown): one is a law-abiding, rational intellectual, and the other is a raving madman bent on the total destruction of the universe. **Lieut. Charlene Masters:** Janet MacLachlan. **Commodore Barstow:** Richard Derr. **Lieut. Leslie:** Eddie Paskey.

SHOW WATCH: The alternative-universe theme is also encountered in the season-two episode "Mirror, Mirror."

CITY ON THE EDGE OF FOREVER
6 April 1967, No. 28
Directed by: Joseph Pevney
Written by: Harlan Ellison
STARDATE: 3134.0
Dr. McCoy goes temporarily insane and transports himself to a planet where he leaps through a time portal – forcing Kirk and Spock to follow after him. **Edith Keeler:** Joan Collins. **Rodent:** John Harmon. **Voice of the Guardian:** Bartell LaRue.

◆ One of the best episode of the classic series, this show won a Hugo Award for Best Dramatic Presentation – with a stunning ending that makes the most of the oft-repeated theme of time-travel and incorporates footage of the Brooklyn Bridge and New York in the 1930s.

MOST HEART-WRENCHING SCENE: Kirk, having fallen in love with Keeler, a social worker, must stop McCoy from saving Keeler's life after he discovers that her survival would alter the course of Earth's history, allowing Hitler to win the Second World War.

SHOW WATCH: London-born Joan Collins' role as visionary Edith Keeler – a sharp contrast to her stint as Alexis Carrington Colby on Dynasty – would become a cornerstone of Star Trek history.

OPERATION – ANNIHILATE!
13 April 1967, No. 29
Directed by: Herschel Daugherty
Written by: Steven W. Carabatsos
STARDATE: 3287.2
After his brother Sam dies of a mysterious ailment on the planet Deneva, Kirk discovers amoeba-like creatures that infiltrate a victim's nervous system and cause insanity. His nephew, Peter, is left orphaned after the disease takes both of his parents. **Kartan:** Dave Armstrong. **Peter Kirk:** Craig Hundley. **Aurelan:** Joan Swift. **Yeoman Zara Jamal:** Maurishka Taliferro.

◆ The final episode of the first season is a race against time as McCoy endeavours to find a cure to a critical disease, while Kirk faces the knowledge that he must destroy a planet if a cure can't be found.

SHOW WATCH: We encounter members – both living and dead – of Capt. Kirk's family. His nephew, Peter (the son of his late brother, Sam) is played by Craig Hundley. Shatner himself (with make-up) assumes the role of his brother's corpse. ✧

CITY ON THE EDGE OF FOREVER: STRANDED ON EARTH IN THE 1930s, CAPT. KIRK (WILLIAM SHATNER) IS MESMERIZED BY THE STARS, AND BY SOCIAL WORKER EDITH KEELER (JOAN COLLINS).

SECOND SEASON

NBC UPROOTED STAR TREK FROM ITS THURSDAY NIGHT BERTH TO FRIDAY IN YEAR TWO, PLACING IT opposite ABC's newcomer western series *Hondo*, and CBS's *Gomer Pyle, U.S.M.C.* and the Friday-night movie. Even though *Star Trek* garnered five major American television awards in its first season, the show still wasn't close to a hit in the ratings.

There were also several personnel changes in the second season: Producer Gene L. Coon left the series and was replaced by John Meredyth Lucas (although Coon would continue to write scripts); script consultant Steven W. Carabatsos departed, leaving that spot open for D.C. Fontana; and Paramount took over full production of the show, which had been produced by Desilu Studios (of Lucille Ball and Desi Arnez fame). The biggest change, though, was the addition of Walter Koenig as Ensign Pavel Chekov. This was a deliberate attempt by *Star Trek* producers to skew the show to a younger audience. The creative team, capitalizing on the popularity of the American hit series *The Monkees*, gave birth to the mop-topped Chekov.

It was also the year that *Star Trek* scripts came of age. Several of the second-season shows were issue-oriented, such as "A Private Little War" and "Patterns of Force." Others were just plain fun, like "The Trouble with Tribbles" and "I, Mudd." The cumulative effect was a second season of outstanding stories that recaptured viewers from the first year and attracted new ones.

AMOK TIME: *IN THE THRALLS OF THE VULCAN PON FARR MATING CYCLE, SPOCK (LEONARD NIMOY) FIGHTS A RELUCTANT KIRK (WILLIAM SHATNER) FOR THE HAND OF SPOCK'S INTENDED VULCAN BRIDE.*

AMOK TIME
15 Sept. 1967, No. 34
Directed by: Joseph Pevney
Written by: Theodore Sturgeon
STARDATE: 3372.7
Spock is uncharacteristically emotional as he's stricken by pon farr, the Vulcan mating cycle that occurs every seven years and dictates that a Vulcan must return home to mate or else die. **T'Pring:** Arlene Martel. **T'Pau:** Celia Lovsky. **Stonn:** Lawrence Montaigne. **Admiral Komack:** Byron Morrow.
✦ Set mostly on the planet Vulcan, this change-of-pace episode provides the first real insight into Spock's ancestral

background and Vulcan physiology. Disobeying Starfleet orders, Kirk proves himself loyal to his friend and first officer by diverting the Enterprise to Spock's home planet – much as Spock risked his career to come to the aid of his former captain in the previous season's "The Menagerie." Kirk and McCoy become the first "out-worlders" to witness the Vulcan marriage ceremony. But when T'Pring, Spock's reluctant betrothed, invokes her right to ritual combat and chooses the captain as her surprise champion, Kirk becomes the second Starfleet regular to be "killed," this time at the hands of his crew mate. In the 24th century, Capt.

Picard would run afoul of Lwaxana Troi's Betazoid mating cycle in ST:TNG's "Manhunt," while Deanna would initially greet her own pre-arranged betrothal with reluctance in "Haven."

BEST SCENE: *Spock's look of overwhelming joy when he realizes that Kirk lives – thanks to a knock-out drug McCoy injected into the captain during his pitched battle with Spock.*

SHOW WATCH: *Watch for Spock giving T'Pau the now-famous Vulcan hand salutation, an unscripted move Leonard Nimoy improvised for the episode. It's also in this episode that we hear for the first time "Live long and prosper."*

WHO MOURNS FOR ADONAIS?
22 Sept. 1967, No. 33
Directed by: Marc Daniels
Written by: Gilbert Ralston
STARDATE: 3468.1
An *Enterprise* landing party encounters a vision of the Greek god Apollo, who commands their collective worship. **Apollo:** Michael Forest. **Lieut. Carolyn Palamas:** Leslie Parrish. **Lieut. Kyle:** John Winston.
✦ *The first of several classic episodes rooted in Greek mythology. In this intriguing story, Apollo is revealed to be an alien space traveller who, along with other gods of Greek mythology, landed on Earth long ago and ruled over its primitive inhabitants from Mount Olympus. The first of Scotty's "unlucky-in-love" infatuations puts him in competition with the god Apollo as they rival for the affections of Lieut. Palamas.*

THE CHANGELING
29 Sept. 1967, No. 37
Directed by: Marc Daniels
Written by: John Meredyth Lucas
STARDATE: 3541.9
Kirk wages a battle of wits with a computer probe named Nomad, which is programmed to eliminate anything impure or inferior. **Lieut. Singh:** Blaisdell Makee. **Lieut. Carlisle:** Arnold Lessing. **Voice of Nomad:** Vic Perrin.
✦ *The notion of technology gone awry underscores this story involving a space probe (launched from Earth) and an alien probe. The encounter leaves the Earth probe drastically changed: It now seeks to eliminate all inferior life forms.*

BEST DIALOGUE: *After Kirk uses pure logic to defeat the alien space probe, he says to Spock, "You didn't think I had it in me, did you Spock?" The ever-truthful Vulcan replies, "No, sir."*

SHOW WATCH: *Twelve years later, this story line would provide part of the inspiration for the V'ger space probe threat of "Star Trek: The Motion Picture."*

MIRROR, MIRROR
6 Oct. 1967, No. 39
Directed by: Marc Daniels
Written by: Jerome Bixby
STARDATE: Unknown
Kirk, Scotty, McCoy and Uhura are transported to a parallel universe in which the *Federation* is evil, Kirk is a despotic captain and Spock a ruthless first officer with eyes on the captain's chair. **Marlena:** Barbara Luna. **Tharn:** Vic Perrin.

◆ *This finely tailored script is the first to introduce the oft-repeated notion of a parallel universe, and in this case we're presented with an inverted Federation – one that's totally malevolent. Kirk faces his other self for the second time (it happened also in "The Enemy Within"). Tremendous attention to detail brings to life the mirror universe in which Kirk imperils his stranded fellow crew members by his show of mercy toward the alternate Halkans. Star Trek humour is scant in this show, whose appeal lies in its pervading darkness.*

SHOW WATCH: *In DS9's "Crossover," the crew would traverse darkly into the universe first viewed in this episode, while Sisko would have the opportunity to save his mirror wife from death in the parallel world in "Through the Looking Glass."*

THE APPLE
13 Oct. 1967, No. 38
Directed by: Joseph Pevney
Written by: Max Ehrlich
and Gene L. Coon
Story by: Max Ehrlich
STARDATE: 3715.3
Kirk leads a landing party to an ancient world ruled by a computer named Vaal, which controls the elements on the planet, as well as its childlike inhabitants. **Akuta:** Keith Andes. **Martha Landon:** Celeste Yarnall. **Sayana:** Shari Nims. **Ensign Mallory:** Jay Jones. **Makora:** David Soul.

◆ *Lush planet setting and fine performances, particularly from Keith Andes as the wide-eyed innocent Akuta.*

SHOW WATCH: *David Soul, as the native Makora, would become an American television star in the '70s weekly police drama Starsky and Hutch.*

THE DOOMSDAY MACHINE
20 Oct. 1967, No. 35
Directed by: Marc Daniels
Written by: Norman Spinrad
STARDATE: 4202.9
The *Enterprise* encounters a giant alien device in space that transmits energy waves capable of destroying entire planets. **Commodore Decker:** William Windom. **Lieut. Palmer:** Elizabeth Rogers. **Elliot:** John Copage. **Washburn:** Richard Compton.

◆ *This show was one of the first Star Trek episodes to draw heavily on special effects and opticals, in this case resulting in the ominous-looking planet killer, making the episode one of the season's strongest. William Windom does a terrific job as Matthew Decker. The horror on his face when he discovers he has inadvertently sent his entire starship crew to death is positively chilling. Edge-of-the-seat suspense all the way through.*

SHOW WATCH: *The doomed commodore's son, Capt. Will Decker, would serve under Admiral Kirk and make a fateful sacrifice of his own in "Star Trek: The Motion Picture."*

CATSPAW
27 Oct. 1967, No. 30
Directed by: Joseph Pevney
Written by: Robert Bloch
and D.C. Fontana
STARDATE: 3018.2
Kirk, Scotty and Spock beam down to Pyris VII, a strange planet overrun with zombies, witches and goblins. **Sylvia:** Antoinette Bower. **Korob:** Theo Marcuse. **Lieut. DeSalle:** Michael Barrier. **Jackson:** Jimmy Jones.

◆ *Intended as a Halloween treat, the off-beat tale is packed with witches, giant cats and things that go bump in the night.*

I, MUDD
3 Nov. 1967, No. 41
Directed by: Marc Daniels
Written by: Stephen Kandel
STARDATE: 4513.3
Devious con man Harry Mudd tricks the *Enterprise* into travelling to an uncharted planet inhabited by androids. **Mudd:** Roger C. Carmel. **Norman:** Richard Tatro. **Lieut. Rowe:** Mike Howden. **Ensign Jordan:** Michael Zaslow. **Stella:** Kay Elliot

◆ *The return of the nefarious Mudd is tremendous fun and is played mostly for laughs, such as the scene in which Kirk and crew outwit the androids by overloading their brains with nonsense. Even Spock gets into the fun, telling two identical androids: "I love you. But I hate you." The only scene funnier is the finale, in which Kirk impishly reveals that Mudd's punishment will be constant vigilance under an entire planet of androids – all of them duplicates of his shrewish wife, Stella.*

METAMORPHOSIS
10 Nov. 1967, No. 31
Directed by: Ralph Senensky
Written by: Gene L. Coon
STARDATE: 3219.8
On the planet Gamma Canaris N, Kirk, Spock and McCoy encounter an Earth scientist who is protected by an energy cloud he calls "The Companion." **Zefram Cochrane:** Glenn Corbett. **Commissioner Nancy Hedford:** Elinor Donahue.

◆ *A truly moving episode that relies very little on special effects or a high-tech storyline. Simply put, it's a surprisingly touching love story between the human scientist Zefram Cochrane and the alien "Companion," a faceless energy cloud with whom the humans are able to communicate by means of the ingenious universal translator.*

SHOW WATCH: *Zefram Cochrane is mentioned in ST:TNG's "New Ground."*

FEDERATION FACTOID: *We learn that Zephram Cochrane discovered space-warp drive more than 100 years earlier. Units of measurement (cochranes and millicochranes) would occasionally be worked into the dialogue of later Star Trek series' episodes as a tribute to this character.*

JOURNEY TO BABEL
17 Nov. 1967, No. 44
Directed by: Joseph Pevney
Written by: D.C. Fontana
STARDATE: 3842.3
A mission to transport passengers to a peace treaty conference becomes very difficult for Spock when he learns that two of the delegates on board are his

own parents. **Sarek:** Mark Lenard. **Amanda:** Jane Wyatt. **Thelev:** William O'Connell. **Shras:** Reggie Nalder. **Gav:** John Wheeler.

✦ *An enjoyable romp with a heartfelt ending, and the first episode to feature a large contingent of on-board aliens. Mark Lenard is appropriately stiff as Spock's Vulcan father, Sarek, and Jane Wyatt is endearing as his Earth-born mother, Amanda. Spock's dilemma: Does he stay on the ship and continue filling in as captain after Kirk is injured, or donate blood to save his dying father?*

BEST DIALOGUE: *Spock to Sarek, referring to his earthly mother: "Emotional, isn't she." Sarek: "She has always been that way." Spock: "Indeed? Why did you marry her?" Sarek: "At the time, it seemed the logical thing to do."*

SHOW WATCH: *The episode marks the second appearance of Mark Lenard, who made his earlier mark as a Romulan commander in "Balance of Terror," and would go on to play a Klingon in "Star Trek: The Motion Picture." Lenard would return as Sarek, his best-known role, in "Star Trek III: The Search for Spock," "Star Trek IV: The Voyage Home" and "Star Trek VI: The Undiscovered Country." He'd then return to the small screen as Sarek in Star Trek: The Next Generation's "Sarek" and "Unification, Part I."*

FRIDAY'S CHILD

1 Dec. 1967, No. 32
Directed by: Joseph Pevney
Written by: D.C. Fontana
STARDATE: 3497.2

Enterprise and Klingon crews clash when they simultaneously try to establish relations with the prosperous planet Capella IV. **Kras:** Tige Andrews. **Maab:** Michael Dante. **Eleen:** Julie Newmar. **Keel:** Cal Bolder. **Duur:** Kirk Raymone. **Akaar:** Ben Gage.

✦ *A quick-paced outing that emphasizes the wisdom of the Prime Directive, which prohibits Federation members from interfering in the development of alien civilizations. Kirk and crew do, in fact, involve themselves with the Capellans, but their motives are genuinely altruistic. This episode is the only one in which Dr. McCoy uses his skills to deliver a baby.*

BEST LINE: *Says an impatient McCoy as he helps the pregnant Eleen up a steep hill: "I'm a doctor, not an escalator."*

SHOW WATCH: *Worf would show similar impatience while helping Keiko deliver her baby (later named Molly), in ST:TNG's "Disaster."*

THE DEADLY YEARS

8 Dec. 1967, No. 40
Directed by: Joseph Pevney
Written by: David P. Harmon
STARDATE: 3478.2

After visiting the planet Gamma Hydra IV, Kirk, Spock, McCoy and Scotty are afflicted with rapid, premature ageing. **Commodore Stocker:** Charles Drake. **Dr. Janet Wallace:** Sarah Marshall. **Lieut. Arlene Galway:** Beverly Washburn. **Johnson:** Felix Locher.

✦ *A thought-provoking look at the ageing process and how it can affect ability. When the four crew members start ageing, it becomes apparent that they do so at markedly different rates and with very different results: Kirk and Spock age more slowly than McCoy and Scotty, who appear positively ancient by comparison. Either way, the make-up and prosthetics are terrific, and the episode benefits from the tense ending in which the rejuvenated Capt. Kirk manages to outwit a hostile Romulan warship.*

BEST LINE: *McCoy, cantankerous and stymied as the disease continues to progress: "I'm a doctor, not a magician."*

SHOW WATCH: *Premature ageing would afflict later Starfleet personnel, including Dr. Pulaski in ST:TNG's "Unnatural Selection," and counsellor Deanna Troi in "Man of the People."*

OBSESSION

15 Dec. 1967, No. 47
Directed by: Ralph Senensky
Written by: Art Wallace
STARDATE: 3619.2

A ghost from Capt. Kirk's past resurfaces in the form of a gaseous cloud creature that feeds on human blood cells. **Ensign Garrovick:** Stephen Brooks. **Ensign Rizzo:** Jerry Ayres

✦ *The script for this episode borrowed a page from Herman Melville's classic "Moby Dick." This is a focal piece for Kirk, whose obsession for destroying the gas creature stems from the fact that it killed half the crew of a ship he was serving on a decade earlier – a direct consequence of the inexperienced Kirk's failure to act soon enough against the creature.*

The episode also reveals more about the biochemistry of Spock, whose blood is found to be distasteful to the creature.

WOLF IN THE FOLD

22 Dec. 1967, No. 36
Directed by: Joseph Pevney
Written by: Robert Bloch
STARDATE: 3614.9

A murder occurs during a mission on Argelius II, with all the evidence pointing to chief engineer Scott. **Hengist:** John Fiedler. **Jaris:** Charles Macaulay. **Sybo:** Pilar Seurat. **Tark:** Joseph Bernard. **Morla:** Charles Dierkop.

✦ *When circumstantial evidence points in his direction, Scotty becomes the first Starfleet officer accused of murder – but not the last. A frightening but intriguing episode, in which the true killer is identified as being the ethereal spirit of Jack the Ripper, in reality an ancient life-form called Redjac. The second of Scotty's "unlucky-in-love" mishaps, with none other than Jack the Ripper as his foil.*

SHOW WATCH: *Scotty's 24th-century counterpart, Geordi La Forge, would find his own encounters with the opposite sex equally unrewarding, when the woman to whom he is drawn in ST:TNG's sixth season "Aquiel" is suspected of murder.*

THE TROUBLE WITH TRIBBLES

29 Dec. 1967, No. 42
Directed by: Joseph Pevney
Written by: David Gerrold
STARDATE: 4523.3

Responding to a distress signal, the *Enterprise* travels to space station K-7, where they are introduced to small, furry creatures called Tribbles. **Nilz Baris:** William Schallert. **Capt. Koloth:** William Campbell. **Cyrano Jones:** Stanley Adams. **Mr. Lurry:** Whit Bissell. **Korax:** Michael Pataki.

✦ *One of the best-loved and most-remembered classic episodes and by far the most whimsical, although the whimsy is interwoven with a clever, well-paced plot. The Tribbles become everyone's best friend – except the Klingons.*

BEST SCENE: *Scotty admits to the bewildered Kirk that he started a fight with the Klingons not because they insulted the captain, but because they called the Enterprise a "garbage scow."*

BEST LINE: *When Kirk asks what happened*

to all the Tribbles, who've disappeared from the ship, Scotty replies: "I transported the whole kit and caboodle into [the Klingon's] engine room, where they'll be no tribble at all."

SHOW WATCH: *William Campbell, the Klingon commander Koloth, first appeared as Trelane in "The Squire of Gothos." And actor Stanley Adams, seen here as Cyrano Jones, would later co-write the third season's "The Mark of Gideon." Also, a prime example of* Star Trek *science rooted in reality: triticale, the parent strain of the genetically engineered quad-rotriticale grain which is devoured by the hungry Tribbles, was actually developed as a cereal crop by scientists in 1954.*

THE TROUBLE WITH TRIBBLES: *KIRK'S TROUBLES MOUNT AS QUICKLY AS THE SMALL, FURRY TRIBBLES CAN MULTIPLY THEMSELVES.*

THE GAMESTERS OF TRISKELION

5 Jan. 1968, No. 46
Directed by: Gene Nelson
Written by: Margaret Armen
STARDATE: 3211.7
Kirk, Uhura and Chekov are mysteriously beamed off the *Enterprise* and onto the warlike planet of Triskelion, where violent gladiator games are the main form of amusement. **Galt:** Joseph Ruskin. **Shahna:** Angelique Pettyjohn. **Lars:** Steve Sandor. **Tamoon:** Jane Ross. **Jana Haines:** Victoria George.
✦ *When Kirk, Uhura and Chekov are abducted, Kirk, as usual, gets the best end of the deal: While Chekov is trapped in his cell with an ugly thrall and Uhura is being mauled unseen by a brute, Kirk is teaching the gorgeous Shahna how to*

kiss and hug. Who says there aren't perks to being a Starfleet captain?

⬟ A PIECE OF THE ACTION
12 Jan. 1968, No. 49
Directed by: James Komack
Written by: David P. Harmon
STARDATE: 4598.0
On the planet Sigma Iotia II, Kirk and crew are shocked to discover the Iotians have adopted a gangster lifestyle right out of Al Capone's heyday. **Oxmyx:** Anthony Caruso. **Krako:** Victor Tayback. **Kalo:** Lee Delano. **Tepo:** John Harmon. **Zabo:** Steve Marlo.
✦ *For camp appeal,* Star Trek *doesn't get much better. The sets and characters are straight out of "The Untouchables," and the story ranks as one of the season's best. Visiting Sigma Iotia II, which the crew of the* Starship Horizon *had visited some 100 years earlier, Kirk finds the Iotians have modelled their culture after a book about Chicago mobs, left behind by the previous starship. Kirk attempts to negotiate peace between rival gangs by adopting the tough guy stance – not to mention lingo – the Iotians have come to respect. Great comedic moments, such as Kirk attempting to drive a vintage Iotian automobile and teach the dim Iotian gangsters to play "fizzbin," a card game the quick-witted captain improvises on the spot.*
SHOW WATCH: *Aliens would be influenced by another book in ST:TNG's second-season episode "The Royale."*

THE IMMUNITY SYNDROME
19 Jan. 1968, No. 48
Directed by: Joseph Pevney
Written by: Robert Sabaroff
STARDATE: 4307.1
The *Enterprise* responds to an emergency in the Gamma 7A solar system, which is being threatened by a massive amoeba-like creature that drains energy from planets and ships.
✦ *Amoeba creature notwithstanding, the strength of this episode comes from the close-up look at the bond of friendship between Kirk and his senior officers and in particular at the sparring relationship between Spock and McCoy – both of whom make impassioned arguments as to why they should risk their lives to pilot the shuttlecraft into the depths of the creature. Kirk, meanwhile, is torn when he has to decide which of his friends he will send on*

the suicide mission. Combined with a nail-biter ending, it's a solid outing.
SHOW WATCH: *The roles would be reversed in the 24th century as* Star Trek: Voyager's *crew exposes an unknown life form to harm in "The Cloud."*

A PRIVATE LITTLE WAR
2 Feb. 1968, No. 45
Directed by: Marc Daniels
Written by: Gene Roddenberry
Story by: Jud Crucis
STARDATE: 4211.4
The *Enterprise* investigates life on the primitive planet Neural, whose inhabitants have adopted a warlike attitude, courtesy of weaponry from the Klingons. **Nona:** Nancy Kovack. **Tyree:** Michael Witney. **Apella:** Arthur Bernard. **Krell:** Ned Romero. **Yutan:** Gary Pillar.
✦ *Intended as a comment on the Vietnam War, which was being waged at the time.*

RETURN TO TOMORROW
9 Feb. 1968, No. 51
Directed by: Ralph Senensky
Written by: John Kingsbridge
STARDATE: 4768.3
Three aliens who have existed for centuries – in a mental state only – request assistance from Kirk to construct android bodies to house their intelligence. **Dr. Ann Mulhall:** Diana Muldaur. **Sargon (voice):** James Doohan. **Sargon (body):** William Shatner. **Nurse:** Cindy Lou.
✦ *An intriguing story with an above-average musical score, the episode is also a showcase for the acting talents of Leonard Nimoy. When the alien Henoch takes over Spock's body, Nimoy – using only his face – shifts from the stoic, thoughtful Vulcan to a sinister-looking villain.*
SHOW WATCH: *Diana Muldaur would return as Dr. Miranda Jones in the third season's "Is There In Truth No Beauty?" and 20 years later as Dr. Kate Pulaski in ST:TNG's second season.*

PATTERNS OF FORCE
16 Feb. 1968, No. 52
Directed by: Vincent McEveety
Written by: John Meredyth Lucas
STARDATE: 2534.0
While investigating the planet Ekos, Kirk and Spock discover the inhabitants have adopted a Nazi-like existence in which the Zeons, an underground group,

are persecuted and exterminated. **John Gill:** David Brian. **Melakon:** Skip Homeier. **Isak:** Richard Evans. **Daras:** Valora Noland.

✦ *This chilling episode is producer Gene Roddenberry's statement on the horrors of Naziism. Once again, the Federation is at fault for creating this ill-advised society, inspired by Earth-born cultural observer John Gill. Despite the subject matter, the episode has its humourous moments, including the scene in which Bones is transported down to Ekos while still getting dressed in his Nazi regalia.*

BY ANY OTHER NAME
23 Feb. 1968, No. 50
Directed by: Marc Daniels
Written by: D.C. Fontana
and Jerome Bixby
STARDATE: 4657.5
Agents of the Kelvan Empire scheme to hijack the *Enterprise* to make a 300-year trip back to the Andromeda Galaxy. **Rojan:** Warren Stevens. **Kelinda:** Barbara Bouchet. **Hanar:** Stewart Moss. **Tomar:** Robert Fortier.

✦ *A thoroughly enjoyable outing in which Kirk and crew have to be at their innovative best in order to outwit aliens that are clearly smarter and stronger. In addition to the frightening sequence in which the Kelvans reduce two Enterprise crew members into small, dry blocks, one of which is crushed by Rojan, there's also a highly amusing scene in which Scotty tries to get the alien Tomar drunk with a bottle of green alien liquor.*

THE OMEGA GLORY
1 March 1968, No. 54
Directed by: Vincent McEveety
Written by: Gene Roddenberry
STARDATE: Unknown
On the planet Omega IV, Kirk discovers that a renegade *Federation* commander, Capt. Tracey, has violated the *Federation's* Prime Directive and interfered with the inhabitants by supplying them with weapons. **Capt. Tracey:** Morgan Woodward. **Cloud William:** Roy Jenson. **Sirah:** Irene Kelly. **Lieut. Galloway:** David L. Ross. **Lieut. Leslie:** Eddie Paskey.

✦ *A well-written story packed with action, where the Yangs battle the Kohms, and in which the Yangs' "worship words" are revealed to be a twisted version*

of the United States Constitution. Actor Morgan Woodward does an excellent turn as Capt. Tracey.*

THE ULTIMATE COMPUTER
8 March 1968, No. 53
Written by: D.C. Fontana
Story by: Laurence N. Wolfe
Directed by: John Meredyth Lucas
STARDATE: 4729.4
Computer genius Dr. Richard Daystrom's plan to test his newest computer development, the M-5, on board the *Starship Enterprise*, brings disastrous results. **Dr. Richard Daystrom:** William Marshall. **Wesley:** Barry Russo. **Harper:** Sean Morgan.

✦ *The recurring Star Trek notion of man being replaced by machine began with this episode. In the early stages, Kirk actually appears to be jealous of the M-5, which seems to do a better job of running the Enterprise than he does.*

ASSIGNMENT: EARTH: IN ANOTHER TIME-TRAVEL EPISODE, GARY SEVEN (ROBERT LANSING) AND HIS DIZZY SECRETARY, ROBERTA (TERI GARR), ENCOUNTER THE EARTH-BOUND KIRK (WILLIAM SHATNER) WITH SOME WONDERFUL ANTICS.

BREAD AND CIRCUSES
15 March 1968, No. 43
Directed by: Ralph Senensky
Written by: Gene Roddenberry
and Gene L. Coon
Written by: John Kneubuhl
STARDATE: 4040.7
On the Planet IV 892, the Kirk-Spock-McCoy trio is captured by a group of Roman soldiers and forced to compete in gladiator games, which are broadcast to the eager citizenry via live television. **Merik:** William Smithers. **Claudius**

Marcus: Logan Ramsey. **Septimus:** Ian Wolfe. **Flavius:** Rhodes Reason. **Drusilla:** Lois Jewell.

✦ *A second-season standout, the episode makes excellent use of the parallel-Earth concept and puts the Enterprise crew up against one of their biggest challenges, making clear the unspoken bond between Kirk, Spock and McCoy. In the final sequence, when Spock and McCoy are battling in the arena, it's Spock who, without reservation, comes to the good doctor's aid.*

ASSIGNMENT: EARTH
29 March 1968, No. 55
Directed by: Marc Daniels
Written by: Art Wallace
Story by: Gene Roddenberry
and Art Wallace
STARDATE: Unknown
After travelling back in time to the 20th century, the *Enterprise* intercepts an enigmatic space traveller named Gary Seven, who claims to be an Earth man trained by aliens to prevent Earth from destroying itself. **Gary Seven:** Robert Lansing. **Roberta Lincoln:** Teri Garr. **Mr. Cromwell:** Jim Keefer. **Col. Nesvig:** Morgan Jones.

✦ *Intended as a spin-off series, the finale for the second season is a prime example of perfect Star Trek story-telling. All the action revolves around the mysterious Gary Seven, who appears more than a match for the crew, and there's a magic blend of humour (from the flighty Roberta, played by Teri Garr), tension (in the spacecraft launch) and wit (great dialogue from Garr and Lansing).*
STAR WATCH: *This was one of the first TV appearances by Teri Garr, who would go on to star in big-league films like "Close Encounters of the Third Kind" and the hilarious "Tootsie."*
SHOW WATCH: *The second appearance of a shape-shifter; Gary Seven's cat, Isis. The shape-shifter concept would be more fully developed on DS9 in the form of Odo.* ✦

THIRD SEASON

The third and final season of *Star Trek* saw the show move to a later time-slot on Friday nights at 10 p.m., pitting it against ABC's legal series *Judd for the Defense* and CBS's Friday-night movie. The move infuriated Gene Roddenberry, who saw *Star Trek* as a show for younger fans, most of whom couldn't watch the show during the later time-slot.

Other significant changes that season: The departure of *Star Trek* cinematographer Gerald P. Finnerman, who was replaced by Al Francis; and the addition of Fred Freiberger (directly from the western series *The Wild, Wild West*) as line producer. The third season is most notable for Spock's shift to the forefront. Unlike the first two years, Spock is by now considered an equal to Capt. James T. Kirk, and is a pivotal character in virtually every third-season episode.

All good things must come to an end, however. The final episode of *Star Trek*, "Turnabout Intruder," aired on 3 June 1969. Yet, despite the ups and downs during the final season, the series had attracted millions of fans in the three-year period. Gene Roddenberry's vision had started to catch on.

SPOCK'S BRAIN

20 Sept. 1968, No. 61
Directed by: Marc Daniels
Written by: Lee Cronin
STARDATE: 5431.4
A mysterious young woman suddenly appears on the *U.S.S. Enterprise* and immediately disappears – taking Spock's brain with her. **Kara:** Marj Dusay. **Luma:** Sheila Leighton. **Morg creature:** James Daris.
✦ *DeForest Kelly has some of his best moments as the unflappable Dr. McCoy begins to lose his nerve – and alien-induced expertise – while attempting to reconnect Spock's brain in his cranium.*

THE ENTERPRISE INCIDENT

27 Sept. 1968, No. 59
Directed by: John Meredyth Lucas
Written by: D.C. Fontana
STARDATE: 5031.3
Capt. Kirk inexplicably takes the *Enterprise* into Romulan territory, where the ship is surrounded by three Romulan battle cruisers. **Romulan commander:** Joanne Linville. **Tal:** Jack Donner.
✦ *A long-overdue Romulan storyline becomes a third-season highlight. The Starship Enterprise's foray into Romulan territory – which is actually a ruse to steal the cloaking device – requires Kirk to be surgically transformed into a Romulan (see photo on page 25). For the second time, Spock appears to kill Capt. Kirk, using the non-existent Vulcan death grip.*
SHOW WATCH: *In the 24th century, an unwilling Counsellor Troi would be surgically altered to resemble a Romulan when conscripted into a spy mission (The Next Generation's "Face of the Enemy.")*

THE PARADISE SYNDROME

4 Oct. 1968, No. 58
Directed by: Jud Taylor
Written by: Margaret Armen
STARDATE: 4842.6
Kirk, while on a planet that's about to be destroyed by an asteroid, is mistaken as a god by the inhabitants, who resemble North American Natives. **Miramanee:** Sabrina Scharf. **Salish:** Rudy Solari. **Goro:** Richard Hale.
✦ *Superb acting by Shatner as an amnesia-stricken Kirk briefly enjoys a life of domestic bliss – something unknown to him as a starship captain.*
SHOW WATCH: *In the 24th century, Picard would also be mistaken for a god in* Star Trek: The Next Generation's *"Who Watches the Watchers?" In the fifth season episode "The Inner Light," Jean-Luc, the victim of probe-induced amnesia, would also experience domestic tranquillity.*

AND THE CHILDREN SHALL LEAD

11 Oct. 1968, No. 60
Written by: Edward J. Lasko
Directed by: Marvin Chomsky
STARDATE: 5027.3
During an expedition to the planet Triacus, a landing party discovers orphaned children whose lives are totally manipulated by an entity they refer to as their "Friendly Angel." **Gorgan:** Melvin Belli. **Professor Starnes:** James Wellman. **Tommy:** Craig Hundley. **Mary:** Pamelyn Ferdin. **Don:** Mark Robert Brown.
✦ *The space-orphan concept introduced in "Charlie X" is revisited in this episode. One of the best scenes takes place early in the show when Kirk initially confronts* Gorgan, the Friendly Angel, *in a cave on Triacus. There are several frightening moments throughout, but particularly haunting is the scene on the bridge where the children, having watched tricorder tapes of themselves at play with their parents, break down after seeing images of the graves of their mothers and fathers, whose deaths were caused by the Angel.*

IS THERE IN TRUTH NO BEAUTY?

18 Oct. 1968, No. 62
Directed by: Ralph Senensky
Written by: Jean Lisette Aroeste
STARDATE: 5630.7
The *Enterprise* is assigned the task of transporting the Medusan ambassador Kollos to his ship. The Medusan race is alleged to be so horrifying to contemplate that one look drives humans insane. **Dr. Miranda Jones:** Diana Muldaur. **Marvick:** David Frankham
✦ *Building suspense by not divulging the nature of Kollos' hideous appearance is key to this script, which serves as a space-age morality tale. The scene in which Spock risks insanity to achieve the Vulcan mind-meld with the alien Kollos is especially effective.*
SHOW WATCH: *This episode marks Diana Muldaur's return to the series after the second season's "Return to Tomorrow."*

SPECTRE OF THE GUN

25 Oct. 1968, No. 56
Directed by: Vincent McEveety
Written by: Lee Cronin
STARDATE: 4385.3
Kirk, Spock, McCoy and Chekov find themselves in the Old West when they land on the strange Melkotian planet. **Wyatt Earp:** Ron Soble. **Morgan Earp:** Rex Holman. **Sylvia:** Bonnie Beecher. **Virgil Earp:** Charles Maxwell. **Doc Holliday:** Sam Gilman.
✦ *The juxtaposition of the two different groups – the* Enterprise *crew in Starfleet uniforms and the Earps in their Western outfits – adds a surreal quality. The* Enterprise *crew takes the place of the losing Clanton gang in the infamous gunfight at the O.K. Corral. Dramatic tension is made all the more eerie by the use of foreboding shadows, inventive camera angles and a disembodied musical score. Chekov is killed prior to the shootout, becoming the third regular crew member to return from the dead.*

DAY OF THE DOVE

1 Nov. 1968, No. 66
Directed by: Marvin Chomsky
Written by: Jerome Bixby
STARDATE: Unknown

After beaming a group of Klingons aboard, Kirk discovers that something else is present – an invisible creature that feeds on hatred and hostility. **Kang:** Michael Ansara. **Mara:** Susan Howard.

✦ *This energetic romp makes the most of a clever script and strong performances. As is usually the case on the Enterprise, Kirk is the first one to realize that an unknown entity has entered the ship. Look for a suitably manic performance from Walter Koenig when Ensign Chekov is briefly possessed by the alien entity.*

BEST SCENE: *Watch the finale in which Kirk can barely resist the urge to thump his Klingon counterpart, all the while pretending to befriend his mortal enemy to drive the alien entity off his ship.*

STAR WATCH: *Actor Michael Ansara would reprise the Klingon character Kang in the Star Trek: Deep Space Nine episode "Blood Oath."*

SHOW WATCH: *The first and only classic episode to feature a female Klingon: Mara, played by Susan Howard.*

FOR THE WORLD IS HOLLOW AND I HAVE TOUCHED THE SKY

8 Nov. 1968, No. 65
Directed by: Tony Leader
Written by: Rik Vollaerts
Stardate: 5476.3

After learning he has less than a year to live, Dr. McCoy meets and marries an alien who controls an asteroid ship that is run by computer. **Natira**: Kate Woodville. **Admiral Westervliet:** Byron Morrow.

✦ *Memorable both as a touching love story and an intriguing sci-fi yarn, this episode offers insight into the background of McCoy, and also reveals the extent of Kirk's friendship with the doctor when it becomes apparent the captain is more interested in McCoy's happiness than in just keeping his starship's surgeon. The asteroid ship's computer is called "The Oracle," which is adapted from the Greek myths about an entity who has the ability to foresee the future.*

THE THOLIAN WEB

15 Nov. 1968, No. 64
Directed by: Herb Wallerstein
Written by: Judy Burns
and Chet Richards

STARDATE: 5693.4

Kirk becomes trapped on the derelict *U.S.S. Defiant*, which then disappears into another dimension, and the captain is believed to be dead.

✦ *Another solo acting showcase for William Shatner, who makes the most of it. The scenes in which Kirk roams around the abandoned* Defiant *are a study in isolation, thanks to some very creative camera work. The episode is also enhanced by the tempestuous scenes between Spock and McCoy, who are left to manage the crew back on the Enterprise after Kirk disappears. There's no end of tension and conflict in this episode.*

SHOW WATCH: *Note the use of spacesuits, rarely seen in the* Star Trek *series or movies. Spock would don a similar suit near the end of "Star Trek: The Motion Picture." Just as the crew in this episode mourned Kirk, who they believed to be dead, the 24th-century crew would hold memorial services for Geordi and Ro, when they were thought to have been killed in ST:TNG's "The Next Phase." The U.S.S. Defiant would be the name given to the ship introduced in* Star Trek: Deep Space Nine's *third season.*

PLATO'S STEPCHILDREN

22 Nov. 1968, No. 67
Directed by: David Alexander
Written by: Meyer Dolinsky
STARDATE: 5784.2

On the planet Platonius, Kirk, Spock and McCoy meet the philosopher king Parmen, who possesses telekinetic powers. **Alexander:** Michael Dunn. **Parmen:** Liam Sullivan. **Philana:** Barbara Babcock. **Eraclitus:** Ted Scott.

✦ *An entertaining story with innumerable highlights. The scenes in which the philosopher king Parmen uses his telekinetic powers to play with the Enterprise crew members are intentionally disconcerting for the viewer: Kirk slaps his own face over and over, and Spock is actually forced to sing a sappy song. On the acting side, Michael Dunn is extremely sympathetic as the jester Alexander, who, though powerless, is clearly the moral superior to his masters.*

STAR WATCH: *Barbara Babcock (Hill Street Blues) made an earlier appearance in "A Taste of Armageddon" and supplied the voice of Trelane's mother in "The Squire of Gothos."*

DAY OF THE DOVE: TO DEFEAT THE ALIEN ENTITY THAT HAS INVADED THE ENTERPRISE, KIRK (WILLIAM SHATNER, CENTRE) AND SPOCK (LEONARD NIMOY, RIGHT) MUST CALL A TEMPORARY TRUCE WITH THEIR KLINGON ADVERSARY (MICHAEL ANSARA, LEFT)

PLATO'S STEPCHILDREN: CONTROLLED BY AN ALIEN'S TELEKINETIC POWERS, LIEUT. UHURA (NICHELLE NICHOLLS) AND CAPT. KIRK (WILLIAM SHATNER) EMBRACE AND KISS.

SHOW WATCH: *The lingering kiss between Kirk and Lieut. Uhura became the first interracial kiss ever shown on North American television.*

WINK OF AN EYE

29 Nov. 1968, No. 68
Directed by: Jud Taylor
Written by: Arthur Heinemann
Story by: Lee Cronin
STARDATE: 5710.5

After an expedition to the planet Scalos – which appears to be deserted – Kirk mistakenly drinks some Scalosian water, which causes his metabolism to escalate. **Deela:** Kathie Browne. **Rael:** Jason Evers. **Ekor:** Eric Holland.
✦ *Shatner makes the most of this storyline, in which the captain, whose metabolism has accelerated to the speed of light, appears to have disappeared from the Enterprise. Strong acting also from Kathie Browne as the alien Deela.*

THE EMPATH

6 Dec. 1968, No. 63
Directed by: John Erman
Written by: Joyce Muskat
STARDATE: 5121.0

Kirk, Spock and McCoy are captured on the planet Minara II by aliens who submit them to a series of experiments with a mute humanoid woman named Gem, whose empathic powers enable her to absorb the pain of others. **Gem:** Kathryn Hays. **Lal:** Alan Bergmann. **Thann:** William Sage. **Dr. Linke:** Jason Wingreen.
✦ *A touching but troubling story in which the aliens' ends – testing Gem's healing powers in an attempt to determine whether her race is worthy of being saved from imminent disaster – are used to justify their means.*

SHOW WATCH: *Crew members would also undergo horrible experiments in ST:TNG's "Schisms."*

ELAAN OF TROYIUS

20 Dec. 1968, No. 57
Directed by: John Meredyth Lucas
Written by: John Meredyth Lucas
STARDATE: 4372.5

The *Enterprise* crew escorts Elaan, a barbaric woman from Elas, to the planet Troyius for an arranged marriage to Lord Petri – a union that's supposed to establish a peace agreement between the two warring planets. While en route, Capt. Kirk falls victim to wily Elaan's chemically-induced tears, as hostile Klingons attack and render the *U.S.S. Enterprise* defenceless.
✦ *A cross between Helen of Troy and "The Taming of the Shrew," this episode delivers the dramatic tale of a woman who doesn't wish to marry, and the war-loving Klingons who are in pursuit of dilithium crystals – contained in the maiden's wedding necklace.*

SHOW WATCH: *In the 24th century, Picard would fall in love with the beautiful Kamala, destined for an arranged marriage in ST:TNG's "The Perfect Mate."*

WHOM GODS DESTROY

3 Jan. 1969, No. 71
Directed by: Herb Wallerstein
Written by: Lee Erwin
Story by: Lee Erwin and Jerry Sohl
STARDATE: 5718.3

Kirk discovers that a facility for the criminally insane on the planet Elba II has been taken over by Garth, a former starship captain gone mad. **Garth:** Steve Ihnat. **Marta:** Yvonne Craig. **Cory:** Keye Luke
✦ *Another woeful tale of a starship captain gone wrong. It seems that Garth's earlier contact with the inhabitants of Antos IV has left him with shape-shifting abilities. Actor Steve Ihnat does a fine job*

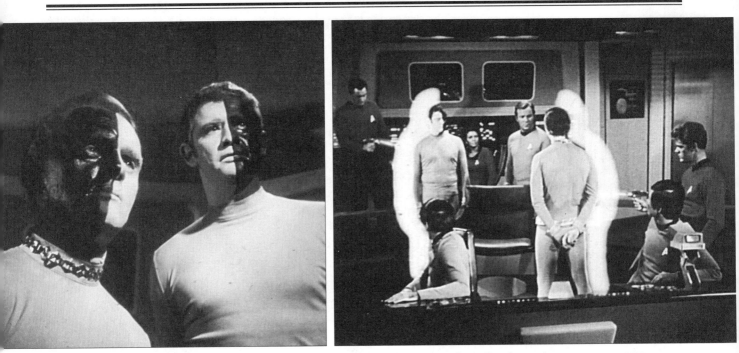

LET THAT BE YOUR LAST BATTLEFIELD: ALL THAT SEPARATES WARRING ALIENS BELE (FRANK GORSHIN) AND LOKAI (LOU ANTONIO) IS WHAT MEETS THE EYE.

as the unhinged Garth and the scene in which he tortures the colony's governor, Cory, is genuinely scary. The climax is thrilling: Spock has to deduce which of the two Kirks is the real captain (one is an impersonation by the deranged Garth).

STAR WATCH: Yvonne Craig went on to play television's Batgirl for two seasons on Batman.

SHOW WATCH: Another early hint at the notion of shape-shifting. Mirroring this episode is "Dagger of the Mind," which similarly featured a character who'd taken control of an asylum.

LET THAT BE YOUR LAST BATTLEFIELD

10 Jan. 1969, No. 70
Directed by: Jud Taylor
Written by: Oliver Crawford
Story by: Lee Cronin
STARDATE: 5730.2

Two aliens appear on the *Enterprise*: a law enforcement agent named Bele, and his prey, Lokai. Each has a half-white, half-black face. **Bele:** Frank Gorshin. **Lokai:** Lou Antonio

◆ A third-season gem, this episode tackles the issue of prejudice head-on. Both Gorshin and Antonio are excellent as the two aliens who hate each other intensely because of their skin colour – even though their appearances are practically identical. When Kirk, always the voice of reason, queries each alien as to the source of such

intense prejudice, neither can actually justify the hateful behaviour.

STAR WATCH: Another veteran of the original Batman TV series comes on set: Frank Gorshin, the maniacal Riddler.

THE MARK OF GIDEON

17 Jan. 1969, No. 72
Directed by: Jud Taylor
Written by: George F. Slavin and Stanley Adams
STARDATE: 5423.4

Kirk suffers a memory lapse when he attempts to beam down to the planet Gideon, and instead ends up back on the *Enterprise* nine minutes later – the only one on the ship. **Odona:** Sharon Acker. **Hodin:** David Hurst. **Krodak:** Gene Dynarski.

◆ The mystery is heightened by the presence of the alien Odona, and what appears to Kirk as the disappearance of his entire crew. Back on the Enterprise, of course, it's Kirk who appears to have disappeared. The ending reveals that Kirk was abducted as a means by which to introduce a deadly virus into a desperately over-populated world.

SHOW WATCH: In the 24th century, Dr. Crusher would similarly experience the loss of the entire crew in ST:TNG's fourth season "Remember Me," while Riker would experience the involuntary use of his DNA by the Mariposans in the second season's "Up the Long Ladder."

THAT WHICH SURVIVES

24 Jan. 1969, No. 69
Directed by: Herb Wallerstein
Written by: John Meredyth Lucas
Story by: Michael Richards
STARDATE: Unknown

Kirk leads a team to an unnamed planet where they encounter a ghostly woman, Losira, whose mere touch brings death. **Losira:** Lee Meriwether. **Lieut. D'Amato:** Arthur Batanides. **Lieut. Rahda:** Naomi Pollack.

◆ Lots of imagination and inventive touches. Lee Meriwether is ethereal as Losira, who keeps appearing and is revealed to be a holographic image.

STAR WATCH: Lee Meriwether, who plays the role of Losira, is a former Miss America. She went on to star in various television series.

THE LIGHTS OF ZETAR

31 Jan. 1969, No. 73
Directed by: Herb Kenwith
Written by: Jeremy Tarcher and Shari Lewis
STARDATE: 5725.3

On her first *Federation* assignment, a young officer is affected by a strange storm that leaves her with the ability to see into the future. **Lieut. Mira Romaine:** Jan Shutan. **Lieut. Kyle:** John Winston. **Kindonian:** Libby Erwin.

◆ A compelling story, providing insight

into the character of Scotty, who — unlucky in love for the third time — becomes infatuated with Mira, only to discover she is possessed by the surviving life forces of the planet Zetar. Still, Scotty remains devoted and defends her and, in the finale, accepts Mira's first devotion to science as she departs.

REQUIEM FOR METHUSELAH

14 Feb. 1969, No. 76
Directed by: Murray Golden
Written by: Jerome Bixby
STARDATE: 5843.7

While on a planet in the Omega system, an *Enterprise* landing party meets a testy man named Flint and his ward, Rayna, to whom Kirk is immediately drawn. **Flint:** James Daly. **Rayna:** Louise Sorel.
✦ *James Daly does a terrific job of playing the cranky Flint, revealed to be a 6,000-year-old multi-talented being who lived on Earth as da Vinci and Brahms, among others. But it's only when Kirk and Rayna begin to fall in love that the full truth comes out: that Rayna is an android built by Flint to provide himself with love and companionship, and that Flint purposely threw Kirk and Rayna together to nurture her emotional response, one that Flint had been unable to spark.*
BEST SCENE: *Spock uses a Vulcan mind-meld to erase Kirk's pain of losing Rayna.*
STAR WATCH: *The late actor James Daly, who plays Flint, is the father of* Cagney & Lacey's *Tyne Daly and* Wings' *Tim Daly. Louise Sorel plays on the American daytime soap* Days of Our Lives *(See page 77).*

THE WAY TO EDEN

21 Feb. 1969, No. 75
Directed by: David Alexander
Written by: Arthur Heinemann
Story by: Michael Richards and Arthur Heinemann
STARDATE: 5832.3

The *Enterprise* transports aboard a group of idealists, in possession of a stolen spaceship, who claim to be searching for a mythical planet called Eden. **Dr. Sevrin:** Skip Homeier. **Adam:** Charles Napier. **Tongo Rad:** Victor Brandt. **Mavig:** Deborah Downey.
✦ *Star Trek's off-beat nod to the '60s hippie movement, complete with costumes, music and beat poetry songs ("I'm jumping for joy, I've got a clean bill of health from*

Dr. McCoy"), with a tidy moral: Paradise is rarely what it seems.
STAR WATCH: *Charles Napier, who plays Adam, would become a character actor with key roles in award-winning films like "The Silence of the Lambs" and "Philadelphia."*

THE CLOUD MINDERS

28 Feb. 1969, No. 74
Directed by: Jud Taylor
Written by: Margaret Armen
Story by: David Gerrold and Oliver Crawford
STARDATE: 5818.4

The *Enterprise* encounters a divisive society on the planet Merak II, in which the elite Stratos live in an idyllic city in the clouds, while the working-class Troglytes labour in hazardous underground caves. **Plasus:** Jeff Corey. **Droxine:** Diana Ewing. **Vanna:** Charlene Polite. **Anka:** Fred Williamson.
✦ *This episode works extremely well by placing Kirk and Spock at opposite ends of the spectrum: While Spock becomes involved in a relationship with Droxine, the daughter of the elitist Stratos leader, Kirk forms an attachment to Vanna, leader of the lowly Troglytes.*
STAR WATCH: *Fred Williamson, the Troglyte Anka, was a former American football star. Jeff Corey was one of Leonard Nimoy's early acting coaches.*

THE SAVAGE CURTAIN

7 March 1969, No. 77
Directed by: Herschel Daugherty
Written by: Arthur Heinemann and Gene Roddenberry
Story by: Gene Roddenberry
STARDATE: 5906.4

A vision of Abraham Lincoln appears on the viewscreen and beseeches Kirk and Spock to transport down to a barren planet, where they are to take part in a battle of good versus evil. **Lincoln:** Lee Bergere. **Col. Green:** Phillip Pine. **Zora:** Carol Daniels Dement. **Surak:** Barry Atwater. **Genghis Khan:** Nathan Jung. **Kahless:** Robert Herron.
✦ *In the ultimate battle, good is represented by Kirk, Spock, Lincoln and Surak (Vulcan's revered leader), while evil is manifested in the figures of Genghis Khan, Col. Green, criminal scientist Zora and the ancient Klingon leader Kahless.*

SHOW WATCH: *First glimpse of Kahless, the legendary Klingon warrior, whom Worf would meet face to face in* Star Trek: The Next Generation's *"Rightful Heir" and who would return in* Deep Space Nine's *"The Sword of Kahless."*

ALL OUR YESTERDAYS

14 March 1969, No. 78
Directed by: Marvin Chomsky
Written by: Jean Lisette Aroeste
STARDATE: 5943.7

While on a rescue mission on the planet Sarpeidon, Kirk, McCoy and Spock slip into a time portal that takes them back in time to different dimensions. **Zarabeth:** Mariette Hartley. **Atoz:** Ian Wolfe. **Prosecutor:** Kermit Murdock.
✦ *The relationship between Spock and McCoy comes to the forefront in an episode that has the two isolated crewmates at each other's throat. After Capt. Kirk is transported to another planet, where he is arrested for witchcraft, Spock and McCoy enter an ice-age dimension where their personalities regress to an earlier, more savage time, and Spock falls in love with Zarabeth. Nimoy does an excellent job of playing the broken-hearted Vulcan, when, in the finale, Spock is forced to leave Zarabeth behind and return to duty.*
SHOW WATCH: *The U.S.S. Enterprise's 24th-century personnel would regress to an earlier stage of evolution in the* Star Trek: The Next Generation *episode "Genesis."*

TURNABOUT INTRUDER

3 June 1969, No. 79
Directed by: Herb Wallerstein
Written by: Arthur Singer
Story by: Gene Roddenberry
Stardate 5928.5

On the planet Camus II, Kirk's old flame, Dr. Janice Lester, is dying from radiation and she employs an alien device that enables her personality to take over the captain's body. **Dr. Janice Lester:** Sandra Smith. **Dr. Coleman:** Harry Landers.
✦ *In what would be the last episode of the classic series, William Shatner has some of his best acting moments as the personality of Janice Lester merges with Capt. Kirk's body. Spock is again court-martialled (this also happened in the first-season episode "The Menagerie").* ✧

Star Trek
The Feature Films

Ten years after the original TV series ended, *Star Trek* resurrected the classic crew on the big screen with spectacular special effects

STAR TREK: THE MOTION PICTURE
Released: 7 Dec. 1979
Directed by: Robert Wise
Screenplay by: Harold Livingston
Story by: Alan Dean Foster
STARDATE: 7412.6

In *Star Trek*'s first big-screen outing, the classic crew returns to the *U.S.S. Enterprise* and heads out to combat an enormous, destructive energy cloud that is making its way toward Earth. **Capt. Willard Decker:** Stephen Collins. **Lieut. Ilia:** Persis Khambatta. **Dr. Christine Chapel:** Majel Barrett. **Transporter Chief Janice Rand:** Grace Lee Whitney. **Klingon Captain:** Mark Lenard.

✦ *Ten years after* Star Trek*'s cancellation, the entire cast returned to a refitted* Enterprise *in a £29-million special-effects adventure, one of the most expensive feature films of its day. It also gave life (long overdue) to the unfilmed* Star Trek II *TV series: The writing team for "*Star Trek: The Motion Picture*" derived its script from* Star Trek II*'s "In Thy Image." Ironically, both Stephen Collins and Persis Khambatta had originally been slated to appear in the aborted TV series, and were then cast in "The Motion Picture" – which brought in a reported £53 million. Fans later lobbied Paramount to re-release the film with footage cut from the original release. Instead, Paramount issued a video version with previously unseen footage – which helped fuel the home video explosion. The film also introduced a new look for the Klingons (which would carry over to* Star Trek: The Next Generation*). And in a fitting gesture, Bjo Trimble, the woman*

who helped orchestrate the 1967 letter-writing campaign that kept Star Trek *on the air, appears as an extra.*

SHOW WATCH: *Capt. Willard Decker is the son of Commodore Matt Decker, seen in the classic-series episode "The Doomsday Machine."*

STAR TREK II:
THE WRATH OF KHAN
Released: 4 June 1982
Directed by: Nicholas Meyer
Screenplay by: Jack B. Sowards
Story by: Harve Bennett
and Jack B. Sowards
STARDATE: 8130.4

Khan Noonian Singh (Ricardo Montalban) and his genetic supermen seek vengeance against Kirk (William Shatner) in this sequel to the classic-series episode "Space Seed." **Dr. Carol Marcus:** Bibi Besch. **Dr. David Marcus:** Merritt Butrick. **Lieut. Saavik:** Kirstie Alley.

✦ *Montalban resurrected Khan with an anger and intensity that stole the show – his image still lingers. Director Meyer further energized the film with his notion to give "*Star Trek II*" the feel of a high-seas adventure. The* Enterprise *was blasted like never before while Khan quoted "Moby Dick," and fans were rendered speechless when Spock died following Khan's savage assault on the ship.*

BEST LINE: *Khan to Kirk, "Time is a luxury you do not have."*

SHOW WATCH: *The late Merritt Butrick, who would reprise his role as Kirk's son in the movie "*Star Trek III: The Search for Spock*," later appeared as T'Jon in* ST:TNG*'s "Symbiosis."*

STAR TREK III:
THE SEARCH FOR SPOCK
Released: 1 June 1984
Directed by: Leonard Nimoy
Screenplay by: Harve Bennett
STARDATE: 8210.3

The *Enterprise* meets a fiery end when Admiral James Kirk and his crew travel to the Genesis planet (created in "Star Trek II: The Wrath of Khan") to retrieve Spock's body – and meet Kruge (Christopher Lloyd), the Klingon commander bent on claiming the secrets of Genesis for himself. **Dr. David Marcus:** Merritt Butrick. **Lieut. Saavik:** Robin Curtis. **Klingon Officer Maltz:** John Larroquette. **Sarek:** Mark Lenard.

✦ *This "*Star Trek II*" sequel explored in great depth the relationships between the characters, and* Star Trek*'s brand of quirky humour (a vital part of the classic series) finally began to shine on the big screen. Memorable example: McCoy's confusion after being infused with Spock's katra (a sort of mental file of one's knowledge and experience – and soul – implanted into his mind by Spock in "*Star Trek II*"), and he can't understand his impulse to try the Vulcan nerve pinch. The Bird-of-Prey also made its first appearance as a Klingon ship – it had been a Romulan vessel in the classic series. Reason for the change: In early working drafts of the "*Star Trek III*" script, Kruge stole the ship from the Romulans, who were eventually cut from the film. The ship, however, remained and became part of* ST:TNG *and* DS9.

SHOW WATCH: *Robin Curtis, who later appeared as Saavik in "*Star Trek IV:*"*

"STAR TREK: THE MOTION PICTURE": *(LEFT TO RIGHT)* GEORGE TAKEI, JAMES DOOHAN, GRACE LEE WHITNEY, NICHELLE NICHOLS, STEPHEN COLLINS, DEFOREST KELLEY, MAJEL BARRETT, WILLIAM SHATNER, LEONARD NIMOY, PERSIS KHAMBATTA AND WALTER KOENIG

The Voyage Home," *would play another Vulcan, Tallera, in the two-part ST:TNG episode "Gambit."*

STAR TREK IV:
THE VOYAGE HOME
Released: 26 Nov. 1986
Directed by: Leonard Nimoy
Screenplay by: Steve Meerson, Peter Krikes, Harve Bennett and Nicholas Meyer
Story by: Leonard Nimoy and Harve Bennett
STARDATE: 8390
When a huge space probe threatens to destroy Earth, Kirk (William Shatner) and crew travel back in time to 20th-century San Francisco to search for a pair of humpback whales, crucial to the planet's survival. **Dr. Gillian Taylor:** Catherine Hicks. **Sarek:** Mark Lenard. **Lieut. Saavik:** Robin Curtis. **Cmdr. Janice Rand:** Grace Lee Whitney. **Cmdr. Christine Chapel:** Majel Barrett.
✦ *The juxtaposition of the Star Trek future and 20th-century Earth creates a wealth of comedic moments in a cautionary tale about environmental exploitation. A continuation of "Star Trek III,"* the film returned Kirk and comrades to duty, aboard the U.S.S. Enterprise-A.

STAR TREK V:
THE FINAL FRONTIER
Released: 9 June 1989
Directed by: William Shatner
Screenplay by: David Loughery
Story by: William Shatner, Harve Bennett and David Loughery
STARDATE: 8454.1
Losing control of the *Enterprise-A* to Sybok (Laurence Luckinbill), Spock's Vulcan half-brother, the crew is taken to an uncharted planet at the centre of the galaxy where God is believed to dwell. **Klingon Capt. Klaa:** Todd Bryant.
✦ *The subtle comfort of the* Enterprise-A *(crafted by Herman Zimmerman, ST:-TNG's production designer) foreshadows the* Enterprise-D, *which would take the notion of quality of life even further (on-board school, bar, arboretum).*
SHOW WATCH: *David Warner (Federation ambassador St. John Talbot) would return as Chancellor Gorkon in the next Star Trek film, then reappear as Picard's Cardassian torturer in ST:TNG's two-part episode "Chain of Command."*

STAR TREK VI:
THE UNDISCOVERED COUNTRY
Released: 6 Dec. 1991
Directed by: Nicholas Meyer
Screenplay by: Nicholas Meyer and Denny Martin Flinn
Story by: Leonard Nimoy, Lawrence Konner, Mark Rosenthal
STARDATE: 9521.6
Kirk and McCoy (DeForest Kelley) are imprisoned for murder when Klingon-Federation peace talks are interrupted by the assassination of a Klingon high official, Chancellor Gorkon (David Warner). **Ambassador Sarek:** Mark Lenard. **Gen. Chang:** Christopher Plummer. **Lieut. Valeris:** Kim Cattrall. **Col. West:** René Auberjonois.
✦ *The sixth movie, which would mark the last time the original cast appears together, is a good chronicle of the events leading up to the Klingon-Federation alliance in ST:TNG. And Michael Dorn was cleverly cast as Worf's grandfather.*
FEDERATION FACTOID: *The proper name of the Klingon homeworld – Qo'noS – was used for the first time.*
STAR WATCH: *Christopher Plummer ("Sound of Music") as Gen. Chang.* ✧

Star Trek: The Next Generation

For seven seasons, Capt. Picard and his *U.S.S. Enterprise-D* crew explored and exploded their way through a universe of new aliens and planets

FIRST SEASON

IT WAS PERHAPS THE MOST ANTICIPATED SERIES PREMIÈRE OF ALL TIME. *STAR TREK: THE NEXT GENERATION* began its syndicated run in America during the week of 28 Sept. 1987, with the two-hour pilot episode "Encounter at Farpoint." Set in the 24th century, some 85 years after the classic *Star Trek* series, the further voyages of the *Starship Enterprise* took up the continuing mission *"to boldly go where no one has gone before."* Outfitted with a host of new technologies – including a holodeck – the new one-of-a-kind *U.S.S. Enterprise (NCC 1701-D)* and its crew of more than 1,000 were off to a promising start. Despite early criticism of plot lines that too closely resembled those of the original series, *Star Trek: The Next Generation* quickly attracted enthusiastic fans around the world and, in North America, climbed in both ratings and in the number of stations airing the program in prime time. By year-end, *Star Trek: The Next Generation* had become the number one first-run hour-long television series in America (the country in which it was first aired) and it gave Paramount Studios the confidence to boost the budget of *Star Trek: The Next Generation* to $1.5 million (U.S.) per episode (approximately £1 million). The space show's rise in popularity proved that Trekkers the world over were once again hooked on the continuing adventures of a crew intent on exploring the unknown universe.

ENCOUNTER AT FARPOINT
Week of 28 Sept. 1987, No. 721
Directed by: Corey Allen
Written by: D.C. Fontana
and Gene Roddenberry
STARDATE: 41153.7
In the series pilot, Capt. Jean-Luc Picard (Patrick Stewart), a new captain for a new *Starship Enterprise*, assembles the crew for its first mission: Discover the secret of Farpoint Station. En route, they encounter the omnipotent being Q, who accuses humanity of barbarism and challenges Picard to prove otherwise. **Groppler Zorn:** Michael Bell. **Lieut. Torres:** Jimmy Ortega.
✦ *Providing a sentimental link to the classic series, DeForest Kelley appears as the irascible Admiral Leonard McCoy, now 137 years old (and still possessing an intense dislike for the transporter). The pilot episode establishes how some of the* crew meet and hints at their backgrounds. *And in what was to become a recurring role, John de Lancie steals the show as the mischievous alien Q. Watch for Colm Meaney (who later becomes Miles O'Brien) as the conn ensign with no name. The pilot first ran as a two-hour program but is repeated in two one-hour segments (numbers 101 and 102).*
BEST DIALOGUE: *McCoy: "I don't see no points on your ears, boy, but you sound like a Vulcan." Data: "No sir, I'm an android." McCoy: "Hmmn, almost as bad."*

THE NAKED NOW
Week of 5 Oct. 1987, No. 103
Directed by: Paul Lynch
Written by: J. Michael Bingham
Story by: John D.F. Black
and J. Micheal Bingham
STARDATE: 41209.2
While investigating the deaths aboard the *Starship Tsiolkovsky*, the *Enterprise* crew becomes infected with a deadly virus that induces intoxicated behaviour – and which the original *Enterprise* crew had contracted decades earlier. **Chief Engineer Sarah MacDougal:** Brooke Bundy. **Assistant Engineer Jim Shimoda:** Benjamin W.S. Lum. **Transporter Chief:** Michael Rider.
✦ *A tribute of sorts, the first regular ST:TNG show – after the pilot episodes – borrows its plot from the classic series' "The Naked Time," and resolves its medical crisis by pulling up the log of the Federation's first Enterprise.*
BEST SCENE: *The unexpected romantic encounter between hot-blooded security chief Tasha Yar and the understandably perplexed android, Lt.-Cmdr. Data, who assures Tasha Yar that he is "fully functional. In every way, of course. I am programmed in multiple techniques, a broad variety of pleasing."*
SHOW WATCH: *Crew members of* Star Trek: Deep Space Nine *would similarly become romantic toward one another due to an intoxicating infection in the third-season episode "Fascination."*

CODE OF HONOR
Week of 12 Oct. 1987, No. 104
Directed by: Russ Mayberry
Written by: Katharyn Powers
and Michael Baron
STARDATE: 41235.25
On a desperate mission to get their hands on a life-saving vaccine from the planet Ligon II, Tasha Yar (Denise Crosby) is kidnapped by the planet's leader. To win her release *and* the vaccine, Picard must follow a strict Ligonian code of honour that requires

FIRST SEASON CAST *(FROM LEFT TO RIGHT)*: WIL WHEATON, DENISE CROSBY, LEVAR BURTON, JONATHAN FRAKES, PATRICK STEWART, GATES McFADDEN, MICHAEL DORN, MARINA SIRTIS AND BRENT SPINER. INSETS: *LATER SEASON CAST* MEMBERS WHOOPI GOLDBERG, DIANA MULDAUR, COLM MEANEY AND MICHELLE FORBES.

Tasha to fight her kidnapper's wife – until one of them is dead. **Lutan:** Jessie Lawrence Ferguson. **Yareena:** Karole Selmon. **Hagon:** James Louis Watkins. **Transporter Chief:** Michael Rider.

THE LAST OUTPOST
Week of 19 Oct. 1987, No. 107
Directed by: Richard Colla
Written by: Herbert Wright
Story by: Richard Krzemien
STARDATE: 41386.4
In a confrontation over an unknown planet, the *Enterprise* and a Ferengi starship are paralysed indefinitely by a powerful creature who insists there is only one escape: They must answer one of his riddles. **Letek:** Armin Shimerman. **Mordoc:** Jake Dengel. **Kayron:** Tracey Walter. **Portal:** Darryl Henriques. **Dai-Mon Taar:** Mike Gomez.
◆ *First appearance of the Ferengi, super capitalists and sexists.*
SHOW WATCH: *Armin Shimerman (Deep*

Space Nine's greedy Quark) in his first of three Ferengi roles.

WHERE NO ONE HAS GONE BEFORE
Week of 26 Oct. 1987, No. 106
Directed by: Rob Bowman
Written by: Diane Duane and Michael Reaves
STARDATE: 41263.1
An arrogant *Starfleet* propulsion expert and his mysterious assistant inadvertently send the *Enterprise* a billion light-years from their galaxy into a region of space where thought becomes reality. **Kosinski:** Stanley Kamel. **Traveller:** Eric Menyuk. **Yvette Gessard Picard:** Herta Ware. **Lt.-Cmdr. Argyle:** Biff Yeager. **Crew Member:** Charles Dayton. **Ballerina:** Victoria Dillard.
◆ *First glimpse of the late Jack Crusher, who appears as a hallucination to both his widow, Beverly, and to Picard. It's during this episode that the captain bestows the*

rank of acting ensign on Wesley Crusher.
SHOW WATCH: *Eric Menyuk – who narrowly missed out on being cast as Data – makes his first appearance as the Traveller, and hints at Wesley's destiny, which won't be resolved until the seventh season's "Journey's End."*

LONELY AMONG US
Week of 2 Nov. 1987, No. 108
Directed by: Cliff Bole
Written by: D.C. Fontana
Story by: Michael Halperin
STARDATE: 41249.3
White transporting two adversarial ambassadors to a *Federation* conference, the *Enterprise* passes through an energy field that takes control of Picard's mind. **Ssestar:** John Durbin. **First Security Guard:** Colm Meaney. **Lt.-Cmdr. Singh:** Kavi Raz.
◆ *First signs of Data's fascination with Sherlock Holmes. The android adopts sleuthing methods of the fictional detective*

to solve a number of puzzling ship mal-functions.

SHOW WATCH: *Marc Alaimo, who has the role of the chief delegate of the Anticans, would appear later in the first season as Romulan Cmdr. Tebok in "The Neutral Zone," as Cardassian Gul Macet in the fourth season's "The Wounded," as the gambler in the fifth season's "Time's Arrow I" and in the recurring role of Cardassian Gul Dukat on DS9.*

JUSTICE

Week of 9 Nov. 1987, No. 109
Directed by: James L. Conway
Written by: Worley Thorne
Story by: Ralph Wills
and Worley Thorne
STARDATE: 41255.6
While vacationing on the blissful planet Rubicun III, Wesley (Wil Weaton) acci-dently breaks a planetary law and is sentenced to death. Picard is then faced with a painful decision: Save Wesley from death or uphold the Prime Directive. **Rivan:** Brenda Bakke. **Liator:** Jay Louden.
✦ *First-rate confrontation between Picard and Dr. Crusher, who urges the cap-tain to violate the Prime Directive to save her son.*

THE BATTLE

Week of 16 Nov. 1987, No. 110
Directed by: Rob Bowman
Written by: Herbert Wright
Story by: Larry Forrester
STARDATE: 41723.9
The Ferengi present Picard with his old starship, the *Stargazer*. Yet havoc ensues: A mind-altering device is planted on board that causes Picard to think he is reliving an old battle – with the *Enterprise* as the enemy. **Kazago:** Doug Warhit. **Rata:** Robert Towers.
✦ *First mention of the Battle of Maxia in which Picard, then in command of the U.S.S. Stargazer, used the famous Picard Manoeuvre to defeat the Ferengi. Bok, driven with vengeance for the death of his son in that battle, would return in the seventh season's "Bloodlines."*

HIDE AND Q

Week of 23 Nov. 1987, No. 111
Directed by: Cliff Bole
Written by: C.J. Holland
and Gene Roddenberry

Story by: C.J. Holland
STARDATE: 41590.5
Q (John de Lancie) toys with the *Enterprise* crew, forcing them to play a Napoleonic war game against boar-faced soldiers.
✦ *Q, in his second appearance, tempts Riker with the omnipotent powers of the Q, and Riker then tempts his crew mates with "gifts" his new powers can provide.*

HAVEN

Week of 30 Nov. 1987, No. 105
Directed by: Richard Compton
Written by: Tracy Tormé
Story by: Tracy Tormé and Lan O'Kun
STARDATE: 41294.5
Counsellor Deanna Troi's mother, the always affectionate and often annoying Lwaxana, makes a sur-prise visit to the *Starship Enterprise* and announces the pre-arranged marriage of Deanna and the son of her late husband's best friend. **Lwaxana:** Majel Barrett. **Wyatt Miller (groom):** Rob Knepper. **Victoria Miller:** Nan Martin. **Steven Miller:** Robert Ellenstein. **Mr. Homn:** Carel Struycken. **Valeda Innis:** Anna Katarina. **Wrenn:** Raye Birk. **Ariana:** Danitza Kingsley.
✦ *Majel Barrett – Nurse Chapel of the classic series (as well as the computer voice throughout Star Trek) and Gene Roddenberry's wife – makes her first scene-stealer as Deanna's mother, the flirtatious Lwaxana, the one individual able to make the even-tempered Deanna lose her cool.*
STAR WATCH: *The late Carel Struycken's first appearance as Mr. Homn. He was Lurch in "The Addams Family" movie.*

THE BIG GOODBYE

Week of 11 Jan. 1988, No. 113
Directed by: Joseph L. Scanlan
Written by: Tracy Tormé
STARDATE: 41997.7
Picard recreates a 1941 San Francisco scenario in the holodeck from one of his favourite Dixon Hill detective novels, and enlists Data and Dr. Crusher in the

fun. But the program malfunctions and they find themselves up against holodeck criminals. **Cyrus Redblock:** Lawrence Tierney. **Felix Leech:** Harvey Jason. **Lieut. Dan Bell:** William Boyett. **Whalen:** David Selburg. **Lieut. Mc-Nary:** Gary Armagnal.
✦ *This episode won a Peabody broadcast award. It was also Picard's first stint as his favourite holodeck character, Dixon Hill, a 1940s private eye from Amazing Detective Stories magazine. The holodeck setting here is reminiscent of the classic "A Piece of the Action."*
BEST LINE: *Recalling many of Kirk's improvised excuses for Spock's ears, Capt. Picard explains the nature of Data's skin tone with an ingenious repartee – "He's from South America."*

THE BIG GOODBYE: DATA (BRENT SPINER) AND CAPT. PICARD (PATRICK STEWART) AS PRIVATE EYES IN 1940s SAN FRANCISCO

DATALORE

Week of 18 Jan. 1988, No. 114
Directed by: Rob Bowman
Written by: Robert Lewin
and Gene Roddenberry
Story by: Robert Lewin
and Maurice Hurley
STARDATE: 41242.4
While visiting Data's home planet, the Away Team discovers a laboratory con-taining android parts that, when assem-bled, form an exact replica of their own Lt.-Cmdr. Data (Brent Spiner). **Lt.-Cmdr. Argyle:** Biff Yeager.
✦ *Brent Spiner shines in a dual role (the first of several) that brings him face to face with his evil twin brother, named Lore, who is the product of Dr. Noonian Soong's earlier attempt to create the ulti-mate android.*

ANGEL ONE

Week of 25 Jan. 1988, No. 115
Directed by: Michael Rhodes
Written by: Patrick Barry
STARDATE: 41636.9

The *Enterprise* crew journeys to a planet dominated by females, and while on Angel One, they discover a group of men – whose *Federation* freighter crashed years earlier – living as fugitives. **Beata:** Karen Montgomery. **Ramsey:** Sam Hennings. **Ariel:** Patricia McPherson. **Trent:** Leonard John Crowfoot.

11001001

Week of 1 Feb. 1988, No. 116
Directed by: Paul Lynch
Written by: Maurice Hurley and Robert Lewin
STARDATE: 41365.9

The *Enterprise*'s computer is scheduled for a rehaul by Bynar technicians while docked in Starbase 74. Instead of improving the system, the Bynars steal the starship to save their own planet. **Minuet:** Carolyn McCormick. **Cmdr. Orfil Quinteros:** Gene Dynarski. **Piano Player:** Jack Sheldon.

◆ *The holodeck, one of ST:TNG's most popular devices, makes its third appearance; Jonathan Frakes shows his stuff on the trombone; Data takes up painting to experience human forms of expression; and Riker, via an infected holodeck, is tempted by his fantasy woman.*

BEST LINE: *An infatuated Riker to the alluring Minuet, "What's a knock-out like you doing in a computer-generated gin joint like this?"*

TOO SHORT A SEASON

Week of 8 Feb. 1988, No. 112
Directed by: Rob Bowman
Written by: Michael Michaelian and D.C. Fontana
Story by: Michael Michaelian
STARDATE: 41309.5

A legendary admiral – on a mission to negotiate the release of *Federation* hostages - is dying. But then he shocks the *Enterprise* crew as he appears to reverse the aging process before their very eyes. **Admiral Mark Jameson:** Clayton Rohner. **Karnas:** Michael Pataki. **Anne Jameson:** Marsha Hunt.

SHOW WATCH: *Michael Pataki appeared as the Klingon Korax in the classic episode "The Trouble with Tribbles."*

WHEN THE BOUGH BREAKS

Week of 15 Feb. 1988, No. 118
Directed by: Kim Manners
Written by: Hannah Louise Shearer
STARDATE: 41509.1

Wesley and other children are kidnapped from the *Enterprise* and taken to the planet Aldea where the inhabitants of the sterile civilization cannot have children of their own. **Radue:** Jerry Hardin. **Rashella:** Brenda Strong. **Katie:** Jandi Swanson. **Melian:** Paul Lambert.

SHOW WATCH: *Wil Wheaton's younger brother, Jeremy, and sister, Amy, turn up in the roles of Mason and Tara. Make-up designer Michael Westmore's daughter, MacKenzie, appears as Roe.*

HOME SOIL

Week of 22 Feb. 1988, No. 117
Directed by: Corey Allen
Written by: Robert Sabaroff
Story by: Karl Guers, Ralph Sanchez and Robert Sabaroff
STARDATE: 41463.9

While investigating the death of a terraformer engineer on Velara III, the Away Team is suddenly faced with the murderous wrath of microscopic inorganic life forms. **Kurt Mandl:** Walter Gotell. **Louisa Kim:** Elizabeth Lindsey. **Bjorn Benson:** Gerard Prendergast. **Arthur Malencon:** Mario Roccuzzo.

◆ *This plot line was inspired by a classic episode titled "Devil in the Dark."*

BEST LINE: *"Ugly bags of mostly water," the Velarans' view of humans.*

COMING OF AGE

Week of 14 March 1988, No. 119
Directed by: Mike Vejar
Written by: Sandy Fries
STARDATE: 41416.2

Picard suddenly finds himself and his career under intense investigation, and Wesley takes the *Starfleet* Academy entrance exam. **Admiral Gregory Quinn:** Ward Costello. **Lt.-Cmdr. Dexter Remmick:** Robert Schenkkan. **Mordock:** John Putch. **Tac Officer Chang:** Robert Ito. **Jake Kurland:** Stephen Gregory. **T'Shanik:** Tasia Valenza. **Oliana Mirren:** Estee Chandler. **Rondon:** Robert Riordan.

◆ *Picard is offered a promotion to the rank of admiral and the position of commandant at Starfleet Academy but chooses to stay aboard his beloved*

Enterprise. The conspiracy plot line would return later in the season in "Conspiracy." Also in this episode, the first Star Trek: The Next Generation *Vulcan in a speaking role.*

HEART OF GLORY

Week of 21 March 1988, No. 120
Directed by: Rob Bowman
Written by: Maurice Hurley
Story by: Maurice Hurley, Herbert Wright and D.C. Fontana
STARDATE: 41503.7

Two renegade, war-hungry Klingons are rescued and beamed aboard the *Starship Enterprise*, which they then try to take over. **Cmdr. Korris:** Vaughn Armstrong. **Lieut. Konmel:** Charles H. Hyman. **K'nera:** David Froman. **Kunivas:** Robert Bauer. **Ramos:** Dennis Madalone.

◆ *Worf's background is introduced (though more fully explored in later episodes), and fans are updated on the state of the Klingon-Federation relationship. This episode marks the end of the "old" Klingon dialogue – which borders on guttural noises. All Klingon characters hereafter speak the "proper" language developed by linguist Marc Okrand, author of "The Klingon Dictionary."*

THE ARSENAL OF FREEDOM

Week of 11 April 1988, No. 121
Directed by: Les Landau
Written by: Richard Manning and Hans Beimler
Story by: Maurice Hurley and Robert Lewin
STARDATE: 41798.2

Destructive energy spheres, sinkholes that swallow, and invisible enemies plague the *Enterprise* as the crew scours the planet Minos for the missing *U.S.S. Drake*. **The Peddler:** Vincent Schiavelli. **Capt. Paul Rice:** Marco Rodriguez. **Chief Engineer Logan:** Vyto Ruginis. **Ensign Lian T'Su:** Julia Nickson. **Lieut. (Junior Grade) Orfil Solis:** George de la Pena.

◆ *Fast-paced episode in which Picard tends to the wounded Dr. Crusher. Much of Beverly's earlier life is revealed during this show.*

BEST LINE: *Riker telling a holographic image of Capt. Rice (a friend and former Starfleet class-mate) that he's from "a good ship," the U.S.S. Lollipop.*

SKIN OF EVIL: TASHA YAR (DENISE CROSBY, THIRD FROM LEFT) FACES DEATH AT THE HANDS OF THE ALIEN ARMUS.

SYMBIOSIS

Week of 18 April 1988, No. 123
Directed by: Win Phelps
Written by: Robert Lewin,
Richard Manning and Hans Beimler
Story by: Robert Lewin
STARDATE: Unknown

The *Enterprise* encounters two civilizations in the Delos system with an unhealthy co-dependency dating back 200 years. Without disobeying the Prime Directive, Picard attempts to break the long-standing co-dependency and prevent all-out war. **Sobi:** Judson Scott. **T'Jon:** Merritt Butrick. **Romas:** Richard Line-back. **Langor:** Kimberly Farr.

◆ *The issue of drug addiction is treated subtly as the planets Brekka and Ornara battle over felecium – a drug produced only on Brekka and presumably a cure to the 200-year-old Ornaran plague.*

SHOW WATCH: *Two guest appearances from "Star Trek II: The Wrath of Khan": the late Merritt Butrick, as Kirk's son, David Marcus; and Judson Scott, as one of Khan's followers.*

SKIN OF EVIL

Week of 25 April 1988, No. 122
Directed by: Joseph L. Scanlan
Written by: Joseph Stefano
and Hannah Louise Shearer
Story by: Joseph Stefano
STARDATE: 41601.3

Counsellor Troi's shuttlecraft crash lands on Vagra II, a planet whose only life form is a sinister creature that enjoys the suffering of humans. Troi's rescue costs the *Enterprise* the life of one of its crew. **Armus:** Mart McChesney. **Asst. Chief Engineer Leland T. Lynch:** Walker Boone. **Nurse:** Brad Zerbst. **Lieut. Ben Prieto:** Raymond Forchion.

◆ *A real Star Trek first: the death of a major character. The tragic loss of security chief Tasha Yar is written into the script as Denise Crosby (above, centre) leaves the show. It's a moving episode for all.*

SHOW WATCH: *Crosby would return in a series of later episodes – as Yar in the third season's "Yesterday's Enterprise," as Tasha's daughter, Romulan Cmdr. Sela, in the two-part episodes "Redemption" and "Unification," and again as Yar in the final episode "All Good Things..."*

WE'LL ALWAYS HAVE PARIS

Week of 2 May 1988, No. 124
Directed by: Robert Becker
Written by: Deborah Dean Davis
and Hannah Louise Shearer
STARDATE: 41697.9

A scientist endangers his own life when his experiments cause a rip in the fabric of time and open up a new dimension. Meanwhile, Picard tries to deal with his feelings for the man's wife, who happens to be the first woman he fell in love with. **Dr. Paul Manheim:** Rod Loomis. **Gabrielle:** Isabel Lorca. **Lieut. Dean:** Dan Kern. **Edouard:** Jean-Paul Vignon. **Transporter Chief Herbert:** Lance Spellerberg.

◆ *The first appearance of a major guest star, Michelle Phillips, who rose to fame in the singing group The Mamas and The Papas. She never quite clicked as Picard's long-lost love, but the episode does serve to humanize Picard and hint at Dr. Crusher's true feelings for the captain.*

CONSPIRACY

Week of 9 May 1988, No. 125
Directed by: Cliff Bole
Written by: Tracy Tormé
Story by: Robert Sabaroff
STARDATE: 41775.5

Picard suspects there is something rotten eating away at the *Federation* when he notices strange behaviour in *Starfleet's* top brass. **Admiral Savar:** Henry Darrow. **Admiral Quinn:** Ward Costello. **Lt.-Cmdr. Dexter Remmick:** Robert Schenkkan. **Admiral Aaron:** Ray Reinhardt. **Capt. Walker Keel:** Jonathan Farwell. **Capt. Rixx:** Michael Berryman. **Capt. Tryla Scott:** Ursaline Bryant.

◆ *One of the goriest* Star Trek: The Next Generation *episodes ever filmed, with unforgettable scenes of death and worm-eating.*

SHOW WATCH: *Henry Darrow appears as the first Vulcan on ST:TNG to deliver the legendary Vulcan nerve pinch.*

THE NEUTRAL ZONE

Week of 16 May 1988, No. 126
Directed by: James L. Conway
Written by: Maurice Hurley
Story by: Deborah McIntyre
and Mona Glee
STARDATE: 41986.0

Three cryogenically-preserved bodies are found on a 20th-century Earth satellite just as the *Enterprise* is ordered to the Neutral Zone to confront Romulans. **Cmdr. Tebok:** Marc Alaimo. **Sub-Cmdr. Thei:** Anthony James. **"Sonny" Clemonds:** Leon Rippy. **Clare Raymond:** Gracie Harrison. **Ralph Offenhouse:** Peter Mark Richman.

◆ *The notion of 20th-century cryogenics first surfaced in the classic episode "Space Seed" and would return in* Star Trek: Voyager's *"The 37's" and "The Thaw."*

FEDERATION FACTOIDS: *The Federation's first contact with the Romulans in 53 years. We learn that the current Earth year is 2364. An interesting cultural note: Television ceases as a form of entertainment by the year 2040.* ◇

SECOND SEASON

NUMEROUS CHANGES WERE ON THE BOARDS FOR CAST AND CHARACTERS ALIKE AT THE BEGINNING OF the second season. Most notable was the absence of Dr. Beverly Crusher. She had accepted a posting at *Starfleet* Medical and was replaced by Dr. Kate Pulaski (Diana Muldaur, a guest-star from the classic series), whose sometimes crusty and stubborn personality was reminiscent of another famous doctor in the classic series. Among the crew, La Forge becomes chief engineer and Worf's promotion to security chief (replacing the late Tasha Yar) is made permanent. Meanwhile, Riker has grown a beard and Deanna adopts a more flattering hairstyle and uniform. And tending bar in the ship's Ten-Forward lounge is Picard's old friend Guinan (Whoopi Goldberg), who, like most bartenders, serves up good advice with two fingers of synthehol. While ambitious plot lines would give way this year to character development and a chance for the cast to have some fun, a 1988 strike in America by the Writers Guild delayed the start of the season and shortened its run from 26 to 22 episodes. The quality, however, did not suffer, with viewers being treated to a much more insightful view of the *Federation* in the 24th century.

THE CHILD

Week of 21 Nov. 1988, No. 127
Directed by: Rob Bowman
Written by: Jaron Summers, Jon Povill and Maurice Hurley
STARDATE: 42073.1
The *U.S.S. Enterprise-D* tries to free the Rachelis system from a deadly plague, and Counsellor Troi shocks everyone with the news that she's pregnant. **Lt.-Cmdr. Hester Dealt:** Seymour Cassel. **Ian Andrew Troi:** R.J. Williams. **Transporter Chief:** Colm Meaney. **Miss Gladstone:** Dawn Arnemann. **Young Ian:** Zachary Benjamin.
✦ *We learn of Troi's attachment to her human father, Ian Andrew, whom we meet in the seventh season's "Dark Page" and in whose memory Troi names her child. Deanna's character is further revealed when she stubbornly refuses to give up her alien baby. Wesley also undergoes some character definition as he ponders, but decides against, joining his mother at Starfleet. The Writers Guild strike threatens to indefinitely delay the start of ST:TNG's second season; consequently this script was the first of two episodes salvaged from the aborted second series, Star Trek II.*

WHERE SILENCE HAS LEASE

Week of 28 Nov. 1988, No. 128
Directed by: Winrich Kolbe
Written by: Jack B. Sowards
STARDATE: 42193.6
Picard is forced to make the most difficult decision of his career when the *Enterprise* enters a mysterious "hole" with no dimensions recognizable to humans. **Nagilum:** Earl Boen.

Ensign Haskell: Charles Douglass. **Transporter Chief:** Colm Meaney.
✦ *First glimpse of Worf's holodeck-enhanced Klingon exercise program. Listen for the fight-scene background music straight out of the classic series.*

⬟ ELEMENTARY, DEAR DATA

Week of 5 Dec. 1988, No.129
Directed by: Rob Bowman
Written by: Brian Alan Lane
STARDATE: 42286.3
During some unexpected time off, Data and Geordi book onto the holodeck and travel back to Victorian England to pay homage to Data's hero, Sherlock Holmes. **Prof. Moriarty:** Daniel Davis. **Lestrade:** Alan Shearman. **Asst. Engineer Clancy:** Anne Elizabeth Ramsey.
✦ *A wonderfully written episode linking Data's fascination with Sherlock Holmes to his ongoing quest to become human. The episode presents the android (Brent Spiner is photographed with LeVar Burton and Diana Muldaur, right) with the oppportunity to display some truly human characteristics, such as loyalty to his friends. We also witness the first instance of Data's obsession with his Holmesian pipe. This episode initiates the debate over the nature of a sentient being, centering in this scenario on the* holodeck-generated Prof. Moriarty and, in a later episode, "The Measure of a Man," on Data himself.
SHOW WATCH: *Daniel Davis would reprise the role of Prof. Moriarty in the sixth season's "Ship in a Bottle."*

THE OUTRAGEOUS OKONA

Week of 12 Dec. 1988, No. 130
Directed by: Robert Becker
Written by: Burton Armus
Story by: Les Menchen, Lance Dickson and David Landsberg
STARDATE: 42402.7
The *Enterprise* takes a disabled ship under its wing but doesn't realize the ship's only resident, Capt. Okona, will put them in the middle of a love triangle. Data attempts to conquer another human trait: humour. **Capt. Thadiun Okona:** William O. Campbell. **Debin:** Douglas Rowe. **Kushell:** Albert Stratton. **Yanar:** Rosalind Ingledew. **Benzan:** Kieran Mulroney. **Lieut. B.G. Robinson:** Teri Hatcher. **The Comic:** Joe Piscopo. **Guinan:** Whoopi Goldberg.
✦ *This light-hearted episode brings to mind some of the best moments of the classic series. Here, the plot takes a back seat to comedy and the interplay between characters, as Data struggles to develop a sense of humour and learn how to tell a joke – aided and abetted by real-life comedian Joe Piscopo, who does a toothy impression of Jerry Lewis.*

ELEMENTARY, DEAR DATA: DATA, GEORDI AND DR. PULASKI ENTER DATA'S SHERLOCK HOLMES-INSPIRED HOLODECK FANTASY.

STAR WATCH: *In pre-fame roles, look for Teri Hatcher (one of the principals in* New Adventures of Superman, *based on the comic book character) and William O. Campbell ("The Rocketeer" and "Bram Stoker's Dracula").*

LOUD AS A WHISPER

Week of 9 Jan. 1989, No. 132
Directed by: Larry Shaw
Written by: Jacqueline Zambrano
STARDATE: 42477.2

The Away Team escorts a well-known deaf mediator to end an ancient conflict on Solaris Five, but tragedy strikes when a disgruntled soldier shoots without warning. **Warrior/Adonis:** Leo Damian. **Woman:** Marnie Mosiman. **The Scholar:** Thomas Oglesby. **Transporter Chief:** Colm Meaney.

✦ *Interesting insight into 24th-century approaches to physical disabilities. Geordi ponders – but ultimately turns down – Dr. Pulaski's offer to restore his sight. Mediator Riva (Howie Seago, who not only is deaf but also originated the story line) uses deafness to his advantage in mediating an end to the conflict.*

THE SCHIZOID MAN

Week of 23 Jan. 1989, No. 131
Directed by: Les Landau
Written by: Tracy Tormé
Story by: Hans Beimler
and Richard Manning
STARDATE: 42437.5

A brilliant scientist dies but his spirit lives on – by taking over Data's mind and body. Instead of being an academic boon, the ghostly presence turns Data violently jealous. **Lieut. Selar:** Suzie Plakson. **Kareen Brianon:** Barbara Alyn Woods. **Dr. Ira Graves:** W. Morgan Sheppard

✦ *Data meets Dr. Ira Graves, the man who was mentor to the android's creator, Dr. Noonian Soong. By implanting himself in Data's mind, Dr. Graves teaches the android more about the human condition. Watch for Data as he tries out a Riker-inspired beard.*

STAR WATCH: *Suzie Plakson makes her first* Star Trek *appearance as Vulcan Lieut. Selar. She would appear later in the season as Worf's mate, K'Ehleyr, in "The Emissary," then reprise that role in the fourth season's "Reunion," which would introduce Worf's son, Alexander.*

UNNATURAL SELECTION

Week of 30 Jan. 1989, No. 133
Directed by: Paul Lynch
Written by: John Mason
and Mike Gray
STARDATE: 42494.8

The *Enterprise* responds to a distress call from a *Federation* supply ship only to find the entire crew has died of old age. **Dr. Sara Kingsley:** Patricia Smith. **Transporter Chief:** Colm Meaney. **Capt. Taggert:** J. Patrick McNamara.

✦ *Another tribute to the classic series, this episode borrows the essence of its plot from "The Deadly Years," while providing a more intriguing technological solution to the ageing epidemic. This is the first central role for Dr. Pulaski.*

A MATTER OF HONOR

Week of 6 Feb. 1989, No. 134
Directed by: Rob Bowman
Written by: Burton Armus
Story by: Wanda M. Haight,
Gregory Amos and Burton Armus
STARDATE: 42506.5

Cmdr. Riker (Jonathan Frakes) is given an opportunity to serve as the first *Starfleet* officer to be posted to a Klingon ship, but a misunderstanding leads to a showdown between Riker and the *Enterprise*. **Ensign Mendon:** John Putch. **Capt. Kargan:** Christopher Collins. **Klag:** Brian Thompson. **Transporter Chief:** Colm Meaney. **Tactics Officer:** Peter Parros. **Vekma:** Laura Drake.

✦ *Solid drama depicting Klingon culture and values. Jonathan Frakes shines as Riker, who must prove his toughness in the eyes of his Klingon hosts and does so by bullying the* Enterprise *into surrender. Colm Meaney's character, Transporter Chief O'Brien, finally gets a last name.*

THE MEASURE OF A MAN

Week of 13 Feb. 1989, No. 135
Directed by: Robert Scheerer
Written by: Melinda M. Snodgrass
STARDATE: 42523.7

Data finds his future on trial when the chief of a new starbase orders the android to be disassembled for research. Picard is forced to defend Data against Riker, who's put into a prosecution role. **Capt. Phillipa Louvois:** Amanda McBroom. **Admiral Nakamura:** Clyde Kusatsu. **Cmdr. Bruce Maddox:** Brian Brophy. **O'Brien:** Colm Meaney. **Guinan:** Whoopi Goldberg.

✦ *Picking up on a theme explored earlier in "Elementary, Dear Data," the android's rights as a sentient being are put to the test. And* Star Trek *fans get their first glimpse of the officers' weekly poker game.*

BEST SCENE: *Riker (Jonathan Frakes, pictured with Brent Spiner's Data, below), as prosecutor, offers proof that Data is only a machine – by switching him off – much as Data would reluctantly do to brother Lore in "Descent, Part II."*

THE DAUPHIN

Week of 20 Feb. 1989, No. 136
Directed by: Rob Bowman
Written by: Scott Rubenstein
and Leonard Mlodinow
STARDATE: 42568.8

The *Enterprise* escorts a young ruler (Jamie Hubbard) and her domineering guardian (Paddi Edwards) to Daled IV without realizing their dangerous metamorphic powers. **Anya:** Paddi Edwards. **O'Brien:** Colm Meaney. **Anya as Girl:** Mädchen Amick. **Anya as Animal:** Cindy Sorenson. **Ensign Gibson:** Jennifer Barlow.

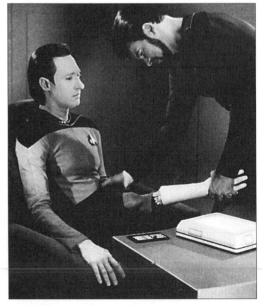

THE MEASURE OF A MAN: PROSECUTOR RIKER (JONATHAN FRAKES, RIGHT) DEMONSTRATES THAT DATA (BRENT SPINER) IS ONLY A MACHINE.

Wesley suffers through his first romance, with the allasomorph (or shape changer) Salia, and has some adult decisions to make after he discovers her true nature. The notion of a shape-shifter would be reintroduced on Star Trek: Deep Space Nine in the character of Odo (played by René Auberjonois). **STAR WATCH:** *Mädchen Amick (Shelly Johnson in the twisted American whodunit* Twin Peaks*) appears as young Anya.*

CONTAGION

Week of 20 March 1989, No. 137
Directed by: Joseph L. Scanlan
Written by: Steve Gerber
and Beth Woods
STARDATE: 42609.1
The Away Team races against time to destroy an eerie power source that has infected the ship's computers, eaten away at Data's software and left the *Enterprise* open to a Romulan attack. **Capt. Donald Varley:** Thalmus Rasulala. **Sub-Cmdr. Taris:** Carolyn Seymour. **O'Brien:** Colm Meaney.
BEST LINE: *Riker commenting on luck: "Fate protects fools, little children, and ships called* Enterprise.*"*

THE ROYALE

Week of 27 March 1989, No. 138
Directed by: Cliff Bole
Written by: Keith Mills
STARDATE: 42625.4
In an uncharted solar system, the Away Team gets trapped in a never-ending story where aliens have replicated human life based on a dramatic novel, "The Hotel Royale." **Texas:** Noble Willingham. **Ass't. Manager:** Sam Anderson. **Vanessa:** Jill Jacobson. **The Bellboy:** Leo Garcia. **Ensign Herbert O'Brien:** Colm Meaney. **Mickey D:** Gregory Beecroft.

TIME SQUARED

Week of 3 April 1989, No. 139
Directed by: Joseph L. Scanlan
Written by: Maurice Hurley
Story by: Kurt Michael Bensmiller
STARDATE: 42679.2
Picard begins to doubt his leadership when the *Enterprise* finds an out-of-control shuttlecraft with the captain's distraught double inside – from six hours in the future. **O'Brien:** Colm Meaney.
◆ *Suspenseful time-travel tale. Patrick*

Stewart in a dual role as Picard in the present and as he appears six hours later.
BEST SCENE: *Picard shoots his future self to stop him from abandoning the* Enterprise *before its destruction.*

THE ICARUS FACTOR: ENTERTAINMENT TONIGHT *ANCHOR* JOHN TESH (FAR LEFT) DONS KLINGON GARB TO TORMENT WORF AS PART OF THE AGE OF ASCENSION RITE.

THE ICARUS FACTOR

Week of 24 April 1989, No. 140
Directed by: Robert Iscove
Written by: David Assael
and Robert L. McCullough
Story by: David Assael
STARDATE: 42686.4
When he is promoted to captain of another *Federation* ship, Riker is eager to get started – until he discovers that he's to be briefed by his estranged father. **O'Brien:** Colm Meaney. **Kyle Riker:** Mitchell Ryan. **Transporter Operator Herbert:** Lance Spellerberg.
◆ *Both Riker and Worf come to terms with the past: Riker with his father's abandonment of him at the age of 15; and Worf with his Klingon heritage. For the second time, Riker will turn down a captaincy to stay aboard the* Enterprise. *We also learn something of Dr. Pulaski's much-married past and her affair with Riker's father. But the best is kept for last: a glimpse of the challenging Klingon Age of Ascension rite as re-created on the holodeck.*

PEN PALS

Week of 1 May 1989, No. 141
Directed by: Winrich Kolbe
Written by:
Melinda M. Snodgrass
Story by:
Hannah Louise Shearer
STARDATE: 42695.3
Wesley cuts his teeth as a *Starfleet* ensign when he's instructed to discover what's causing the earthquakes and volcanic eruptions on Drema IV where Data's young pen-pal lives. **Davies:** Nicholas Cascone. **Sarjenka:** Nikki Cox. **Hildebrandt:** Anne H. Gillespie. **O'Brien:** Colm Meaney. **Alans:** Whitney Rydbeck.

Q WHO?

Week of 8 May 1989, No. 142
Directed by: Rob Bowman
Written by: Maurice Hurley
STARDATE: 42761.3
The *Enterprise* is attacked by the Borg after being hurled into a distant part of the galaxy by an angry Q (John de Lancie). As the aliens close in for the kill, Q returns and offers his help – if Picard swallows his pride. **Ensign Sonya Gomez:** Lycia Naff. **O'Brien:** Colm Meaney. **Guinan:** Whoopi Goldberg.
◆ *Q's third appearance leads to the Federation's first encounter with the Borg – a half-humanoid, half-robotic race living as a single collective entity whose sole purpose is to assimilate other cultures for the sake of gaining new technologies. This episode establishes the Borg as the most powerful and destructive enemy in Federation history and sets the tone for future confrontations – many of these among the most exciting ST:TNG episodes filmed. We learn that the Borg were responsible for almost totally destroying Guinan's race a century earlier. As Guinan, Whoopi Goldberg shines in a heated exchange with Q over her hatred of the Borg – a confrontation that will come back to haunt the mischievous alien in the third season's "Déjà Q."*

SAMARITAN SNARE

Week of May 15, 1989, No. 143
Directed by: Les Landau
Written by: Robert L. McCullough
STARDATE: 42779.1

As Capt. Picard lies near death on an operating table, the crew tries to outsmart the dim-witted Pakleds who are holding Geordi hostage. **Grebnedlog:** Christopher Collins. **Reginod:** Leslie Morris. **Surgeon:** Daniel Benzali. **Ensign Sonya Gomez:** Lycia Naff. **Biomolecular Physiologist:** Tzi Ma.

◆ *In this episode, Picard tells Wesley that as a 21-year-old ensign he lost his heart – which had to be replaced by an artificial one – in a bar fight with a Nausicaan. Courtesy of Q, Picard would later relive the fight in the sixth season's "Tapestry."*

STAR WATCH: *Christopher Collins appeared as a Klingon in "A Matter of Honor."*

UP THE LONG LADDER

Week of 22 May 1989, No. 144
Directed by: Winrich Kolbe
Written by: Melinda M. Snodgrass
STARDATE: 42823.2

Picard must convince two dying civilizations that their only chance for survival lies in cohabitating. But one of the cultures would much rather clone Riker and Dr. Pulaski. **Danilo Odell:** Barrie Ingham. **Granger:** Jon de Vries. **Brenna Odell:** Rosalyn Landor. **O'Brien:** Colm Meaney.

◆ *This episode is sheer fun, with Riker again playing ladies' man. The Bringloidis – who don't mind a wee drop or two – prove to be almost as much trouble as the wee Tribbles once were. This particular show stands a notch above the rest.*

BEST SCENE: *The leader of the chaste Mariposans – who haven't had sex in decades and find the mere thought of physical intimacy repugnant – contemplates a future breeding with the earthy, fun-loving Bringloidis in a resettlement world.*

MANHUNT

Week of 19 June 1989, No. 145
Directed by: Rob Bowman
Written by: Terry Devereaux
STARDATE: 42859.2

On her way to a *Federation* conference, Lwaxana Troi, Counsellor Troi's mother, searches for a man to satisfy her insatiable appetite. **Lwaxana Troi:** Majel Barrett. **Slade Bender:** Robert Costanza. **Mr. Homn:** Carel Struycken. **Rex:** Rod Arrants. **O'Brien:** Colm Meaney. **Scarface:** Robert O'Reilly. **Madeline:** Rhonda Aldrich. **Antidean Dignitary:** Mick Fleetwood. **Transport Pilot:** Wren T. Brown.

◆ *Comedy is the name of the game in this episode as Lwaxana – making her second Star Trek appearance – goes on the prowl for Picard. The captain tries to flee her advances by assuming the holodeck persona of detective Dixon Hill – also for the second time. Lwaxana, in the throes of a female Betazoid mid-life cycle that quadruples her sex drive, falls instead for the bartender.*

STAR WATCH: *A heavily made-up Mick Fleetwood of Fleetwood Mac has a cameo as an Antidean dignitary.*

MANHUNT: *THE EPISODE FEATURES A CAMEO BY MICK FLEETWOOD OF FLEETWOOD MAC.*

THE EMISSARY

Week of 26 June 1989, No. 146
Directed by: Cliff Bole
Written by: Richard Manning and Hans Beimler
Story by: Thomas H. Calder
STARDATE: 42901.3

Worf is reluctantly reunited with a past lover when the *Enterprise* is ordered to intercept a Klingon ship whose crew has been in stasis for 100 years. **K'Temoc:** Lance le Gault. **Admiral Gromek:** Georgann Johnson. **O'Brien:** Colm Meaney. **Ensign Clancy:** Anne Elizabeth Ramsey. **Tactical Crewman:** Dietrich Bader.

◆ *Second appearance of actor Suzie Plakson, this time as Worf's former lover and future mate, K'Ehleyr, a half-human, half-Klingon diplomat for the Klingon Empire. As a consequence of their "union" on the holodeck, K'Ehleyr would return – with son Alexander – in the fourth season's "Reunion" to change Worf's life. A half-human, half-Klingon character, in the person of Lieut. B'Elanna Torres (Roxann Biggs-Dawson), would be reintroduced in Star Trek: Voyager.*

PEAK PERFORMANCE

Week of 10 July 1989, No. 147
Directed by: Robert Scheerer
Written by: David Kemper
STARDATE: 42923.4

Cmdr. Riker and Capt. Picard compete in a *Starfleet* battle simulation program. But the fun ends when a Ferengi warship stumbles across the game and starts firing on them for real. **Sirna Kolrami:** Roy Brocksmith. **Bractor:** Armin Shimerman. **Ferengi Tactician:** David L. Lander. **Ensign Nagel:** Leslie Neale. **Ensign Burke:** Glenn Morshower.

◆ *Armin Shimerman's second appearance as a Ferengi.*

STAR WATCH: *David L. Lander (Squiggy on Laverne & Shirley) appears as a Ferengi.*

SHADES OF GRAY

Week of 17 July 1989, No. 148
Directed by: Rob Bowman
Written by: Maurice Hurley, Richard Manning and Hans Beimler
Story by: Maurice Hurley
STARDATE: 42976.1

Riker is infected with an alien organism that quickly takes control of his brain. To fight the fatal bug, Dr. Pulaski must lead Riker's mind back to its most primitive memories of survival. **Transporter Chief O'Brien:** Colm Meaney.

◆ *The second-season finale uses Cmdr. Riker's coma-induced dream state as a plot device to replay virtually every significant Riker clip from earlier episodes of Star Trek: The Next Generation. These include: "Encounter at Farpoint," "The Naked Now," "The Last Outpost," "Justice," "Angel One," "11001001," "Heart of Glory," "Symbiosis," "Skin of Evil," "Conspiracy," "The Child," "Loud as a Whisper," "Unnatural Selection," "A Matter of Honor," "The Dauphin," "The Icarus Factor" and "Up the Long Ladder."* ✧

THIRD SEASON

THE THIRD SEASON WOULD MARK STAR TREK: THE NEXT GENERATION'S EMERGENCE FROM THE SHADOW of its predecessor. The new series' writing staff matured under the leadership of Michael Piller, and the day-to-day operations passed from Gene Roddenberry to new executive producer Rick Berman. This season's plot lines would emphasize character development, humour, and scripts with a social conscience – stories that would attract a new legion of faithful fans. And, thanks in part to a vigourous letter-writing campaign waged by devoted fans, the third-season start saw yet another change in medical officers, as Gates McFadden returned to the role of Dr. Beverly Crusher (just back from a year-long assignment at *Starfleet* Medical). The look of *ST:TNG* changed as well, as new costume designer Robert Blackman replaced the men's one-piece jumpsuit – that had so constrained *Starfleet* staff – with the striking and flexible two-piece uniforms still worn by crew today. That, of course, led to the "Picard manoeuvre" – the small tug Patrick Stewart gives to his uniform top when it starts riding up on him. A small gesture, certainly, but the trademark tug somehow defined the captain in a manner no other script detail ever could.

EVOLUTION
Week of 25 Sept. 1989, No. 150
Directed by: Winrich Kolbe
Written by: Michael Piller
Story by: Michael Piller
and Michael Wagner
STARDATE: 43125.8
While escorting a scientist to the site of an exploding star in the Kavis Alpha Sector, a computer malfunction on the *U.S.S. Enterprise-D* jeopardizes lives and research. **Dr. Paul Stubbs:** Ken Jenkins. **Eric:** Scott Grimes. **Annette:** Amy O'Neill. **Guinan:** Whoopi Goldberg. **Nurse:** Mary McCusker. **Crewman No. 1:** Randal Patrick.
✦ *What begins as a science experiment for Wesley almost destroys Dr. Stubbs' once-in-a-lifetime project aboard the* Enterprise*. The nature-of-a-sentient-being debate is renewed: Data realizes he is not alone as a non-organic being when the microbiotic Nanites begin to evolve and become sentient. Though they threaten both the* Starship Enterprise *and the experiment to which Dr. Stubbs has dedicated his entire life, Data refuses to destroy the creatures – instead offering himself as a conduit to communicate with the rapidly evolving Nanites. Data's actions save the ship, the experiment and the Nanites' lives. The episode also notes Dr. Crusher's return to the* Enterprise*, hints at Guinan's past and reveals that Wesley learned about baseball – which ceases as a professional sport in the year 2042 – from his father, much as* Star Trek: Deep Space Nine's *Jake Sisko would learn about the game of baseball from his father.*
STAR WATCH: *Ken Jenkins* (Homefront) *appears in the role of Dr. Stubbs.*

THE ENSIGNS OF COMMAND
Week of 2 Oct. 1989, No. 149
Directed by: Cliff Bole
Written by: Melinda M. Snodgrass
STARDATE: 43133.3
The *Enterprise* organizes a massive evacuation when an alien race reclaims a planet and orders the removal of all humans within four days – or face annihilation. **Ard'rian McKenzie:** Eileen Seeley. **Noe:** Richard Allen. **Haritath:** Mark L. Taylor. **O'Brien:** Colm Meaney. **Gosheven:** Grainger Hines. **Sheliak:** Mart McChesney.
✦ *Seeking to understand human creativity, Data takes up the violin.*
FEDERATION FACTOID: *Scenic art supervisor Michael Okuda named Data's shuttlepod "Onizuka" in honour of U.S. astronaut Ellison Onizuka, who died in the tragic January 1986 Challenger explosion.*

THE SURVIVORS
Week of 9 Oct. 1989, No. 151
Directed by: Les Landau
Written by: Michael Wagner
STARDATE: 43152.4
The *Enterprise* arrives at Rana IV and discovers that the planet's entire population has been destroyed, with the exception of an elderly couple who refuses to leave. **Kevin Uxbridge:** John Anderson. **Rishon Uxbridge:** Anne Haney.
✦ *Sobering episode on shame, guilt and punishment as Picard discovers that Kevin – who is actually a Douwd, an immortal being disguised as a human – destroyed the entire Husnock race*

with a single regrettable thought out of rage over the death of his wife.

WHO WATCHES THE WATCHERS?
Week of 16 Oct. 1989, No. 152
Directed by: Robert Wiemer
Written by: Richard Manning
and Hans Beimler
STARDATE: 43173.5
While assisting *Federation* anthropologists injured during an explosion on Mintaka III, the Away Team inadvertently causes its primitive people to view Picard as a god. **Nuria:** Kathryn Leigh Scott. **Liko:** Ray Wise. **Dr. Barron:** James Greene. **Oji:** Pamela Segall. **Fento:** John McLiam. **Hali:** James McIntire. **Mary Warren:** Lois Hall.
✦ *The Prime Directive gets another airing when Dr. Crusher beams up an inhabitant from a strange planet to save his life.*
STAR WATCH: *Ray Wise* (Twin Peaks) *turns in a convincing performance as the Picard-fearing Liko.*

THE BONDING
Week of 23 Oct. 1989, No. 153
Directed by: Winrich Kolbe
Written by: Ronald D. Moore
STARDATE: 43198.7
Worf and Wesley help a 12-year-old boy cope with the death of his mother, an archeologist killed during an Away Team investigation of a deserted planet. **Jeremy Aster:** Gabriel Damon. **Lieut. Marla Aster:** Susan Powell. **Transporter Chief O'Brien:** Colm Meaney. **Teacher:** Raymond D. Turner.

THE BONDING: ORPHAN JEREMY (GABRIEL DAMON) IS TAKEN UNDER WORF'S WING.

♦ In a compelling episode dealing with the loss of a parent, young Jeremy finds comfort in the memories of Worf and Wesley, who both lost parents in childhood – Worf at 6, when his parents were killed during the Khitomer massacre by the Romulans, and Wesley at 5, when his father Jack was killed during an Away Team mission commanded by Picard.

BEST SCENE: *Worf leads Jeremy (previous page) through the Klingon R'uustai bonding ceremony, making him a brother.*

BOOBY TRAP

Week of 30 Oct. 1989, No. 154
Directed by: Gabrielle Beaumont
Written by: Ron Roman,
Michael Piller and Richard Danus
Story by: Michael Wagner
and Ron Roman
STARDATE: 43205.6
The *Enterprise* sends an Away Team to investigate an ancient warship, and is trapped in the same energy-draining field that snared the derelict ship during a battle a thousand years before. **Dr. Leah Brahms:** Susan Gibney. **O'Brien:** Colm Meaney. **Guinan:** Whoopi Goldberg. **Galek Dar:** Albert Hall. **Christy Henshaw:** Julie Warner.

♦ Picard is at his most human, revealing his enthusiastic interest in ancient cultures and technology, an interest that resurfaces in later episodes. To spring the ship from the radiation trap, Geordi calls up the holographic projection of the original designer of the starship, Dr. Leah Brahms, who becomes his dream girl.

BEST LINE: "You have used the asteroid belt's gravitational pull as a slingshot. Excellent!" marvels Data as Picard takes the helm to steer the ship free of the trap.

STAR WATCH: Julie Warner (Pride & Joy, "Doc Hollywood") as crew member Christy Henshaw, who would reprise that role later in the season in "Transfigurations."

THE ENEMY

Week of 6 Nov. 1989, No. 155
Directed by: David Carson
Written by: David Kemper
and Michael Piller
STARDATE: 43349.2
A Romulan ship hinders attempts to rescue Geordi, who is stranded on the Federation planet Galorndon Core, along with the survivor of a downed Romulan vessel. **Centurion Bochra:**

John Snyder. **Cmdr. Tomalak:** Andreas Katsulas. **O'Brien:** Colm Meaney. **Patahk:** Steve Rankin.

♦ LeVar Burton gets the chance to deliver a stellar performance when Geordi must convince the injured Romulan to combine forces with him to save both their lives. We learn more of the deep-seated hatred between the Klingons and the Romulans when Worf – who was orphaned at Khitomer in the Romulan raid – refuses to give blood to save an injured Romulan's life. Showing profound respect for Worf's culture and feelings, Picard, in turn, refuses to order Worf to save his enemy. Picard's respect for Worf's integrity and Klingon heritage will come into play in later episodes when Worf's family honour is questioned. Andreas Katsulas would return as Tomalak later in this season's "The Defector" and in the fourth season's "Future Imperfect."

THE PRICE

Week of 13 Nov. 1989, No. 156
Directed by: Robert Scheerer
Written by: Hannah Louise Shearer
STARDATE: 43385.6
Duplicity and subterfuge abound as the *Enterprise* hosts negotiations for rights to a newly-discovered wormhole, which is coveted by both the Barzan and the Ferengi. **Devinoni Ral:** Matt McCoy. **Premier Bhavani:** Elizabeth Hoffman. **Dr. Mendoza:** Castulo Guerra. **DaiMon Goss:** Scott Thompson. **Dr. Arridor:** Dan Shor. **Leyor:** Kevin Peter Hall. **O'Brien:** Colm Meaney.

♦ The writers toss a few comical subplots into this episode that raises an ethical debate between Troi and Devinoni over the use of Betazoid powers on humans: Riker gets his first chance to act the diplomat when the Ferengi make the Federation delegate too ill to work; and Troi not only reveals her passion for chocolate but also has ST:TNG's first bed scene. And watch for the late Kevin Peter Hall ("Predator," "Harry and the Hendersons") as the 7-foot, 4-inch Leyor.

BEST SCENE: *The look on the Ferengi's faces as the* Enterprise *crew disappears back through the closing wormhole. The notion of a stable wormhole would later return as a central feature on* Deep Space Nine. *In "Star Trek: The Motion Picture," an unbalanced warp drive system created an artificial – and dangerous – wormhole.*

THE VENGEANCE FACTOR

Week of 20 Nov. 1989, 157
Directed by: Timothy Bond
Written by: Sam Rolfe
STARDATE: 43421.9
The crew attempts to reconcile the Acamarians and the rebel group known as the Gatherers, a faction which broke away from the Acamarians during clan wars more than 100 years earlier. **Yuta:** Lisa Wilcox. **Brull:** Joey Aresco. **Marouk:** Nancy Parsons. **Chorgan:** Stephen Lee. **Volnoth:** Marc Lawrence. **Temarek:** Elkanah Burns.

♦ Powerful scene in which Riker must overcome his feelings for the beautiful Yuta, who's really an assassin, and kill her before she can start another civil war.

FEDERATION FACTOID: We learn that Data is stronger than Worf.

STAR WATCH: Stephen Lee reappeared as an alien bartender in "Gambit, Part 1." The non-speaking Gatherer is played by Michael Lamper, Marina Sirtis's husband.

THE DEFECTOR

Week of 1 Jan. 1990, No. 158
Directed by: Robert Scheerer
Written by: Ronald D. Moore
STARDATE: 43462.5
A defecting Romulan pilot warns the crew of the *Enterprise* about an impending assault from a Romulan base being established in the Neutral Zone. **Sub.-Lt. Setal/Alidar Jarok:** James Sloyan. **Cmdr. Tomalak:** Andreas Katsulas. **Admiral Haden:** John Hancock. **John Bates:** S.A. Templeman.

♦ Admiral Jarok's defection provides insight into internal Romulan treachery. Riker makes reference to the U.S.S. Hood, his previous assignment.

STAR WATCH: Look closely to spot Patrick Stewart heavily made up as holodeck character Michael Williams.

SHOW WATCH: James Sloyan would return as the Klingon K'Mtar in the seventh season's "Firstborn," as Bajoran scientist Dr. Mora Pol in DS9's "The Alternate," and as Neelix's nemesis in Star Trek: Voyager's "Jetrel" episode.

THE HUNTED

Week of 8 Jan. 1990, No. 159
Directed by: Cliff Bole
Written by: Robin Bernheim
STARDATE: 43489.2
The planet Angosia III seeks to become a

member of the *Federation*, and asks for assistance in their efforts to capture a prison escapee (Jeff McCarthy) who has a reputation for extreme violence. **Roga Danar:** Jeff McCarthy. **Nayrok:** James Cromwell. **O'Brien:** Colm Meaney. **Zaynar:** J. Michael Flynn. **Wagnor:** Andrew Bicknell.

✦ *Explosive episode dealing with government-sponsored experiments in mind control and biochemical alteration. High-action chase scenes through little-seen sections of the Starship Enterprise are cleverly juxtaposed with an ongoing debate over the ethics of the experiments and the subsequent incarceration of their subjects.*

BEST DIALOGUE: *"A matter for internal security,"* muses Picard when the Angosian prime minister warns him not to interfere. *"The age-old cry of the oppressor."* And as the prisoner escapes, Worf says, *"Danar, you are cunning. You must have Klingon blood."*

SHOW WATCH: *British actor James Cromwell (who was nominated for an Oscar for the popular "Babe" movie, about a pig and his animal cohorts) returns in the sixth season's two-part "Birthright" to lead Worf on a search for his father, and as Hanok in* Star Trek: Deep Space Nine's *"Starship Down."*

THE HIGH GROUND
Week of 29 Jan. 1990, No. 160
Directed by: Gabrielle Beaumont
Written by: Melinda M. Snodgrass
STARDATE: 43510.7
Dr. Crusher is kidnapped by terrorists while delivering much-needed medical supplies to a planet torn by civil war. **Kyril Finn:** Richard Cox. **Waiter (Katik Shaw):** Marc Buckland. **Policeman:** Fred G. Smith. **Boy (Ansata):** Christopher Pettiet.
✦ *This action-packed episode gives Picard the chance to finally use his fists on the face of a terrorist. The Jean-Luc Picard and Dr. Beverley Crusher relationship is further explored after the captain is also kidnapped.*

DÉJÀ Q
Week of 5 Feb. 1990, No. 161
Directed by: Les Landau
Written by: Richard Danus
STARDATE: 43539.1
A suddenly powerless Q is forced to request sanctuary on the *Starship Enterprise* when a Calamarian seeks revenge against him. **Q:** John de Lancie. **Guinan:** Whoopi Goldberg. **Dr. Garin:** Richard Cansino. **Bre'el Scientist:** Betty Muramoto. **Q2:** Corbin Bernsen.
✦ *Comical episode in which Q, in his fourth appearance, finally gets what's coming to him: He loses his powers, and his very survival depends on those he has always treated as playthings.*
BEST SCENES: *Q orders ten chocolate sundaes to calm his terrifying new-found hunger; Guinan nearly stabs Q with a fork; Q rewards his new* Enterprise *friends with a band, cigars, even women, while saving the best reward for Data – an honest-to-goodness human belly laugh.*
BEST LINE: *"Oh, you're so stolid,"* says Q to Riker, who rejects Q's offer of female companionship. *"You weren't like that before the beard."*
STAR WATCH: *Corbin Bernsen, a long-time Star Trek fan, does a terrific turn as Q2.*

A MATTER OF PERSPECTIVE
Week of 12 Feb. 1990, No. 162
Directed by: Cliff Bole
Written by: Ed Zuckerman
STARDATE: 43610.4
While on Tanuga IV, Riker must defend himself against accusations of murder when a research scientist (Mark Margolis) is killed in an explosion, and Picard uses the *Enterprise*'s holodeck to prove his commander's innocence. **Krag:** Craig Richard Nelson. **Manua Apgar:** Gina Hecht. **O'Brien:** Colm Meaney. **Tayna:** Juli Donald.
✦ *Riker is not the first* Starfleet *officer to be accused of murder – that dubious honour belongs to the classic series' Scotty ("Wolf in the Fold"). For the first time, however, the holodeck is used to reconstruct the crime, reminiscent of the Talosians re-creating events during Spock's court martial in the classic series' "The Menagerie."*

YESTERDAY'S ENTERPRISE
Week of 19 Feb. 1990, No. 163
Directed by: David Carson
Written by: Ira Steven Behr,

THE OFFSPRING: *HALLIE TODD (WITH WHOOPI GOLDBERG) STARS AS DATA'S DAUGHTER, LAL.*

Richard Manning, Hans Beimler and Ronald D. Moore
Story by: Trent Christopher Ganino and Eric A. Stillwell
STARDATE: 43625.2
A rift in space and time brings the *Enterprise* into contact with a ship that was destroyed 20 years earlier, and leads to a reunion with ex-security chief Tasha Yar (Denise Crosby). **Capt. Rachel Garrett:** Tricia O'Neil. **Lieut. (Junior Grade) Richard Castillo:** Christopher McDonald.
✦ *One of ST:TNG's best episodes, with a clever twist that resurrects Tasha Yar (Denise Crosby) by means of an alternate time line. A fascinating look at what might have been: In the alternate universe, there has been no Klingon-Federation détente and the ensuing war continues. Note the absence of Worf and Counsellor Troi – not to mention the warlike ambience of the alternate Enterprise-D. And in a shocking scene, Riker dies an "alternate death." Once again, Guinan proves her wisdom – and her influence with Picard – when she convinces him to send the U.S.S. Enterprise-C back through the time rift to put things right. And in a final gesture, Picard allows Tasha to return with the Enterprise-C, saving her from the death she faced in the first season's "Skin of Evil." It's not the last we'll hear of her.*

THE OFFSPRING
Week of 12 March 1990, No. 164
Directed by: Jonathan Frakes
Written by: René Echevarria
STARDATE: 43657.0
Data becomes a daddy when he creates

an android daughter named Lal, whom he enrols in school so she can learn human behaviour. **Lal:** Hallie Todd. **Admiral Haftel:** Nicholas Coster. **Lieut. Ballard:** Judyann Elder. **Lal as Robot:** Leonard John Crowfoot.

✦ *First episode directed by Jonathan Frakes, a tear-jerker on the life and death of Lal, who brings out Data's fatherly traits: stubbornness when he refuses to let Lal leave the Enterprise to live at Starfleet Research; and protectiveness, when – in a lighter moment – he confronts the dumbfounded Riker over the first officer's intentions regarding his daughter. Her death, however, gives Data his most poignant human experience to date.*

STAR WATCH: *Hallie Todd (with Whoopi Goldberg, previous page), daughter of Ann Morgan Gilbert (The Nanny, The Dick Van Dyke Show) appears as Lal.*

SINS OF THE FATHER
Week of 19 March 1990, No. 165
Directed by: Les Landau
Written by: Ronald D. Moore and W. Reed Moran
Story by: Drew Deighan
STARDATE: 43685.2
Worf meets his long-lost brother and learns that his father has been charged with treason for aiding the Romulans during the Khitomer assault. Together, they confront the Klingon High Council and challenge the charges against their father. **K'mpec:** Charles Cooper. **Kurn:** Tony Todd. **Duras:** Patrick Massett. **Kahlest:** Thelma Lee.

✦ *One of Michael Dorn's finest acting turns, as Worf finally meets the brother he never knew. The best Klingon episode to date, shedding light on the complex Klingon world, its culture and ceremonies. Worf shows great respect for his captain when he asks Picard to return to Qo'noS with him, and even greater courage when he allows the lie about his father's treason to stand – thereby averting a Klingon civil war, even though, in so doing, Worf is publicly branded an outcast and a coward. The stage is thus set for the fourth-season The Next Generation cliff-hanger, in which Worf sets out to redeem his family's honour. The "new" Klingon language as developed by linguist Marc Okrand starts with this episode.*

BEST LINE: *In response to Worf's request*

that they return with him to Qo'noS, Picard and Kurn reply, "jIlajneS. ghIj qet jaghmeyjaj." ("I accept with honour. May your enemies run with fear.")

SHOW WATCH: *Following a fifth-season appearance as Kurn in "Redemption," actor Tony Todd would return as Worf's Klingon brother in DS9's "Sons of Mogh," and as the grown-up Jake Sisko in "The Visitor."*

ALLEGIANCE
Week of 26 March 1990, No. 166
Directed by: Winrich Kolbe
Written by: Richard Manning and Hans Beimler
STARDATE: 43714.1
An alien energy beam kidnaps Picard from his quarters and replaces him with a look-alike, whose strange behaviour gives the crew just cause to relieve him of his command. **Kova Tholl:** Stephen Markel. **Esoqq:** Reiner Schöne. **Cadet Mitena Haro:** Joycelyn O'Brien. **Alien No. 1:** Jerry Rector. **Alien No. 2:** Jeff Rector.

✦ *Picard is kidnapped for the second time. Patrick Stewart, as the impostor, puts a comical spin on the show as he courts a puzzled Dr. Crusher and leads the Ten-Forward crowd in a rousing drinking song.*

CAPTAIN'S HOLIDAY
Week of 2 April 1990, No. 167
Directed by: Chip Chalmers
Written by: Ira Steven Behr
STARDATE: 43745.2
Picard's tropical vacation is interrupted by time-travelling Vorgons from the 27th century who say they're a security team searching for a powerful weapon hidden on the paradise planet. **Vash:** Jennifer Hetrick. **Ajur:** Karen Landry. **Boratus:** Michael Champion. **Sovak:** Max Grodenchik. **Joval:** Deirdre Imershein.

✦ *The captain's much-needed R&R on the fantasy planet Risa is quashed when he meets Vash, the infamous seductress/con artist who steals his heart. This episode marks the first appearance of Vash, and also shows Picard in a much more relaxed state. His bare chest gets equal air time.*

SHOW WATCH: *Jennifer Hetrick (L.A. Law) returns as Vash in the fourth season's "Qpid" and in "Q-Less" on DS9. Max Grodénchik, seen here as the Ferengi who helps spark the romance between Vash*

and Picard, would become better known as Rom, Quark's brother on DS9.

TIN MAN
Week of 23 April 1990, No. 168
Directed by: Robert Scheerer
Written by: Dennis Putnam Bailey and David Bischoff
STARDATE: 43779.3
The *Enterprise* risks hostile Romulan Warbirds and a star on the verge of exploding in order to bring a Betazoid *Federation* emissary (Harry Groener) into contact with Tin Man, a newly-discovered alien intelligence. **Capt. Robert DeSoto:** Michael Cavanaugh. **Romulan Commander:** Peter Vogt. **O'Brien:** Colm Meaney.

STAR WATCH: *Harry Groener (Dear John) guests as the Betazoid Tam Elbrun.*

HOLLOW PURSUITS
Week of 30 April 1990, No. 169
Directed by: Cliff Bole
Written by: Sally Caves
STARDATE: 43807.4
A timid and ineffectual crew member uses the holodeck to act out his fantasies and vent his frustrations, but places the *Enterprise* in jeopardy when he neglects his duties in engineering. **Lieut. Barclay:** Dwight Schultz. **Lieut. Duffy:** Charley Lang. **O'Brien:** Colm Meaney.

✦ *Dwight Schultz (The A Team) steals the show as Lieut. Barclay, the fuzzy-headed engineering officer – Geordi calls him Lieut. Broccoli – who ducks onto the holodeck whenever life gets too stressful. There, he indulges in his favourite fantasies: Dating Troi and duelling with Picard. Some comic moments: the holodeck version of a bewitching Troi in flowing robes, and a Three Musketeers-style gaggle of officers, including Picard, Data, Geordi and Riker. But Geordi's question – and perhaps the most puzzling mystery in Starfleet history – remains unanswered: How did Broccoli ever get through Starfleet Academy?*

FEDERATION FACTOID: *We learn that the Enterprise has 4,000 power systems.*

THE MOST TOYS
Week of 7 May 1990, No. 170
Directed by: Timothy Bond
Written by: Shari Goodhartz
STARDATE: 43872.2
The crew is convinced Data is dead after

his shuttlecraft explodes but they are forced to leave on a mission before confirming what has happened to the android. **Kivas Fajo:** Saul Rubinek. **Palor Toff:** Nehemiah Persoff. **Varria:** Jane Daly. **O'Brien:** Colm Meaney.

✦ *For the second time, Worf is asked to replace a crew member who has "died." We also learn that Data has never killed a living creature, a fact which will change in the sixth season's "Descent."*

SHOW WATCH: *Actor Saul Rubinek ("Unforgiven," "Getting Even with Dad"), in the role of Kivas Fajo, is darkly reminiscent of Harry Mudd, the amusing wag who exasperated the classic-series crew in "Mudd's Women" and "I, Mudd." Data's decision to fire upon Fajo in order to end his ordeal is heart-stopping.*

SAREK

Week of 14 May 1990, No. 171
Directed by: Les Landau
Written by: Peter S. Beagle
Story by: Marc Cushman
and Jake Jacobs
STARDATE: 43917.4

Tempers flare during a visit by the Vulcan ambassador Sarek (Mark Lenard), who boards the *Enterprise* to negotiate diplomatic ties with the Legaran. **Perrin:** Joanna Miles. **Ki Mendrossen:** William Denis. **Sakkath:** Rocco Sisto. **O'Brien:** Colm Meaney. **Science Crewman:** John H. Francis.

✦ *The second episode to feature a character from the classic series – this time, Sarek, Spock's Vulcan father. In a long-overdue Vulcan story-line, the aging Sarek – who has contracted the Alzheimer-like Bendii syndrome – struggles to contain his emotions. Patrick Stewart has some fine moments as Picard confronts Sarek over his loss of control and deals with the overpowering emotions Sarek temporarily bestows on him via the Vulcan mind-meld. Picard's bond with Sarek will resurface in the fifth season's two-part "Unification."*

MÉNAGE À TROI

Week of 28 May 1990, No. 172
Directed by: Robert Legato
Written by: Fred Bronson
and Susan Sackett
STARDATE: 43930.7

Riker and Troi's shore leave on Betazed suddenly goes awry: First they are interrupted by Deanna Troi's mother,

Lwaxana (Majel Barrett), and then all three are kidnapped by the greedy Ferengi, who want to study Lwaxana Troi's telepathic powers. **DaiMon Tog:** Frank Corsentino. **Dr. Farek:** Ethan Phillips. **Nibor:** Peter Slutsker. **Reittan Grax:** Rudolph Willrich. **Mr. Homn:** Carel Struycken.

✦ *Riker and Deanna indulge in an all-too-rare romantic shore leave on the planet where they first met and fell in love. Third appearance of the inimitable Lwaxana Troi – always good for a dose of high camp, particularly after kidnapper DaiMon Tog is smitten with her charm. Note the Ferengi custom of forbidding females, in this case Lwaxana and Troi, to wear clothes. And Wesley gets a second field promotion to full ensign.*

BEST SCENE: *Capt. Picard having to feign jealousy (much to his chagrin) over Lwaxana, and spout his beloved Shakespeare to gain her release.*

SHOW WATCH: *Viewers should listen carefully for the voice of Ethan Phillips – almost unrecognizable beneath Ferengi make-up – better known as* Star Trek: Voyager's *Neelix, the first of three ST:TNG actors who would be cast on the fourth* Star Trek *series.*

TRANSFIGURATIONS

Week of 4 June 1990, No. 173
Directed by: Tom Benko
Written by: Rene Echevarria
STARDATE: 43957.2

After they succeed in rescuing a severely injured humanoid from a crippled escape pod, the entire crew of the *Starship Enterprise* is overcome with feelings of serenity, and witness the alien's healing powers. **John Doe:** Mark LaMura. **Cmdr. Sunad:** Charles Dennis. **Christy Henshaw:** Julie Warner. **Transporter Chief O'Brien:** Colm Meaney. **Nurse Temple:** Patti Tippo.

✦ *Worf is killed in a fall but is brought back to life by the mysterious alien.*

THE BEST OF BOTH WORLDS, PART I

Week of 18 June 1990, No. 174
Directed by: Cliff Bole
Written by: Michael Piller
STARDATE: 43989.1

An ambitious *Starfleet* officer (Elizabeth Dennehy) arrives on the *Enterprise* to assist in an investigation of the disappear-

THE BEST OF BOTH WORLDS, PART I: SHELBY (ELIZABETH DENNEHY) AND RIKER (JONATHAN FRAKES) CONFRONT THE BORG.

ance of a *Federation* colony, and leads an Away Team effort to rescue Picard, who has been kidnapped by the Borg. Part 1 of two. **Admiral J.P. Hanson:** George Murdock. **Guinan:** Whoopi Goldberg. **O'Brien:** Colm Meaney.

✦ *The third season closes with a spine-chilling cliff-hanger: The return appearance of the dreaded Borg, who, having kidnapped Picard, transform him into the machine-like Locutus of Borg. Every adrenaline-drenched moment is filled with suspense: Will Picard die? Will the Borg destroy the* Federation? ST:TNG *had finally come into its own with this rivetting episode. In a secondary plot line, Riker is pitted against the ambitious Lt.-Cmdr. Shelby, who claims Riker is lazy because he turns down the command of a ship, the U.S.S. Melbourne (this being his third refusal of the captain's chair).* ✧

FOURTH SEASON

TREKKERS IMPATIENTLY AWAITED THE RESOLUTION OF SEASON THREE'S CLIFFHANGER. COULD PICARD BE rescued from the Borg? Was it possible to stop the Borg from destroying the *Federation*? The suspense only added to the success of "The Best of Both Worlds, Part II." The fanfare over that episode had barely died down when "Legacy," *Star Trek: The Next Generation*'s record-setting 80th episode, aired in North America in late October, breaking the mark set by the original series' 79-episode run. The fourth season would also mark the return of many previous guests, including Q, Lwaxana Troi, Lieut. Barclay, Dr. Leah Brahms and the Traveller. And, in what was to become the season's dominant theme, nine of the first 11 episodes dealt with family: Worf introduces his foster parents, meets his son and then avenges his lover's death; Picard returns home to reconcile with the brother he hasn't seen in 20 years; and Data meets his father, battles his evil twin brother and learns about love. This was also the season of maturity: Wesley takes his leave of the *U.S.S. Enterprise-D* to study at *Starfleet* Academy; O'Brien gets married; and Worf takes responsibility for his son – and his life as a Klingon. Altogether, the fourth season featured the greatest number of episodes ever to deal with character development and would become – in our opinion – one of the best *Star Trek* seasons.

THE BEST OF BOTH WORLDS, PART II

Week of 24 Sept. 1990, No. 175
Directed by: Cliff Bole
Written by: Michael Piller
STARDATE: 44001.4
Conclusion. Riker must try everything he can to save Earth, including destroying Picard, who has been assimilated by the Borg and is being used for his knowledge of Federation defences. **Lt.-Cmdr.**

THE BEST OF BOTH WORLDS, PART II: *PICARD (PATRICK STEWART) IS TRANSFORMED INTO LOCUTUS OF BORG.*

Shelby: Elizabeth Dennehy. **Admiral Hanson:** George Murdock. **O'Brien:** Colm Meaney. **Guinan:** Whoopi Goldberg. **Ensign Gleason:** Todd Merrill.

✦ *In a conclusion as suspenseful and well-written as the previous season's cliffhanger, the action is neatly interwoven with the all-too-human dilemmas faced by members of the crew: Riker, for his part, must take command of the ship while contending with his overly ambitious first officer; and Guinan, who can't bear to witness the Borg destroying the human race like they destroyed her people, still manages to give Riker some excellent advice. Shedding a single tear to signal Picard's presence, Patrick Stewart (left) gives a commanding performance as Locutus of Borg, a creation of the Borg's cybernetic implants and his own hot-wired DNA, who leads a devastating attack against Starfleet's armada, destroying 39 ships, including the U.S.S. Melbourne, and costing more than 10,000 lives. The saviour is Data, who sends the Borg into regeneration when he correctly interprets Picard's single utterance ("Sleep"). It will take the Federation a year to rebuild the fleet, and the consequences of the*

tragedy would return in the pilot episode of Star Trek: Deep Space Nine, *when Picard must face the animosity of Cmdr. Benjamin Sisko, whose wife was killed during the captain's Locutus-led attack.*

FAMILY

Week of 1 Oct. 1990, No. 178
Directed by: Les Landau
Written by: Ronald D. Moore
Premise by: Susanne Lambdin and Bryan Stewart
STARDATE: 44012.3
Picard reunites with his older brother on Earth (France, to be exact) and considers leaving *Starfleet*. On the *Enterprise*, Worf's adoptive parents embarrass him with their displays of affection. **Robert Picard:** Jeremy Kemp. **Marie Picard:** Samantha Eggar. **Sergey Rozhenko:** Theodore Bikel. **Helena Rozhenko:** Georgia Brown. **Louis:** Dennis Creaghan. **O'Brien:** Colm Meaney. **Guinan:** Whoopi Goldberg. **Jack R. Crusher:** Doug Wert. **René Picard**: David Tristan Birkin.

✦ *A bevy of guest stars joins the cast in an episode dealing with families. Jeremy Kemp is outstanding as the older brother with whom Picard had a falling-out 20 years earlier, and who goads Jean-Luc into the memorable mud tussle while helping him face his guilt over the Borg disaster. In a more comedic vein, Theodore Bikel and Georgia Brown are brilliant as Worf's adoptive parents, who, while supportive of their son over his recent Klingon "discommendation," can still make Worf blush as only a parent can. And in the most touching storyline, Wesley learns something of his late father, Jack, when Beverly finally lets him view the haunting holotape her husband made just after Wesley was born.*
SHOW WATCH: *The wine Robert gives Jean-Luc would be shared in the subsequent fourth-season episodes "Legacy" and "First Contact." Also, we finally get the complete name of Colm Meaney's character, Miles Edward O'Brien.*

BROTHERS

Week of 8 Oct. 1990, No. 177
Directed by: Rob Bowman
Written by: Rick Berman
STARDATE: 44085.7
While rushing a seriously ill boy to a nearby Starbase for life-saving treat-

BROTHERS: *BRENT SPINER STARS AS DATA'S CREATOR, DR. NOONIAN SOONG.*

ment, Data inexplicably seizes control of the *Enterprise*, taking it to a remote planet. **Jake Potts:** Cory Danziger. **O'Brien:** Colm Meaney. **Willie (Potts):** Adam Ryen. **Ensign Kopf:** James Lashly. **Lore/Dr. Noonian Soong:** Brent Spiner.

✦ *Executive producer Rick Berman wrote this episode in which Brent Spiner outdoes himself in a triple role as Data; as Data's creator, Dr. Noonian Soong (above); and as Data's evil twin, Lore, first encountered in the first season's "Datalore." Called home by his creator – long since presumed dead – Data meets the reclusive genius, who has at last perfected a chip that will grant Data human emotions. That opportunity vanishes when Lore – who also turns up – tricks Soong, steals the chip and leaves the inventor fatally injured.*

BEST SCENE: *In saying goodbye, Data calls Soong "Father" and is left to ponder what he might have learned. While Data would be reunited with a dream-induced image of his father in the sixth season's "Birthright I," he would not re-encounter evil Lore until the seventh season's "Descent II."*

SUDDENLY HUMAN

Week of 15 Oct. 1990, No. 176
Directed by: Gabrielle Beaumont
Written by: John Whelpley and Jeri Taylor
Story by: Ralph Phillips
STARDATE: 44143.7

A human boy showing signs of abuse is found on a Talarian ship in distress. When the child's adoptive Talarian father asks for his return, Picard risks war by refusing to surrender him. **Capt. Endar:** Sherman Howard. **Admiral Connaught Rossa:** Barbara Townsend.

✦ *Picard's edgy relationship with children is examined when the captain must determine why Jono, the human child raised by Talarians, doesn't wish to go home to his human family. Chad Allen (Dr. Quinn, Medicine Woman) gives an honest portrayal of Jono, a child torn apart when forced to choose between the alien father he respects and the human family seeking his return.*

✦ REMEMBER ME

Week of 22 Oct. 1990, No. 179
Directed by: Cliff Bole
Written by: Lee Sheldon
STARDATE: 44161.2

When crew on the *Enterprise* begin to disappear, Dr. Crusher finds she's the only one who can remember them. **Traveller:** Eric Menyuk. **Commander Dalen Quaice, M.D.:** Bill Erwin. **O'Brien:** Colm Meaney.

✦ *Stellar performance by Gates McFadden, who carries the storyline solo for part of the episode. Left to solve the mystery or die in the incredibly shrinking universe that – from her perspective – has invaded the Enterprise, Dr. Crusher argues with the computer while her crewmates double talk and disappear. She begins to doubt her sanity as she is left entirely alone. The recurring Star Trek theme of an alternative universe provides the opportunity here to learn more about Beverly's background, her thoughts and feelings as she works to discover the key to the mystery.*

SHOW WATCH: *In his second appearance, Eric Menyuk returns as the Traveller to help Wesley save his mother.*

LEGACY

Week of 29 Oct. 1990, No. 180
Directed by: Robert Scheerer
Written by: Joe Menosky
STARDATE: 44215.2

The *Enterprise* crew gets caught in the middle of a war on the home planet of the late Tasha Yar where they meet Tasha's sister – a member of one of the warring factions. **Ishara Yar:** Beth Toussaint.

Hayne: Don Mirault. **O'Brien:** Colm Meaney. **Tan Tsu:** Vladimir Velasco. **Coalition Lieut.:** Christopher Michael.

✦ *The milestone 80th ST:TNG episode surpasses the 79-episode run of the classic series. Picking up on the Tasha Yar storyline, the crew encounters Tasha's long-lost younger sister, Ishara, who befriends the crew to penetrate the defences of her enemies. Both Picard and Data are drawn to Ishara out of friendship for Tasha, but it is Data who gets an unexpected lesson in betrayal when the younger Yar nearly kills him in pursuit of her mission.*

✦ REUNION

Week of 5 Nov. 1990, No. 181
Directed by: Jonathan Frakes
Written by: Thomas Perry, Jo Perry, Ronald D. Moore and Brannon Braga
Story by: Drew Deighan, Thomas Perry and Jo Perry
STARDATE: 44246.3

Klingon leader K'mpec (Charles Cooper) asks Picard to choose between two contenders to succeed him as head of the Klingons and determine which has been poisoning him. And Worf receives startling news from his former lover. **K'Ehleyr:** Suzie Plakson. **Gowron:** Robert O'Reilly. **Duras:** Patrick Massett. **Alexander:** Jon Steuer. **Security Guard:** Michael Rider. **Transporter Chief Hubbel:** April Grace. Klingon **Guard No. 1:** Basil Wallace. **Klingon Guard No. 2:** Mirron E. Willis.

✦ *In Jonathan Frakes' second directorial stint, actor Suzie Plakson (with Michael Dorn, next page) returns in the role of Klingon Ambassador K'Ehleyr – Worf's half-human former love and the mother of his son, Alexander. The episode is rife with passion and political intrigue as Worf rekindles his romance with K'Ehleyr, and Picard assists the dying K'mpec with the ritual selection of a new Klingon leader – and then attempts to unmask his assassin. Duras – the Klingon who implicated Worf's father in the Khitomer massacre and now a contender to succeed K'mpec – kills K'Ehleyr when she rightly suspects him of the crime. Crossing the thin line of his restraint, Worf finally gives in to his Klingon rage and kills Duras for murdering his lover and dishonouring his father. While not yet at liberty to reclaim his family's honour – that would wait until the season's*

REUNION: WORF (MICHAEL DORN) REKINDLES HIS ROMANCE WITH K'EHLEYR, PLAYED BY SUZIE PLAKSON.

cliff-hanger, "Redemption, Part I" – Worf cannot publicly acknowledge Alexander as his son and sends him to live with his own foster parents to spare the youngster the shame of Worf's humiliating "discommendation."

SHOW WATCH: *Alexander, later played by Brian Bonsall ("Blank Check," Family Ties), would return to live with Worf in the fifth season's "New Ground."*

FUTURE IMPERFECT

Week of 12 Nov. 1990, No. 182
Directed by: Les Landau
Written by: J. Larry Carroll
and David Bennett Carren
STARDATE: 44286.5

After an aborted mission, Riker awakens to a universe 16 years in the future where he is the captain of the *Enterprise* in the midst of negotiating a treaty with the Romulans – and has no memory of how he got there. **Ambassador Tomalak:** Andreas Katsulas. **Jean-Luc/Ethan:** Chris Demetral. **Minuet:** Carolyn McCormick. **Nurse Alyssa Ogawa:** Patti Yasutake. **Transporter Chief Hubbell:** April Grace. **Barash:** Chris Demetral.

✦ *Riker briefly experiences what it's like to be both captain of the* Enterprise *and the father of a teen-age son. His fantasy love, Minuet, makes a return appearance in a holotape, enabling Riker to discover the truth about his surroundings, which have been devised by the alien Barash posing as Riker's fantasy son, who wishes to keep the first officer as a permanent guest (much as Trelane attempted to keep Kirk and crew for company on the origi-*

nal Star Trek's "The Squire of Gothos"). Riker's fantasy future serves as a neat device to catch a glimpse of the Federation as it could evolve 16 years hence – including a bearded Admiral Picard and a married Troi.

SHOW WATCH: *Third appearance by Andreas Katsulas as Tomalak.*

FINAL MISSION

Week of 19 Nov. 1990, No. 183
Directed by: Corey Allen
Written by: Kacey Arnold-Ince
and Jeri Taylor
Story by: Kacey Arnold-Ince
STARDATE: 44307.3

On a final mission before entering *Starfleet* Academy, Wesley must save the life of his mentor, Capt. Picard, when their shuttle crashes on a lifeless moon. **Dirgo:** Nick Tate. **Chairman Songi:** Kim Hamilton. **Ensign Tess Allenby:** Mary Kohnert.

✦ *Wil Wheaton gives his best performance in this episode, which marks his departure from the regular cast. Wesley Crusher – like Jean-Luc Picard many years earlier – is finally accepted into* Starfleet *Academy on his second attempt. There are touching moments as Wesley comforts an injured Picard while awaiting the rescue team. The captain in turn admits how proud he is of Wesley (who's like a son to him in many ways), and talks to him of Boothby, the Academy groundsman and Picard's mentor, who shows up in the fifth-season episode "The First Duty."*

STAR WATCH: *Nick Tate (Space: 1999) turns up as Dirgo.*

THE LOSS

Week of 31 Dec. 1990, No. 184
Directed by: Chip Chalmers
Written by: Hilary J. Bader,
Alan J. Adler and Vanessa Greene
Story by: Hilary J. Bader
STARDATE: 44356.9

Deanna Troi is horrified when she loses her empathic powers and is unable to help the *Enterprise*, which is caught in a gravitational pull and is headed towards a black hole-like phenomena. **Ensign Janet Brooks:** Kim Braden. **Ensign Tess Allenby:** Mary Kohnert. **Guinan:** Whoopi Goldberg.

✦ *In an episode that focusses on Troi's crisis of confidence over the loss of her empathic powers, Marina Sirtis provides her character with depth and vulnerability – in contrast to Deanna's normal self-control. We also witness the enduring strength of the Riker-Troi relationship.*

DATA'S DAY

Week of 7 Jan. 1991, No. 185
Directed by: Robert Wiemer
Written by: Harold Apter
and Ronald D. Moore
Story by: Harold Apter
STARDATE: 44390.1

Data is saddled with problems: First he's faced with a jittery bride on the day of her wedding, and then a Vulcan ambassador headed for treaty negotiations with the Romulans starts behaving oddly. **O'Brien:** Colm Meaney. **Ambassador T'Pel (Sub-Commander Selok):** Sierra Pecheur. **Admiral Mendak:** Alan Scarfe. **Transporter Chief Hubbell:** April Grace. **V'Sal:** Shelly Desai. **Keiko:** Rosalind Chao.

✦ *In a very creative day-in-the-life episode, the action unfolds from the perspective of a very busy Data, the only round-the-clock being on the ship. He must deal with bride Keiko's change of heart on the eve of her wedding to Miles O'Brien, in addition to monitoring Ambassador T'Pel's attempt to extract security information for which she has not been given clearance. Following the ambassador's apparent death in a transporter accident, the android turns once again to his Sherlock Holmes persona (the third time he does so) to unravel the mystery. Data is successful on all counts, and ends his day by walking Keiko down the aisle in a marriage ceremony performed by Picard.*

BEST SCENE: *Dr. Crusher teaching Data how to dance before the wedding.*

SHOW WATCH: *Behind Romulan make-up as Admiral Mendak, actor Alan Scarfe (married to Barbara March, who plays Lursa, one half of the infamous Duras sisters) would return as the Romulan prison-camp commandant Tokath in the sixth season's "Birthright, Part II," then as Augris in Star Trek: Voyager's second season-episode "Resistance." Also: First glimpse of Data's cat, possibly Riker's least favourite creature.*

THE WOUNDED

Week of 28 Jan. 1991, No. 186
Directed by: Chip Chalmers
Written by: Jeri Taylor
Story by: Stuart Charno, Sara Charno and Cy Chermak
STARDATE: 44429.6
Fearing the Cardassians are rearming, a *Federation* captain takes matters into his own hands and attacks their ships. The *Enterprise* must help their former enemies stop the renegade. **Keiko Ishikawa O'Brien:** Rosalind Chao. **Gul Macet:** Marc Alaimo. **Miles O'Brien:** Colm Meaney. **Glinn Telle:** Marco Rodriguez. **Glinn Daro:** Time Winters. **Admiral Haden:** John Hancock.
✦ *First real insight into the* Federation's *newest enemies, the Cardassians. Colm Meaney does a star turn as Miles O'Brien, who, in this revealing episode, is the only one able to convince his former captain, Benjamin Maxwell, to stand down in the face of war.*

DEVIL'S DUE

Week of 4 Feb. 1991, No. 187
Directed by: Tom Benko
Written by: Philip Lazebnick
Story by: Philip Lazebnick and William Douglas Lansford
STARDATE: 44474.5
Picard must defend his soul and the planet Ventax from a woman claiming to be the devil. **Ardra:** Marta DuBois. **Dr. Clarke:** Paul Lambert. **Jared:** Marcello Tubert. **Devil Monster:** Thad Lamey. **Klingon Monster:** Tom Magee. **Marley:** William Glover.
STAR WATCH: *Marta DuBois (Magnum's ex on* Magnum, P.I.) *appears as the con-artist-cum-devil Ardra, whose sexual advances Picard refuses. She retaliates by making the* Enterprise *disappear.*

SHOW WATCH: *This is the second of two episodes originally scripted for the aborted* Star Trek II *series.*

CLUES

Week of 11 Feb. 1991, No. 188
Directed by: Les Landau
Written by: Bruce D. Arthurs and Joe Menosky
Story by: Bruce D. Arthurs
STARDATE: 44502.7
The crew suspects Data is lying about a wormhole, so Picard orders a covert investigation. **O'Brien:** Colm Meaney. **Ensign McKnight:** Pamela Winslow. **Madeline:** Rhonda Aldrich. **Guinan:** Whoopi Goldberg. **Nurse Alyssa Ogawa:** Patti Yasutake. **Gunman:** Thomas Knickerbocker.
SHOW WATCH: *Third appearance of Capt. Picard's favourite holodeck persona, the private eye Dixon Hill.*

FIRST CONTACT: *RIKER (JONATHAN FRAKES) HAS A CLOSE ENCOUNTER WITH AMOROUS ALIEN LANEL (BEBE NEUWIRTH).*

FIRST CONTACT

Week of 18 Feb. 1991, No. 189
Directed by: Cliff Bole
Written by: Dennis Russell Bailey, David Bischoff, Joe Menosky, Ronald D. Moore and Michael Piller
Story by: Marc Scott Zicree
STARDATE: Unknown
On a first contact mission, Riker is captured by xenophobic people who fear he is an advance scout for an invading force. **Chancellor Avel Durken:** George

Coe. **Mirasta:** Carolyn Seymour. **Berel:** George Hearn. **Krola:** Michael Ensign. **Nilrem:** Steven Anderson. **Dr. Tava:** Sachi Parker. **Lanel:** Bebe Neuwirth.
✦ *In a philosophical twist, we get an examination of the fear of aliens from the subject's point of view – instead of the* Federation's *perspective. A future footnote: In a later episode ("The Drumhead"), Admiral Satie accuses Picard of breaking the Prime Directive, citing his behaviour here (in "The First Contact") as the most recent of nine occasions on which the captain breaks the* Federation *rule. We also learn that the unsuccessful first-contact mission long ago led to years of Federation-Klingon enmity. Watch for Sachi Parker, Shirley MacLaine's daughter, as Dr. Tava.*
STAR WATCH: *Bebe Neuwirth (Lilith on* Cheers) *has a memorable cameo as a nurse whose greatest fantasy is to have sex with an alien – and the injured Riker (Jonathan Frakes with Neuwirth, left) is in no position to refuse.*

GALAXY'S CHILD

Week of 11 March 1991, No. 190
Directed by: Winrich Kolbe
Written by: Maurice Hurley
Story by: Thomas Kartozian
STARDATE: 44614.6
Geordi is dejected upon meeting his dream woman, Dr. Leah Brahms, who has no interest in him. However, the two must work together to detach a parasitic life form that thinks the *Enterprise* is its mother. **Dr. Leah Brahms:** Susan Gibney. **Ensign Rager:** Lanei Chapman. **Ensign Pavlik:** Jana Marie Hupp. **Guinan:** Whoopi Goldberg. **Transporter Chief Hubbell:** April Grace.
✦ *Second appearance of Geordi's fantasy woman, Dr. Leah Brahms – in the flesh this time, as opposed to the holodeck version. Alas, Brahms, who happens to be an original designer of the* Enterprise, *turns out to be very different from Geordi's holodeck creation. Not only is she married, but the woman is a tad more critical than in his fantasy ("Booby Trap"). Geordi's struggle to overcome his discomfort around women is more apparent, and he does make friends with Leah – even after she learns of his fantasy.*
SHOW WATCH: *First glimpse of the Jefferies Tubes, named after the original series art director Matt Jefferies.*

NIGHT TERRORS

Week of 18 March 1991, No. 191
Directed by: Les Landau
Written by: Pamela Douglas
and Jeri Taylor
Story by: Shari Goodhartz
STARDATE: 44631.2

The *Enterprise* gets trapped in a rift in space where Troi is tormented by a recurring nightmare while the rest of the crew slip into insanity from dream deprivation. **Keiko O'Brien:** Rosalind Chao. **Andrus Hagan:** John Vickery. **Ensign Gillespie:** Duke Mooseikian. **Ensign Peeples:** Craig Hurley. **Ensign Kenny Lin:** Brian Tochi. **Ensign Rager:** Lanei Chapman. **O'Brien:** Colm Meaney. **Guinan:** Whoopi Goldberg. **Capt. Chantal Zaheva:** Deborah Taylor.

◆ *The ship is saved this time by Troi's empathic powers.*

SHOW WATCH: *Brian Tochi (Leonardo of "The Teenage Mutant Ninja Turtles") plays Ensign Kenny Lin. He appeared earlier as young Ray Tsingtao on the classic series' "And the Children Shall Lead."*

IDENTITY CRISIS

Week of 25 March 1991, No. 192
Directed by: Winrich Kolbe
Written by: Brannon Braga
Premise by: Timothy DeHaas
STARDATE: 44664.5

Geordi and a former shipmate exhibit symptoms of genetic transformation when drawn to a planet they investigated five years earlier. **Lt.-Cmdr. Susanna Leitjen:** Maryann Plunkett. **Nurse Alyssa Ogawa:** Patti Yasutake. **Lieut. Hickman:** Amick Byram. **Transporter Chief Hendrick:** Dennis Madalone. **Ensign Graham:** Mona Grudt. **Brevelle:** Paul Tompkins.

◆ *A strong episode for LeVar Burton, in which Geordi La Forge is reunited with a former U.S.S. Victory shipmate – who, with Geordi, participated in an Away Team mission to the planet Tarchannen III, where a parasite entered their bodies.*

NTH DEGREE

Week of 1 April 1991, No. 193
Directed by: Robert Legato
Written by: Joe Menosky
STARDATE: 44704.2

An alien probe turns the shy and timid Lieut. Barclay into a genius who can argue theoretical mathematics with Einstein and interface with the ship's computer. **Einstein:** Jim Morton. **Cytherian:** Kay E. Kuter. **Lieut. Linda Larson:** Saxon Trainor. **Ensign April Anaya:** Page Leong. **Lieut. Reginald Barclay:** Dwight Schultz. **Ensign Brower:** David Coburn.

SHOW WATCH: *Dwight Schultz returns as Lieut. Barclay in an episode that bears a passing resemblance to the classic series' "Where No Man Has Gone Before."*

QPID

Week of 22 April 1991, No. 194
Directed by: Cliff Bole
Written by: Ira Steven Behr
Story by: Randee Russell
and Ira Steven Behr
STARDATE: 44741.9

Q (John de Lancie) transforms Vash into a condemned Maid Marian and Picard into Robin Hood. **Vash:** Jennifer Hetrick. **Sir Guy:** Clive Revill.

◆ *A fantasy episode in the tradition of the classic series' "Shore Leave," and one of ST:TNG's most humourous outings. In his fifth appearance, John de Lancie (below) is at his mischievous best as Q, and Jennifer Hetrick returns as Picard's love interest, Vash. To repay the favour Picard did him in the previous season's "Déjà Q," the bad boy of the universe simulates the Sherwood Forest fantasy to get Picard and Vash to admit their true feelings for one another. But in a promising twist of fate – to be explored in "Q-Less," a first-season episode of Star Trek: Deep Space Nine – Vash declares her intention to travel the galaxy with Q, not stay with Picard.*

BEST LINE: *Forced to join Robin Hood's band of thieves, a protesting Worf declares, "I am not a merry man!"*

THE DRUMHEAD

Week of 29 April 1991, No. 195
Directed by: Jonathan Frakes
Written by: Jeri Taylor
STARDATE: 44769.2

An explosion aboard the *Enterprise* leads to an investigation headed by a retired *Starfleet* admiral who accuses Picard of treason. **Admiral Norah Satie:** Jean Simmons. **Sabin Genestra:** Bruce French. **Simon Tarses:** Spencer Garrett. **Lieut. J'Ddan:** Henry Woronicz. **Admiral Thomas Henry:** Earl Billings. **Nellen Tore:** Ann Shea.

◆ *In a chilling episode – Jonathan Frakes' third as director – Admiral Norah Satie leads a 24th-century witch hunt for non-existent conspirators. The admiral accuses Picard of violating the Prime Directive nine times, citing a litany of infractions ("Justice," "Angel One," "Pen Pals," "Up the Long Ladder," "The Ensigns of Command," "Who Watches the Watchers?" "The High Ground," "Legacy" and "First Contact"). Jean Simmons gives an extremely convincing portrayal of a woman whose bitter rage overwhelms her sense of justice. The notion of conspiracy among Federation officers would resurface in the DS9 episode "Paradise Lost."*

QPID: *SHERWOOD FOREST PROVES AN APPROPRIATE SETTING FOR MISCHIEF-MAKER Q (JOHN DE LANCIE).*

HALF A LIFE

Week of 6 May 1991, No. 196
Directed by: Les Landau
Written by: Peter Allan Fields
Story by: Ted Roberts
and Peter Allan Fields
STARDATE: 44805.3

Troi's mother, Lwaxana (Majel Barrett), falls in love with a scientist, Dr. Timicin (David Ogden Stiers), who must return to his home planet to commit ritual suicide, as required by his society. **Dara:** Michelle Forbes. **B'Tardat:** Terrence McNally. **O'Brien:** Colm Meaney. **Mr. Homn:** Carel Struycken.

HALF A LIFE: DAVID OGDEN STIERS IN A TOUCHING GUEST APPEARANCE AS THE DOOMED SCIENTIST TIMICIN.

✦ *In this sad, sweet episode, David Ogden Stiers (M*A*S*H) and Majel Barrett are well-paired as lovers forced to separate when Timicin must return home to die. On board to conduct an experiment that may save his world's dying star, the reserved Dr. Timicin is at first bewildered, then enchanted, by the vivacious Lwaxana Troi, on her fourth visit to the Enterprise. Persuaded by his new-found love to seek asylum rather than abandon his work and life to ritual suicide, the 60-year-old Timicin is confronted by his daughter, Dara (Michelle Forbes, set to return in the fifth season as Ensign Ro). She begs her father to remain true to his heritage and go through with their culture's "resolution." In a tearful exchange that allows Majel Barrett to display her dramatic talents, Timicin tells Lwaxana of his decision to embrace his proscribed destiny, and thus remain honourable to his people. In the episode's touching final scene, Lwaxana – as one of Timicin's loved ones – decides to accompany him to the planet to be with the scientist in his final moments.*

THE HOST

Week of 13 May 1991, No. 197
Directed by: Marvin Rush
Written by: Michel Horvat
STARDATE: 44821.3

Dr. Crusher's love for a Trillan ambassador (Franc Luz) is tested when she discovers he is actually an alien creature living inside a humanoid host. **Governor Leka Trion:** Barbara Tarbuck. **Kareel:** Nicole Orth-Pallavicini. **Kalin Trose:** William Newman. **Nurse Ogawa:** Patti Yasutake. **Lathal Bine:** Robert Harper.

✦ *Dr. Beverly Crusher finally gets to display her passionate side when she falls in love with Odan, a Trillian diplomat (played by Franc Luz), and is torn when she discovers the true nature of his symbiotic relationship with his host body.*

BEST SCENE: *Odan, after being temporarily housed in Cmdr. Riker when his first body dies, convinces Beverly to continue their affair, and they spend one more night together.*

SHOW WATCH: *The Trill species would return on Star Trek: Deep Space Nine in the character of Jadzia Dax (played by Terry Farrell).*

THE MIND'S EYE

Week of 27 May 1991, No. 198
Directed by: David Livingston
Written by: René Echevarria
Story by: Ken Schafer
and Rene Echevarria
STARDATE: 44885.5

En route to the blissful planet Risa for his vacation, Geordi is kidnapped by a group of hostile Romulans and is brainwashed into being their assassin. **Ambassador Kell:** Larry Dobkin. **Taibak:** John Fleck. **Governor Vagh:** Edward Wiley. **O'Brien:** Colm Meaney. **Computer Voice:** Majel Barrett.

IN THEORY

Week of 3 June 1991, No. 199
Directed by: Patrick Stewart
Written by: Joe Menosky
and Ronald D. Moore
STARDATE: 44932.3

Data (Brent Spiner) struggles with the intricacies of love when he becomes romantically involved with a crew-mate (Michele Scarabelli). **Keiko O'Brien:** Rosalind Chao. **Transporter Chief O'Brien:** Colm Meaney. **Ensign McKnight:** Pamela Winslow. **Guinan:** Whoopi Goldberg.

✦ *In a serio-comic episode that marks Patrick Stewart's debut in the director's seat, Data comes close to learning, first-hand, the meaning of love. Despite his well-intentioned attempt to create a program to provide himself with a guide to love, the android doesn't quite get with the program, and when Ensign Jenna D'Sora realizes that she can't fall in love with a machine, Data's left holding his cat, Spot, as D'Sora walks away.*

REDEMPTION, PART I

Week of 17 June 1991, No. 200
Directed by: Cliff Bole
Written by: Ronald D. Moore
STARDATE: 44995.3

Worf (Michael Dorn) is torn between his duty to the *Federation* and his Klingon heritage when civil war threatens the Klingon Empire. **Gowron:** Robert O'Reilly. **Cmdr. Kurn:** Tony Todd. **Lursa:** Barbara March. **B'Etor:** Gwynyth Walsh. **K'Tal:** Ben Slack. **General Movar:** Nicholas Kepros. **Toral:** J.D. Cullum. **Guinan:** Whoopi Goldberg. **Klingon First Officer:** Tom Ormeny. **Computer Voice:** Majel Barrett. **Cmdr. Sela:** Denise Crosby. **Helmsman:** Clifton Jones.

✦ *The series' second cliff-hanger pits Worf against traitors on his home world in the final chapter of the saga that began in the earlier "Sins of the Father" and "Reunion" episodes. Michael Dorn has some of his best moments as Worf reclaims his father's honour and resigns his Starfleet commission to fight for Gowron in the Klingon civil war. And in ST:TNG's most surprising plot twist, Denise Crosby returns as Romulan Cmdr. Sela, Tasha Yar's daughter by her forced marriage to her Romulan abductor – an explanation that wouldn't be shared with Star Trek viewers until the fifth season.*

SHOW WATCH: *Actors Barbara March and Gwynyth Walsh (see photograph, next page) make a lasting impression as the Klingon sisters of Duras, who would return to threaten Worf and the Klingon Empire's peace with the Federation in part two of "Redemption" and DS9's "Past Prologue," before meeting their demise in "Star Trek Generations."* ✧

FIFTH SEASON

THE FIFTH SEASON WAS LAUNCHED WITH GREAT FANFARE TO CELEBRATE *STAR TREK*'S 25TH ANNIVERSARY – not bad for a show that NBC tried to kill more than once. By the autumn of 1991, *Star Trek: The Next Generation* was achieving weekly American ratings that would have placed it as a top prime-time show every week – had it been televised on network TV. The season boasted top-notch scripts and consistently credible performances. Even in the absence of a network berth, the show still had managed to capture a handful of major television awards for technical excellence.

Stories this season would shift their emphasis to character development, social commentary and the importance of overcoming personal differences to fight for a common goal. Issues such as vengeance, sexual preference, euthanasia and genetic engineering were explored without succumbing to preachiness or forsaking the action-adventure mode that was *Star Trek*'s hallmark. Fans noted the absence this season of Q – the roguish mischief-maker and fan favourite. And, on a much sadder note, the world bid farewell to *Star Trek* creator Gene Roddenberry, who died in October 1991. Even with the death of the Great Bird of the Galaxy, no one doubted that his vision would continue to *live long and prosper*.

REDEMPTION, PART II: GWYNYTH WALSH (B'ETOR) AND BARBARA MARCH (LURSA) ARE UNFORGETTABLE AS THE NASTY KLINGON SISTERS OF DURAS.

REDEMPTION, PART II
Week of 23 Sept. 1991, No. 201
Directed by: David Carson
Written by: Ronald D. Moore
STARDATE: 45020.4
Picard suspects the Romulans are stirring up the civil war that threatens the *Federation*-Klingon alliance, and convinces the *Federation* to impose a blockade against the Romulan Empire. **Cmdr. Sela:** Denise Crosby. **Cmdr. Kurn:** Tony Todd. **Lursa:** Barbara March. **B'Etor:** Gwynyth Walsh. **Toral:** J.D. Cullum. **Gowron:** Robert O'Reilly. **Capt. Larg:** Michael G. Hagerty. **Admiral Shanthii** Fran Bennett. **Gen. Movar:** Nicholas Kepros. **O'Brien:** Colm Meaney. **Lt.-Cmdr.**
Christopher Hobson: Timothy Carhart. **Guinan:** Whoopi Goldberg. **Kulge:** Jordan Lund. **Ensign Craig:** Clifton Jones.
◆ *An action-packed wrap-up to last season's gripping finale, with one of the most entertaining plot twists ever developed for a science-fiction series: Seemingly back from the dead, Denise Crosby pops up in the role of Tasha Yar's half-Romulan daughter, Sela, who plots with the sisters of Duras to initiate civil war in the Klingon Empire and destroy the Federation. Another fine performance by Michael Dorn, who plays both sides of Worf's loyalties to his Klingon home world and to the Federation – with equal conviction. And Data finally commands a*

ship in this episode, handling the crew's resistance to his orders admirably well.
BEST SCENE: *In explaining her uncanny resemblance to Tasha Yar, Sela reveals her lingering guilt over betraying her mother for trying to escape the Romulans.*

DARMOK
Week of 30 Sept. 1991, No. 202
Directed by: Winrich Kolbe
Written by: Joe Menosky
Story by: Philip Lazebnik and Joe Menosky
STARDATE: 45047.2
The *Enterprise* makes contact with the Tamarians, a non-violent race of aliens whose language is incomprehensible to humans – but the two groups are forced to find a way to communicate when Picard and the Tamarian Captain (Paul Winfield) unite to defend themselves against an angry creature. **Tamarian First Officer:** Richard James. **O'Brien:** Colm Meaney.
◆ *With the two captains co-operating – rather than fighting, as with Kirk and the Gorn in the classic series' "Arena" – Picard learns a tough lesson on the value of communication when his new-found ally is killed by the beastly enemy – and he must use his limited knowledge of the Tamarian language to praise the dead captain's courage, lest the Tamarian crew open fire on the Enterprise. Paul Winfield first appeared in "Star Trek II: The Wrath of Khan" as Capt. Terrell.*
STAR WATCH: *Ashley Judd ("Heat") turns up as Ensign Lefler, who would appear later in the season as Wesley's love interest in "The Game."*

ENSIGN RO
Week of 7 Oct. 1991, No. 203
Directed by: Les Landau
Written by: Michael Piller
Story by: Rick Berman and Michael Piller
STARDATE: 45076.3
While investigating a terrorist attack on the Solarion planet, Capt. Jean-Luc Picard uncovers evidence of a conspiracy to wipe out the Bajorans, and exposes the dastardly deed with the help of a new officer, Ro Laren (Michelle Forbes). **Keeve Falor:** Scott Marlowe. **Gul Dolak:** Frank Collison. **Orta:** Jeffrey Hayenga. **Transporter Technician Collins:** Harley Venton. **Barber Mot:**

Ken Thorley. **Admiral Kennelly:** Cliff Potts. **Guinan:** Whoopi Goldberg.

◆ *Michelle Forbes, Dr. Timicin's daughter in the fourth season's "Half a Life," appears as Ro Laren, the strong-willed Bajoran with a troubled past. Ro is the first recurring crew member to display traits of aggression and impatience, which brings into question her suitability as a Federation officer. Guinan reveals her intuitive side in seeing through Ro's tough façade to the vulnerable person within. The appearance of the Bajorans lays the foundation for much of DS9.*

SHOW WATCH: *The Bajoran ear-ring, as introduced by Ro and later worn by Major Kira on DS9, would emerge as a fashion favourite among Trekkers.*

SILICON AVATAR

Week of 14 Oct. 1991, No. 204
Directed by: Cliff Bole
Written by: Jeri Taylor
Story by: Lawrence V. Conley
STARDATE: 45122.3
During a survey mission on Melona IV, the *Enterprise* is approached by the Crystalline Entity, a life form responsible for numerous deaths. While Picard attempts to communicate with the entity, an *Enterprise* scientist (Ellen Geer) insists that it should be detroyed. **Carmen Davila:** Susan Diol.

◆ *The return of the Crystalline Entity ("Datalore") sets the stage for a clash between Picard (faithful to his mission to seek out new life) and Dr. Kila Marr (obsessed with avenging her son's death at the hands of the entity on Omicron Theta, Data's home planet). Although initially hostile to Data – accusing him of luring the entity to Melona IV as Lore had done on Omicron Theta – Marr bonds with the android after realizing that his programming contains the memories of Omicron Theta's inhabitants, including those of her son. Brent Spiner goes solo on guitar as Data pursues his interest in music.*

DISASTER

Week of 21 Oct. 1991, No. 205
Directed by: Gabrielle Beaumont
Written by: Ronald D. Moore
Story by: Ron Jarvis
and Philip A. Scorza
STARDATE: 45156.1
The *Enterprise* is caught in the path of a rare natural phenomenon, which severe-ly damages the ship and leaves Troi (Marina Sirtis) in command on the bridge, Picard trapped in a turbolift with three children, and O'Brien's wife about to give birth in Ten-Forward. **Keiko O'Brien:** Rosalind Chao. **Miles O'Brien:** Colm Meaney. **Ensign Ro:** Michelle Forbes. **Marissa:** Erika Flores. **Jay Gordon:** John Christian Graas. **Patterson:** Max Supera. **Ensign Mandel:** Cameron Arnett. **Lieut. Monroe:** Jana Marie Hupp.

◆ *Splendid high-tension episode bringing out the crew's lesser-known strengths: The injured Picard must comfort three frightened children; Worf must tend to the wounded and deliver Keiko's baby; and an uncertain Troi must take command, finding the courage to make crucial decisions in the nick of time.*

BEST SCENE: *A panicky Worf orders Keiko to give birth "immediately."*

STAR WATCH: *Erika Flores (Dr. Quinn, Medicine Woman) appears as Marissa.*

THE GAME

Week of 28 Oct. 1991, No. 206
Directed by: Corey Allen
Written by: Brannon Braga
Story by: Susan Sackett, Fred Bronson and Brannon Braga
STARDATE: 45208.2
When Wesley (Wil Wheaton) returns to the *Enterprise* on a vacation from *Starfleet* Academy, he finds the entire crew has become addicted to an electronic mind game which tampers with an individual's ability to reason. **Ensign Robin Lefler:** Ashley Judd. **Etana Jol:** Katherine Moffat. **O'Brien:** Colm

---

UNIFICATION I: MARC LENARD REPRISES HIS CLASSIC STAR TREK ROLE OF SAREK, SPOCK'S FATHER.

Meaney. **Nurse Alyssa Ogawa:** Patti Yasutake. **Ensign:** Diane M. Hurley.

◆ *Wil Wheaton's first guest appearance on Star Trek: The Next Generation series since leaving the show in the fourth season. Ashley Judd's second appearance as Ensign Lefler, to whom the vacationing Wesley takes an immediate shine.*

UNIFICATION, PART I

Week of 4 Nov. 1991, No. 208
Directed by: Les Landau
Written by: Jeri Taylor
Story by: Rick Berman and Michael Piller
STARDATE: 45236.4
After learning that the Vulcan ambassador Mr. Spock has travelled to Romulus for a secret meeting with the Romulan Senator, Picard and Data follow – disguised as Romulans – to determine his intentions. **Perrin:** Joanna Miles. **Capt. K'Vada:** Stephen D. Root. **Klim Dokachin:** Graham Jarvis. **Senator Pardek:** Malachi Throne. **Proconsul Neral:** Norman Large. **B'iJik:** Erick Avari. **Admiral Brackett:** Karen Hensel. **Sarek:** Mark Lenard. **Soup Woman:** Mimi Cozzens. **Computer Voice:** Majel Barrett.

◆ *The third and perhaps best appearance of a character carried over from the classic* Star Trek *series, the incomparable Mr. Spock (Leonard Nimoy, next page), who, with his father, Sarek (Mark Lenard, below), links the present Federation to its past. Make-up and costumes are used to great effect as Picard becomes the second Federation captain to masquerade as a Romulan – James T. Kirk was the first (in* Star Trek's *original-series episode "The Enterprise Incident"). This will develop into a trend on* Star Trek.

BEST SCENE: *Sarek, while on his deathbed, confides to Capt. Picard his love for his ever-distant son, Spock.*

SHOW WATCH: *Malachi Throne, appearing in this episode as Romulan Senator Pardek, played Commodore Mendez in the classic series' "The Menagerie."*

UNIFICATION, PART II

Week of 11 Nov. 1991, No. 207
Directed by: Cliff Bole
Written by: Michael Piller
Story by: Rick Berman and Michael Piller
STARDATE: 45245.8

Conclusion. Picard and Data locate Spock, who reveals the reason for his journey to Romulus – an attempt to unify the Romulans and the Vulcans – but his efforts are thwarted with the discovery of a Romulan plot to invade Vulcan. **Cmdr. Sela:** Denise Crosby. **Capt. K'Vada:** Stephen D. Root. **Senator Pardek:** Malachi Throne. **Proconsul Neral:** Norman Large. **Omag:** William Bastiani. **D'Tan:** Vidal Peterson. **Amarie:** Harriet Leider.

✦ *Solid plot and great acting add to the suspense of this episode. And in a neatly written bridge to an earlier plot line, the half-Romulan Cmdr. Sela (Denise Crosby, in her fourth guest appearance) returns to cause trouble for the Federation. In a touching moment, Picard allows Spock to use the Vulcan mind-meld to access the late Sarek's innermost feelings.*

BEST SCENE: *Data and Spock meet for the first time, allowing Data – forever driven to be human – to ask the Vulcan: Why did Spock choose to reject his human half instead of his Vulcan side?*

UNIFICATION, PART II: LEONARD NIMOY AS THE INCOMPARABLE AMBASSADOR SPOCK.

A MATTER OF TIME
Week of 18 Nov. 1991, No. 209
Directed by: Paul Lynch
Written by: Rick Berman
STARDATE: 45349.1
While on a mercy mission to the Penthara IV planet, which has been struck by a massive asteroid, the *Enterprise* is visited by a man "from the future." **Rasmussen:** Matt Frewer. **Dr. Hal Moseley:** Stefan Gierasch. **Ensign Felton:** Sheila Franklin. **Female Scientist:** Shay Garner.

✦ *The role of the time-travelling Berlingoff Rasmussen in this light-hearted episode was originally written for Robin Williams, who bowed out to play Peter Pan in "Hook." Successor to the role, Matt Frewer ("Honey, I Shrunk the Kids") became a cult sensation in the late '80s as M-M-M-M-Max Headroom.*

NEW GROUND
Week of 6 Jan. 1992, No. 210
Directed by: Robert Scheerer
Written by: Grant Rosenberg
Story by: Sara Charno and Stuart Charno
STARDATE: 45376.3
As the *Enterprise* makes its way to Bilana III to test a new propulsion system, Worf's son, Alexander (Brian Bonsall), arrives on the *Enterprise* – intending to stay permanently. **Helena Rozhenko:** Georgia Brown. **Dr. Ja'Dar:** Richard McGonagle. **Kyle:** Jennifer Edwards. **Ensign Felton:** Sheila Franklin. **Computer Voice:** Majel Barrett.
✦ *This episode adds dimension to Worf's character as he struggles to become a father to Alexander (Brian Bonsall of "Blank Check," Family Ties), tapping unsuspected reserves of love and patience. Worf and Troi discover their common interest in Alexander and – for the first time, but not the last – in each other.*

HERO WORSHIP
Week of 27 Jan. 1992, No. 211
Directed by: Patrick Stewart
Written by: Joe Menosky
Story by: Hilary J. Bader
STARDATE: 45397.3
After rescuing a traumatized young boy from the wreckage of a research vessel, the *Enterprise* crew strives to discover what caused the destruction of the small ship. **Timothy:** Joshua Harris. **Transporter Chief:** Harley Venton. **Ensign Felton:** Sheila Franklin. **Teacher:** Steven Einspahr.
✦ *In the second episode directed by Patrick Stewart, the crew again tends to a young orphan who, while traumatized by the destruction of his ship and the loss of his parents, makes a friend in Data and begins to mimic his every move – which is sometimes humourous. As Data and Troi struggle to reach young Timothy, Geordi recalls his own terror at the fire that nearly killed him when he was 5.*

VIOLATIONS
Week of 3 Feb. 1992, No. 212
Directed by: Robert Wiemer
Written by: Pamela Gray and Jeri Taylor
Story by: Shari Goodhartz, T. Michael Gray and Pamela Gray
STARDATE: 45429.3
As the *Enterprise* escorts a group of telepathic Ullians to Kaldra IV planet, crew members begin to lapse into comas, which are seemingly caused by the delegation of telepathic aliens. **Keiko O'Brien:** Rosalind Chao. **Jev:** Ben Lemon. **Tarmin:** David Sage. **Dr. Martin:** Rick Fitts. **Inad:** Eve Brenner. **Lt.-Cmdr. Jack Crusher:** Doug Wert. **Crewman Davis:** Craig Benton. **Computer Voice:** Majel Barrett.
✦ *An episode brimming with fear and violence. The notion of assault is taken one step further – into the mind. Before lapsing into comas, Troi, Riker and Crusher are repeatedly subjected to violent, horrifying memories, caused by Jev, a telepathic violator posing as a historian.*

SCARIEST SCENE: *Beverly Crusher is forced to peer into her husband's coffin, only to find Jev waiting there for her.*

THE MASTERPIECE SOCIETY
Week of 10 Feb. 1992, No. 213
Directed by: Winrich Kolbe
Written by: Adam Belanoff and Michael Piller
Story by: James Kahn and Adam Belanoff
STARDATE: 45470.1
A stellar core fragment threatens to destroy a genetically engineered human colony on an otherwise deserted planet. The crew of the *Enterprise* attempts to avert the natural disaster, without realizing that their assistance could be just as damaging. **Aaron Conor:** John Snyder. **Hannah Bates:** Dey Young. **Martin Benbeck:** Ron Canada. **Ensign Felton:** Sheila Franklin.
✦ *A thought-provoking episode on genetic engineering with Deanna Troi and Geordi playing central roles in the debate. While Troi immediately regrets her brief, "genetically incorrect" affair with the human colony's leader, Geordi works to solve their engineering problem, fully realizing that, being blind, he would never have been allowed to live in their society – which considered him imperfect.*

CONUNDRUM

Week of 17 Feb. 1992, No. 214
Directed by: Les Landau
Written by: Barry M. Schkolnick
Story by: Paul Schiffer
STARDATE: 45494.2

After being scanned by an alien ship, the *Enterprise* crew members lose their memories and find they have a new officer on board, one who insists they are at war. **Cmdr. Kieran MacDuff:** Erich Anderson. **Ensign Ro Laren:** Michelle Forbes. **Kristin:** Liz Vassey. **Crewman:** Erick Weiss.

◆ *Intriguing glimpse at what might have been. Suffering complete memory loss, the crew begins to assume the identities that feel most comfortable to them: Worf decides he must be the captain of the* Enterprise, *while Picard becomes the navigator; Ro and Riker, meanwhile, share a mutual attraction.*

POWER PLAY

Week of 24 Feb. 1992, No. 215
Directed by: David Livingston
Written by: Rene Balcer,
Herbert J. Wright and Brannon Braga
Story by: Paul Ruben
and Maurice Hurley
STARDATE: 45571.2

After investigating a sub-space distress signal coming from an uninhabited moon, Troi, Data and O'Brien stage a violent takeover on the bridge and force Picard to change the direction of the *Enterprise*. **Keiko O'Brien:** Rosalind Chao. **Miles O'Brien:** Colm Meaney. **Ensign Ro Laren:** Michelle Forbes. **Transporter Technician:** Ryan Reid. **Computer Voice:** Majel Barrett.

◆ *Marina Sirtis, Brent Spiner and Colm Meaney get to step out of character when Troi, Data and O'Brien are possessed by disembodied entities, prisoners of an unsuspected penal colony located on the "uninhabited" moon.*

ETHICS

Week of 2 March 1992, No. 216
Directed by: Chip Chalmers
Written by: Ronald D. Moore
Story by: Sara Charno
and Stuart Charno
STARDATE: 45587.3

Dr. Crusher (Gates McFadden) calls in a neurogeneticist after Worf (Michael Dorn) is paralysed in an accident, but she

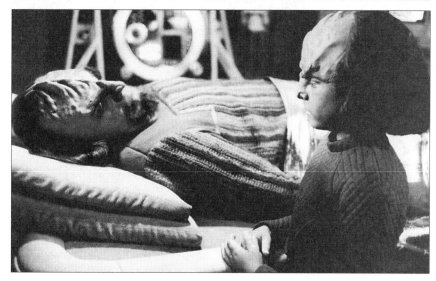

ETHICS: *AFTER BEING PARALYSED IN AN ACCIDENT, WORF ASKS HIS SON, ALEXANDER (BRIAN BONSALL), TO ASSIST HIM IN COMMITTING RITUAL SUICIDE.*

begins to regret the decision after Dr. Russell suggests experimental surgery that could cost Worf his life. **Dr. Toby Russell:** Caroline Kava. **Alexander:** Brian Bonsall. **Nurse Alyssa Ogawa:** Patti Yasutake.

◆ *Ethical issues force Worf and Dr. Crusher to re-examine their values, and places them in conflict with their colleagues. After Riker refuses to assist him in ritual suicide, Worf turns to his son, Alexander – but, in his reluctance to put the 7-year-old boy through the ordeal, he begins to question his Klingon resolve. Beverly, meanwhile, objects vehemently to Dr. Russell's determination to risk her patients' lives to prove her theories. Worf dies, for the second time, in surgery just before his Klingon anatomy – featuring a backup synaptic system – kicks in to resuscitate him.*

THE OUTCAST

Week of 16 March 1992, No. 217
Directed by: Robert Scheerer
Written by: Jeri Taylor
STARDATE: 45614.6

While working together to locate a missing shuttlecraft, Riker and a J'naii member (Melinda Culea) become attracted to each other, despite the fact that a relationship is prohibited because the androgynous J'naii race prohibits male-female relationships. **Krite:** Callan White. **Noor:** Megan Cole.

◆ *Issues of sexual preference and tolerance are put to the test in one of* Star Trek's *most controversial episodes. When*

Soren *is put on trial for her involvement with Riker, the first officer assumes full responsibility for their liaison while defending his lover's right to choose to be female. In a heart-wrenching scene, Riker must deal with the brainwashing cure she is forced to undergo as punishment. Placing both himself and his career at risk, he attempts to rescue Soren only to have her renounce him as her brainwashing takes hold.*

CAUSE AND EFFECT

Week of 23 March 1992, No. 218
Directed by: Jonathan Frakes
Written by: Brannon Braga
STARDATE: 45652.1

The *Enterprise* is caught in a time warp while charting the unexplored region known as the Typhon Expanse, inducing dizziness and déjà vu in the crew, and causing the *Enterprise* to collide repeatedly with another ship. **Ensign Ro Laren:** Michelle Forbes. **Nurse Alyssa Ogawa:** Patti Yasutake. **Capt. Morgan Bateman:** Kelsey Grammer.

◆ *In the fourth episode directed by Jonathan Frakes, a sequence of events leading to the ship's destruction is repeated again and again, and the* Enterprise *falls into a time loop that steals 17 days out of the ship's history.*

STAR WATCH: *Kelsey Grammer (of television's* Frasier) *has a letter-perfect cameo as the bemused Capt. Morgan Bateman of the Starship* Bozeman, *the other time-looped ship, which has been trapped for 90 years. Note his 23rd-century uniform,* *which was introduced in the movie "Star Trek II: The Wrath of Khan."*

THE FIRST DUTY
Week of 30 March 1992, No. 219
Directed by: Paul Lynch
Written by: Ronald Moore
and Naren Shankar
STARDATE: 45703.9
Wesley (Wil Wheaton) becomes involved in a coverup during the investigation of an in-flight accident which destroyed five *Starfleet* Academy ships and caused the death of his friend Joshua Albert. **Boothby:** Ray Walston. **Cadet First Class Nicholas Locarno:** Robert Duncan McNeill. **Lt.-Cmdr. Albert:** Ed Lauter. **Capt. Satelk:** Richard Fancy. **Supt. Admiral Brand:** Jacqueline Brookes. **Cadet Second Class Jean Hajar:** Walker Brandt. **Cadet Second Class Sito:** Shannon Fill.

✦ *In Wil Wheaton's second guest appearance since leaving* The Next Generation *series, Wesley comes of age when he realizes that loyalty to the truth – which is the first duty of a Starfleet officer, Picard reminds him – is worth more than friendship, leading him to testify against his squadron after one of his team is killed during an ill-fated attempt at a banned flight manoeuvre. A first glimpse at Starfleet Academy in San Francisco, where Picard catches up with Boothby (Ray Walston of "My Favourite Martian" and "Picket Fences," in photograph with Patrick Stewart, right), the Academy groundsman and his mentor.*
SHOW WATCH: *Robert Duncan McNeill – better known as Lieut. Tom Paris, the second of three ST:TNG actors to be cast in the Star Trek: Voyager series – appears as Cadet Locarno. Shannon Fill, as Cadet Second Class Sito, would reprise her*

Bajoran character in ST:TNG's seventh season episode "Lower Decks," and Richard Fancy's character, Satelk, is the first appearance of a Vulcan captain on ST:TNG.

COST OF LIVING
Week of 20 April 1992, No. 220
Directed by: Winrich Kolbe
Written by: Peter Allan Fields
STARDATE: 45733.6
After the *Enterprise* destroys an asteroid, a cloud of parasitic particles begins to destroy the ship's hull. Meanwhile, Lwaxana Troi (Majel Barrett), Deanna's impossible mother, arrives on board with startling news for Troi: She plans to marry a man she has never met. **Campio:** Tony Jay. **Mr. Homn:** Carel Struycken. **Young Man:** David Oliver. **Juggler:** Albie Selznick. **Erko:** Patrick Cronin. **Young Woman:** Tracey D'Arcy. **Poet:** George Edie. **First Learner:** Christopher Halste.

✦ *Another first-rate Lwaxana storyline with Majel Barrett pulling out all stops. As usual, her visits are accompanied by humour, conflict and near-disaster. On board to be married to a man she hasn't met, the high-spirited Betazoid befriends young Alexander – to the consternation of both Worf and Deanna – and teaches the youth something about life while learning a lesson of her own.*
BEST SCENE: *The audacious Lwaxana arrives for her marriage ceremony in traditional Betazoid wedding attire – the nude – much to the embarrassment of her guests, not to mention her stuffy fiancé, who flees in panic.*

SHOW WATCH: *Listen carefully during the scene outside the holodeck where Majel Barrett as Lwaxana Troi talks to Majel Barrett, the voice of the ship's computer.*

THE PERFECT MATE
Week of 27 April 1992, No. 221
Directed by: Cliff Bole
Written by: Gary Percante
and Michael Piller
Story by: René Echevarria
and Gary Percante
STARDATE: 45761.3
A Ceremony of Reconciliation is scheduled to take place on the *Starship Enterprise*, but the peace process between the Kriosians and the Valtese is jeopardized when the troublesome Ferengi try to steal the peace offering (Famke Janssen). **Briam:** Tim O'Connor. **Par Lenor:** Max Grodénchik. **Alrik:** Mickey Cottrell. **Qol:** Michael Snyder. **Transporter Chief Hubbell:** April Grace. **Computer Voice:** Majel Barrett.

✦ *Bittersweet tale of true love lost, with Jean-Luc Picard as the unhappy protagonist in this case. Interesting debate arises between the captain and Dr. Crusher as to whether Kamala's cultural obligations amount to prostitution, and whether on moral grounds the Federation has the right to interfere with those obligations. First glimpse of the breakfast and tea that Picard and Crusher are in the habit of sharing. Kamala's spotted temples and hairline will later be seen on the host body of Jadzia Dax in Star Trek: Deep Space Nine.*
STAR WATCH: *Famke Janssen (the latest Bond girl in "Goldeneye") as Kamala.*

THE FIRST DUTY: ROBERT DUNCAN MCNEILL, LATER CAST ON VOYAGER, GUEST STARS AS WESLEY'S (WIL WHEATON) ACADEMY CLASS-MATE, IN THE SAME EPISODE, RAY WALSTON (WITH PATRICK STEWART) DOES A FINE TURN AS ACADEMY GROUNDSMAN BOOTHBY.

IMAGINARY FRIEND

Week of 4 May 1992, No. 222
Directed by: Gabrielle Beaumont
Written by: Edithe Swensen
and Brannon Braga
Story by: Ronald Wilderson,
Jean Matthias and Richard Fliegel
STARDATE: 45832.1

A little girl's imaginary friend comes to life and threatens the ship and crew when the *Enterprise* enters a region of space containing a strange energy form. **Isabella:** Shay Astar. **Ensign Daniel Sutter:** Jeff Allin. **Clara Sutter:** Noley Thornton. **Alexander:** Brian Bonsall. **Nurse Alyssa Ogawa:** Patti Yasutake. **Ensign Felton:** Sheila Franklin. **Guinan:** Whoopi Goldberg.

◆ *First mention of Geordi La Forge's parents, who will appear in the seventh season's "Interface."*

I, BORG

Week of 11 May 1992, No. 223
Directed by: Robert Lederman
Written by: Rene Echevarria
STARDATE: 45854.2

The *Enterprise* discovers an injured adolescent Borg who exhibits human qualities, but reactions among the crew are not favourable when the youngster is brought on board. **Hugh:** Jonathan Del Arco. **Guinan:** Whoopi Goldberg.

◆ *In one of ST:TNG's most popular Borg episodes, Dr. Crusher saves the life of an injured Borg, whom Geordi befriends and names Hugh. The crew is divided over the young Borg, forcing Picard to make the critical decision: Should Hugh be destroyed or returned to the collective which would expose the Federation to future risk? Picard will face the consequences of his decision in the sixth season's "Descent, Part I." Jonathan Del Arco gives a rivetting performance as the young Borg who learns to become an individual.*

THE NEXT PHASE

Week of 18 May 1992, No. 224
Directed by: David Carson
Written by: Ronald D. Moore
STARDATE: 45092.4

After the *Enterprise* offers assistance to a Romulan science ship in distress, La Forge and Ro (LeVar Burton, Michelle Forbes) disappear during transport between the ships, and are assumed

dead. **Mirok:** Thomas Kopache. **Varel:** Susanna Thompson. **Transporter Chief Brossmer:** Shelby Leverington. **Parem:** Brian Cousins. **Ensign McDowell:** Kenneth Meseroll.

◆ *Imaginative special effects, as Geordi and Ro – accidentally cloaked through Romulan chicanery – walk through walls. While Data searches for an appropriate memorial service by which to mark his comrades' deaths, we observe different cultural traditions: for Worf, an honourable death is cause to celebrate, whereas Ro would prefer the two-hour Bajoran death chant for her borhyas, or soul. Jonathan Frakes once again sets forth with his own trombone-playing number as Riker gets into the spirit of the Mardi Gras-style wake Data finally settles on.*

THE INNER LIGHT

Week of 1 June 1992, No. 225
Directed by: Peter Lauritson
Written by: Peter Allan Fields
and Morgan Gendel
Story by: Morgan Gendel
STARDATE: 45944.1

Picard (Patrick Stewart) is struck by a primitive alien probe which renders him unconscious, and wakens to find himself on the planet Kataan, living the simple life of an iron weaver on the drought-stricken planet. **Eline:** Margot Rose. **Batai:** Richard Riehle. **Administrator:** Scott Jaeck. **Meribor:** Jennifer Nash. **Nurse Alyssa Ogawa:** Patti Yasutake. **Young Batai:** Daniel Stewart.

◆ *In a wonderfully touching change-of-pace episode – a Hugo Science Fiction*

Award-winner for Best Dramatic Presentation – Picard lives another man's life while under the influence of the space probe. As Kamin the iron weaver, Picard has a wife, a loving relationship with his children, and a lifelong – but ultimately futile – mission to save the planet from drought. As Kamin nears the end of his own life, the significance of the probe becomes clear: It was launched by the long-dead Kataanians to record their story, and Picard was used as the witness through whom that story might be told. Having lived Kataan's demise through Kamin's eyes, Picard awakens on the Enterprise 25 minutes later a changed man – with Kamin's flute and the memories of that lifetime to carry forward.

SHOW WATCH: *Patrick Stewart's son, Daniel (with his father, left), has a minor role as Batai, Kamin's son on Kataan.*

TIME'S ARROW, PART I

Week of 15 June 1992, No. 226
Directed by: Les Landau
Written by: Joe Menosky
and Michael Piller
Story by: Joe Menosky
STARDATE: 45959.1

The *Enterprise* travels to Earth to investigate archeological evidence of aliens living on the planet as early as the 19th century. When they uncover a very unusual artifact – Data's head – the Away Team transports itself to the late 1890s San Francisco to investigate. Part one of two. **Samuel Clemens:** Jerry Hardin. **Bellboy:** Michael Aron. **Doorman:** Barry Kivel. **Seaman:** Ken Thorley. Joe **Falling Hawk:** Sheldon Peters. Wolfchild. **Gambler/Frederick La Rouque:** Marc Alaimo. **Scientist:** Milt Tarver. **Guinan:** Whoopi Goldberg. **Roughneck:** Michael Hungerford. **Beggar:** John M. Murdock.

◆ *Another season-ending cliff-hanger with a fascinating twist: While searching for clues to the artifact, Data is sucked back in time to 1890s San Francisco – where he promptly meets Mark Twain (Clemens) and discovers a Guinan – living as a wealthy socialite – who does not recognize him. Jerry Hardin is amusing as the irrepressible Samuel Clemens, who eavesdrops on Guinan and Data and earns himself a trip to the future. And, as the season ends, we're left to ponder: What ever happened to Data's head?* ✧

SIXTH SEASON

WITH RUMOURS ALREADY CIRCULATING THAT *STAR TREK: THE NEXT GENERATION*'S SIXTH SEASON MIGHT well be its last, the year was marked by story-lines that brought closure to earlier episodes, and allowed several characters a sense of completeness in their lives: Data, in seeking his father, again meets up with his evil twin; Worf, undertaking his own paternal quest, explores the spiritual side to his Klingon nature; Riker, while encountering his other self, gets a second chance to build a life with Deanna; and Picard, on a journey to the afterlife, is tempted to undo his past mistakes. And while Q – to fans' delight – resurfaces in the sixth season to resume his mischief-making, Lwaxana Troi – another fan favourite – unfortunately does not return. It's a season packed with emotion. Great excitement surrounds the launch of *Star Trek: Deep Space Nine* – the third *Star Trek* incarnation – while *The Next Generation* series experiences its own score of sentimental high notes, including the return of Lt.-Cmdr. Montgomery Scott to the *Federation* fold and the guest appearance of physicist Stephen Hawking in the season finale. With the cast eventually signed to a seventh year, the sixth season would emerge as one of superb storytelling, stories that allowed the crew to seek out new life, as well as explore within.

TIME'S ARROW, PART II

Week of 21 Sept. 1992, No. 227
Directed by: Les Landau
Written by: Jeri Taylor
Story by: Joe Menosky
STARDATE: 46001.3
Conclusion. The crew's efforts to find Data in 19th-century San Francisco and stop alien time travellers from tampering with the future is hindered by a distrustful Samuel Clemens (Jerry Hardin). **Guinan:** Whoopi Goldberg. **Mrs. Carmichael:** Pamela Kosh. **Young Reporter:** Alexander Enberg. **Morgue Attendant:** Van Epperson. **Dr. Appollinaire:** James Gleason. **Male Patient:** Bill Cho Lee. **Policeman:** William Boyett. **Alien Nurse:** Mary Stein. **Jack London:** Michael Aron.
✦ *In the life-or-death conclusion to the fifth-season finale, we learn why Data's head – blown off in an explosion – was separated from his body in the first place. In the wake of Worf's miraculous fifth-season recovery, Data is the second ST:TNG crew member brought back from the dead. Picard, meanwhile, finally discovers how he really met Guinan, and the meddlesome Sam Clemens earns a quick trip to the 24th century. Unlike other aliens in the* Federation *universe, the soul-stealers of this episode are deemed evil – without being given the usual opportunity to redeem themselves.*

REALM OF FEAR

Week of 28 Sept. 1992, No. 228
Directed by: Cliff Bole
Written by: Brannon Braga
STARDATE: 46041.4

Lieut. Barclay's fear of transporting is compounded when he encounters a creature inside the transporter stream during an away mission. **Lieut. Barclay:** Dwight Schultz. **Admiral Hayes:** Renata Scott. **Transporter Chief Miles O'Brien:** Colm Meaney. **Nurse Ogawa:** Patti Yasutake. **Crew Member:** Thomas Velgrey. **Computer Voice:** Majel Barrett.
✦ *Dwight Schultz makes his third appearance as the phobia-afflicted Barclay, who this time suffers from a well-justified fear of transporters. The hapless Barclay must overcome his fear to save his own life and the lives of four missing* U.S.S. Yosemite *crew members. Watch for inventive special effects when a shapeless being bites Barclay just before he emerges from the transporter buffer.*

MAN OF THE PEOPLE

Week of 5 Oct. 1992, No. 229
Directed by: Winrich Kolbe
Written by: Frank Abatemarco
STARDATE: 46071.6
Deanna Troi is attracted to a Lumerian ambassador (Chip Lucia) while becoming increasingly hostile to the crew and demonstrates signs of rapid aging. **Jarth:** Rick Scarry. **Maylor:** Susan French. **Ensign Janeway:** Lucy Boryer. **Admiral Simons:** George D. Wallace. **Liva:** Stephanie Erb.
✦ *Not the first* Starfleet *officer to undergo rapid aging (see the classic episode* "The Deadly Years" *and ST:TNG's* "Unnatural Selection"*), Troi is also subjected to a number of disturbing personality changes, seducing men at random,*

raging with jealousy and assaulting people. In a chilling discovery, Ambassador Alkar is found responsible for Troi's deteriorating condition, having chosen her as the receptacle for his own negative emotions to free himself up to be the perfect diplomat – a condition he has repeatedly and remorselessly imposed on others. Deanna becomes the third crew member revived after death.
SHOW WATCH: *Worf leads the Mak'bahr, a Klingon meditation exercise.*

RELICS: *JAMES DOOHAN HAS A MEMORABLE GUEST APPEARANCE AS THE 147-YEAR-OLD SCOTTY*

RELICS

Week of 12 Oct. 1992, No. 230
Directed by: Alexander Singer
Written by: Ronald D. Moore
STARDATE: 46125.3
A veteran of the original *U.S.S. Enterprise*, Montgomery "Scotty" Scott (James Doohan), is discovered suspended in the transporter system of a 75-year-old wreck. However, the legendary *Starfleet* figure is dejected when it seems that he is no more than a relic on the *U.S.S. Enterprise-D*. **Ensign Rager:** Lanei Chapman. **Ensign Kane:** Erick Weiss. **Engineer Bartel:** Stacie Foster. **Waiter:** Ernie Mirich. **Computer Voice:** Majel Barrett.
✦ *A clever means to bring back a beloved character – the fourth so far – from the classic series. James Doohan does an entertaining turn as the 147-year-old Scotty trying to prove his usefulness in a society that's changed beyond recognition – which of course, given his resourcefulness, he does.*

BEST SCENE: *The holodeck's re-creation of the original Enterprise bridge – background beeps and all.*

BEST LINE: *Scotty to La Forge, "Geordi, I've spent my whole life tryin' to figure out crazy ways to do things. I'm tellin' ya – one engineer to another – I can do this."*

SCHISMS

Week of 19 Oct. 1992, No. 231
Directed by: Robert Wiemer
Written by: Brannon Braga
Story by: Jean Louise Matthias and Ron Wilkerson
STARDATE: 46154.2

When an alien energy source is discovered in a cargo bay, some members of the crew are shocked to discover they had temporarily vanished from the ship and had been used for medical experiments without remembering any of it. **Ensign Rager:** Lanei Chapman. **Mot:** Ken Thorley. **Lieut. Shipley:** Scott T. Trost. **Crewman:** Angelo McCabe. **Kaminer:** Angelina Fiordellisi. **Medical Technician:** John Nelson. **Computer Voice:** Majel Barrett.

✦ *Another just-in-the-nick-of-time solution by Geordi, who saves the crew and ship from the machinations of the antimatter aliens. Again, the holodeck is used to great effect to re-create the terrifying recollections of the four crew members – Riker, Worf, Geordi and Ensign Rager – who were painfully cut apart and examined by the unfriendly aliens.*

BEST SCENE: *Data reads a comedic poem dedicated to his cat, Spot.*

TRUE Q

Week of 26 Oct. 1992, No. 232
Directed by: Robert Scheerer
Written by: René Echevarria
Premise by: Matthew Corey
STARDATE: 46192.3

A young intern (Olivia D'abo) attracts the attention of Q when she shows signs of omnipotence. **Q:** John de Lancie. **Lote:** John P. Connolly.

✦ *In the sixth Q episode, the troublesome alien shows up to train the interning Amanda, who is as surprised as the crew to discover she is the orphan of two former members of the Q Continuum. Amanda's parents chose to leave the Continuum only to be killed by a freak tornado that struck their home in – are you ready, Dorothy? – Kansas! Under Q's guidance, Amanda* turns out to be a precocious student, as Riker – every alien's favourite boy toy – is quick to discover.

BEST SCENE: *The 24th-century wizard Q is at his arrogant best when he justifies the possible termination of Amanda, insisting to Capt. Picard that it just wouldn't do to have omnipotent beings running around the universe.*

RASCALS

Week of 2 Nov. 1992, No. 233
Directed by: Adam Nimoy
Written by: Allison Hock
Story by: Ward Botsford, Diana Dru Botsford and Michael Piller
STARDATE: 46235.7

Picard relinquishes his command when a transporter accident physically transforms him, along with Guinan, Ensign Ro and Keiko, into 12-year-olds. But when the Ferengi seize the *Enterprise*, Picard shows he can still lead. **Guinan:** Whoopi Goldberg. **Ensign Ro:** Michelle Forbes. **Keiko:** Rosalind Chao. **Berik:** Tracey Walter. **Morta:** Michael Snyder. **Alexander:** Brian Bonsall. **Young Picard:** David Tristan Birkin. **Young Guinan:** Isis Jones. **Young Keiko:** Caroline Junko King. **Lurin:** Mike Gomez. **O'Brien:** Colm Meaney. **Young Ro:** Megan Parlen. **Kid No. 1:** Morgan Nagler. **Molly:** Hana Hatae. **Computer Voice:** Majel Barrett.

✦ *Leonard Nimoy's son, Adam, directed this quirky reversal of the rapid-aging storyline. Watch for David Tristan Birkin – who shows up here as the 12-year-old Jean-Luc – as Picard's nephew René in the fourth season's "Family."*

SHOW WATCH: *Final ST:TNG appearance of Colm Meaney as Chief O'Brien and Rosalind Chao as O'Brien's wife, Keiko – both off to join the cast of DS9 whose debut would air the following January.*

A FISTFUL OF DATAS

Week of 9 Nov. 1992, No. 234
Directed by: Patrick Stewart
Written by: Robert Hewitt Wolfe and Brannon Braga
Story by: Robert Hewitt Wolfe
STARDATE: 46271.5

It's a deadly showdown in the holodeck when Worf (Michael Dorn) and son Alexander (Brian Bonsall) are trapped in a malfunctioning Wild West program and have to tackle a couple of gunslingers with Data's face and android abilities. **Annie:** Joy Garrett. **Bandito:** Jorge Cervera. **Eli Hollander:** John Pyper-Ferguson.

✦ *Patrick Stewart's third episode as director. Brent Spiner does a terrific job in five roles, playing nearly all the characters in Worf's holodeck melodrama. The fully functional android does a great comedic turn when transformed into a robotic-looking Miss Annie – who performs "her" best show in gratitude to Worf after the mighty Klingon warrior saves the day.*

THE QUALITY OF LIFE

Week of 16 Nov. 1992, No. 235
Directed by: Jonathan Frakes
Written by: Naren Shankar
STARDATE: 46307.2

Data risks the lives of Capt. Picard and Geordi when he prevents the use of machines known as "exocomps" in their rescue, believing the machines are alive and wouldn't survive the attempt. **Dr. Farallon:** Ellen Bry. **Transporter Chief Kelso:** J. Downing. **Computer Voice:** Majel Barrett.

✦ *Fifth episode directed by Jonathan Frakes. Chalk one up for the android when, once again, Data correctly realizes that the exocomps – like the Nanites of the third season's "Evolution" – are sentient beings, and he stubbornly refuses to send them into danger, even under threat of court-martial and with the captain's life at stake.*

BEST SCENE: *Picard, having escaped with his life thanks to the exocomps' decision to help, tells Data that his decision to fight for the exocomps's right to life was "the most human decision you've ever made."*

CHAIN OF COMMAND, PART I

Week of 14 Dec. 1992, No. 236
Directed by: Robert Scheerer
Written by: Ronald D. Moore
Story by: Frank Abatemarco
STARDATE: 46357.4

Picard resigns his command of the *Enterprise* to lead Worf and Dr. Crusher in an ultra-secret espionage mission against the Cardassians. Part one of two. **Capt. Jellico:** Ronny Cox. **Gul Lemec:** John Durbin. **Gul Madred:** David Warner. **Admiral Nechayev:** Natalija Nogulich. **Solok:** Lou Wagner.

♦ *Picard is assigned a kamikaze mission to determine whether the Cardassians are manufacturing a metagenic weapon – the biological equivalent of a neutron bomb – as Capt. Jellico assumes command of the* Enterprise *in a transition that is anything but smooth for Jellico, Riker and the entire crew. Meanwhile, Picard, an expert in the theta-band subspace waves required by the weapon (from his days in command of the U.S.S.* Stargazer*), leads a commando team consisting of himself, Worf and Dr. Crusher into the Cardassian installation on Celtris III, thought to be a metagenic production facility. The suspense mounts as the trio enters a Cardassian trap and Picard is captured (right). Part I ends as Picard,*

CHAIN OF COMMAND, PART I: *PICARD (PATRICK STEWART) IS TAKEN CAPTIVE BY THE CARDASSIANS.*

serial number SP-937-215, *prepares to be interrogated by his Cardassian captors.*

SHOW WATCH: *Troi dons a regulation* Starfleet *uniform at the request of Capt. Jellico. Actor David Warner made earlier appearances in "Star Trek V: The Final Frontier," and as Chancellor Gorkon of the Klingon Empire in "Star Trek VI: The Undiscovered Country."*

⟨⟩ CHAIN OF COMMAND, PART II

Week of 14 Dec. 1992, No. 237
Directed by: Les Landau
Written by: Frank Abatemarco
STARDATE: 46360.8
Conclusion. Picard's will is pushed to its limit when he is captured by the Cardassians and tortured by Gul Madred (David Warner). Meanwhile, the unpopular Capt. Jellico dismisses Riker and plans a first strike on the Cardassians. **Capt. Jellico:** Ronny Cox. **Gul Lemec:** John Durbin. **Jil Orra:** Heather Lauren Olson.
♦ *Powerful conclusion as Picard is brought to the brink of brainwashing by repeated torture. Patrick Stewart, who prepared for the demanding script by watching tapes provided by Amnesty International, gives a painfully accurate performance of a man punished again and*

again until he very nearly succumbs to his captors. Aboard the Enterprise, tension mounts as Data becomes acting first officer when Riker is relieved of his duties for challenging Jellico's judgment. In the end, of course, Jellico must ask for Riker's help in piloting the shuttle on a mission to plant mines on the Cardassian ships – the success of which leads to the Cardassians' withdrawal and Picard's release. Not a moment too soon for Picard who was close to believing his torturer's taunts, as the shaken captain confides to Troi in the episode's final scene. The episode's Cardassian storyline, with Cardassia's withdrawal from Bajoran space, provided a timely bridge to DS9, whose world première airs the following month.

SHIP IN A BOTTLE

Week of 25 Jan. 1993, No. 238
Directed by: Alexander Singer
Written by: René Echevarria
STARDATE: 46424.1
Professor Moriarty (Daniel Davis), a character in Data's Sherlock Holmes holodeck fantasy created to match the android wit for wit, shocks and bewilders the crew when the nasty one comes to life and steps into the real world. **Lieut. Barclay:** Dwight Schultz. **Countess:** Stephanie Beacham. **Gentleman:**

Clement von Franckenstein. **Computer Voice:** Majel Barrett.
♦ *A light-hearted break from the serious episodes of recent weeks. In Dwight Schultz's fourth appearance, Lieut. Barclay accidentally releases Prof. Moriarty from the holodeck program in which he was stored four years earlier ("Elementary, Dear Data"). Moriarty amazes himself and the entire crew when he appears to live and breathe outside the holodeck and, as before, seeks to gain control of the* Enterprise. *A neat mirror-within-a-mirror episode which blurs the line between reality and imagination.*
STAR WATCH: *Daniel Davis (The Nanny) makes a return appearance as Moriarty, and Stephanie Beacham (No Bananas star) turns up as his beloved Countess Regina Barthalomew.*

AQUIEL

Week of 1 Feb. 1993, No. 239
Directed by: Cliff Bole
Written by: Brannon Braga and Ronald D. Moore
Story by: Jeri Taylor
STARDATE: 46461.3
Geordi (LeVar Burton) falls in love with a *Starfleet* lieutenant who's suspected of murdering a fellow officer. **Lieut. Aquiel:** Renee Jones. **Torak:** Wayne Grace. **Morag:** Reg E. Cathey. **Computer Voice:** Majel Barrett.
♦ *Geordi finally falls for a woman who returns his interest, only to have her accused of murder, in an episode tied to a Klingon storyline. The loveless La Forge saves the day – and Aquiel's career – when he destroys the murderous alien masquerading as Aquiel's pet dog.*

FACE OF THE ENEMY

Week of 8 Feb. 1993, No. 240
Directed by: Gabrielle Beaumont
Written by: Naren Shankar
Story by: René Echevarria
STARDATE: 46519.1
Troi awakens to find herself on a Romulan warbird and looking like a Romulan. Turns out she's been conscripted into a plot to smuggle high-ranking Romulan defectors to the *Federation.* **N'Vek:** Scott MacDonald. **Toreth:** Carolyn Seymour. **DeSeve:** Barry Lynch. **Alien Captain:** Dennis Cockrum. **Pilot:** Robertson Dean. **Ensign McKnight:** Pamela Winslow.

◆ Another opportunity for a Starfleet officer – this time Troi, kidnapped for the second time – to go undercover as a Romulan, recalling Kirk's similar assignment in the classic series' "The Enterprise Incident." Marina Sirtis does an excellent job as the unwilling Troi, who has been surgically altered to become Maj. Rakal of the Tal Shiar (the Romulan intelligence) and who, when her cover is threatened, is forced to project command abilities or die. The episode provides an intriguing link to the covert diplomatic mission initiated by Ambassador Spock in the fifth season's two-part "Unification."

TAPESTRY
Week of 15 Feb. 1993, No. 241
Directed by: Les Landau
Written: Ronald D. Moore
STARDATE: Unknown
Picard, lying in limbo after being mortally wounded in an alien attack, is manipulated by Q (John de Lancie) into reliving a regrettable part of his life.
Corey: Ned Vaughn. **Marta:** J.C. Brandy. **Penny Muroc:** Rendé Rae Norman. **Nausicaan No. 1:** Clint Carmichael. **Maurice Picard:** Clive Church. **Young Picard:** Marcus Nash. **Computer Voice:** Majel Barrett.
◆ In his seventh episode, Q tempts Picard with a chance to undo his life's mistakes, taking him back to the moment when, as a 22-year-old ensign, he was stabbed through the heart by a Nausicaan in a bar fight. But Picard's refusal to be goaded a second time into the fight that

cost him his heart – replaced surgically by an artificial one – costs him his passion, his courage, his friends and his captain's bars. Realizing that he would rather die a courageous man than play it safe, Picard asks Q for one more chance to put things back the way they were and quickly finds himself impaled once again on the Nausicaan's blade. For once, Picard finds himself grateful to Q for showing him that the good and the bad of his past were essential to his growth. Picard is the fourth ST:TNG crew member to be resurrected from the dead.

BIRTHRIGHT, PART I
Week of 22 Feb. 1993, No. 242
Directed by: Winrich Kolbe
Written by: Brannon Braga
STARDATE: 46578.4
While on a layover on *Deep Space Nine*, Worf learns that his father is still alive and being held prisoner by the Romulans, and Data has a vision of his father/creator, Dr. Noonian Soong. Part one of two. **L'Kor:** Richard Herd. **Dr. Bashir:** Siddig El Fadil. **Shrek:** James Cromwell. **Ba'el:** Jennifer Gatti. **Gi'ral:** Christine Rose.
◆ In the first ST:TNG episode with a direct link to DS9, Data learns to dream, and Worf learns to combat his prejudices, as each begins a journey to find their fathers and their pasts. In Part 1, Data is the primary focus when, as the result of an accidental plasma shock, dream circuits – designed to be activated only when Data has reached a certain level of awareness – kick in early. As the

metaphorical bird of his dreams, Data is set free by his new knowledge, even as Worf is captured and held – along with 73 Klingon prisoners, survivors of the raid on Khitomer and their descendants – inside an unsuspected Romulan prisoner-of-war camp. Also in this episode, Worf begins to sport a more warrior-like ponytail. Data's new-found ability to dream – which allows him to meet his father for the second time – would be explored further in the seventh season's "Phantasms." **SHOW WATCH:** Siddig El Fadil, DS9's Dr. Bashir, has a brief guest appearance in an episode that marks the return of actor James Cromwell, who would be back in DS9's "Starship Down."

BIRTHRIGHT, PART II
Week of 1 March 1993, No. 243
Directed by: Dan Curry
Written by: René Echevarria
STARDATE: 46759.2
Conclusion. Worf (Michael Dorn) suffers a fate worse than death for Klingons – he is captured and imprisoned in a Romulan camp. Adding to his disgust, he finds Klingon prisoners living in peaceful coexistence with their captors. **Ba'el:** Jennifer Gatti. **Gi'ral:** Cristine Rose. **L'Kor:** Richard Herd. **Tokath:** Alan Scarfe. **Shrek:** James Cromwell. **Toq:** Sterling Macer Jr.
◆ In Part 2, the focus shifts to Worf, who learns that his father did in fact die at Khitomer, but the survivors of that raid – whose existence the Klingon High Council refused to acknowledge – have lived ever since as docile, peaceful prisoners of the Romulans. Worf's shock turns to disgust as he realizes that the children of the once-mighty warriors know nothing of their heritage. While plotting his escape, Worf begins to train the offspring in the ways of a Klingon, teaching them the Mok'bara – a meditation exercise that is at the basis of all Klingon fighting techniques – and telling them of Kahless, the greatest Klingon warrior. But even as he rouses the younger generation to challenge their fate and assert their freedom, Worf must also come to respect their parents' wish to remain as prisoners rather than return to the outside world, which would dishonour their families. Michael Dorn is superb as Worf struggles to come to terms with his father's past while leading the descendants of Khitomer to a free and more honourable

SHIP IN A BOTTLE: DANIEL DAVIS RETURNS AS MORIARTY IN DATA'S HOLODECK FANTASY GONE AWRY, WITH STEPHANIE BEACHAM AS THE COUNTESS

future – swearing the young Klingons to secrecy over the camp's existence, in honour of their parents' sacrifice. And again, Picard will demonstrate his loyalty and respect for Worf in keeping that secret. Later this season, in "Rightful Heir," Worf will come face to come with the legendary Kahless.

SHOW WATCH: *The first Klingon kiss between Worf and Ba'el.*

STAR WATCH: *Alan Scarfe, previously seen in the fourth season's "Data's Day," returns as the Romulan prison-camp commander, Tokath.*

⬡ STARSHIP MINE
Week of 29 March 1993, No. 244
Directed by: Cliff Bole
Written by: Morgan Gendel
STARDATE: 46682.4
The crew evacuates the *Enterprise* so it may be cleansed by a lethal baryon sweep, but Picard gets trapped aboard his ship and must face a group of terrorists alone. **Kelsey:** Marie Marshall. **Hutchinson:** David Spielberg. **Devor:** Tim Russ. **Orton:** Glenn Morshower. **Kiros:** Patricia Tallman. **Neil:** Tom Nibley. **Satler:** Tim deZarn. **Waiter:** Arlee Reed. **Pomet:** Alan Altshuld.

✦ *Another dynamic episode as Picard – returning to the* Enterprise *to fetch his riding gear – discovers the ship commandeered by political terrorists out to steal trilithium resin for use as a weapon. Trapped alone with the terrorists as the deadly baryon sweep gets under way, Picard – who passes himself off as Mot, the ship's second-rate barber – works to booby trap their every escape route, leaving only Ten-Forward as the final battlefield. Unable to negotiate with Kelsey, the terrorists' leader – who has betrayed her comrades and is now stealing the resin for its commercial value – Picard plants a final snare by removing the resin's control rod, and watches sadly as Kelsey's escaping ship explodes as a result. Many humourous moments early in the episode as Data attempts to learn the art of small talk by imitating the extremely dull Cmdr. Hutchinson.*

SHOW WATCH: *Tim Russ, better known as the Vulcan Tuvok, the third ST:TNG actor to be cast in Star Trek: Voyager, has a brief stint as the terrorist Devor. Russ (who earlier lost out to LeVar Burton for the role of Geordi La Forge) also*

appears as a Klingon in DS9's "Invasive Procedures," and as crew member of the U.S.S. Enterprise in the feature film "Star Trek Generations."

⬡ LESSONS
Week of 5 April 1993, No. 245
Directed by: Robert Wiemer
Written by: Ronald Wilkerson
and Jean Louise Matthias
STARDATE: 46693.1
Capt. Picard is torn when he falls in love with a woman under his command (Wendy Hughes) and must send her on a potentially deadly mission.

✦ *In an episode that provides a welcome change of pace and picks up the storyline started in the fifth season's "The Inner Light," Picard enters into a relationship with Lt.-Cmdr. Nella Daren, sharing with her his love of music – something he acquired on the planet Kataan – as well as his life there as Kamin. When Picard is called upon to send his new love on a life-threatening mission, the captain finds himself – for the first time – torn between his personal feelings and his duty, and sadly realizes that he cannot have one without risking the other.*

STAR WATCH: *Australian actor Wendy Hughes (Homicide: Life on the Street) is memorable as Nella Daren.*

⬡ THE CHASE
Week of 26 April 1993, No. 246
Directed by: Jonathan Frakes
Written by: Joe Menosky
Story by: Joe Menosky
and Ronald D. Moore
STARDATE: 46731.5
When Picard's old archeology professor is killed, a four-billion-year old genetic puzzle is discovered and the crew finds itself racing against the Cardassians, Klingons and Romulans to solve it. **Humanoid:** Salome Jens. **Capt. Nu'Daq:** John Cothran Jr. **Gul Ocett:** Linda Thorson. **Romulan Captain:** Maurice Roeves. **Prof. Galen:** Norman Lloyd.

✦ *Jonathan Frakes' sixth episode as director. A science-driven, action-packed episode reunites Picard with Galen (Norman Lloyd, known as Dr. Auschlander on St. Elsewhere) – his old archeology professor – and pits the Enterprise against the Cardassians, Klingons and Romulans in a chase to uncover Galen's monumental discovery,*

the nature of which adds credence to the notion first raised in the classic episode "The Paradise Syndrome" that the galaxy was genetically seeded by the same originating species.

STAR WATCH: *Linda Thorson (who, in the late 1960s, played Tara King on* The Avengers) *appears as the first female Cardassian, Gul Ocett.*

FRAME OF MIND
Week of 3 May 1993, No. 247
Directed by: James L. Conway
Written by: Brannon Braga
STARDATE: 46778.1
Riker (Jonathan Frakes) struggles to maintain his sanity as his perception of reality shifts between a play he is performing on the *Enterprise* and an alien mental asylum where it seems he is a patient. **Dr. Syrus:** David Selburg. **Mavek:** Gary Werntz. **Administrator:** Andrew Prine. **Inmate:** Susanna Thompson.

✦ *A tour-de-force performance by Jonathan Frakes when, on a covert mission, Riker is captured and subjected to neural torture.*

SUSPICIONS
Week of 10 May 1993, No. 248
Directed by: Cliff Bole
Written by: Joe Menosky
and Naren Shankar
STARDATE: 46830.1
Dr. Beverly Crusher (Gates McFadden) risks her life and career in order to clear the name of a murdered Ferengi scientist whose controversial invention might allow starships to enter a sun's corona. **Dr. Kurak:** Tricia O'Neil. **Dr. Jo'Bril:** James Horan. **Dr. T'Pan:** Joan Stuart Morris. **Dr. Reyga:** Peter Slutsker. **Dr. Christopher:** John S. Ragin. **Ogawa:** Patti Yasutake. **Guinan:** Whoopi Goldberg.

✦ *Gates McFadden is marvellous when Dr. Crusher – under threat of court-martial – performs an illegal autopsy, relying on her judgement and stubborn determination to prove her suspicions of murder. The use of a shield strong enough to prevent the* Enterprise *from melting inside a star would resurface in the seventh season's "Descent, Part II." Whoopi Goldberg also returns as Guinan, in only her third appearance this season.*

SHOW WATCH: *Tricia O'Neil, who played*

Capt. Rachel Garrett in the third season's "Yesterday's Enterprise," plays the Klingon scientist Kurak.

RIGHTFUL HEIR
Week of 17 May 1993, No. 249
Directed by: Winrich Kolbe
Written by: Ronald D. Moore
Story by: James Brooks
STARDATE: 46852.2
Worf visits the planet Boreth on a spiritual quest to summon a vision of Klingon's greatest warrior, Kahless. He finds his faith tested, however, when the real Kahless returns from the dead to lead the Empire. **Koroth:** Alan Oppenheimer. **Gowron:** Robert O'Reilly. **Torin:** Norman Snow. **Divok:** Charles Esten. **Kahless:** Kevin Conway.
✦ *Another powerful episode centering on Worf's quest to explore his Klingon spirituality, a theme first broached in the two-part "Birthright." Worf's faith is tested when he doubts, then believes, then doubts again that Kahless, the legendary Klingon warrior and true leader of the Klingon Empire, has actually returned. Discovering that this Kahless is in fact a clone of the original, Worf finally appreciates that it's the belief in the teachings of Kahless that really matters, rather than in Kahless himself. Resolved to avert a new civil war, Worf forces Gowron to accept Kahless as spiritual leader and figure-head emperor, while leaving the secular power in the hands of Gowron and the High Council. Kahless, whose story was told in "Birthright, Part II," was first seen in the classic Star Trek episode "The Savage Curtain" and would later return in Deep Space Nine's "The Sword of Kahless."*

SECOND CHANCES
Week of 24 May 1993, No. 250
Directed by: LeVar Burton
Written by: René Echevarria
Story by: Michael A. Medlock
STARDATE: 46915.2
Riker (Jonathan Frakes) returns to a mission site from which he barely escaped eight years earlier to discover that a transporter accident had created an exact duplicate of himself, and the alternate Riker is still in love with Troi. **Ensign Palmer:** Dr. Mae Jemison.

✦ *In LeVar Burton's first episode as director, Jonathan Frakes does double duty as the Riker who serves aboard the Enterprise and the Will Thomas Riker who served eight years earlier on the U.S.S. Potemkin. The second Riker, created by a pair of transporter beams used to break through Nervala IV's distortion field, is as real as the first, but different in nature, and still in love with Deanna. For the second time, a Will Riker proposes to Deanna, but this time Troi turns him down – realizing that this Riker, like the first, will renege on his promise. A neat twist to the Riker-Troi romance, as Thomas Riker, still a lieutenant, leaves to take up his new posting aboard the U.S.S. Gandhi. Thomas Riker would return in DS9's "Defiant."*
STAR WATCH: *Dr. Mae Jemison – the first female African-American astronaut in space – has a cameo as Ensign Palmer. Jemison was inspired at an early age by original-series actor Nichelle Nichols.*

SECOND CHANCES: FORMER ASTRONAUT DR. MAE JEMISON IN A CAMEO AS ENSIGN PALMER.

TIMESCAPE
Week of 14 June 1993, No. 251
Directed by: Adam Nimoy
Written by: Brannon Braga
STARDATE: 46944.2
Picard, Troi, Data and Geordi are faced with a baffling mystery when they return from a Federation conference to find the U.S.S. Enterprise frozen in time – along with a Romulan Warbird which is firing a disruptor beam at the starship. **Romulan/Alien:** Michael Bofshever.
✦ *A second episode directed by Adam Nimoy, son of Leonard, with a suspenseful, clever plot that has Picard and associates seeking to control the space-time continuum by first moving time backward and then forward to save the Enterprise from a deadly engine core breach.*

DESCENT, PART I
Week of 21 June 1993, No. 252
Directed by: Alexander Singer
Written by: Ronald D. Moore
Story by: Jeri Taylor
STARDATE: 46982.1
The Borg returns with a new sense of individuality, and Data (Brent Spiner) is mystified when he experiences pleasure after killing one of them, furthering his quest to understand human emotions. Part one of two. **Professor Stephen Hawking:** Himself. **Sir Isaac Newton:** John Neville. **Albert Einstein:** Jim Norton. **Crosis:** Brian J. Cousins. **Admiral Nechayev:** Natalija Nogulich.
✦ *The second season-ender to feature the Borg. Capt. Picard must face the consequences of his earlier decision to return Hugh to the collective ("I, Borg"). A startling shift toward "individual" personalities seems to have occurred and, in an even more surprising development, Data kills out of anger, a feeling – like all other emotions – thought impossible for his android circuitry. Taunted by a Borg prisoner, Data confirms the pleasure he felt in killing and admits that he would kill even Geordi if it meant he could experience that feeling once again. With that, Data frees the Borg, and together they head for a planet that may have fallen to the collective. In pursuit, Picard leads an Away Team to the planet and straight into a Borg ambush – led not by Hugh, as Picard had feared, but by Lore, Data's evil twin brother. There he is joined by Data, who chillingly promises that "The sons of Soong have joined together – and together, we will destroy the Federation." On that gut-twisting line, the season comes to an end.*
STAR WATCH: *The opening scene features world-renowned physicist Stephen Hawking as himself – as the fourth in a holodeck-created poker game with Sir Isaac Newton, Albert Einstein and Data. Renowned English stage actor John Neville ("Oscar Wilde," "A Study in Terror") plays Sir Isaac Newton.* ✧

SEVENTH SEASON

As the seventh season began, family re-emerged as *Star Trek: The Next Generation's* dominant theme, with several earlier (fourth-season) storylines brought full circle. The focus on father-child relationships in earlier episodes would switch in the seventh season as crew members – particularly Geordi, Data and Deanna – sought to define their relationships with their mothers. On the romantic front, two simmering relationships – Picard and Crusher, Troi and Worf – were at last reignited. The year would also be marked by a number of clever science-driven episodes, one of them ("Genesis") allowing Gates McFadden to make her directorial debut. But all good things must come to an end – as the title of the final TV episode would underscore. When Paramount confirmed in early November that the seventh season would be the last, the series – that was always about so much more than phasers and warp speed – began to tie up loose ends. And while setting the stage for the fourth TV series – *Star Trek: Voyager* – *Star Trek: The Next Generation* finished its run in the same position in which it started: Number one.

DESCENT, PART II
Week of 20 Sept. 1993, No. 253
Directed by: Alexander Singer
Written by: René Echevarria
STARDATE: 47025.4
Conclusion. After deserting the *U.S.S. Enterprise-D* to join his brother, Lore, at the helm of a Borg ship, Data captures Capt. Picard, Deanna Troi and Geordi La Forge and holds them prisoner, enjoying the evil emotions fed to him by his brother. **Hugh:** Jonathan Del Arco. **Taitt:** Alex Datcher. **Barnaby:** James Horan. **Crosis:** Brian J. Cousins.
♦ *With Lore in control of both Data and the Borg, the sons of Soong begin to make good their threat, as the Enterprise, under Dr. Crusher's command, makes its escape. Back on the planet, Data – who has learned to feel anger and hate – subjects Geordi to dangerous neurological experiments at Lore's urging. Realizing that Lore has dismantled Data's ethical program, Geordi, Picard and Troi struggle to reactivate it by means of a crudely rigged kedion pulse. As the tension mounts, the action shifts to Riker and Worf, who are captured by a second group of Borg, led by the now-bitter Hugh. Meanwhile, using only the ship's metaphasic shields for protection, Beverly orders the Enterprise to fly directly into the sun's corona as the crew devises a dangerous plan to destroy the Borg ship by creating a solar fusion eruption. With Geordi's kedion pulse beginning to take effect, Lore orders his brother to prove his loyalty by killing Picard. Data refuses, and just as Lore turns to kill his twin, Hugh – who has led Riker and Worf to the Borg compound out of friendship for Geordi – steps forward to knock the* weapon from Lore's hand. As the Borg's sixth and final ST:TNG episode concludes, Data is forced to fire on the escaping Lore, whom he then deactivates, while Hugh becomes the Borg group's new leader. Watch for terrific special effects as the Enterprise blows the Borg ship away with a refractive shot into the sun.

LIAISONS
Week of 27 Sept. 1993, No. 254
Directed by: Cliff Bole
Written by: Jeanne Carrigan Fauci and Lisa Rich
Story by: Roger Eschbacher and Jaq Greenspon
STARDATE: Unknown
During a cultural exchange program, two Lyaaran ambassadors visit the *Enterprise* while Picard journeys to Iyar. Picard's shuttlecraft crashes on an unknown planet and he is rescued by a woman (Barbara Williams) who crashed there several years earlier. **Voval:** Eric Pierpoint. **Loquel:** Paul Eiding. **Byleth:** Michael Harris.
♦ *Worf learns a valuable lesson in diplomacy, and Capt. Picard teaches the notion of love to Anna, the apparent sole survivor of a Terellian cargo freighter crash seven years earlier – though she is not what she appears.*

INTERFACE
Week of 4 Oct. 1993, No. 255
Directed by: Robert Wiemer
Written by: Joe Menosky
STARDATE: 47215.5
Geordi La Forge learns that his mother (Madge Sinclair) has been reported missing, but believes that he could find her using an experimental interfacing probe, and defies Picard's direct orders by attempting to save her. **Admiral Holt:** Warren Munson. **Dr. La Forge:** Ben Vereen.
♦ *LeVar Burton shines in this episode as Geordi risks his life and career defying both his father and his captain in a desperate search for his mother, Capt. Silva La Forge, whose ship, the U.S.S. Hera, has disappeared without a trace. Using an interface unit, a type of virtual reality device, Geordi appears to find his mother aboard the U.S.S. Raman, a science vessel trapped inside the turbulent atmosphere of an unusually gaseous planet. Though shocked to discover an alien masquerading as Silva La Forge, Geordi makes a courageous decision to risk his life to save the life forms who will die if not returned to the planet's lower atmosphere. Geordi is revived from his life-threatening interface to face an angry Picard, and the episode concludes as Geordi realizes that his experience with his "alien" mother actually helped him say goodbye.*
STAR WATCH: *At the urging of LeVar Burton, Star Trek fan Ben Vereen took a brief sabbatical from his then Broadway show to tape a guest stint as Geordi's father.*

GAMBIT, PART I
Week of 11 Oct. 1993, No. 256
Directed by: Peter Lauritson
Written by: Naren Shankar
Story by: Christopher Hatton and Naren Shankar
STARDATE: 47135.2
After he's kidnapped, Riker (Jonathan Frakes) is shocked to find the missing-and-presumed-dead Picard (Patrick Stewart) among the crew of a mercenary ship which has been looting archeological sites. Part one of two. **Baran:** Richard Lynch. **Tallera:** Robin Curtis. **Vekor:** Caitlin Brown. **Narik:** Cameron Thor. **Yranac:** Alan Altshuld. **Admiral Chekote:** Bruce Gray.
♦ *In this quick-paced two-part adventure, Picard's interest in archeology leads to his fifth abduction, this time by mercenaries searching for a number of mysterious and highly dangerous artifacts.*
SHOW WATCH: *Robin Curtis, who earlier appeared as Lieut. Saavik in "Star Trek IV: The Voyage Home," turns up in this episode as the Romulan Tallera.*

GAMBIT, PART II

Week of 18 Oct. 1993, No. 257
Directed by: Alexander Singer
Written by: Ronald D. Moore
Story by: Naren Shankar
STARDATE: 47160.1

Conclusion. Picard and Riker become an integral part of the mercenary crew, and secretly work to undermine Baran's leadership while trying to determine the real reason behind the archeological looting. **Baran:** Richard Lynch. **Tallera:** Robin Curtis. **Vekor:** Caitlin Brown. **Narik:** Cameron Thor. **Koral:** James Worthy. **Ensign Giusti:** Sabrina LeBeauf.

✦ *Intrigue and conspiracy abound as the search for the final artifact – believed to be Romulan – leads the mercenaries to rendezvous with a Klingon transport ship – resulting in a frantic pursuit back to the Enterprise. The chase becomes a race to the finish to prevent disaster when the artifacts turn out to be Vulcan, fragments of the mythical Stone of Gol – a psionic resonator that, when reassembled, has the power to eliminate the entire Vulcan council in a single thought.*

STAR WATCH: *At six feet nine inches, American basketball star James Worthy (Los Angeles Lakers) is undoubtedly the tallest Klingon roaming the galaxy.*

PHANTASMS

Week of 25 Oct. 1993, No. 258
Directed by: Patrick Stewart
Written by: Brannon Braga
STARDATE: 47225.7

Data (Brent Spiner) tests his new dream program and is subsequently plagued by bizarre nightmares which dangerously affect his behaviour and endanger his fellow crew, but provide clues to other strange events on board the *Starship Enterprise.* **Ensign Tyler:** Gina Ravarra. **Sigmund Freud:** Bernard Kates. **Admiral Nakamura**: Clyde Kusatsu. **Workman:** David L. Crowley.

✦ *Patrick Stewart's fourth episode as director. As Data pursues the dream state he experienced in "Birthright, Part I," symbolic metaphors replace reality when the android can't stop dreaming about violent images. Watch for great special effects in Data's dream sequences as Deanna's shoulder gets sliced up like a piece of cake and the android reaches into his own stomach to answer a ringing phone.*

DARK PAGE

Week of 1 Nov. 1993, No. 259
Directed by: Les Landau
Written by: Hilary J. Bader
STARDATE: 47254.1

Lwaxana Troi (Majel Barrett) collapses and Counsellor Deanna Troi is forced to explore the darkest regions of her mother's psyche to determine what is killing her. **Maques:** Norman Large. **Hedril:** Kirsten Dunst. **Ian Andrew Troi:** Amick Byram. **Kestra Troi:** Andreana Weiner.

✦ *In her sixth appearance, Majel Barrett delivers an intensely dramatic performance as Lwaxana Troi, who, suffering from repressed memory syndrome, collapses into a coma. Aided by Maques, one of the telepathic Cairn, Deanna enters her mother's mind and is confronted by a series of barriers sent by Lwaxana to prevent her daughter from going any further – including the image of her dead father, who pleads with her to stay with him but whose urging Deanna tearfully resists. On a second penetration into her mother's mind, Troi is shocked to encounter Kestra – the sister she never knew she had, whose accidental drowning at age 7 has been a repressed memory for Lwaxana. One of ST:TNG's saddest episodes, as Deanna must fight to save her mother's life.*

STAR WATCH: *Kirsten Dunst ("Little Women," "Interview with a Vampire"), with Majel Barrett, turns up here as Hedril, a Cairn girl.*

ATTACHED

Week of 8 Nov. 1993, No. 260
Directed by: Jonathan Frakes
Written by: Nicholas Sagan
STARDATE: 47304.2

While on a diplomatic mission, Picard and Dr. Beverly Crusher are forced to share their true feelings for each other when they are imprisoned and linked together with a telepathic shackling device. **Mauric:** Robin Gammell. **Lorin:** Lenore Kasdorf.

✦ *The seventh episode directed by Jonathan Frakes. Forced together by telepathic link, Picard and Crusher finally explore the long-simmering attraction between them. After the captain explains that his love for Beverly was the real reason he did not want her assigned to the Enterprise seven years earlier, Picard suggests they pursue their relationship. This time, it's Beverly's turn to admit she's not ready yet. The episode was written by Nicholas Sagan, son of renowned physicist Carl Sagan.*

DARK PAGE: MAJEL BARRETT AS EMPATH LWAXANA TROI DELIVERS AN INTENSELY DRAMATIC PERFORMANCE SPARKED BY THE ENCOUNTER WITH THE CAIRN GIRL HEDRIL (PLAYED BY KIRSTEN DUNST).

FORCE OF NATURE

Week of 15 Nov. 1993, No. 261
Directed by: Robert Lederman
Written by: Naren Shankar
STARDATE: 47310.2

The *Enterprise* encounters a couple of unlikely terrorists – a brother and sister – who have been disabling starships in order to draw attention to their claim that warp travel is destroying their region of space. **Dr. Rabal:** Michael Corbett. **Dr. Serova:** Margaret Reed. **DaiMon Prak:** Lee Arenberg.

✦ *An insightful story-line on the potential of advanced technologies to damage the environment. Picard and Geordi gradually realize that by exploring the universe they love, they may have inadvertently been contributing to its destruction. Issuing a new directive, the Federation*

Council agrees to limit all Federation vessels to a speed of warp 5, except in emergency situations.

SHOW WATCH: *Lee Arenberg would return as Ferengi DaiMon Bok later in the seventh season.*

INHERITANCE

Week of 22 Nov. 1993, No. 262
Directed by: Robert Scheerer
Written by: Dan Koeppel
and René Echevarria
Story by: Dan Koepel
STARDATE: 47410.2

Data is troubled when he meets a brilliant scientist (Fionnula Flanagan) who claims to be Noonian Soong's ex-wife, and therefore Data's mother. **Pran:** William Lithgow.

✦ *In the third episode this season to deal with the mother of a crew member, Data gets to complete his family circle with the appearance of Juliana Tainer, remarried since her divorce from Data's father/creator, Noonian Soong. Data learns he was deactivated and intentionally left behind on Omicron Theta because Juliana feared he would become evil like Lore – which prompts him to wonder whether Juliana would have abandoned him had he been her biological child. But when he discovers that Juliana is also an android – created after the Crystalline Entity killed the real Juliana – Data learns a lesson in compassion as the pleading image of Dr. Soong begs him not to tell Juliana the truth about her android self.*

SHOW WATCH: *Actor Fionnula Flanagan*

would return in the Star Trek: Deep Space Nine *episode "Dax."*

PARALLELS

Week of 29 Nov. 1993, No. 263
Directed by: Robert Wiemer
Written by: Brannon Braga
STARDATE: 47391.2

Worf (Michael Dorn) returns from a Klingon warrior competition to find himself shifting into multiple realities – including a marriage to Troi. **Ogawa:** Patti Yasutake. **Gul Nador:** Mark Bramhall. **Wesley:** Wil Wheaton.

✦ *Wil Wheaton's third guest appearance since leaving the regular cast in the fourth season. This clever episode brings back the parallel universe theme, this time with Worf as the very confused protagonist, who – while he unknowingly jumps from one universe into the next – hears Troi tell him that she's his wife and the mother of his two children. The episode features terrific special effects as Worf, attempting to return to his rightful universe by flying his shuttlecraft through a time rift in space, encounters dozens of other Worfs doing the same thing, and thousands of Enterprises.*

MOST UNSETTLING SCENE: *A desperate Riker begs not to be sent back to his universe, which has been overtaken by the Borg, and decides instead to destroy his ship.*

THE PEGASUS

Week of 10 Jan. 1994, No. 264
Directed by: LeVar Burton
Written by: Ronald D. Moore
STARDATE: 47457.1

Cmdr. Riker is torn when his former captain (Terry O'Quinn), now an admiral, orders him to not to tell Picard the true nature of a dangerous mission to salvage their old ship – a mission which could destroy the *Federation*'s treaty with the Romulans. **Admiral Blackwell:** Nancy Vawter.

✦ *A high-tension episode, LeVar Burton's second as director. Jonathan Frakes gives another terrific performance as Riker is torn between his loyalty to his first captain, now Admiral Pressman (Terry O'Quinn), and Picard. Twelve years earlier, the U.S.S. Pegasus – Riker's first assignment after leaving Starfleet Academy – was lost with most of its crew, the result of Pressman's deployment of an experimen-*

tal device. When that turns out to be a prototype for a cloaking device that allows ships to travel through solid rock – a technology banned by a Federation treaty – Picard learns from Riker that its use aboard the Pegasus led to mutiny by the crew and disaster for the ship.

BEST SCENE: *Having been sealed into an asteroid by the Romulans – who are also searching for the prototype – the Enterprise uses the banned device to phase through the asteroid and escape, much to the surprise of the Romulan Warbird waiting on the other side.*

HOMEWARD

Week of 17 Jan. 1994, No. 265
Directed by: Alexander Singer
Written by: Naren Shankar
Story by: Spike Steingasser
STARDATE: 47423.9

Worf clashes with his adoptive brother, Nikolai Rozhenko (Paul Sorvino), who violates the Prime Directive by rescuing a primitive alien society whose planet is on the verge of dying. **Dobara:** Penny Johnson. **Vorin:** Brian Markinson. **Kateras:** Edward Penn.

✦ *Another fine episode focussing on the Prime Directive as the Enterprise responds to a distress call from Nikolai Rozhenko (Paul Sorvino, in a terrific guest appearance), Worf's adopted human brother and a cultural observer on Boraal II. The episode provides an interesting commentary on loyalty to one's family as Worf discovers that Nikolai is not only trying to save the Boraalan people but also the Boraalan mother of his unborn child.*

SHOW WATCH: *Michael Dorn appears in this episode without his Klingon make-up as Worf is disguised as a Boraalan.*

SUB ROSA

Week of 31 Jan. 1994, No. 266
Directed by: Jonathan Frakes
Written by: Brannon Braga
Story by: Jeri Taylor
STARDATE: Unknown

After attending her grandmother's funeral, Dr. Crusher is seduced by a ghost (Duncan Regehr) who has romanced the women of her family for hundreds of years. **Maturin:** Michael Keenan. **Ned Quint:** Shay Duffin.

✦ *This haunting story – Jonathan Frakes' eighth episode as director – explores*

Sub Rosa: Dr. Crusher (Gates McFadden) gets more than she bargained for when she returns to Caldos IV for the funeral of her maternal grandmother.

Beverly's background and family history as she travels to Caldos IV to attend the funeral of her maternal grandmother, Felisa Howard. There she finds love and passion with Ronin, an apparent ghost who's loved the women in Beverly's family for more than 800 years. But as Crusher resigns her Enterprise *post, she discovers that Ronin is, in fact, an anaphasic life form that has been using the women in her family to stay alive. Gates McFadden delivers a splendid portrayal of a woman in the agonizing position of having to kill her lover when she realizes he means to kill her crew-mates.*

STAR WATCH: *Duncan Regehr would return as the Bajoran leader Shakaar in DS9's third-season episode "Shakaar," then reprise the role in DS9's fourth-season episode "Crossfire."*

LOWER DECKS
Week of 7 Feb. 1994, No. 267
Directed by: Gabrielle Beaumont
Written by: René Echevarria
Story by: Ronald Wilkerson and Jean Louise Matthias
STARDATE: 47566.7
Four young officers, one of whom was involved in a *Starfleet* Academy cover-up three years earlier, are struggling to prove themselves during an evaluation process when they suddenly find themselves involved in a top-secret and extremely dangerous mission. **Sam Lavelle:** Dan Gauthier. **Sito Jaxa:** Shannon Fill. **Taurik:** Alexander Enberg. **Ben:** Bruce Beatty. **Ogawa:** Patti Yasutake. **Joret:** Don Reilly.
✦ *An intriguing episode that offers a snapshot of what life as a young officer must have been like for Picard or Riker. And Worf must deal with the death of Sito, the young officer he had recently taken under his wing – and who had been involved in the cadet coverup of Wesley Crusher's* Starfleet Academy *flight team in the fifth season's "The First Duty."*

THINE OWN SELF
Week of 14 Feb. 1994, No. 268
Directed by: Winrich Kolbe
Written by: Ronald D. Moore
Story by: Christopher Halton
STARDATE: 47611.2
Suffering from amnesia, Data finds himself stranded on a primitive planet where the inhabitants identify him as the source of a strange plague. Meanwhile, back on the *Enterprise*, Counsellor Deanna Troi takes the Bridge Officer's test. **Talur:** Ronnie Claire Edwards. **Garvin:** Michael Rothhaar. **Gia:** Kimberly Cullum. **Skoran:** Michael G. Hagerty.
✦ *Data learns the meaning of friendship – as well as its power to overcome ignorance and fear – when, in a state of amnesia, he is befriended by a young girl and her father over the objections and threats of the other villagers. Data risks his life to save them all from the radiation poisoning he inadvertently caused. It's an emotional episode for cast and audience alike. Meanwhile, Deanna Troi faces her own test of strength when, to pass the bridge officers' test, she must knowingly send a crew member to his death.*

MASKS
Week of 21 Feb. 1994, No. 269
Directed by: Robert Wiemer
Written by: Joe Menosky
STARDATE: 47615.2
When an alien archive is discovered, Data becomes possessed by several different personalities while the *Starship Enterprise* is transformed into an ancient temple.
✦ *In another extraordinary performance, Brent Spiner plays all of the alien personalities discovered in the ancient archive, as Data develops the android equivalent of multiple-personality syndrome.*

EYE OF THE BEHOLDER
Week of 28 Feb. 1994, No. 270
Directed by: Cliff Bole
Written by: René Echevarria
Story by: Brannon Braga
STARDATE: 47622.1
Troi and Worf (Marina Sirtis, Michael Dorn) find themselves becoming romantically involved while investigating the mysterious suicide of a crew member. **Lieut. Walter Pierce:** Mark Rolston. **Lieut. Nara:** Nancy Harewood. **Lieut. Kwan:** Tim Lounibos. **Ensign Calloway:** Johanna McCloy.
✦ *High drama: suicide, then murder and back to suicide. Troi and Worf conduct an investigation into events that transpired eight years earlier during the construction of the* Enterprise *at the Utopia Planitia Fleet Yards, in orbit around the planet Mars. The episode allows Troi to explore her attraction to Worf that began in the fifth season's "New Ground."*

GENESIS
Week of 21 March 1994, No. 271
Directed by: Gates McFadden
Written by: Brannon Braga
STARDATE: 47653.2
Picard and Data (Patrick Stewart, Brent Spiner) return to the *Enterprise* after a routine mission, only to find the ship drifting in space while the crew seems to be de-evolving – Worf into a primal beast, Troi into a reptile and Riker into a primitive man. **Ogawa:** Patti Yasutake. **Barclay:** Dwight Schultz.
✦ *Gates McFadden's directorial debut marks Dwight Schultz's fifth guest appearance as Lieut. Barclay. And if ever there were an episode to make Trekkers wonder how Starfleet's finest could possibly get out*

of this one, this is it. Make-up is used to great effect to turn Deanna into an amphibian, Riker into a prehistoric man, Worf into an early Klingon and Barclay into a half-man, half-spider (pictured below). As Data races to find a cure to the virus that is causing the crew to de-evolve, Picard – absent from the Enterprise when the virus first took hold – begins to feel unfamiliar pangs of fear and panic as he, too, starts to de-evolve, leading to an extraordinary scene as the captain is chased through the bowels of the Enterprise by a venom-spitting Worf. Fast action, eerie effects and a rather neat conclusion (thanks to a clue left by Spot, Data's pregnant cat) as the virus is traced back to a synthetic T-cell given to hypochondriac Barclay, for whom the disease – Barclay's Protomorphosis Syndrome – is then named.

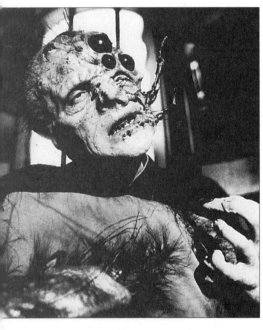

GENESIS: *DWIGHT SCHULTZ AS BARCLAY DE-EVOLVING INTO A HALF-MAN, HALF-SPIDER.*

JOURNEY'S END

Week of 28 March 1994, No. 272
Directed by: Corey Allen
Written by: Ronald D. Moore
Premise by: Shawn Piller
and Antonio Napoli
STARDATE: 47751.2
After the Cardassians and the *Federation* reach a settlement, Picard is ordered to remove a colony of native Americans from an annexed planet using any means necessary, but Wesley (Wil Wheaton) urges the natives to resist efforts to displace them. **Lakanta:** Tom Jackson.

Admiral Necheyev: Natalija Nogulich.
Anthwarta: Ned Romero. **Wakasa:** George Aguilar. **Gul Evek:** Richard Poe.
Traveler: Eric Menyuk. **Lieut. Jack Crusher:** Jack Wert.

✦ *Wil Wheaton returns in his fourth guest appearance as Wesley, unhappy at the Academy, stumbles onto his true destiny, as revealed by the Traveller. Meanwhile, Picard is challenged to reverse a stain of blood worn by his family for 23 generations. Watch for return appearances by Eric Menyuk as the Traveller and Doug Wert as Jack Crusher. A Native American character, Cmdr. Chakotay (Robert Beltran), would be reintroduced with the debut of Star Trek: Voyager in January 1995.*

STAR WATCH: *Tom Jackson (Billy Two-feathers in the PBS children's show* Shining Time Station, *which featured Ringo Starr) is terrific as Lakanta.*

FIRSTBORN

Week of 25 April 1994, No. 273
Directed by: Jonathan West
Written by: Christopher Halton and Ronald D. Moore
Story by: Mark Kalbfeld
STARDATE: 47779.4
The time comes for Alexander (Brian Bonsall) to undergo his First Rite of Ascension, but his lack of interest in the Klingon warrior heritage troubles Worf (Michael Dorn). **Lursa:** Barbara March.
B'Etor: Gwynyth Walsh. **Molor:** John Kenton Shull. **K'Mtar:** James Sloyan.
Quark: Armin Shimerman.

✦ *Worf's family storyline continues. Armin Shimerman makes a brief appearance as Quark, his third and best-known Ferengi role, as the Enterprise contacts Deep Space Nine.*

SHOW WATCH: *James Sloyan (who played Romulan Admiral Jarok in the third season's "The Defector") shows up here as the Klingon K'Mtar – who turns out to be none other than a grown-up Alexander, travelling from the future to save his father, Worf, from murder. Also, listen for mention of the compound magnesite, the substance used by Capt. Kirk to generate light in the classic-series' episode "Friday's Child."*

FEDERATION FACTOID: *We learn that Lursa is pregnant – but never discover if she gives birth prior to her demise in "Star Trek Generations."*

BLOODLINES

Week of 2 May 1994, No. 274
Directed by: Les Landau
Written by: Nicholas Sagan
STARDATE: 47829.1
Picard sets the *Enterprise* on a course for Camor Five to save his recently discovered son (Ken Olandt) from DaiMon Bok, a renegade Ferengi with an old grievance against Picard. **Birta:** Peter Slutsker.
DaiMon Bok: Lee Arenberg.

✦ *Tampering with evidence as he did in the first season's "The Battle," DaiMon Bok returns to exact vengeance on Picard for the death of Bok's son years earlier at the Battle of Maxia. Bok's plans go awry when, having resequenced Jason Vigo's DNA to match Picard's, his duplicity is discovered and (for the second time) his Ferengi shipmates turn against him.*

EMERGENCE

Week of 9 May 1994, No. 275
Directed by: Cliff Bole
Written by: Joe Menosky
Story by: Brannon Braga
STARDATE: 47869.2
A string of unexplained malfunctions in the *Enterprise*'s systems leads the crew to believe the ship may be developing its own intelligence – and creating a new life form at the same time. **Conductor:** David Huddleston. **Hitman:** Vinny Argiro. **Engineer:** Thomas Kopache.
Hayseed: Arlee Reed.

✦ *The holodeck is put to clever use in an imaginative episode in which the U.S.S. Enterprise gives birth to a new life form.*

PREEMPTIVE STRIKE

Week of 16 May 1994, No. 276
Directed by: Patrick Stewart
Written by: René Echevarria
Story by: Naren Shankar
STARDATE: 47941.7
Ro Laren (Michelle Forbes) poses as a *Starfleet* deserter to infiltrate and trap the vigilante group known as the Maquis, but finds her orders difficult to carry out as she becomes increasingly sympathetic to the group's cause. **Gul Evek:** Richard Poe. **Kalita:** Shannon Cochran. **Macias:** John Franklin-Robbins. **Santos:** William Thomas Jr.

✦ *Fifth episode directed by Patrick Stewart. Michelle Forbes makes her eighth appearance as Ro Laren, who returns to the Enterprise after completing*

Starfleet's *Advanced Tactical Training,* only to be assigned to join the Maquis as an undercover operative. But as the Bajoran begins to sympathize with the vigilantes' cause, Ro Laren is forced to choose between them and her loyalty to Picard and the Federation. The Maquis, introduced earlier this season in the two-part DS9 episode of the same name, would return to play a prominent role in Star Trek: Voyager.

ALL GOOD THINGS...
Week of 23 May 1994, No. 277
Directed by: Winrich Kolbe
Written by: Brannon Braga and Ronald D. Moore
STARDATE: 47988.0

Picard's arch-nemesis Q (John de Lancie) returns to put the captain on trial for the crimes of mankind. **Tasha Yar:** Denise Crosby. **O'Brien:** Colm Meaney.
✦ In the two-hour series finale, Q, in his eighth ST:TNG appearance, is back where he started – putting Picard on trial, as he did seven years earlier, and taking the captain on a quantum leap through the past, present and 25 years

ALL GOOD THINGS: 25 YEARS IN THE FUTURE, GEORDI (LEVAR BURTON), PICARD (PATRICK STEWART), CRUSHER (GATES MCFADDEN) AND DATA (BRENT SPINER) REUNITE TO SAVE EARTH FROM ANNIHILATION.

into the future – where Picard, having married and divorced Dr. Crusher, is now a retired farmer living on his family's vineyard in France; Data has become a professor at Cambridge; Worf is a high-ranking member of the Klingon council; and Riker and Crusher both captain their own starships. Familiar faces (including those of Denise Crosby and Colm Meaney reprising their early ST:TNG roles) add an element of history to this episode that brings closure to the Enterprise-D's very first encounter. A Hugo Science Fiction Award-winner for Best Dramatic Presentation, the finale repeats as two one-hour segments (numbers 277 and 278).

STAR TREK GENERATIONS
Released: Nov. 18, 1994
Directed by: David Carson
Screenplay by: Ronald D. Moore and Brannon Braga
STARDATE: 48632.4

When a mad scientist, Dr. Tolian Soran (Malcolm McDowell), alters the path of a spatial energy ribbon, causing stellar obliteration, Capt. Jean-Luc Picard (Patrick Stewart) enlists the aid of a legendary Starfleet officer – none other than Capt. James T. Kirk (William Shatner). **Scotty:** James Doohan. **Chekov:** Walter Koenig. **Lursa:** Barbara March. **B'Etor:** Gwynyth Walsh. **Capt. Harriman:** Alan Ruck. **1701-B Lieut.:** Tim Russ.
✦ "Star Trek Generations" was first in a series of films planned for The Next Generation crew, and opened at the box office with greater success than any previous Star Trek film – mostly because it promised to unite the ST:TNG cast with the Kirk-Scotty-Chekov trio of the classic series. (Leonard Nimoy and DeForest Kelly declined.) "Star Trek Generations" was considered by many to be the swan song for the original cast, and the much-

rumoured climax involving Kirk's death was another draw for Trekkers. The hit film was visually stunning from start to finish, with a renovated Enterprise-D (complete with a stellar cartography lab) and outstanding special effects – topped by the amazing saucer-section crash. In terms of dramatic appeal, there were riveting scenes between the steely-edged Picard (while mourning the loss of his brother and nephew) and the hot-tempered Kirk as they confront the evil Dr. Soran, who is deliciously played by science-fiction veteran Malcolm McDowell. Brent Spiner does another fine turn as Data, who, equipped with an emotion-chip, loses control and succumbs to fits of laughter, cowardice and remorse. Also neatly woven into the story line are the Klingon Duras sisters, who meet their demise in a spectacular battle with the Enterprise-D.
SHOW WATCH: Tim Russ, who'd soon be cast as Star Trek: Voyager's Tuvok, appears briefly in the opening sequence aboard the U.S.S. Enterprise-B. And actors Barbara March and Gwynyth Walsh, as the Duras sisters, taunt and

terrorize for the last time. Watch for the crew's next mission, which pits them against the Borg in "Star Trek: First Contact" (the scheduled release is November 1996). ✧

STAR TREK GENERATIONS: TWO LEGENDARY CAPTAINS MEET FACE TO FACE, KIRK (WILLIAM SHATNER) AND PICARD (PATRICK STEWART)

![logo] STARTREK 30 YEARS

Star Trek: Deep Space Nine

Sisko and company's four seasons on the sinister-looking space station have made for a grittier, conflict-ridden Star Trek

FIRST SEASON

WHEN STAR TREK: DEEP SPACE NINE MADE ITS WORLD DEBUT IN JANUARY 1993, IN THE MIDDLE OF STAR Trek: The Next Generation's sixth season, two questions were being asked: Firstly, could two Star Trek series actually co-exist, and secondly, would the third venture have anything new to offer? The challenge to co-creators Rick Berman and Michael Piller was to remain true to Gene Roddenberry's optimistic vision of the future while introducing a degree of tension and conflict to make DS9 a grittier show. From the outset, DS9 sought to distinguish itself from its older sibling – whereas Capt. Jean-Luc Picard assumed command of the impressive U.S.S. Enterprise-D, the pristine flagship of the Federation, Cmdr. Benjamin Sisko would inherit a dark and sinister-looking station, in utter shambles, where nothing worked properly. Where Picard assembled an elite crew of unquestionable loyalty, Sisko would be saddled with a collection of Federation and non-Federation personnel – more than one of them with a hidden agenda – set in an atmosphere of animosity. The Bajoran-Cardassian conflict would be a main component of the series, and on-going tension between characters would be the key element that, from the very start, would set DS9 apart from its illustrious predecessor.

EMISSARY

Week of 2 Jan. 1993, No. 721
Directed by: David Carson
Written by: Michael Piller
Story by: Rick Berman
and Michael Piller
STARDATE: 46379.1
In the series' two-hour première, Cmdr. Benjamin Sisko (Avery Brooks) is charged with overseeing the former Cardassian space station orbiting the planet Bajor, but his already difficult assignment takes a turn for the unexpected when a stable wormhole is discovered near the station, and Bajor's religious leader declares Sisko to be her people's long-awaited spiritual emissary. **Capt. Picard:** Patrick Stewart. **Jennifer Sisko:** Felicia Bell. **Gul Dukat:** Marc Alaimo. **Kai Opaka:** Camille Saviola.
✦ Tension and animosity grip the newly-installed Cmdr. Sisko – whose wife was

killed during Picard's Locutus-led attack on the Federation nearly three years earlier – as the commander meets his briefing officer – none other than Jean-Luc Picard himself. This episode introduces a grittier, darker corner of the Star Trek universe. Not to mention a new kind of commander – who's seething inside over the tragic loss of his wife. The spectacular battle with the Borg in the opening scene provides a dramatic link to ST:TNG, and details the extent to which Starfleet was damaged as a result (only the aftermath of the battle was shown in ST:TNG's "The Best of Both Worlds, Part II"). While familiar faces, such as Chief Operations Officer Miles O'Brien (Colm Meaney) and his wife, Keiko (Rosalind Chao), take up their new assignment on DS9, new characters would quickly capture viewers' attention: shape-shifter Odo (René Auberjonois) and symbiotic Jadzia Dax (Terry Farrell). But leave

it to Quark (Armin Shimerman, an early Ferengi on ST:TNG) and his race to provide comic relief. The pilot also delves into Bajoran spiritual beliefs. And in a fitting denouement – though Gene Roddenberry would not live to see his original wish fulfilled – some 29 years after the taping of the original pilot, "The Cage," a woman would be installed as first officer: Maj. Kira Nerys (Nana Visitor), who had proved herself in the Bajoran underground. The pilot repeats as two one-hour episodes.
SHOW WATCH: The long-standing Bajoran-Cardassian conflict was first seen in ST:TNG's fifth season "Ensign Ro," a year before DS9's debut. Meanwhile, Marc Alaimo, first seen as Romulan Cmdr. Tebok on ST:TNG's "The Neutral Zone," would frequently return to DS9 as Cardassian Gul Dukat.

PAST PROLOGUE

Week of 9 Jan. 1993, No. 404
Directed by: Winrich Kolbe
Written by: Peter Allan Fields
Story by: Kathryn Powers
STARDATE: Unknown
Still an unknown entity in Federation circles, Major Kira's loyalty is questioned after she helps a suspected terrorist – a comrade from her days in the Bajoran underground – seek asylum on DS9. **Tahna:** Jeffrey Nordling. **Garak:** Andrew Robinson. **Lursa:** Barbara March. **B'Etor:** Gwynyth Walsh. **Gul Dunar:** Vaughn Armstrong.
✦ When Michelle Forbes (Ro Laren) wouldn't commit to a long-running role on DS9, the character of Maj. Kira was created to replace Forbes' strong-willed Bajoran. Kira not only dishes out as much attitude,

but also exhibits a shaky allegiance to the Federation. *First appearance of Garak, the Cardassian tailor with a mysterious past.*

SHOW WATCH: *The Duras sisters would reappear in ST:TNG's "Firstborn" before their demise in "Star Trek Generations."*

A MAN ALONE

Week of 16 Jan. 1993, No. 403
Directed by: Paul Lynch
Written by: Michael Piller
Story by: Gerald Sanford and Michael Piller
STARDATE: 46421.5
While Keiko (Rosalind Chao) attempts to bring a semblance of normality to the station by starting a school, the inhabitants turn against Odo (René Auberjonois) when he is a prime suspect in the murder of a Bajoran. **Ibudan:** Stephen James Carver. **Zayra:** Edward Laurance Albert. **Nog:** Aron Eisenberg.

✦ *Odo joins a growing list of regulars – including Scotty from the classic series and Riker from ST:TNG – accused of murder. Mob hysteria prevails as the citizens respond to the murder, reinforcing the notion that* Deep Space Nine *is not a typical, cohesive Federation installation.*

SHOW WATCH: *Dax would be up on suspicion of murder later in the season in "Dax," while Maj. Kira would fall under suspicion in the second season's "Necessary Evil." Star Trek: Voyager's Tom Paris would also be accused – and convicted – of murder in "Ex Post Facto."*

FEDERATION FACTOID: *We learn that the shape-shifting Odo must return to his natural liquid state every 16 hours to regenerate – in a pail in his office.*

BABEL

Week of 23 Jan. 1993, No. 405
Directed by: Paul Lynch
Written by: Michael McGreevey and Naren Shankar
Story by: Sally Caves and Ira Steven Behr
STARDATE: 46423.7
O'Brien (Colm Meaney) unknowingly triggers a virus-releasing device that

STAR TREK: DEEP SPACE NINE: *FIRST-SEASON CAST (BACK ROW, FROM LEFT TO RIGHT): NANA VISITOR, SIDDIG EL FADIL, AVERY BROOKS, RENÉ AUBERJONOIS, TERRY FARRELL. (FRONT ROW, LEFT TO RIGHT): COLM MEANEY, CIRROC LOFTON, ARMIN SHIMERMAN. INSET: MICHAEL DORN, WHO JOINED THE CAST AT THE OUTSET OF THE FOURTH SEASON.*

causes the crew to speak gibberish. **Jaheel:** Jack Kehler. **Surmak Ren:** Matthew Faison. **Nurse Jabara:** Ann Gillespie. **Galis Blin:** Geraldine Farrell. **Asoth:** Bo Zenga.

✦ *The love-hate relationship between Odo and Quark, introduced in the pilot, is taken further in some great scenes involving Auberjonois and Shimerman.*

FEDERATION FACTOID: *Deep Space Nine, the former Cardassian mining station, was once known as Terek Nor. In the mirror universe, visited in DS9's "Crossover," "Through the Looking Glass" and "Shattered Mirror," the mirror station is still called Terek Nor.*

CAPTIVE PURSUIT

Week of 30 Jan. 1993, No. 406
Directed by: Corey Allen
Written by: Jill Sherman Donner and Michael Piller
Story by: Jill Sherman Donner
STARDATE: Unknown
O'Brien befriends an alien whose people are raised to be the blood-sport prey for another alien race. **Tosk:** Scott

MacDonald. **The Hunter:** Gerrit Graham. **Miss Sarda:** Kelly Curtis.

✦ *Tosk, a reptile bred to be hunted by another race, is the first life form to appear from the Gamma Quadrant.*

STAR WATCH: *Gerrit Graham would make a memorable appearance as a suicidal member of the Q Continuum on Star Trek: Voyager's "Death Wish"; Scott MacDonald appeared as N'Vek in Star Trek: The Next Generation's "Face of the Enemy."*

SHOW WATCH: *The subjugation of one race by another, usually explained as a cultural tradition, first surfaced in the classic Star Trek episode "The Cloudminders" and again in ST:TNG's "Symbiosis."*

✦ Q-LESS

Week of 6 Feb. 1993, No. 407
Directed by: Paul Lynch
Written by: Robert Hewitt Wolfe
Story by: Hannah Louise Shearer
STARDATE: 46531.2
The station experiences a critical loss of power when Vash (Jennifer Hetrick) arrives on *Deep Space Nine*, fresh from

her adventures in the Gamma Quadrant with none other than Q (John de Lancie). **Kolos:** Tom McCleister.

◆ *Up to his old tricks, the irrepressible Q (John de Lancie, in his first DS9 appearance) makes the most of the chaos that permeates* Deep Space Nine *to sow further disarray ("Picard and his lackeys would have solved all this technobabble hours ago") and conflict among the crew.*

BEST LINE: *As they battle over Vash and Sisko punches him in the face, Q declares: "You hit me! Picard never hit me."*

STAR WATCH: *Jennifer Hetrick (from television's* L.A. Law*) makes her first crossover appearance as Vash, the seductress-con artist who first romanced Capt. Picard in* ST:TNG's *"Captain's Holiday" and again in the fourth-season episode "Qpid."*

DAX
Week of 13 Feb. 1993, No. 408
Directed by: David Carson
Written by: D.C. Fontana
and Peter Allan Fields
Story by: Peter Allan Fields
STARDATE: 46910.1
Jadzia (Terry Farrell) refuses to act in her own defence when her previous Trill identity, Curzon Dax, is accused of having murdered a Klaestron general 30 years earlier. **Tandro:** Gregory Itzin. **Enina:** Fionnula Flanagan. **Selin Peers:** Richard Linebeck.

◆ *Dax is the second* Deep Space Nine *character accused of murder and her trial provides an excellent opportunity to learn more about the Trill-symbiont connection. Although Jadzia Dax (Terry Farrell) is a different entity from Curzon Dax, she feels honour-bound to protect Curzon, given his disturbing alibi: Curzon couldn't have murdered the general because, at the time of the said crime, he was in bed with the general's wife.*

SHOW WATCH: *Fionnula Flanagan made a seventh-season appearance as Data's mother in* ST:TNG's *"Inheritance."*

THE PASSENGER
Week of 20 Feb. 1993, No. 409
Directed by: Paul Lynch
Written by: Morgan Gendel, Robert Hewitt Wolfe and Michael Piller
Story by: Morgan Gendel
STARDATE: Unknown
The crew must contend with a criminal

Q-LESS: ON THE HEELS OF THEIR TOUR OF THE GAMMA QUADRANT, Q (JOHN DE LANCIE) AND VASH (JENNIFER HETRICK) MAKE AN UNEXPECTED, TROUBLE-FILLED STOPOVER ON THE DEEP SPACE NINE SPACE STATION.

alien (James Harper) who is determined to steal vital cargo and who can hide his consciousness in the unused parts of the crew's brains. **Ty Kajada:** Caitlin Brown. **Lieut. Primmin:** James Lashly. **Durg:** Christopher Collins.

◆ *Bashir (Siddig El Fadil) takes centre stage in this engaging story of alien possession. At this early point in the series, characters are still finding their form.*

SHOW WATCH: *Alien possession would return later in the season to pit Sisko and Kira against each other in "Dramatis Personae." In the classic* Star Trek *episode "Turnabout Intruder," Kirk was possessed by a vengeful Dr. Janice Lester, while in "Wolf in the Fold," Scotty was framed for a murder committed by the spirit of the infamous Jack the Ripper. In* ST:TNG's *"The Schizoid Man," the dying mentor of Dr. Noonian Soong dumps his consciousness into Data's neural net, while numerous members of* Star Trek: Voyager's *crew would suffer the intrusion of alien possession in "Cathexis."*

MOVE ALONG HOME
Week of 13 March 1993, No. 410
Directed by: David Carson
Written by: Frederick Rappaport, Lisa Rich and Jeanne Carrigan-Fauci
Story by: Michael Piller
STARDATE: Unknown
When Quark (Armin Shimerman) is caught trying to cheat a delegation from

the Gamma Quadrant out of its winnings, the aliens take revenge by turning the senior staff into playing pieces on a deadly board game, and force Quark to play in order to save their lives. **Falow:** Joel Brooks. **Lieut. George Primmin:** James Lashly. **Chandra:** Clara Bryant.

◆ *An imaginative story, the episode cost almost as much to produce as the pilot. Quark must use his Ferengi cunning to save his crew-mates.*

THE NAGUS
Week of 20 March 1993, No. 411
Directed by: David Livingston
Written by: Ira Steven Behr
Story by: David Livingston
STARDATE: Unknown
When the leader (Wallace Shawn) of the Ferengi empire unexpectedly retires, he shocks his followers by appointing *Deep Space Nine's* Quark as his successor. **Rom:** Max Grodénchik. **Nog:** Aron Eisenberg. **Krax:** Lou Wagner. **Nava:** Barry Gordon. **Maihar'du:** Tiny Ron.

◆ *Great episode for Ferengi fans, the first to feature the Ferengi in a story-line of their own – not merely acting as antagonists in a* Federation *plot line.*

BEST LINE: *Grand Nagus Zek on his retirement: "I'm old. The fire dims. I'm just not as greedy as I used to be."*

STAR WATCH: *Wallace Shawn (who starred in the movie "The Princess Bride") steals everything but the scenery in his first appearance as the Grand Nagus Zek. He would return to worry Quark in the* Star Trek: Deep Space Nine *episode "Prophet Motive."*

SHOW WATCH: *Actor Max Grodénchik, as Quark's brother Rom, gets more air time in this episode. He first appeared in Ferengi garb on* Star Trek: The Next Generation *as the one who helped spark the romance between Picard and Vash in the episode "Captain's Holiday," and as Par Lenor, a Ferengi character featured in the background of a less successful Picard romance in "The Perfect Mate."*

RULES OF ACQUISITION: *No. 1: "Once you have their money, you never give it back." No. 6: "Never allow family to stand in the way of opportunity."*

VORTEX

Week of 17 April 1993, No. 412
Directed by: Winrich Kolbe
Written by: Sam Rolfe
STARDATE: Unknown

Odo (René Auberjonois) arrests a Gamma Quadrant criminal (Cliff DeYoung) who offers to lead him to other shape-shifters on the other side of the wormhole. **Ah-Kel/Ro-Kel:** Randy Oglesby. **Hadran:** Gordon Clapp. **Vulcan Captain:** Kathleen Garrett. **Yareth:** Leslie Engelberg.

◆ *All four* Star Trek *series have one main character who serves as a vehicle for the exploration of human nature: In* Star Trek: Deep Space Nine, *it's the shape-shifting Odo (René Auberjonois). Like* Star Trek: The Next Generation's *Data, Odo has assumed humanoid form but he can't quite get the details right. He is constantly questioning human behaviour in order to understand it. While not wanting to be human, he does display a rather human desire to understand himself. Without a past of his own, he yearns to discover where he comes from and who he really is. Shape-shifter Odo's story-line will be continued in the second season's "The Alternate."*

STAR WATCH: *Cliff De Young ("Manhattan") appears as the criminal who tempts shape-shifter Odo with knowledge of his roots.*

SHOW WATCH: *Odo would discover his ancestry in the two-part third season DS9 episode "The Search."*

BATTLE LINES

Week of 24 April 1993, No. 413
Directed by: Paul Lynch
Written by: Richard Danus and Evan Carlos Somers
Story by: Hilary Bader
STARDATE: Unknown

Sisko, Kira and Bashir are stranded on a planet where the inhabitants are in a state of perpetual warfare but can never die. **Shel-La:** Jonathan Banks. **Kai Opaka:** Camille Saviola. **Zlangco:** Paul Collins.

◆ *Unlike the classic episode "A Taste of Armageddon," in which two planets have been able to wage a perpetual war with computers, this episode's hostilities are messy and very painful, and immortality is seen as a curse. The ending offers no simple solution, only the hope of peace through Kai Opaka acting as mediator.*

THE STORYTELLER

Week of 1 May 1993, No. 414
Directed by: David Livingston
Written by: Kurt Michael Bensmiller and Ira Steven Behr
Story by: Kurt Michael Bensmiller
STARDATE: 46729.1

When Bashir (Siddig El Fadil) and O'Brien (Colm Meaney) fail to save the life of the spiritual leader of a Bajoran village, a reluctant Miles O'Brien is made their new leader, and it's up to him to try and save the Bajoran villagers from a mysterious, destructive force. **The Sirah:** Kay E. Kuter. **Hovath:** Lawrence Monoson. **Varis:** Gina Philips. **Faren:** Jim Jansen. **Woban:** Jordan Lund.

◆ *One of the first episodes to develop the Bashir-O'Brien camaraderie, which will grow through weekly darts matches and numerous holosuite adventures.*

RULE OF ACQUISITION: No. 9: *"Opportunity plus instinct equals profit."*

PROGRESS

Week of 8 May 1993, No. 415
Directed by: Les Landau
Written by: Peter Allan Fields
STARDATE: 46844.3

While on an evacuation mission, Kira (Nana Visitor) encounters a stubborn, old Bajoran farmer (Brian Keith) who contends that time spent with the *Federation* is causing the major to lose touch with her true Bajoran identity. **Toran:** Michael Bofshever. **Baltrim:** Terrence Evans. **Keena:** Annie O'Donnell. **Alien Captain:** Nicholas Worth.

◆ *Further insight into the personality of Kira, who, as a member of the underground, fought against those with power – and now finds herself on the other side.*

STAR WATCH: *Veteran actor Brian Keith (Family Affair, "Parent Trap") does a masterful job as the free-spirited Bajoran farmer who resists authority.*

SHOW WATCH: *Kira is not the first or the last Starfleet officer to find a father figure in an unexpected person; Ro Laren became so emotionally attached to senior resistance fighter Macias that she abandoned Starfleet to join his Maquis cause in ST:TNG's "Preemptive Strike." On* Star Trek: Voyager, *Janeway would find her own father figure in Caylem, who mistakes the captain for his daughter in the "Resistance" episode.*

IF WISHES WERE HORSES

Week of 15 May 1993, No. 416
Directed by: Robert Legato
Written by: Nell McCue Crawford, William L. Crawford, Michael Piller
Story by: Nell McCue Crawford and William L. Crawford
STARDATE: 46853.2

The *Deep Space Nine* crew is bewildered when their wildest fantasies become real, but the phenomenon is only a prelude to catastrophe. **Keiko:** Rosalind Chao. **Buck Bokai:** Keone Young. **Rumpelstiltskin:** Michael John Anderson. **Molly:** Hana Hatae.

THE NAGUS: QUARK (ARMIN SHIMERMAN, CENTRE) AND ROM (MAX GRODÉNCHIK, RIGHT) ARE BOTH STUNNED WHEN GRAND NAGUS ZEK APPOINTS QUARK AS HIS SUCCESSOR.

◆ *Wonderfully comic show, borrowing the "be careful what you wish for" notion from the classic episode "Shore Leave" and ST:TNG's "Where No One Has Gone Before."*

BEST DIALOGUE: *Odo to Quark: "You're disgusting." Quark's response: "It's a living."*

FEDERATION FACTOID: *Baseball great Buck Bokai, first mentioned in ST:TNG's "The Big Goodbye," played for the London Kings and broke Joe DiMaggio's consecutive hitting streak in 2026.*

DRAMATIS PERSONAE: INFLUENCED BY AN ALIEN FORCE, SISKO (AVERY BROOKS) BATTLES KIRA (NANA VISITOR) FOR CONTROL OF THE STATION.

THE FORSAKEN

Week of 22 May 1993, No. 417
Directed by: Les Landau
Written by: Don Carlos Dunaway and Michael Piller
Story by: Jim Trombetta
STARDATE: 46925.1
Lwaxana Troi (Majel Barrett) visits *Deep Space Nine* and quickly sets her sights on Odo. Meanwhile, the station's computer begins to misbehave like an attention-hungry child. **Ambassador Taxco:** Constance Towers. **Ambassador Lojal:** Michael Ensign. **Ambassador Vadosia:** Jack Shearer. **Anara:** Benita Andre.
◆ *Majel Barrett, having made appearances in every Star Trek series except for Star Trek: Voyager – though she's the voice of the computer for that series – gives another splendid performance. In one heart-warming scene, she and Odo share some private revelations as they're trapped in a turbolift. With only moments remaining before Odo has to return to liquid form, Lwaxana ingeniously catches him in a makeshift bucket – using her dress – and saves him.*

BEST DIALOGUE: *Trying to halt Lwaxana's advances, Odo protests: "Every 16 hours, I turn into a liquid." Replies Lwaxana, undeterred: "I can swim."*

SHOW WATCH: *Barrett's Lwaxana would return in the third season's "Fascination" and in the fourth season's "The Muse." Jack Shearer would appear as an alien sent to keep an eye on Harry Kim in Voyager's "Non Sequitur."*

FEDERATION FACTOID: *We learn that the shape-shifting Odo was found in the Denorios Belt, then brought back to Bajor and placed in a research institute under the care of Dr. Mora Pol, on whom Odo modelled his humanoid appearance and behaviour. We meet Pol in the second season episode "The Alternate."*

DRAMATIS PERSONAE

Week of 29 May 1993, No. 418
Directed by: Cliff Bole
Written by: Joe Menosky
STARDATE: 46922.3
Under the influence of an alien force, Cmdr. Benjamin Sisko (Avery Brooks) and Major Kira Nerys (Nana Visitor) fight each other for control of *Deep Space Nine*. **Klingon:** Tom Towles. **Valerian:** Stephen Parr. **Guard:** Randy Pflug. **Ensign:** Jeff Pruitt.
◆ *The subconscious jealousies and overt rivalries brewing since the start of the season come to a head in this conflict-ridden episode as an alien archive takes possession of the Deep Space Nine crew, forcing them to re-create the power struggle that destroyed the alien's race.*

SHOW WATCH: *In ST:TNG's "Masks," an alien archive took possession of Data. The Saltah'na clock, built by Sisko while under the influence of the mind control device, would frequently reappear in subsequent episodes.*

DUET

Week of 12 June 1993, No. 419
Directed by: James L. Conway
Written by: Peter Allan Fields
Story by: Lisa Rich and Jeanne Carrigan-Fauci
STARDATE: Unknown
Major Kira Nerys (Nana Visitor) tries to uncover the identity of a Cardassian she believes is a war criminal, but her investigation leads to an even more shocking revelation. **Marritza:** Harris Yulin. **Gul Dukat:** Marc Alaimo. **Kaval:** Ted Sorel.

Kainon: Tony Rizzoli. **The Captain:** Norman Large. **Neela:** Robin Christopher.
◆ *Nana Visitor does an excellent job in this gripping story about Cardassian war crimes. Major Kira's hatred of the Cardassians makes her highly alert to any opportunity for vengeance. Yet, as she discovers, she is not totally blinded by anger and will not kill a Cardassian merely because the opportunity presents itself. Harris Yulin delivers one of the most memorable guest performances of the DS9 season: Playing a cowardly clerk who passes himself off as the sadistic Cardassian war criminal Gul Darhe'el ("The Butcher of Gallitep"), Yulin draws contempt then sympathy in this brilliant plot twist examining the secret shame of his people at their treatment of the Bajorans.*

SHOW WATCH: *The issue of war crimes was first raised in the original Star Trek series episode "The Conscience of the King." Actor Norman Large would reappear as a Kazon in several Star Trek: Voyager episodes, including "State of Flux" and "Cold Fire."*

IN THE HANDS OF THE PROPHETS

Week of 19 June 1993, No. 420
Directed by: David Livingston
Written by: Robert Hewitt Wolfe
STARDATE: Unknown
Keiko's secular teachings about the wormhole are the catalyst for a spiritual leader's threat to destroy the Bajoran-*Federation* alliance. **Keiko:** Rosalind Chao. **Vedek Winn:** Louise Fletcher. **Vedek Bareil:** Philip Anglim. **Neela:** Robin Christopher.
◆ *The final conflict of the first Star Trek: Deep Space Nine season: The secular ideals of the Federation versus the deeply spiritual and theocratic convictions of the Bajorans. Major Kira Nerys, at first sympathetic to Vedek Winn's spiritual crusade, continues to find herself torn between two worlds and must ultimately decide where her duty lies.*

STAR WATCH: *Oscar Award-winner Louise Fletcher ("One Flew Over the Cuckoo's Nest") appears for the first time as the rigid Vedek Winn, who would go on to play a key role in the Bajoran conspiracy plot lines of the second season in Deep Space Nine.*

RULE OF ACQUISITION: *No. 7: "Keep your ears open."* ✧

SECOND SEASON

WITH *STAR TREK: DEEP SPACE NINE'S* SECOND SEASON BARELY UNDER WAY, THE NEWS THAT *STAR TREK* FANS had been fearing for more than a year finally broke: *Star Trek: The Next Generation's* seventh season would be its last. Despite the attention that immediately shifted back to its older sibling, *Deep Space Nine* managed to be one of the top-rated shows in American television, with a production budget reported to be $1.5 million (US) per episode (approximately £1 million). Story-lines rife with political intrigue and turmoil would place its evolving characters in increasingly well-written and complex plots, and hone the defining characteristics of its second season. On Bajor, where church and state are one and the same, a conspiracy unfolds as spiritual leaders manoeuvre to become the next Kai. Meanwhile, the *Federation* also suffers from discord as the Maquis, a terrorist group of *Federation* civilians and renegade *Starfleet* officers, threaten the uneasy peace with the Cardassian Union by launching attacks against the former oppressor of Bajor. In what has become the *Star Trek: Deep Space Nine* trademark style, life is not black and white but shades of grey. The lines between hero and villain become increasingly blurred, compromises are made and unscrupulous foes live to fight another day.

THE HOMECOMING

Week of 25 Sept. 1993, No. 421
Directed by: Winrich Kolbe
Written by: Ira Steven Behr
Story by: Jeri Taylor, Ira Steven Behr
STARDATE: Unknown
Seeking a leader to bring stability to the increasingly factionalized Bajorans, Kira and O'Brien (Nana Visitor, Colm Meaney) set off to rescue a legendary Bajoran resistance fighter (Richard Beymer), who is being held in a Cardassian slave-labour colony. **Borum:** Michael Bell. **Rom:** Max Grodénchik. **Gul Dukat:** Marc Alaimo. **Minister Jaro:** Frank Langella.
✦ *Bajor's deteriorating internal struggles are the focus of an ambitious second-season-opening trilogy which, at the outset, takes viewers back to the earlier Bajoran-Cardassian conflict. But after Kira rescues Li Nalas, the revered Bajoran resistance fighter believed to have been killed ten years earlier, she learns his prowess has been greatly exaggerated, and – to Sisko's consternation – the major is relieved of her position as Bajoran liaison to DS9.*
STAR WATCH: *Frank Langella, who had the title role in the 1979 movie "Dracula," puts his talent for nefarious characters to good use as Jaro, minister for the Bajoran provisional government. And Richard Beymer ("West Side Story"), last seen on* Twin Peaks, *is quietly effective as the reluctant hero Li Nalas.*
SHOW WATCH: *The Bajoran prison camp detainees in this episode echo Worf's discovery of Klingons being held in a secret Romulan prison camp in ST:TNG's two-part "Birthright."*

RULE OF ACQUISITION: *No. 76: "Every once in a while, declare peace. It confuses the hell out of your enemies."*

THE CIRCLE

Week of 2 Oct. 1993, No. 422
Directed by: Corey Allen
Written by: Peter Allan Fields
STARDATE: Unknown
Relieved of her post on *Deep Space Nine*, Kira returns to Bajor where she helps expose the leaders of the terrorist group known as The Circle. **Minister Jaro:** Frank Langella. **Vedek Winn:** Louise Fletcher. **Krim:** Stephen Macht. **Vedek Bareil:** Philip Anglim. **Zef'no:** Mike Genovese.
✦ *Powerful episode for Nana Visitor as Kira is kidnapped and tortured by agents of The Circle, secretly led by Minister Jaro. Despite the serious tone of the opening trilogy's second instalment, watch for the early scene of comedic confusion as Odo, Dax, Bashir, O'Brien and Quark stage an impromptu gathering in Kira's quarters as she prepares to depart DS9.*
STAR WATCH: *Oscar winner Louise Fletcher returns as the self-righteous Vedek Winn.*
SHOW WATCH: *Picard was subjected to Cardassian torture in ST:TNG's two-part "Chain of Command."*

THE SIEGE

Week of 9 Oct. 1993, No. 423
Directed by: Winrich Kolbe
Written by: Michael Piller
STARDATE: Unknown
With the Bajoran civil war turning in favour of the terrorists, Cmdr. Benjamin Sisko (Avery Brooks) is ordered to evac-

uate *Deep Space Nine* before invasion forces arrive, but he remains aboard to delay the station's takeover while Kira and Dax try to expose the true nature of The Circle's leadership. **Vedek Winn:** Louise Fletcher. **Minister Jaro:** Frank Langella. **Col. Day:** Steven Weber. **Li Nalas:** Richard Beymer. **Krim:** Stephen Macht. **Vedek Bareil:** Philip Anglim.
✦ *The crew prepare for an all-out battle with the Bajoran terrorists. Plenty of action scenes.*
RULE OF ACQUISITION: *No. 31: "Never make fun of a Ferengi's mother...insult something he cares about instead."*

INVASIVE PROCEDURES

Week of 16 Oct. 1993, No. 424
Directed by: Les Landau
Written by: John Whelpley
and Robert Hewitt Wolfe
Story by: John Whelpley
STARDATE: 47182.1
With *Deep Space Nine* operating under a skeleton crew, a desperate Trill (John Glover) takes the crew hostage and steals the Dax symbiont from Jadzia, determined to join it with himself. **Mareel:** Megan Gallagher. **T'Kar:** Tim Russ. **Yeto:** Steve Rankin.
✦ *Insight into the Trill-symbiont selection process and the eight lifetimes that Dax has shared with his Trill hosts, including the most recent, Jadzia. John Glover portrays his Trill personality before and after being joined with Dax.*
SHOW WATCH: *Making his first DS9 appearance as a Klingon, Tim Russ – who was cast in ST:TNG's "Starship Mine" – would come back as a nameless officer in "Star Trek Generations" before landing the role of the Vulcan Tuvok on the Star Trek: Voyager series. Russ would also appear as Tuvok in DS9's third-season episode "Through the Looking Glass."*

CARDASSIANS

Week of 23 Oct. 1993, No. 425
Directed by: Cliff Bole
Written by: James Crocker
Story by: Gene Wolande
and John Wright
STARDATE: 47177.2
An odd custody battle takes place aboard the station when the Cardassians try to reclaim an orphaned Cardassian boy (Vidal Peterson) who was raised by Bajoran parents. **Kotan Pa'Dar:** Robert

Mandan. **Proka:** Terrence Evans. **Gul Dukat:** Marc Alaimo. **Garak:** Andrew Robinson. **Zolan:** Dion Anderson. **Keiko:** Rosalind Chao.

◆ *Effective treatment of the consequences and casualties of war, specifically the orphans Cardassia left behind on Bajor upon withdrawing from the planet. More intriguing hints as to the likely background of Garak, the secretive Cardassian working as DS9's tailor.*

SHOW WATCH: *We learn that the Cardassians murdered ten million Bajorans during more than 30 years of occupation. The issue of child custody – and the possibility of parental abuse – was raised in ST:TNG's "Suddenly Human." Gul Dukat's deception in hiding the Cardassian orphan will find a parallel in the fourth season's "Indiscretion."*

STAR WATCH: *Robert Mandan (Soap) appears as Pa'Dar, one of Cardassia's most prominent politicians and the natural father of the teen-age boy, Rugal.*

MELORA
Week of 30 Oct. 1993, No. 426
Directed by: Winrich Kolbe
Written by: Evan Carlos Somers, Steven Baum, Michael Piller and James Crocker
Story by: Evan Carlos Somers
STARDATE: 47229.1
Bashir (Siddig El Fadil) falls in love with a woman (Daphne Ashbrook) from a low gravity planet, who cannot walk in DS9's gravitational conditions. Bashir is determined to find a way to free the woman from her wheelchair. **Fallit Kot:** Peter Crombie. **Ashrock:** Don Stark.

◆ *Dr. Bashir's love for the wheelchair-bound woman inspires a bitter-sweet tale when Melora decides to discontinue the treatment that would allow her mobility but would also remove her ability to return home to her own planet.*

RULE OF ACQUISITION: *No. 16: "A deal is a deal...until a better one comes along."*

RULES OF ACQUISITION
Week of 6 Nov. 1993, No. 427
Directed by: David Livingston
Written by: Ira Steven Behr
Story by: Hilary Bader
STARDATE: Unknown
An ambitious Ferengi female (Helene Udy) disguises herself as a male to help Quark (Armin Shimerman) with busi-

ness negotiations in the Gamma Quadrant, but she has to hide more than her gender when she falls in love with him. **Inglatu:** Brian Thompson. **Zek:** Wallace Shawn. **Zyree:** Emilia Crow. **Maihar'u:** Tiny Ron. **Rom:** Max Grodenchik.

◆ *Gender inequality among the Ferengi is explored in an often humourous manner. Second appearance of Grand Nagus Zek.*

SHOW WATCH: *Quark's mother, Ishka (Andrea Martin) would also oppose Ferengi tradition by making a profit in season three's "Family Business."*

RULES OF ACQUISITION: *No. 22: "A wise man can hear profit in the wind." No. 33: "It never hurts to suck up to the boss." No. 48: "The bigger the smile, the sharper the knife." No. 62: "The riskier the road, the greater the profit" (also heard in the fourth season's "Little Green Men").*

🖖 NECESSARY EVIL
Week of 13 Nov. 1993, No. 428
Directed by: James L. Conway
Written by: Peter Allan Fields
STARDATE: 47282.5
When Quark is wounded in an attack, Odo believes it is related to a five-year-old unsolved murder case, in which Kira was the prime suspect. **Pallra:** Katherine Moffat. **Rom:** Max Grodenchik. **Gul Dukat:** Marc Alaimo.

◆ *Kira becomes the third DS9 crew member suspected of murder – albeit one that was committed five years earlier.*

SECOND SIGHT
Week of 20 Nov. 1993, No. 429
Directed by: Alexander Singer
Written by: Mark Gehred-O'Connell, Ira Steven Behr and Robert Hewitt Wolfe
Story by: Mark Gehred-O'Connell
STARDATE: 47329.4
Sisko (Avery Brooks) falls in love for the first time since his wife's death, but his dream woman seems to suffer from a peculiar form of split personality. **Fenna/Nidell:** Salli Elise Richardson. **Seyetik:** Richard Kiley.

◆ *A visually stunning episode that allows Sisko to engage in his first taste of romance since the death of his wife.*

STAR WATCH: *Broadway star Richard Kiley brings to life the egocentric character of Gideon Seyetik. As he's about to crash his ship into a dead sun, his character's last*

words – "Let there be light" – echo those of Slim Pickens in "Dr. Strangelove."

SANCTUARY
Week of 27 Nov. 1993, No. 430
Directed by: Les Landau
Written by: Frederick Rappaport
Story by: Gabe Escoe and Kelley Miles
STARDATE: 47391.2
Kira's tolerance is put to the test when a group of refugees escaping from the Gamma Quadrant claim Bajor to be their mythical homeland. **Haneek:** Deborah May. **Tumak:** Andrew Koenig. **General Hazar:** Michael Durrell. **Rozahn:** Kitty Swink. **Vedek Sorad:** Robert Curtis-Brown. **Varani:** William Schallert.

◆ *The touching, terrifying plight of political refugees, the Skrreeans, who are fleeing from the Dominion.*

SHOW WATCH: *Kitty Swink, who plays Rozahn, is Armin Shimerman's wife; Andrew Koenig, who portrays the teenage Tumak, is the son of Walter Koenig.*

RIVALS
Week of 1 Jan. 1994, No. 431
Directed by: David Livingston
Written by: Joe Menosky
Story by: Jim Trombetta and Michael Piller
STARDATE: Unknown
Quark discovers he is not the only game in town when a con man (Chris Sarandon) opens a competing bar on the station featuring an unusual gambling device. **Cos:** Albert Henderson. **Roana:** Barbara Bosson. **Alsia:** K Callan. **Keiko:** Rosalind Chao.

NECESSARY EVIL: ODO (RENÉ AUBERJONOIS) INVESTIGATES A FIVE-YEAR-OLD MURDER CHARGE AGAINST MAJOR KIRA NERYS.

◆ *A light-hearted episode about rivalry. Quark isn't sporting a smile after a competitor opens a new bar. Dr. Bashir and O'Brien play some intense racquet-ball.*

STAR WATCH: *Chris Sarandon (who starred in "The Princess Bride" with Wallace Shawn), Barbara Bosson (Hill Street Blues) and K. Callan (The New Adventures of Superman).*

RULE OF ACQUISITION: *No. 109: "Dignity and an empty sack is worth the sack."*

THE ALTERNATE

Week of 8 Jan. 1994, No. 432
Directed by: David Carson
Written by: Bill Dial
Story by: Jim Trombetta and Bill Dial
STARDATE: 47391.7

Odo (René Auberjonois) has mixed feelings when the Bajoran scientist (James Sloyan) who first studied him announces he may have found Odo's true home in the Gamma Quadrant.

◆ *An excellent episode that allows Odo to resume the search for his roots which he began in the first season's "Vortex."*

SHOW WATCH: *On Star Trek: Voyager's "Jetrel," Neelix meets a scientist from his past, also played by James Sloyan.*

ARMAGEDDON GAME

Week of 29 Jan. 1994, No. 433
Directed by: Winrich Kolbe
Written by: Morgan Gendel, Ira Steven Behr and James Crocker
Story by: Morgan Gendel
STARDATE: Unknown

While working to rid a warring planet of a deadly biochemical weapon, Bashir and O'Brien (Siddig El Fadil, Colm Meaney) are attacked by the people they are trying to help. **E'Tyshra:** Darleen Carr. **Sharat:** Peter White. **Nydrom:** Larry Cedar. **Keiko:** Rosalind Chao.

◆ *Bashir and O'Brien's friendship is put to the test when they are forced into hiding after their good intentions are somehow misconstrued.*

RULE OF ACQUISITION: *No. 57: "Good customers are as rare as latinum. Treasure them."*

WHISPERS

Week of 5 Feb. 1994, No. 434
Directed by: Les Landau
Written by: Paul Coyle
STARDATE: 47581.2

O'Brien (Colm Meaney) returns from a mission only to find he has been locked out of every security feature on the station and everyone, including his wife (Rosalind Chao), has turned against him. **DeCurtis:** Todd Waring. **Admiral Rollman:** Susan Bay. **Coutu:** Philip LeStrange.

◆ *Well-written mystery that at first suggests a mysterious conspiracy or a possible alternate universe. Viewers are kept guessing right to the end.*

RULE OF ACQUISITION: *No. 194: "It's always good business to know about new customers before they walk in your door."*

PARADISE

Week of 12 Feb. 1994, No. 435
Directed by: Corey Allen
Written by: Jeff King, Richard Manning and Hans Beimler
Story by: Jim Trombetta and James Crocker
STARDATE: 47573.1

Sisko and O'Brien are stranded on a planet where they encounter a human colony whose leader (Gail Strickland) has forbidden any form of technology. **Cassandra:** Julia Nickson. **Joseph:** Steve Vinovich. **Vinod:** Michael Buchman Silver. **Stephan:** Erick Weiss.

◆ *The workings of cult worship are investigated in this episode as Sisko and O'Brien crash-land on a planet where inhabitants follow a charismatic scientist.*

SHADOWPLAY

Week of 19 Feb. 1994, No. 436
Directed by: Robert Scheerer
Written by: Robert Hewitt Wolfe
STARDATE: 47603.3

Odo and Dax (René Auberjonois, Terry Farrell) discover that the inhabitants on an unexplored planet are vanishing. **Colyus:** Kenneth Mars. **Rurigan:** Kenneth Tobey. **Taya:** Noley Thornton. **Vedek Bareil:** Philip Anglim.

◆ *Intriguing denouement that reveals the inhabitants of the planet to be holograms, who are disappearing as a result of a program glitch. First opportunity for the gruff Odo to reveal his tender side as he comforts the frightened young Yaderan, Taya. Meanwhile, Vedek Bareil turns up at the station hoping to pursue Kira. The attraction – much to the grief of Odo, whose love for Kira has remained silent – would build through the third season.*

STAR WATCH: *Veteran performer Kenneth Mars ("The Parallax View") appears as Colyus, the protector of the settlement.*

SHOW WATCH: *Noley Thornton, who plays Taya, earlier appeared as Clara Sutter in ST:TNG's "Imaginary Friend." Like Odo, Data would also find a friend in a young girl (Gia) in ST:TNG's seventh-season episode "Thine Own Self."*

PLAYING GOD

Week of 26 Feb. 1994, No. 437
Directed by: David Livingston
Written by: Jim Trombetta and Michael Piller
Story by: Jim Trombetta
STARDATE: Unknown

While playing host to a nervous Trill initiate, Jadzia (Terry Farrell) discovers a small universe growing out of a piece of protoplasm in the science lab that threatens to destroy the station. **Arjin:** Geoffrey Blake. **Klingon Host:** Ron Taylor. **Cardassian:** Richard Poe.

◆ *Terry Farrell is front and centre as Jadzia judges a would-be symbiont host.*

FEDERATION FACTOID: *We learn that over the past 200 years, Dax has personally eliminated 57 host candidates from the Initiate programme, and that Jadzia herself was once eliminated from the programme by Curzon Dax, her training supervisor.*

RULE OF ACQUISITION: *No. 112: "Never have sex with the boss's sister."*

PROFIT AND LOSS

Week of 19 March 1994, No. 438
Directed by: Robert Wiemer
Written by: Flip Kobler and Cindy Marcus
STARDATE: Unknown

Quark risks everything to win back the love of his life (Mary Crosby), a fugitive Cardassian woman suspected of terrorism on her homeworld. **Hogue:** Michael Reilly Burke. **Garak:** Andrew Robinson. **Rekelen:** Heidi Swedberg. **Gul Toran:** Edward Wiley.

◆ *Quark momentarily sheds his selfish nature to stay with the woman he loves. His second such opportunity this season.*

STAR WATCH: *Mary Crosby, who plays Quark's lost love, Natima, became famous as the vixen who shot J.R. on Dallas. She is the daughter of Bing Crosby, whose granddaughter, Denise, played Tasha Yar on ST:TNG. And Heidi Swedberg (George's fiancée, Susan, on Seinfeld) plays Rekelen.*

BLOOD OATH: *TO FULFILL AN OATH MADE BY CURZON DAX, JADZIA (TERRY FARRELL) JOINS THREE LEGENDARY KLINGON WARRIORS (PLAYED BY WILLIAM CAMPBELL, MICHAEL ANSARA AND JOHN COLICOS) IN BATTLE.*

BLOOD OATH

Week of 26 March 1994, No. 439
Directed by: Winrich Kolbe
Written by: Peter Allan Fields
STARDATE: Unknown
Jadzia risks her career in *Starfleet* in order to fulfill a blood oath Curzon Dax made years ago with three Klingons. **Kor:** John Colicos. **Kang:** Michael Ansara. **Koloth:** William Campbell. **The Albino:** Bill Bolender.

✦ *In a clever carry-over of characters from the classic series – 27 years later – three notorious Klingons (Kor, Kang and Koloth) are reunited aboard DS9 to avenge the death of one of their sons.*

STAR WATCH: *John Colicos (the first Klingon, "Errand of Mercy") would return as Kor in the fourth season's "The Sword of Kahless." William Campbell (Trelane in "The Squire of Gothos") played Koloth in "The Trouble with Tribbles." Michael Ansara (Jeyal in DS9's fourth season "The Muse") was Kang in the classic episode "Day of the Dove."*

THE MAQUIS, PART I

Week of 23 April 1994, No. 440
Directed by: David Livingston
Written by: James Crocker
Story by: Rick Berman, Michael Piller and Jeri Taylor
STARDATE: Unknown
Federation-Cardassian peace is threatened when a group of renegade *Federation* colonists in the Demilitarized Zone attack Cardassian vessels. **Cal Hudson:** Bernie Casey. **Gul Evek:** Richard Poe. **Amaros:** Tony Plana. **Sakonna:** Bertila Damas. **Samuels:** Michael A. Krawic. **Kobb:** Amanda Carlin. **Gul Dukat:** Marc Alaimo.

✦ *The appearance here of the renegade terrorist group known as the Maquis provides background to the Federation's relationship with Cardassia, first introduced in Star Trek: The Next Generation's "The Wounded," and lays the groundwork for the Star Trek: Voyager series.*

RULE OF ACQUISITION: *No. 214: "Never begin a negotiation on an empty stomach."*

THE MAQUIS, PART II

Week of 30 April 1994, No. 441
Directed by: Corey Allen
Written by: Ira Steven Behr
Story by: Rick Berman, Michael Piller and Jeri Taylor
STARDATE: Unknown
Sisko's old friend Cmdr. Cal Hudson (Bernie Casey) turns enemy when he quits *Starfleet* to join the Maquis in their war against Cardassia. **Amaros:** Tony Plana. **Legate Parn:** John Schuck. **Admiral Necheyev:** Natalija Nogulich. **Sakonna:** Bertila Damas. **Xepolite:** Michael Bell. **Kobb:** Amanda Carlin. **Gul Dukat:** Marc Alaimo.

✦ *Although the Maquis story-line throws a wrinkle into the seemingly harmonious Federation universe, it also serves to further develop the Gul Dukat character, skilfully played by Marc Alaimo.*

SHOW WATCH: *Cal Hudson would not be the last Starfleet officer to join the Maquis: Ro Laren would take up that cause in ST:TNG's "Preemptive Strike," as would Thomas Riker in "Defiant." After numerous appearances on ST:TNG, Natalija Nogulich returns in the role of Admiral Necheyev. First mention of the Cardassian judicial system, in which the verdict is decided before the trial. Cardassians are given mind-training from the age of four, enabling Dukat to shield his thoughts from a Vulcan mind-meld. Although Dukat claims to have seven children, we don't meet the Bajoran offspring he has kept in hiding until the fourth-season episode "Indiscretion."*

THE WIRE

Week of 7 May 1994, No. 442
Directed by: Kim Friedman
Written by: Robert Hewitt Wolfe
STARDATE: Unknown
Bashir (Siddig El Fadil) fights to save the life of his Cardassian friend Garak (Andrew Robinson), who is suffering from an unusual addiction. **Glinn Boheeka:** Jimmie F. Skaggs. **Enabran Tain:** Paul Dooley. **Jabara:** Ann Gillespie.

◆ *Andrew Robinson shines in an episode that sheds light on DS9's mysterious Cardassian tailor, Garak. A former member of the Obsidian Order, Cardassia's secret police, Garak is now suffering intense withdrawal symptoms from a pain-killer implant designed to release its drug in the event the Cardassian is caught and tortured.*

BEST LINE: *Not unlike an earlier* Starfleet *physician, the even-tempered Bashir snaps, "I'm a doctor, not a botanist."*

STAR WATCH: *Paul Dooley (Grace Under Fire) appears as Garak's former mentor, Enabran Tain, who'd reprise the role later in the third season.*

SHOW WATCH: *The issue of drug addiction, also addressed in* ST:TNG's *first-season episode "Symbiosis," will return in the fourth season's "Hippocratic Oath."*

⬩ CROSSOVER

Week of 14 May 1994, No. 443
Directed by: David Livingston
Written by: Peter Allan Fields and Michael Piller
Story by: Peter Allan Fields
STARDATE: 47891.1
A wormhole accident sends Major Kira Nerys (Nana Visitor) and Bashir (Siddig

CROSSOVER: *BASHIR (SIDDIG EL FADIL) FINDS AN ALTERED REALITY AT QUARK'S BAR.*

El Fadil) to an alternate universe where the humans are slaves. **Garak:** Andrew Robinson. **Telok:** John Cothran Jr.
◆ *In an inspired second carry-over from the classic series, fans get to see what happened to the evil alternate universe Kirk visited nearly 100 years earlier in "Mirror, Mirror." In the timeline of that universe, the alternate Spock pacified Earth's Galactic Empire, leading to its eventual defeat at the hands of the Klingon-Cardassian alliance. Nana Visitor delivers a provocative performance as Kira's seductive double.*

THE COLLABORATOR

Week of 21 May 1994, No. 444
Directed by: Cliff Bole
Written by: Gary Holland, Ira Steven Behr and Robert Hewitt Wolfe
Story by: Gary Holland
STARDATE: Unknown
Major Kira discovers that the man she loves (Philip Anglim), a leading candidate for the Bajoran spiritual leadership, might have been responsible for the massacre of 43 Bajoran freedom fighters. **Vedek Winn:** Louise Fletcher.

Kubus: Bert Remsen. **Kai Opaka:** Camille Saviola.
◆ *Excellent insight into the Bajoran culture where church and politics are one. The conspiracy, which began in the first season and was heightened at the outset of the second, roars back to life. Louise Fletcher gives a suitably understated performance as the villainous Winn.*

TRIBUNAL

Week of 4 June 1994, No. 445
Directed by: Avery Brooks
Written by: Bill Dial
STARDATE: 47944.2
While on holiday, Operations Chief Miles O'Brien is arrested by the Cardassians and is horrified to discover that, under Cardassian law, he is already proven guilty and now faces the death penalty. **Keiko:** Rosalind Chao. **Makbar:** Caroline Lagerfelt. **Boone:** John Beck. **Gul Evek:** Richard Poe. **Kovat:** Fritz Weaver.
◆ *Avery Brooks' first turn at directing gives viewers a taste of the totalitarian authority of the Cardassians.*

SHOW WATCH: *O'Brien would again suffer brutal justice in* Star Trek: Deep Space Nine's *fourth-season episode "Hard Time."*

⬩ THE JEM'HADAR

Week of 11 June 1994 , No. 446
Directed by: Kim Friedman
Written by: Ira Steven Behr
STARDATE: Unknown
On a trip to the Gamma Quadrant, Cmdr. Benjamin Sisko and Quark are taken prisoner by the Jem'Hadar, storm troopers for a powerful new enemy known as the Dominion. **Eris:** Molly Hagan. **Talak'talan:** Cress Williams. **Capt. Keogh:** Alan Oppenheimer. **Nog:** Aron Eisenberg.
◆ *Although not a cliff-hanger in the traditional* Star Trek *sense, the introduction of a mysterious new enemy intent on keeping the Gamma Quadrant for itself gives the final episode of* Deep Space Nine's *second season a rivetting air of suspense, and a promise of a threat to come in the third season, as foreshadowed by Cmdr. Benjamin Sisko's deliberate words: "If the Dominion come through the wormhole, the first battle will be fought here, and I intend to be ready for them."*

RULE OF ACQUISITION: *No. 102: "Nature decays, but latinum is forever."* ✧

THE JEM'HADAR: *SISKO (AVERY BROOKS) PROTECTS QUARK FROM THE ADVANCING FORCES OF THE JEM'HADAR.*

THIRD SEASON

Star Trek: Deep Space Nine's third season brought significant changes to Avery Brooks's character. Sisko would be made over with an authoritative beard and moustache toward the end of the season (a look which would prevail throughout the show's fourth season), and he'd develop a new hobby, Bajoran antiquities (reminiscent of Patrick Stewart's interest in archeology in *Star Trek: The Next Generation*). It would also be a season of closure. Sisko would have a chance to lay to rest his lingering grief over the death of his wife, Jennifer. Major Kira would purge herself of the despair left after the death of her beloved Bajoran, Vedek Bareil, and Jadzia Dax would finally understand why Curzon had thrown her out of the Trill Initiate programme. The bonds of family would strengthen in many heart-warming episodes, and it would be a year of discovery, with Odo finally getting in touch with his own race. Yet, danger would rear before them as well. Furnished with a new Valiant-class starship, the *U.S.S. Defiant*, the station crew – with the *DS9* actors carrying the *Star Trek* mantle alone for the first time since *ST:TNG* signed off American TV in May 1994 – would prevent Romulan aggression against the Dominion, only to fall prey to the Dominion itself.

THE SEARCH, PART I

Week of 24 Sept. 1994, No. 447
Directed by: Kim Friedman
Written by: Ronald D. Moore
Story by: Ira Steven Behr and Robert Hewitt Wolfe
STARDATE: 48212.4
Sisko (Avery Brooks) and crew venture into the Gamma Quadrant to make peace with the Dominion, but the peace initiative falls apart after an attack by the Jem'Hadar, whose onslaught leaves the *Defiant* dead in space and Kira alone in a shuttle with Odo, who is compelled to abandon the *Defiant* to explore the strange Omarion Nebula. **T'Rul:** Martha Hackett. **Ornithar:** John Fleck. **Eddington:** Kenneth Marshall. **The Female Shape-Shifter:** Salome Jens.
◆ *The Jem'Hadar attack on the* Defiant *kicks off the two-part season-opener as Sisko takes his offensive against the Founders of the Dominion into the Gamma Quadrant. In a revealing sub-plot, Odo's fascination with the Omarion Nebula leads him to discover his homeworld.*
SHOW WATCH: *Martha Hackett (Romulan T'Rul) would return in Star Trek: Voyager as Seska. Kenneth Marshall's Eddington reappears in DS9 seasons three and four.*

THE SEARCH, PART II

Week of 1 Oct. 1994, No. 448
Directed by: Jonathan Frakes
Written by: Ira Steven Behr
Story by: Ira Steven Behr and Robert Hewitt Wolfe
STARDATE: Unknown
Conclusion: Sisko learns that the Dominion and the *Federation* are signing a peace treaty that would place the Bajorans under Dominion control. **Garak:** Andrew Robinson. **Admiral Necheyev:** Natalija Nogulich. **T'Rul:** Martha Hackett. **Eddington:** Kenneth Marshall. **Borath:** Dennis Christopher.
◆ *In a shocking turn of events, Odo struggles to deal with his Changeling heritage when he finally encounters his own kind and discovers that his shape-shifting brethren are the Founders of the Dominion, who control and subjugate other races. While the DS9 crew struggles to collapse the wormhole to prevent a Dominion invasion, the episode climaxes on a tense note as Odo makes the difficult decision to stay on DS9 after he discovers that the Dominion's attack was illusionary, induced in the minds of the DS9 crew by Borath (Dennis Christopher).*
FEDERATION FACTOID: *Odo was sent from his homeworld as one of 100 infant Changelings programmed to explore the galaxy then return home. Odo wasn't expected to reappear for another 300 years.*

THE HOUSE OF QUARK

Week of 8 Oct. 1994, No. 449
Directed by: Les Landau
Written by: Ronald D. Moore
Story by: Tom Benko
STARDATE: Unknown
To enhance his reputation, Quark lies about killing a drunken Klingon – then gets more than he bargained for when the warrior's widow (Mary Kay Adams) forces Quark to become her new husband. **Keiko:** Rosalind Chao. **D'Ghor:** Carlos Carrasco. **Rom:** Max Grodénchik. **Gowron:** Robert O'Reilly. **Tumek:** Joseph Ruskin.
◆ *A quick-witted episode underscoring*

Klingon-Ferengi differences. Action and comedy are served in equal measure as Quark breaks out of Ferengi character to come to the aid of a woman – albeit a fierce, knife-wielding Klingon female named Grilka. Putting aside his profit-seeking motives, the newly-married Quark earns the respect of the High Council by proving his courage in combat against D'Ghor, his Klingon adversary.
SHOW WATCH: *Joseph Ruskin (Klingon Tumek) first appeared as Galt, the master thrall, in the classic episode "The Gamesters of Triskelion," and would return in this season's "Improbable Cause."*
RULE OF ACQUISITION: *Quark's Rule No. 286: "When Morn leaves, it's all over."*

EQUILIBRIUM

Week of 15 Oct. 1994, No. 450
Directed by: Cliff Bole
Written by: René Echevarria
Story by: Christopher Teague
STARDATE: Unknown
Jadzia (Terry Farrell) suffers a breakdown and must fight for her life after she is stalked by a mysterious figure from her past. **Dr. Renhol:** Lisa Banes. **Joran Belar:** Jeff Magnus McBride.
◆ *Trill society, including the symbiont breeding habits and selection process, is further explained in this eerie drama that places Jadzia's life on the line as she struggles with the repressed memories of an earlier host.*
SHOW WATCH: *Jay Chattaway composed the haunting melody hummed by Jadzia.*

SECOND SKIN

Week of 22 Oct. 1994, No. 451
Directed by: Les Landau
Written by: Robert Hewitt Wolfe
STARDATE: Unknown
Kira is shocked to learn that she may be a Cardassian operative who was surgically altered to look Bajoran. **Garak:** Andrew Robinson. **Entek:** Gregory Sierra. **Yeln:** Tony Papenfuss. **Yteppa:** Cindy Katz. **Tekeny Ghemor:** Lawrence Pressman.
◆ *Nana Visitor does a terrific job of balancing the hostility Kira feels toward her Cardassian kidnappers and the sympathy she feels for the man who thinks he's her Cardassian father, forcing her to confront her past and question her very identity.*
STAR WATCH: *Gregory Sierra (Barney Miller) plays Entek, a sinister member of the Cardassian secret police. Lawrence*

Pressman (Doogie Howser, M.D.) is touching as Kira's would-be father.

FEDERATION FACTOID: *We learn Kira is from the Bajoran province Dahkur, and her parents died in Bajoran refugee camps.*

THE ABANDONED

Week of 29 Oct. 1994, No. 452
Directed by: Avery Brooks
Written by: D. Thomas Maio and Steve Warnek
STARDATE: Unknown

Odo tries to alter the violent behaviour of a Jem'Hadar child (Bumper Robinson).
Boslic Captain: Leslie Bevis.

✦ *Odo attempts to connect with his people by collecting statues of all shapes and sizes to explore new forms and textures. He no longer rests in his bucket, but keeps it as a reminder.*

FEDERATION FACTOID: *Secret to Jem'Hadar's submission: An isogenic enzyme is missing from their genes and is provided by an addictive drug – supplied by the Dominion.*

CIVIL DEFENSE

Week of 5 Nov. 1994, No. 453
Directed by: Reza Badiyi
Written by: Mike Krohn
STARDATE: Unknown

When a security program is activated, the crew must work together to prevent the destruction of the station. **Garak:** Andrew Robinson. **Gul Dukat:** Marc Alaimo. **Legate Kell:** Danny Goldring.

✦ *Long-time adversaries Odo and Quark are forced to co-operate, and Jake disobeys his father's orders in order to save O'Brien's life.*

BEST DIALOGUE: *After discovering that he's described in his security file as "a self-important con artist who's nowhere near as clever as he thinks he is," a horrified Quark says to Odo, "Two hours ago, you told me I was the most devious Ferengi you ever met." Replies Odo: "I thought we were going to die. I was trying to be nice."*

RULE OF ACQUISITION: *No. 75: "Home is where the heart is, but the stars are made of latinum."*

MERIDIAN

Week of 12 Nov. 1994, No. 454
Directed by: Jonathan Frakes
Written by: Mark Gehred-O'Connell
Story by: Hilary Bader and Evan Carlos Somers
STARDATE: 48423.2

Jadzia falls in love with a Meridian scientist (Brett Cullen) only to discover that he and his planet are about to disappear into another dimension. **Seltin:** Christine Healy. **Tiron:** Jeffrey Combs.

✦ *While Dax, the Trill symbiont, has had many romantic encounters, it's a first for Jadzia. Her attempts to join the scientist in his dimension are unsuccessful. In a humourous secondary story, Quark promises to create a Kira-based holodeck fantasy for an infatuated customer – but Odo foils the holo-program and places Quark's head on Kira's body.*

RULE OF ACQUISITION: *No. 19: "Satisfaction is not guaranteed."*

DEFIANT

Week of 19 Nov. 1994, No. 455
Directed by: Cliff Bole
Written by: Ronald D. Moore
STARDATE: 48467.3

When Cmdr. Riker (Jonathan Frakes) arrives unexpectedly at the station, neither he nor his intentions towards Kira are what they appear to be. **Gul Dukat:** Marc Alaimo. **Korinas:** Tricia O'Neil. **Kalita:** Shannon Cochran.

✦ *Coinciding with the première of "Star Trek Generations," Jonathan Frakes makes a cross-over appearance on DS9 (though he had already directed twice this season). Picking up the Thomas Riker story-line (ST:TNG's "Second Chances"), Riker's alter ego struggles to carve his own identity by joining the Maquis, stealing the Defiant and attacking a Cardassian base. Although Thomas was in love with Deanna last time around, he's now attracted to Kira. They share an undeniable attraction – plus a passionate kiss – and Kira promises to get him out of the Cardassian labour camp.*

SHOW WATCH: *Tricia O'Neil (Korinas) was Capt. Garrett in ST:TNG's "Yesterday's Enterprise," then played Klingon Kurak in the sixth season's "Suspicions."*

FASCINATION

Week of 26 Nov. 1994, No. 456
Directed by: Avery Brooks
Written by: Phillip LaZebnik
Story by: Ira Steven Behr and James Crocker
STARDATE: Unknown

SECOND SKIN: *MAJOR KIRA NERYS (NANA VISITOR) IS SHOCKED TO DISCOVER SHE MAY ACTUALLY BE A CARDASSIAN OPERATIVE.*

Station personnel express latent feelings of love toward one another after Lwaxana Troi (Majel Barrett) arrives to attend the Bajoran Gratitude Festival and infects everyone with Zanthi Fever, a condition that releases one's hidden passions. **Bareil:** Philip Anglim.

✦ *Avery Brooks's third time in the director chair coincides with Majel Barret's second cross-over appearance as the outrageous Lwaxana Troi, whose odd Betazoid fever induces an epidemic of unexpected romantic attractions – Jake to Kira, Quark to Keiko, Bareil to Dax, Dax to Sisko, Bashir to Kira and, of course, Lwaxana to Odo.*

SHOW WATCH: *We get a closer look at Quark's alien barfly, Morn, when Dax becomes fascinated with the wiry hairs sticking out of his huge head.*

PAST TENSE, PART I

Week of 31 Dec. 1994, No. 457
Directed by: Reza Badiyi
Written by: Robert Hewitt Wolfe
Story by: Ira Steven Behr and Robert Hewitt Wolfe
STARDATE: 48481.2

A transporter accident strands Sisko, Dax and Bashir in San Francisco in the year 2024 – a period of riots and rebellion – where their presence alters the future. **Chris Brynner:** Jim Metzler. **Webb:** Bill Smitrovich. **B.C.:** Frank Military.

◆ An oft-repeated plot: Crew keeps past Earth experiences on course according to the real time line. DS9 also deals with homelessness in the 21st century as Sisko, Bashir and Dax discover ghettos, called "Sanctuary Districts," for people with nowhere to go.

RULE OF ACQUISITION: No. 111: "Treat people in your debt like family...exploit them."

PAST TENSE, PART II

Week of 7 Jan. 1995, No. 458
Directed by: Jonathan Frakes
Written by: Ira Steven Behr
and René Echevarria
STARDATE: Unknown
Conclusion. In order to restore the time line, Sisko must pose as a key historic figure and risk his life to prevent bloodshed during a hostage crisis. **Webb:** Bill Smitrovich. **B.C.:** Frank Military. **Grady:** Clint Howard.

◆ Despite the episode's dark look at poverty and homelessness, light moments are woven into the sub-plot which has Kira and O'Brien beaming in and out of 1960s San Francisco as they search for Bashir, Dax and Sisko (leaving several confused hippies in their wake). The episode also has some nice retro-futuristic touches, with Sisko logging onto "the Net" to inform the public about the terrible conditions of the "Sanctuary Districts."

STAR WATCH: Clint Howard (Gentle Ben), who appeared 29 years earlier as Balok in the classic episode "The Corbomite Maneuver," appears as Grady.

LIFE SUPPORT

Week of 28 Jan. 1995, No. 459
Directed by: Reza Badiyi
Written by: Ronald D. Moore
Story by: Christian Ford
and Roger Soffer
STARDATE: 48498.4
A serious injury to mediator Vedek Bareil (Philip Anglim) threatens peace talks between Bajor and Cardassia, especially when it's learned that the operation to save him will transform Bareil into a half-human, half-machine. **Kai Winn:** Louise Fletcher. **Leanne.** Lark Voorhies.

◆ Once again, enduring love eludes

Starfleet members: Kira Nerys sheds tears as she's helpless to prevent her beloved Bareil from dying. This episode marks Academy Award-winner Louise Fletcher's fifth appearance as Kai Winn.

🚀 HEART OF STONE

Week of 4 Feb. 1995, No. 460
Directed by: Alexander Singer
Written by: Ira Steven Behr
and Robert Hewitt Wolfe
STARDATE: 48521.5
Tracking a lone Maquis to a deserted moon, shape-shifter Odo and Major Kira Nerys quickly forget the fugitive when Kira becomes trapped by a crystalline formation. **Rom:** Max Grodénchik. **Nog:** Aron Eisenberg.

◆ Odo finally makes the confession that has long burned within him. Trying to free Maj. Kira Nerys from her crystal cage, Odo bravely confesses his love for her when it appears that she's going to die, but cruel barbs of betrayal are the shape-shifter's only reward. Bewildered by Kira's admission of love for him, Odo discovers that the Kira trapped in the crystal is actually the female shape-shifter he met in the Omarion Nebula ("The Search, Part I"), and her Kira disguise is intended to crush Odo's love for the real Kira so he'll consider returning to his homeworld. Meanwhile back at the Deep Space Nine station, the assimilating Nog tells Cmdr. Sisko that he wants to join Starfleet and study at the Academy.

RULE OF ACQUISITION: No. 18: "A Ferengi without profit is no Ferengi at all."

DESTINY

Week of 11 Feb. 1995, No. 461
Directed by: Les Landau
Written by: David S. Cohen
and Martin A. Winer
STARDATE: 48543.2
An ancient Bajoran prophecy of doom seems to be coming true when the DS9 crew cannot stop a rogue comet threatening to collapse the Bajoran-Idran wormhole. **Gilora:** Tracy Scoggins. **Ulani:** Wendy Robie. **Vedek Yarka:** Erick Avari. **Dejar:** Jessica Hendra.

◆ Sisko gains respect for Bajoran beliefs in this episode, which highlights the shaky Federation-Cardassian treaty.

RULES OF ACQUISITION: No. 34: "Peace is good for business." No. 35: "War is good for business."

PROPHET MOTIVE

Week of 18 Feb. 1995, No. 462
Directed by: René Auberjonois
Written by: Ira Steven Behr
and Robert Hewitt Wolfe
STARDATE: Unknown
When Grand Nagus Zek (Wallace Shawn) arrives at Deep Space Nine, Quark and Rom are stunned to hear that he has come up with a plan that may ultimately lead to the downfall of the Ferengi people. **Rom:** Max Grodénchik. **Emi:** Juliana Donald.

◆ Wallace Shawn – memorable for his comic debut as the Ferengi leader in "The Nagus" – makes his third appearance as Grand Nagus Zek, whose unexpected vision of a kinder Ferengi race is com-

PAST TENSE: A TRANSPORTER ACCIDENT STRANDS SISKO (AVERY BROOKS) AND BASHIR (SIDDIG EL FADIL) IN SAN FRANCISCO – IN THE YEAR 2024.

pletely insane according to Quark, who can barely stomach the Nagus's new book: "The Rules of Acquisition Revised for the Modern Ferengi." Among the revised rules: No. 1: "If they want their money back, give it to them." Armin Shimerman is in top form as a Ferengi determined to return the Nagus to his old greedy self.

BEST DIALOGUE: *Quark to Rom: "You embezzled money from the Nagus? Father would be proud."*

FEDERATION FACTOID: *We learn that Bashir is the youngest doctor ever nominated for the Federation's prestigious Carrington Award, given to one who has made significant medical contributions.*

RULE OF ACQUISITION: *No. 10: "Greed is eternal."*

VISIONARY

Week of 25 Feb. 1995, No. 463
Directed by: Reza Badiyi
Written by: John Shirley
Story by: Ethan H. Calk
STARDATE: Unknown
After being exposed to a mild form of radiation, O'Brien is able to shift through time to see events before they actually occur – including his own death and the station's destruction. **Ruwon:** Jack Shearer. **Karina:** Annette Helde.

✦ *Another distortion in the time-space continuum where the Federation finally makes payment for the U.S.S. Defiant's cloaking technology by providing information about the Dominion to the Romulans, who attempt to destroy the wormhole in order to secure a hold on the Alpha Quadrant. In the familiar back-from-the-dead tradition: O'Brien time-shifts to the past to prevent his future death by providing Bashir with vital medical information.*

BEST DIALOGUE: *Curious about the provider of the medical information, which O'Brien brought from the future, Bashir remarks, "Oh? Well, who am I to argue with me?" after hearing it was himself.*

SHOW WATCH: *Miles O'Brien teaches his friends the 20th-century game of darts.*

DISTANT VOICES

Week of 8 April 1995, No. 464
Directed by: Alexander Singer
Written by: Ira Steven Behr and Robert Hewitt Wolfe
Story by: Joe Menosky
STARDATE: Unknown
Left in a coma following an alien attack,

Bashir takes an inner journey through his own mind as he fights to regain consciousness by calling upon different aspects of his personality, represented by various station crew members. **Garak:** Andrew Robinson. **Altovar:** Victor Rivers.

✦ *Garnering a major American television award for Outstanding Individual Achievement in Make-Up for a Series, the episode introduces a Lethean, a previously unknown alien, who manages to physically affect Bashir's deterioration by existing right within his mind.*

SHOW WATCH: *The Ullians possess a similar ability to project themselves into the minds of others, which threw Deanna Troi, Cmdr. Riker and Dr. Beverley Crusher into comas after Jev invaded their minds in ST:TNG's "Violations."*

THROUGH THE LOOKING GLASS

Week of 15 April 1995, No. 466
Directed by: Winrich Kolbe
Written by: Ira Steven Behr and Robert Hewitt Wolfe
STARDATE: Unknown
Abducted into a mirror universe by Miles O'Brien's double, Sisko is forced to assume the identity of the mirror Sisko to lead a rebellion against the Klingon-Cardassian Alliance. **Tuvok:** Tim Russ.

✦ *The third Star Trek adventure in the mirror universe, first visited by Capt. James Kirk and crew in the classic series episode "Mirror, Mirror," then by Sisko and staff in DS9's second-season "Crossover." This time, Sisko gets the opportunity to find inner peace. Where he couldn't save his wife, Jennifer, during the Locutus-led attack against the Federation (ST:TNG's two-part "The Best of Both Worlds"), Sisko now has the chance to save the mirror Jennifer from assassins and bid goodbye the way he needs to.*

SHOW WATCH: *In the first direct cross-over from Star Trek: Voyager to DS9, Tim Russ appears as the mirror Tuvok. Felicia Bell, first seen as Jennifer Sisko in DS9's "Emissary," makes her second appearance, this time as the mirror Jennifer.*

FEDERATION FACTOID: *Quark's words to Sisko, following the confiscation of 27 Cardassian voles – "Poor Morn. This is going to break his hearts" – suggests Morn's race has at least as many hearts as Klingons have livers (two, noted in ST:TNG's "Ethics").*

IMPROBABLE CAUSE

Week of 22 April 1995, No. 465
Directed by: Avery Brooks
Written by: René Echevarria
Story by: Robert Lederman and David R. Long
STARDATE: Unknown
When an attempt is made on the life of Garak (Andrew Robinson), Odo's investigation points to the Romulans. **Enabran Tain:** Paul Dooley. **Retaya:** Carlos LaCamara. **Informant:** Joseph Ruskin. **Romulan:** Darwyn Carson. **Mila:** Julianna McCarthy.

✦ *The Romulan effort to crush the Dominion continues, with the former head of the Obsidian Order – Enabran Tain – behind a joint Cardassian-Romulan plan to destroy the Founders. The first of a two-part tale where Garak's loyalties fall under suspicion after Odo and Garak are taken aboard a Romulan Warbird and Garak sides with Tain, leaving Odo to the uncertainty of Romulan incarceration.*

BEST DIALOGUE: *Tain to Garak: "Always burn your bridges behind you. You never know who might be following."*

SHOW WATCH: *Paul Dooley (Grace Under Fire) returns as Garak's former mentor and current tormentor, Enabran Tain.*

THE DIE IS CAST

Week of 29 April 1995, No. 467
Directed by: David Livingston
Written by: Ronald D. Moore
STARDATE: Unknown
On the eve of a joint Romulan-Cardassian attack against the Founders, Garak must decide whether to spare Odo's life or kill him to please his former mentor, Enabran Tain. **Lovok:** Leland Orser. **Eddington:** Kenneth Marshall. **Toddman:** Leon Russom.

✦ *The consequences of a shape-shifter's inability to revert to a liquid state at the end of the "solid" cycle are graphically displayed as Odo – interrogated by Garak while being held in solid form by Cardassian technology – begins to crumble apart. Odo admits his secret desire to return to his homeworld, but later decides to stay aboard the station after being rescued by the Defiant. The Romulan-Cardassian alliance is left in ruins, no longer a threat to the Dominion.*

SHOW WATCH: *Kenneth Marshall returns as Eddington, last seen in "The Search," parts one and two.*

EXPLORERS

Week of 6 May 1995, No. 468
Directed by: Cliff Bole
Written by: René Echevarria
Story by: Hilary J. Bader
STARDATE: Unknown

Intrigued by the legend that Bajorans were exploring their star system eight centuries ago, Sisko builds a replica of an ancient Bajoran sail-powered spacecraft and pilots it into space with Jake – right into Cardassian territory. **Gul Dukat:** Marc Alaimo. **Dr. Elizabeth Lense:** Bari Hochwald. **Leeta:** Chase Masterson.

✦ *Sisko's beard and moustache appear in this Sisko-Jake story which explores the close father-son bond. Jake has been offered a writing fellowship at the Pennington School in New Zealand, but is worried about his father being alone and suggests that he consider dating a certain "freighter captain" – the first mention of Kasidy Yates (Penny Johnson), who would steal Sisko's heart and appear throughout DS9's fourth season.*

SHOW WATCH: *Chase Masterson ("Married People, Single Sex") would reprise her role as the feisty Dabo girl Leeta in "Facets," then return as Leeta in "Bar Association."*

FEDERATION FACTOID: *Bashir would have been class valedictorian at Starfleet Medical instead of runner-up salutatorian had he not mistaken a pre-ganglionic fibre for a post-ganglionic nerve on an exam.*

⬟ FAMILY BUSINESS

Week of 13 May 1995, No. 469
Directed by: René Auberjonois
Written by: Ira Steven Behr
and Robert Hewitt Wolfe
STARDATE: Unknown

Quark faces financial ruin when it's discovered that his mother, Ishka (Andrea Martin), has defied Ferengi law and made herself a profit through a secret business deal. **Kasidy Yates:** Penny Johnson. **Brunt:** Jeffrey Combs.

✦ *Andrea Martin ("Club Paradise") became an instant fan favourite as Ishka, mother to Rom and Quark, who breaks every Ferengi rule when she makes a profit (in a beetle farm), speaks for herself – and wears clothes. Rom's discontent with Ferengi law also begins to stir, and would erupt in "Bar Association."*

SHOW WATCH: *Penny Johnson's first appearance as Sisko's love interest, Kasidy Yates.*

FEDERATION FACTOID: *The name of the Ferengi homeworld is Ferenginar.*

SHAKAAR

Week of 20 May 1995, No. 470
Directed by: Jonathan West
Written by: Gordon Dawson
STARDATE: Unknown

Kai Winn (Louise Fletcher) is appointed First Minister of Bajor's Provisional Government, but when a small group threatens to disrupt her transition to power, Kira intervenes – siding with the dissenters – when she finds that the head of the resistance (Duncan Regehr) is an old friend.

✦ *Kira's mistrust of Kai Winn erupts into outright defiance, and her noble nature shines as she defends poor farmers against the government. Kira also deals with the lingering pain wrought by the death of Vedek Bareil ("Life Support").*

STAR WATCH: *Duncan Regehr (Shakaar) first appeared as the ghostly Ronin in ST:TNG's "Sub Rosa." Shakaar would return to ignite Kira's passion in the fourth season's "Crossfire."*

FACETS

Week of 10 June 1995, No. 471
Directed by: Cliff Bole
Written by: René Echevarria
STARDATE: Unknown

After Odo agrees to temporarily host the

FAMILY BUSINESS: COMIC STAR ANDREA MARTIN MAKES A GUTSY BID FOR EQUALITY AS SHE BREAKS EVERY KNOWN RULE RESTRICTING FERENGI WOMEN

spirit of Curzon as part of the Trill Rite of Closure, which enables Jadzia (Terry Farrell) a chance to meet all of her previous hosts, Curzon refuses to leave Odo's body. **Guardian:** Jefrey Alan Chandler. **Nog:** Aron Eisenberg.

✦ *Odo's quest to further his understanding of the human condition is greatly enhanced through his temporary joining with the spirit of Curzon Dax, who soon has the normally-reserved constable drinking and laughing as no one's ever seen him, and Rom's self-confidence continues to grow following Quark's attempt to ruin Nog's efforts to pass a Starfleet Academy Preparatory entrance exam.*

BEST DIALOGUE: *Quark to Nog, who orders an unlikely beverage: "A root beer? This is the end of Ferengi civilization."*

SHOW WATCH: *The second appearance by Chase Masterson as Leeta the Dabo girl.*

FEDERATION FACTOID: *Jadzia is the only Trill ever to be readmitted to the Initiate program after being washed out.*

THE ADVERSARY

Week of 17 June 1995, No. 472
Directed by: Alexander Singer
Written by: Ira Steven Behr
and Robert Hewitt Wolfe
STARDATE: 48959.1

Aboard the *Defiant*, Sisko and crew fall prey to a shape-shifting saboteur, intent on throwing the *Federation* into a war with the Tzenkethi homeworld – a prelude to the Dominion invasion. **Krajensky:** Lawrence Pressman. **Eddington:** Kenneth Marshall.

✦ *The Federation feared they would come. The Founders are everywhere in the Alpha Quadrant in this suspenseful season-ender where no one can be trusted. Sisko rises in rank to captain.*

BEST DIALOGUE: *With the ship's auto-destruct sequence less than seven minutes to detonation, Sisko asks O'Brien, "How long will it take?" (to disengage a saboteur's force field). O'Brien's reply: "I guess it's going to have to be less than seven minutes, won't it?"*

SHOW WATCH: *Lawrence Pressman (Krajensky) first turned up this season as Ghemor, Kira's would-be Cardassian father ("Second Skin"). And it's the last credit for Siddig El Fadil. The actor would change his name to Alexander Siddig (and become romantically involved with Nana Visitor) before season four.* ✦

FOURTH SEASON

SEASON FOUR HAS AN EXPLOSIVE START AS THE KLINGONS END THEIR ALLIANCE WITH THE *FEDERATION* AND resume their warrior conduct in an effort to establish a hold on the Alpha Quadrant. Boarding the station to investigate the Klingon aggression is Lt.-Cmdr. Worf (Michael Dorn), who joins the *Star Trek: Deep Space Nine* crew to bolster the shaky Klingon-*Federation* truce. (Producers hoped that some of *Star Trek: The Next Generation's* stardust might rub off to expand *Star Trek: Deep Space Nine's* audience.) There's also a change in the credits this season: Siddig El Fadil, who plays Dr. Julian Bashir, changes his name to Alexander Siddig.

THE WAY OF THE WARRIOR: *EVER THE AMIABLE HOST, QUARK (ARMIN SHIMERMAN) IS EAGER TO WELCOME NEWCOMER (AND POTENTIAL CUSTOMER) WORF (MICHAEL DORN) TO HIS BAR ON DEEP SPACE NINE.*

THE WAY OF THE WARRIOR
Week of 30 Sept. 1995, No. 718
Directed by: James L. Conway
Written by: Ira Steven Behr and Robert Hewitt Wolfe
STARDATE: 49011.4
The Klingons attack Cardassia in a bid to overthrow the planet's new civilian government, and the station becomes a Klingon target after Sisko (Avery Brooks) and crew save members of Cardassia's new government from falling into Klingon hands. **Gul Dukat:** Marc Alaimo. **Gowron:** Robert O'Reilly. **Martok:** J.G. Hertzler. **Drex:** Obi Ndefo. **Kaybok:** Christopher Darga. **Huraga:** William Dennis Hunt.
✦ A dynamite season-opener from the writing team of Behr and Wolfe, who would script many of the season's best action pieces. The Klingons are back, doing what they do best – flexing their spirit of conquest, which does nothing for Worf's sense of isolation (a problem that began

during ST:TNG). Still feeling like an outsider among humans, Worf comes to the station to avert an all-out war between the Klingons and the Federation – but in the process, he exiles himself from the Klingons, bringing disgrace to his family and fuelling his burning desire for vengeance – an issue central to this season's "Rules of Engagement" episode in which Worf faces extradition. (Repeats as two one-hour episodes, Nos. 473 and 474.)
BEST DIALOGUE: *Garak (Andrew Robinson) about to be attacked by four Klingons: "Let me guess. You're either lost or desperately searching for a good tailor." Quark, agreeing that root beer is vile: "It's so bubbly and cloying and happy."*
SHOW WATCH: *Sisko gives his love interest, Kasidy Yates (Penny Johnson), a scarf made of Tholian silk. The Tholians (mentioned in ST:TNG's "The Icarus Factor," "Peak Performance" and "Reunion") were first encountered in the classic episode "The Tholian Web."*

THE VISITOR
Week of 7 Oct. 1995, No. 476
Directed by: David Livingston
Written by: Michael Taylor
STARDATE: Unknown
A warp core accident traps Capt. Benjamin Sisko (Avery Brooks) in subspace, causing Jake (Cirroc Lofton) to spend most of his life trying to get his father back. **Adult Jake:** Tony Todd. **Melanie:** Rachel Robinson. **Korena:** Galyn Görg. **Nog:** Aron Eisenberg.
✦ *Tony Todd (who played Worf's younger brother, Kurn, in several ST:TNG episodes) plays an elderly Jake Sisko in this touching story focussing on the deep love between father and son. Set more than 50 years in the future, the story is told in flashbacks as Jake imparts to an aspiring writer (Rachel Robinson) the sad tale of how his father disappeared during an accident aboard the U.S.S. Defiant.*
SHOW WATCH: *Jake's mission to rescue his only parent is reminiscent of the experiences of ST:TNG's Deanna ("Dark Page"), Geordi ("Interface"), Wesley Crusher ("Remember Me") and the grown-up Alexander in "Firstborn."*
FEDERATION FACTOID: *In this episode's future time line, Jake published two books ("Anslem" and "Collected Stories"), Nog rose to the rank of Starfleet captain and Morn became the owner of Quark's bar.*

HIPPOCRATIC OATH
Week of 14 Oct. 1995, No. 475
Directed by: René Auberjonois
Written by: Lisa Klink
STARDATE: 49066.5
Bashir and O'Brien (Alexander Siddig, Colm Meaney) are captured by Jem'Hadar soldiers, who threaten to kill the two unless the Jem'Hadar are cured of their drug addiction, which is fed by the Dominion. **Goran'Agar:** Scott MacDonald. **Arak'Taral:** Stephen Davies. **Meso'Clan:** Jerry Roberts. **Temo'Zuma:** Marshall Teague.
✦ Star Trek once again deals with the issue of drug addiction. (DS9 addressed the issue in the second-season episode "The Wire," while ST:TNG dealt with the issue in its first-season episode "Symbiosis.") This time, the Jem'Hadar are central to the issue, and we're given a look at the terrible pain a Jem'Hadar experiences when the Dominion drug is withheld. This is also the first evidence that a

Jem'Hadar's genetic make-up can evolve, allowing the aliens to live without the drug, as Goran'Agar has succeeded in doing. Although the encounter doesn't end in friendship between the Federation and the Jem'Hadar, the two organizations would meet and co-operate again in this season's "To the Death."

FEDERATION FACTOID: *The opaque liquid the Jem'Hadar need to survive is called Ketracel-white.*

INDISCRETION
Week of 21 Oct. 1995, No. 477
Directed by: LeVar Burton
Teleplay by: Nicholas Corea
Story by: Toni Marberry
and Jack Treviño
STARDATE: Unknown
When Gul Dukat (Marc Alaimo) asks to accompany Kira on a search for long lost Bajoran prisoners of war, the major discovers his motives are not as innocent as they first appeared. **Kasidy Yates:** Penny Johnson. **Razka:** Roy Brocksmith. **Ziyal:** Cyia Batten.
✦ *The lingering hostility between Bajor and Cardassia is exemplified in the verbal exchanges between Dukat and Kira, whose search for a missing Cardassian transport forces her to re-evaluate her anti-Cardassian feelings. It's a story full of surprises, with a bit of Dukat's compassion shining through his cold exterior.*
FEDERATION FACTOID: *Dukat's half-Cardassian, half-Bajoran daughter, Ziyal, was born of his secret love affair with the Bajoran woman Tora Naprem, whom he met during the occupation.*

REJOINED
Week of 28 Oct. 1995, No. 478
Directed by: Avery Brooks
Written by: Ronald D. Moore
and René Echevarria
Story by: René Echevarria
STARDATE: 49195.5
Jadzia (Terry Farrell) faces exile from her homeland – and the death of the symbiont – when the spirit of a former male host meets his former wife and falls in love again. **Lenara:** Susanna Thompson. **Bejal:** Tim Ryan. **Pren:** James Noah. **Eddington:** Kenneth Marshall.
✦ *Overcome by emotions felt by former host Torias Dax, Jadzia and a female Trill wrestle within the constraints of Trill law before allowing old feelings to surface,*

resulting in Star Trek's much-talked-about kiss between two females, echoing the Kirk-Uhura interracial kiss 27 years earlier in "Plato's Stepchildren."

SHOW WATCH: *Kenneth Marshall would return as Eddington in "Our Man Bashir."*

LITTLE GREEN MEN
Week of 4 Nov. 1995, No. 480
Directed by: James L. Conway
Written by: Ira Steven Behr
and Robert Hewitt Wolfe
Story by: Tony Marberry
and Jack Treviño
STARDATE: Unknown
En route to *Starfleet* Academy aboard a shuttle, Quark, Rom and Nog are transported back in time and are forced to land at Roswell, New Mexico, in the year 1947, where they are mistaken for invaders from Mars. **Rom:** Max Grodénchik. **Nog:** Aron Eisenberg. **Nurse Garland:** Megan Gallagher. **Denning:** Charles Napier. **Carlson:** Conor O'Farrell.
✦ *Another example of crew members experiencing real Earth events by being carried back in time. An entertaining take on the real-life controversy surrounding Roswell, New Mexico, where many believe a real UFO landed in 1947.*
FEDERATION FACTOID: *The Ferengi equivalent to heaven is "The Divine Treasury," where Ferengi can bid for new lives, thus supporting the notion that their race believes in the*

"after life." Their equivalent to hell is "The Vault of Eternal Destitution."

RULE OF ACQUISITION: *No. 203: "New customers are like razor-toothed Greeworms. They can be succulent, but sometimes they bite back."*

STARSHIP DOWN
Week of 11 Nov. 1995, No. 479
Directed by: Alexander Singer
Written by: David Mack
and John J. Ordover
STARDATE: 49263.5
When a Jem'Hadar attack injures Sisko and leaves the *Defiant* crippled inside a remote planet's turbulent atmosphere, Kira (Nana Visitor) draws upon her Bajoran faith in her efforts to keep Sisko alive. **Hanok:** James Cromwell. **Muniz:** F.J. Rio. **Stevens:** Jay Baker.
✦ *Sisko and Kira begin a relationship as true friends – not as commander to second or Emissary to Bajoran – when Kira prevents Sisko from slipping into a coma while the Defiant drifts helplessly. A great action-filled episode with Worf struggling to deal with engineers who, to his frustration, do not perform their duties in a manner he had grown accustomed to as a member of the U.S.S. Enterprise-D.*
SHOW WATCH: *James Cromwell ("Babe") plays the Karemma trader Hanok.*
FEDERATION FACTOID: *We learn that Morn has 17 brothers and sisters.*

LITTLE GREEN MEN: NO SOONER DO QUARK (ARMIN SHIMERMAN), NOG (ARON EISENBERG) AND ROM (MAX GRODÉNCHIK) ACCIDENTALLY LAND ON EARTH IN THE YEAR 1947 THAN THEY'RE MISTAKEN FOR LITTLE GREEN MEN FROM MARS.

THE SWORD OF KAHLESS

Week of 18 Nov. 1995, No. 481
Directed by: LeVar Burton
Written by: Hans Beimler
Story by: Richard Danus
STARDATE: Unknown

Worf and Jadzia accompany the legendary Klingon warrior Kor (John Colicos) in search of a mythical sword they believe will unite the Klingon Empire. **Toral:** Rick Pasqualone. **Soto:** Tom Morga.

✦ *Kahless, who united the Klingon Empire some 1,500 years earlier, was first introduced in the classic-episode "The Savage Curtain."*

SHOW WATCH: *John Colicos, the first Klingon, Kor, in the classic-episode "Errand of Mercy," also appeared as Kor in DS9's second-season "Blood Oath."*

OUR MAN BASHIR

Week of 25 Nov. 1995, No. 482
Directed by: Winrich Kolbe
Written by: Ronald D. Moore
Story by: Robert Gillan
STARDATE: Unknown

Bashir becomes embroiled in a life-and-death situation after a transporter accident traps crew members in the holo-suite computer memory. **Rom:** Max Grodénchik. **Eddington:** Kenneth Marshall. **Garak:** Andrew Robinson.

✦ *A tongue-in-cheek tribute to the James Bond films of the '60s, with Bashir playing a secret agent trying to foil plans of world domination by the power-hungry scientist Dr. Noah (Sisko, whose holosuite character sounds a lot like "Dr. No") and his accomplice, Professor Bare (Dax).*

HOMEFRONT

Week of 30 Dec. 1995, No. 483
Directed by: David Livingston
Written by: Ira Steven Behr
and Robert Hewitt Wolfe
STARDATE: 49170.6

Odo and Sisko head planetary security after the *Federation* informs them that Changelings may have invaded Earth. Part one of two. **Admiral Leyton:** Robert Foxworth. **Joseph Sisko:** Brock Peters.

✦ *While on Earth to oversee Starfleet security measures to prevent planetary infiltration by the Founders, Sisko visits his father, Joseph – only to widen the gulf between himself and his only parent when he suspects his father of being a*

Changeling. Joseph's stubborn refusal to submit to a blood test dramatically demonstrates the deterioration of a relationship in the absence of trust. ("Paradise Lost" is the conclusion of this two-part tale.)

PARADISE LOST

Week of 6 Jan. 1996, No. 484
Directed by: Reza Badiyi
Written by: Ira Steven Behr
and Robert Hewitt Wolfe
Story by: Ronald D. Moore
STARDATE: Unknown

Conclusion. Earth is under martial law and *Starfleet* troops are stationed around the planet in anticipation of a Dominion invasion. **Leyton:** Robert Foxworth. **Jaresh-Inyo:** Herschel Sparber. **Benteen:** Susan Gibney. **Riley Shepard:** David Drew Gallagher.

✦ *Earth endures its own power struggle, mirroring recent developments on Cardassia where the military government was overthrown by civilians in "The Way of the Warrior."*

CROSSFIRE

Week of 27 Jan. 1996, No. 485
Directed by: Les Landau
Written by: René Echevarria
STARDATE: Unknown

Odo is assigned to protect the Bajoran First Minister Shakaar (Duncan Regehr), but the shape-shifter's hidden feelings for Kira come to a head when Shakaar becomes attracted to the major – and she to him. **Sarish:** Bruce Wright.

✦ *Matters of the heart begin to affect Odo's performance in his duties. He uses whatever small opportunities he can to watch Kira and Shakaar together, but soon realizes the futility of what he's doing, becomes frustrated and, in an uncharacteristic show of anger, trashes his quarters. Still more unusual is Odo taking advice from Quark.*

RETURN TO GRACE

Week of 3 Feb. 1996, No. 486
Directed by: Jonathan West
Written by: Hans Beimler
Story by: Tom Benko
Stardate: Unknown

To regain his former status in the Cardassian government, a demoted Gul Dukat (Marc Alaimo) seeks Kira's help in hunting down the Klingon ship responsible for destroying a Cardassian

outpost. **Ziyal:** Cyia Batten. **Damar:** Casey Biggs. **K'Temang:** John K. Shull.

✦ *Having briefly revealed his compassionate side to both Kira and his half-Bajoran, half-Cardassian daughter, Ziyal, in "Indiscretion," Dukat refocusses on his career as one whose lust for power will always be a driving passion.*

SONS OF MOGH

Week of 10 Feb. 1996, No. 487
Directed by: David Livingston
Written by: Ronald D. Moore
STARDATE: 49556.2

An outcast of the Klingon Empire because brother Worf decided to side with the *Federation*, Kurn (Tony Todd) arrives at *Deep Space Nine* with one thought in mind – to ask Worf to kill him in order to die an honourable death. **Noggra:** Robert DoQui. **Tilikia:** Dell Yount. **Klingon Officer:** Elliot Woods.

✦ *One of the most detailed displays of Klingon family culture: Tony Todd returns to Star Trek as Worf's brother, Kurn, who tries to end his life rather than live with the shame of his brother's actions during the battle fought in DS9's "The Way of the Warrior." Although Klingons condemn suicide as an option, they have a ritual Mok TuVor which allows family members to kill one another honourably.*

BEST DIALOGUE: *After his memory is erased, Kurn turns to Worf, whom he no longer recognizes, and asks, "Are you part of my family?" Worf replies, "I have no family," echoing his long-standing sense of alienation within the Federation.*

BAR ASSOCIATION

Week of 17 Feb. 1996, No. 488
Directed by: LeVar Burton
Written by: Robert Hewitt Wolfe
and Ira Steven Behr
Story by: Barbara J. Lee, Jenifer A. Lee
STARDATE: Unknown

Exasperated by Quark's abuse and the terrible working conditions at the bar, Rom (Max Grodénchik) organizes his fellow employees into a union and leads them all on strike. **Leeta:** Chase Masterson. **Grimp:** Jason Marsden. **Frool:** Emilio Borelli. **Brunt:** Jeffrey Combs.

✦ *Rom finally asserts his independence, which has been steadily growing over the course of the series. (He revealed his intolerance of Ferengi tradition in DS9's* third-season episode "Family Business.") Braving the iron fist of the oppressive Ferengi Commerce Authority, Rom wins respect and fair treatment for Quark's employees.

BEST SCENE: *Quark using faulty holographic images of himself in an attempt to run his bar single-handedly.*

RULE OF ACQUISITION: *No. 211: "Employees are the rungs on the ladder of success – don't hesitate to step on them."*

ACCESSION

Week of 24 Feb. 1996, No. 489
Directed by: Les Landau
Written by: Jane Espenson
STARDATE: Unknown
Sisko steps down as Emissary when an ancient poet (Richard Libertini) from planet Bajor emerges from the wormhole more than 200 years after his disappearance and claims to be the true Emissary.
Keiko: Rosalind Chao. **Vedek Porta:** Robert Symonds. **Kai Opaka:** Camille Saviola. **Molly O'Brien:** Hana Hatae.

✦ *Relieved to surrender the duties of Emissary, Sisko rethinks his decision when the new Emissary reinstates a Bajoran caste system which jeopardizes Bajor's application to enter the Federation.*

BEST DIALOGUE: *Quark to Worf, "Did you hear? Keiko's going to have another baby," to which an alarmed Worf (who delivered Keiko's first child, Molly) responds, "Now?"*

SHOW WATCH: *The Bajoran sail-powered spacecraft flown by the new Emissary is similar to the ancient Bajoran spacecraft built by Sisko in "Explorers."*

FEDERATION FACTOID: *Although Kira descends from artists, she can't divine such talent in herself. Her frustrated efforts to sculpt a clay bird cause her to question the wisdom of the new Emissary.*

RULES OF ENGAGEMENT

Week of 6 April 1996, No. 490
Directed by: LeVar Burton
Written by: Ronald D. Moore
Story by: Bradley Thompson and David Weddle
STARDATE: Unknown
Worf faces extradition to his homeworld when he accidentally destroys a Klingon transport and kills all 441 passengers.
Ch'Pok: Ron Canada. **T'Lara:** Deborah Strang.

✦ *Worf is further alienated from his own*

kind when the Klingons use him to discredit the Federation and expand their control in the Alpha Quadrant. An intriguing study of the Klingon need to conquer.

HARD TIME

Week of 13 April 1996, No. 491
Directed by: Alexander Singer
Written by: Robert Hewitt Wolfe
Story by: Daniel Keys Moran and Lynn Barker
STARDATE: Unknown
Wrongly charged with espionage by the Argrathi, O'Brien suffers an alien mind implant – which makes him think he's served a 20-year prison sentence.
Ee'char: Craig Wasson. **Muniz:** F.J.

RULES OF ENGAGEMENT: WORF (MICHAEL DORN) IS INTERROGATED BY CH'POK (RON CANADA) DURING AN EXTRADITION HEARING AFTER A KLINGON TRANSPORT SHIP AND ITS 441 CIVILIAN PASSENGERS ARE OBLITERATED. THE EXPERIENCE FURTHER UNDERSCORES WORF'S ALIENATION FROM HIS OWN RACE.

Rio. **Keiko:** Rosalind Chao. **Molly:** Hana Hatae. **Rinn:** Margot Rose.

✦ *Where Capt. Jean-Luc Picard was enriched by an alien mind probe (ST:TNG's "The Inner Light"), O'Brien is nearly destroyed by his memories of 20 years in one small cell with no one for company but his friendly cell-mate, Ee'char, the Argrathi who keeps O'Brien sane through his friendship – and the one whom O'Brien kills out of the madness brought on by hunger. It's a dark road to recovery when O'Brien is released back to the station. Tortured by guilt, the typically friendly engineer lashes out at everyone, nearly striking Molly, then points a phas-*

er to his head when he sees suicide as the only way he can atone for his supposed sins, before he comes to his senses.

SHATTERED MIRROR

Week of 20 April 1996, No. 492
Directed by: James L. Conway
Written by: Ira Steven Behr and Hans Beimler
STARDATE: Unknown
Capt. Benjamin Sisko (Avery Brooks) is forced to help rebels fight a Klingon-Cardassian alliance in a parallel universe.
Jennifer: Felicia Bell. **Garak:** Andrew Robinson.

✦ *In the fourth adventure to the mirror universe first discovered in the original*

Star Trek episode "Mirror, Mirror," Sisko must ready a mirror Defiant so the rebels (who recently captured the mirror Deep Space Nine space station) can defend against a Klingon-Cardassian Alliance assault led by the mirror Worf. The final space battle scenes in this show are spectacular, drawing on amazing special effects and musical arrangements.

BEST DIALOGUE: *In command of a Klingon ship, the mirror Worf says, "Make it so."*

SHOW WATCH: *Actor Felicia Bell makes her third Star Trek appearance. In the Star Trek: Deep Space Nine opener, "Emissary," she played the role of Jennifer*

Sisko, the wife of Capt. Benjamin Sisko. In "Through the Looking Glass," she played the mirror version of Jennifer.

THE MUSE

Week of 27 April 1996, No. 493
Directed by: David Livingston
Written by: René Echevarria
Story by: Majel Barrett
and René Echevarria
STARDATE: Unknown

When a pregnant Lwaxana Troi (Majel Barrett) arrives at the station, Odo (René Auberjonois) marries her in order to prevent the baby from being taken away after birth by the Tavnian father. **Jeyal:** Michael Ansara. **Onaya:** Meg Foster.

✦ *Majel Barrett (who appeared in DS9's third-season episode "Fascination") co-developed this tender story in which wedding bells finally chime for the alluring Betazoid, but not under the most romantic of conditions. Pregnant by a Tavnian named Jeyal (with whom Lwaxana was joined prior to her pregnancy), the Betazoid cannot abide by the Tavnian law which would allow Jeyal to take her child back to the Tavnian homeworld after the baby's birth, and she is caught off guard – and more than a little flattered – when Odo offers to marry her in order to annul the union with Jeyal and grant her custody of the unborn baby. It's one of Odo's most noble acts, and with the announcement of Lwaxana's pregnancy the Star Trek nursery continues to expand.*

STAR WATCH: *Michael Ansara (Jeyal) played the Klingon Kang in the classic episode "Day of the Dove" and in DS9's "Blood Oath."*

SHOW WATCH: *Chakotay unexpectedly became a father after Seska impregnated herself with some of his DNA as an act of retaliation in Star Trek: Voyager's "Maneuvers," and Keiko O'Brien's second pregnancy is revealed in this season's episode "Accession."*

FOR THE CAUSE

Week of 4 May 1996, No. 494
Directed by: James L. Conway
Written by: Ronald D. Moore
Story by: Mark Gehred-O'Connell
STARDATE: Unknown

Sisko (Avery Brooks) is alarmed to discover that the woman he loves, Kasidy Yates (Penny Johnson), may actually be a

Maquis smuggler. **Eddington:** Kenneth Marshall. **Ziyal:** Tracy Middendorf. **Brathaw:** John Prosky. **Lt. Reese:** Steven Vincent Leigh. **Garak:** Andrew Robinson.

✦ *Love continues to crash around Capt. Benjamin Sisko. Still recovering from the death of the mirror Jennifer in "Shattered Mirror," the captain is further crushed to learn that Yates is in league with the Maquis who, as a plot element, have been dormant since "Heart of Stone."*

SHOW WATCH: *Star Trek throws a curve when the Eddington character (played by Kenneth Marshall) reveals himself as a Federation traitor.*

TO THE DEATH

Week of 11 May 1996, No. 496
Directed by: LeVar Burton
Written by: Ira Steven Behr
andRobert Hewitt Wolfe
STARDATE: 49904.2

When Jem'Hadar rebels discover an ancient gateway through an instant transportation device, the safety of the *Deep Space Nine* station – and the future of the entire *Federation* itself – is in jeopardy. **Toman'torax:** Brian Thompson. **Virak'kara:** Scott Haven. **Omet'iklan:** Clarence Williams III.

✦ *In a surprising development, the Dominion is threatened by rebel Jem'-Hadar soldiers, which bodes a dark future for the safety of the station. The Klingons, Romulans and Cardassians have all expressed interest in conquering the Dominion, which is beginning to crumble from within. Deep Space Nine may need every defence possible to prevent itself from getting blown away in a rush for the wormhole. An action-packed episode which, unfortunately, doesn't result in friendship between the Jem'Hadar and the Federation.*

STAR WATCH: *Clarence Williams III (a youthful undercover agent in The Mod Squad) is found behind Jem'Hadar make-up as the soldier Omet'ikian.*

THE QUICKENING

Week of 18 May 1996, No. 495
Directed by: René Auberjonois
Written by: Naren Shankar
STARDATE: Unknown

Doctor Bashir and Jadzia (Alexander Siddig, Terry Farrell) try to save the inhabitants of a Gamma Quadrant plan-

et infected with a disease introduced by the Jem'Hadar. **Ekoria:** Ellen Wheeler. **Epran:** Dylan Haggerty. **Trevean:** Michael Sarrazin.

✦ *The so-called "healer" of the planet, Trevean (who dispenses poison to sufferers of the seemingly incurable disease), raises a controversial question: Should the terminally ill be allowed to die quickly and painlessly when faced with a painful, agonizing decline? It's a question Bashir must address as he works to cure the afflicted.*

BODY PARTS

Week of 10 June 1996, No. 497
Written by: Ira Steven Behr
and Robert Hewitt Wolfe
STARDATE: Unknown

Quark believes he's dying and, in true Ferengi tradition, sells his body in advance for a profit. Upon discovering he's going to live, he is faced with breaking that contract – a definite taboo in the Ferengi culture. Keiko's developing baby (her second child) is transferred into Major Kira's womb after the expectant mother is injured in an accident. **Brunt:** Jeffrey Combs. **Rom:** Max Grodénchik. **Garak:** Andrew Robinson. **Keiko:** Rosalind Chao.

✦ *Scripting around the real-life pregnancy of Nana Visitor (the father is Alexander Siddig), the producers cleverly came up with "Body Parts" to explain why Kira would be with child at the start of DS9's fifth season.*

BROKEN LINK

Week of 15 June 1996, No. 498
Directed by: Les Landau
Written by: Ira Steven Behr
and Robert Hewitt Wolfe
Story by: George A. Brozak
STARDATE: Unknown

Odo is returned to his homeworld and tried for the murder of another shape-shifter. **Garak:** Andrew Robinson. **Female Shape-Shifter:** Salome Jens.

✦ Bad times for *Deep Space Nine* only get worse when Garak, waiting for the outcome of Odo's trial, tries to annihilate the Founders and start an all-out war with the Jem'Hadar in this suspenseful fourth-season finale.

SHOW WATCH: *Actor Salome Jens reprises her female shape-shifter role first introduced in Star Trek: Deep Space Nine's "The Search."* ✧

Star Trek: Voyager

With Capt. Kathryn Janeway at the helm, the *U.S.S. Voyager* wraps up its second season of adventure in the unknown reaches of the galaxy

FIRST SEASON

FOR AN AUDIENCE THAT WAS PINING FOR THE CREW OF *STAR TREK: THE NEXT GENERATION* AND ITS WEEKLY adventures in uncharted space, which wasn't always integral to the *Star Trek: Deep Space Nine* theme, *Star Trek: Voyager* was a welcome return to the unknown reaches of the galaxy. *Star Trek*'s fourth venture into the final frontier made it out of spacedock intact and on time – despite the abrupt eleventh-hour departure of actor Geneviève Bujold, whose sudden exit threatened to delay the January 1995 debut of *Star Trek: Voyager* and prompted the last-minute casting of Kate Mulgrew as *Star Trek*'s first female lead in a series (Capt. Kathryn Janeway). And despite the stress of her abrupt promotion into the pivotal lead role, Mulgrew quickly and deftly settled into the captain's chair seemingly made for her. Indeed, the entire cast seemed to fit their characters perfectly, gelling faster than any *Star Trek* ensemble since the classic series. And while the show would make the most of the state-of-the-art *U.S.S. Voyager*, its premise would owe more to its roots: Stranded in the Delta Quadrant, with no choice but to seek out new worlds and new civilizations, *Star Trek: Voyager* would be off to one of the best first seasons since the original series.

CARETAKER
Week of 16 Jan. 1995, No. 721
Directed by: Winrich Kolbe
Written by: Michael Piller
and Jeri Taylor
Story by: Rick Berman,
Michael Piller and Jeri Taylor
STARDATE: 48315.6
While investigating the disappearance of a Maquis ship in the territory of space known as the Badlands, the *U.S.S. Voyager*, captained by Kathryn Janeway (Kate Mulgrew), is swept 70,000 light-years from home, suffering the same fate as the ship it came looking for. **Lieut. Stadi:** Alicia Coppola. **Quark:** Armin Shimerman. **Carey:** Josh Clark. **Rollins:** Scott MacDonald. **Cavit:** Scott Jaeck. **Ocampa Doctor:** Bruce French. **Jabin:** Gavan O'Herlihy. **Gul Evek:** Richard Poe. **Banjo Man:** Basil Langton.
◆ In an explosive two-hour pilot, *Star Trek*'s fourth series establishes the *Voyager*'s forlorn plight in the distant,

uncharted space of the Delta Quadrant. Isolated and vulnerable, the crews of the Maquis – some of whom are former Starfleet officers – and Federation ships are forced to co-operate in order to survive and find a way home. While the patchwork crew are fodder for potential conflict, so too are some of the alien races native to the Delta Quadrant, such as the Talaxians (most notably Neelix), the Ocampa (the underground race to which Kes belongs) and the Kazons (who occupy the barren surface of the Ocampa homeworld and who promise to become one of *Voyager*'s deadliest enemies). But the most promising newcomer would be one of Starfleet's own: a holographic doctor with no name and an attitude (perfectly executed by actor Robert Picardo). In one of Star Trek's best climax scenes, the dying Caretaker tells Janeway that if she uses his Array technology to get home, it will leave the Ocampa defenceless from the Kazons. The captain reluctantly but nobly

destroys the Array, a decision which preserves both her integrity and the Ocampa, but strands the Maquis and Starfleet crew 70,000 light-years from home. Originally a two-hour program, the pilot repeats as two one-hour segments.

SHOW WATCH: *The Maquis resistance fighters were first introduced in DS9's two-part episode "The Maquis" and again in ST:TNG's "Preemptive Strike," when Bajoran Ro Laren abruptly deserted Starfleet to take up the Maquis cause. In Voyager's second-season episode "Cold Fire," the Caretaker's mate, Suspiria, would seek vengeance against Janeway and crew.*

PARALLAX
Week of 23 Jan. 1995, No. 103
Directed by: Kim Friedman
Written by: Brannon Braga
Story by: Jim Trombetta
STARDATE: 48439.7
Answering the distress call of another ship, *Voyager* becomes trapped in the gravitational pull of a collapsing star – only to realize that the other ship appears to be *Voyager* itself. **Seska:** Martha Hackett. **Carey:** Josh Clark. **Jarvin:** Justin Williams.
◆ *Once cool toward B'Elanna Torres (Roxann Biggs-Dawson), Janeway begins to bond with the spirited Maquis engineer, whose half-Klingon side makes her fiery and unpredictable. Torres broke the nose of Starfleet engineer Carey when he and Torres disagreed while solving a problem, but the action didn't prevent Torres from being promoted to Chief Engineer, the second-highest ranking Maquis on Voyager after Chakotay.*

STAR TREK: VOYAGER: *THE FIRST-SEASON CAST (FROM RIGHT TO LEFT):* ETHAN PHILLIPS, ROBERT BELTRAN, GARRETT WANG, KATE MULGREW, JENNIFER LIEN, ROBERT DUNCAN MCNEILL, TIM RUSS, ROBERT PICARDO *AND* ROXANN BIGGS-DAWSON.

TIME AND AGAIN

Week of 30 Jan. 1995, No. 104
Directed by: Les Landau
Written by: Michael Piller
and David Kemper
Story by: David Kemper
STARDATE: Unknown

Voyager discovers a planet whose entire civilization has recently been destroyed by a massive explosion, possibly triggered by *Voyager*'s own interference. **Makull:** Nicolas Surovy. **Terla:** Joel Polis. **Latika:** Brady Bluhm.

✦ *Janeway and Paris become the first two members of Voyager's crew resurrected from death in an episode that underscores the importance of the Prime Directive.*

PHAGE

Week of 6 Feb. 1995, No. 105
Directed by: Winrich Kolbe
Written by: Skye Dent
and Brannon Braga
Story by: Timothy DeHaas
STARDATE: 48532.4

Neelix (Ethan Phillips) lies near death when his lungs are stolen by the disease-ridden Vidiians, who harvest organs to replace their own. **Seska:** Martha Hackett. **Alien No.1:** Cully Fredericksen. **Alien No. 2:** Stephen Rappaport.

✦ *Early in the episode, Neelix converts the captain's private dining room into a galley and installs himself as head chef when the food replicators become energy-consuming conveniences which the ship can ill afford to run. His creations, rarely delectable to anyone but himself, become something of a running gag in the series as Neelix concocts and serves one questionable dish after another. But his cooking career is cut short when he's robbed of his lungs by the Vidiians. It's all Neelix can do to breathe with a set of holographic replacements, which the Doctor devises to keep the Talaxian alive until his lungs are replaced. And laying the groundwork for the Neelix-Kes-Paris triangle that will explode in the second season's "Parturition," a jealous Neelix describes rival Paris – who volunteers his shoulder for Kes to cry on – as "just one big hormone walking around the ship." In a gripping conclusion, Kes donates one of her lungs to save her beloved Neelix. The life-threatening emergency also forges a bond between Kes and the Doctor, who offers to train the young Ocampan as a medical assistant to replace Paris.*

BEST DIALOGUE: *Neelix: "If I'm going to be in here a while, now's as good a time as any to tell you your ceiling is hideous." Replies the Doctor, in a bedside manner reminiscent of an earlier Starfleet medical man: "I'm a doctor, Mr. Neelix, not a decorator."*

THE CLOUD

Week of 13 Feb. 1995, No. 106
Directed by: David Livingston
Written by: Tom Szollosi
and Michael Piller
Story by: Brannon Braga
STARDATE: 48546.2

To replenish the ship's diminishing energy reserves, Capt. Janeway decides to mine an energy-rich nebula – which

Voyager injures prior to discovering the nebula is a living creature. **Gaunt Gary:** Larry Hankin. **Ricky:** Angela Dohrmann. **Sandrine:** Judy Geeson. **The Gigolo:** Luigi Amodeo.

✦ *Brimming with rich dialogue and character conflicts, this episode highlights the risks exposed to unknown life forms by Voyager – and vice versa – as the ship continues through unknown space. Meanwhile, as Neelix appoints himself morale officer in order to energize the lives of those on Voyager, everyone turns to their own devices to replenish their personal energy reserves: Chakotay, to his Native American spiritual beliefs; and Paris, to the holodeck re-creation of his favourite cafe outside Marseilles. As the classic series' officers turned to chess, ST:TNG's to poker and DS9's to darts, Voyager's finest will turn to pool as a recreational pursuit.*

BEST LINES: *Says a caffeine-deprived Janeway:* "There's coffee in that nebula!" *And to a perturbed Neelix several scenes later:* "Dismissed. That's a Starfleet expression for 'get out.'"

STAR WATCH: *Angela Dohrmann (Donna Chang of* Seinfeld *fame) plays Ricky, the fetching woman who appears in all of Paris's holo-programs.*

FEDERATION FACTOID: *We learn that Voyager has a complement of 38 photon torpedoes – and no way to replace them after they're gone.*

EYE OF THE NEEDLE
Week of 20 Feb. 1995, No. 107
Directed by: Winrich Kolbe
Written by: Bill Dial and Jeri Taylor
Story by: Hilary Bader
STARDATE: 48579.4
Scanning space for anomalies, Ensign Kim (Garrett Wang) discovers a tiny wormhole that may offer a way home for *Voyager*. **Lord Burleigh:** Michael Cumpsty. **Mrs. Templeton:** Carolyn Seymour. **Telek:** Vaughn Armstrong. **Baxter:** Tom Virtue.

✦ *Voyager's second opportunity to get home (which results in the crew's first encounter with a Romulan) leads to bitter disappointment when they discover the wormhole is a distortion in space and time, too small to afford passage to the ship. The crew, hoping to send messages home to their families through their Romulan contact, Telek R'Mor, learn*

he's operating on a different time-frame. In fact, they discover the Romulan died in 2367, four years before their messages are due to be delivered. Meanwhile, the Doctor gets his first kiss from Kes when she's overcome with sadness at the thought of leaving him behind with the ship.

EX POST FACTO
Week of 27 Feb. 1995, No. 108
Directed by: LeVar Burton
Written by: Evan Carlos Somers and Michael Piller
Story by: Evan Carlos Somers
STARDATE: Unknown
Tuvok and Janeway (Tim Russ, Kate Mulgrew) struggle to prove the innocence of Lieut. Paris (Robert Duncan McNeill), who is convicted of murder while on an away mission and, through an alien mind implant, is forced to continually relive the victim's final moments. **Lidell:** Robin McKee. **Numiri Captain:** Henry Brown. **Tolen Ren:** Ray Reinhardt. **Minister Kray:** Francis Guinan. **Doctor:** Aaron Lustig.

✦ *Paris becomes the first of Voyager's crew to be accused of murder when an away-mission romance with a beautiful Banean named Lidell leads to the murder of her scientist husband, Tolen Ren. The difficult task of proving Paris's innocence falls to Tuvok, whose diligent pursuit of the truth behind the murder earns the eternal respect and gratitude of Paris. Meanwhile, Kes encourages the Doctor to take a name for himself. Among the names considered: Dr. Galen, Dr. Salk and – you guessed it – Dr. Spock.*

FEDERATION FACTOID: *We learn Tuvok and his wife have been married for 67 years, quite an achievement considering that long-term marriages – or even enduring romantic liaisons – are rare in Starfleet.*

EMANATIONS
Week of 13 March 1995, No. 109
Directed by: David Livingston
Written by: Brannon Braga
STARDATE: 48623.5
Kim investigates an alien burial ground and goes missing when a subspace anomaly causes him to materialize on the aliens' homeworld – where he appears to have returned from the dead. **Hatil:** Jefrey Alan Chandler. **Dr. Neria:** Jerry Hardin. **Alien No. 1:** John Cirigliano. **Seska:** Martha Hackett.

Hatil's wife: Robin Groves. **Ptera:** Cecile Callan.

✦ *Kim becomes the third member of Voyager's crew to be brought back from the dead when a mission to investigate the apparent discovery of a new element – the 247th element in Federation science – leads to Voyager's first encounter with the Vhnori. It also fuels a fascinating life-after-death story line, touching on notions of euthanasia and the afterlife.*

SHOW WATCH: *Jerry Hardin, who appears as the dumbfounded Dr. Neria, appeared earlier as the Aldean Radue in* Star Trek: The Next Generation's *"When the Bough Breaks" and as the cantankerous Samuel Clemens in the two-part "Time's Arrow."*

PRIME FACTORS
Week of 20 March 1995, No. 110
Directed by: Les Landau
Written by: Michael Perricone, Greg Elliot and Jeri Taylor
Story by: David R. George III, Eric A. Stillwell, Michael Perricone and Greg Elliot.
STARDATE: 48642.5
Voyager's crew is invited to enjoy the hedonistic pleasures of the planet Sikaris, whose inhabitants have a technology that could instantaneously transport Voyager 40,000 light-years closer to home. **Gath:** Ronald Guttman. **Eudana:** Yvonne Suhor. **Seska:** Martha Hackett. **Carey:** Josh Clark. **Jaret:** Andrew Hill Newman.

✦ *It's a case of the Federation being on the receiving end of the Prime Directive. The law of Sikaris, unfortunately, prevents its inhabitants from sharing technology with Capt. Kathryn Janeway and crew, who are only welcome to the planet in the interests of romance. Yet the law of Sikaris proves too much of an irritating obstacle for some of Voyager's team. Working behind Janeway's back, Torres, Carey and Seska (an individual who would rise to greater treachery) illegally acquire the tantalizing Sikaris technology – only to discover the matrix is incompatible with Voyager. The captain's wrath boils over when she discovers that Tuvok himself ignored his duties as head of ship security and assisted Torres, Carey and Seska in their misdeed. As a result, Tuvok becomes the first Voyager crew member to face the possibility of court-martial.*

HEROES AND DEMONS: *THE DOCTOR (ROBERT PICARDO) IMPRESSES VIKING WARRIOR FREYA (MARJORIE MONAGHAN) WITH HIS KNOWLEDGE OF HERBAL MEDICINES*

BEST DIALOGUE: *Reminiscent of the human-Vulcan bond between Kirk and Spock, Janeway says to Tuvok, "I realize you made a sacrifice for me, but it is not one I would have allowed you to make. You can use logic to justify almost anything. That's its power – and its flaw. From now on, bring your logic to me. Don't act on it behind my back." Replies a chastened Tuvok, "You have my word. My logic was not in error, but I was."*

STATE OF FLUX

Week of 10 April 1995, No. 111
Directed by: Robert Sheerer
Written by: Chris Abbott
Story by: Paul Coyle
STARDATE: 48658.2
Capt. Kathryn Janeway (Kate Mulgrew) launches an investigation to uncover an on-board traitor after *Voyager* discovers a Kazon warship which has disabled itself through the use of *Federation* technology. **Seska:** Martha Hackett. **Carey:** Josh Clark. **Kazon:** Norman Large. **Kazon First Maje Culluh:** Anthony De Longis.
✦ *Voyager's second encounter with the Kazon leads to the first act of treason and and first defection by one of its members: Ensign Seska, formerly of the Maquis. It's also a powerful episode for Robert Beltran, who, as Chakotay, defends his former lover – only to discover her true identity is that of a Cardassian operative, surgically altered to look Bajoran. Guest star Martha Hackett creates a powerful*

persona in Seska, who, prior to beaming off Voyager *to join the Kazon, openly rebukes the captain for the "incomprehensible decision" that led to Voyager's current fate. But the episode's top honours go to Kate Mulgrew, whose face and eyes convey Janeway's vulnerability and self-doubt in a manner her male counterparts rarely allowed themselves.*

HEROES AND DEMONS

Week of 24 April 1995, No. 112
Directed by: Les Landau
Written by: Naren Shankar
Story by: John Sayers
STARDATE: 48693.2
The Doctor (Robert Picardo) becomes an unlikely hero when crew members become trapped in a malfunctioning holo-novel based on the Old English epic poem "Beowulf." **Freya:** Marjorie Monaghan. **Unferth:** Christopher Neame. **Hrothgar:** Michael Keenan.
✦ *The first season's most imaginative episode leads to the Doctor's first adventure out of Sickbay – and unexpectedly to his first romance and second kiss. Wonderfully humourous and touchingly sad, the story provides Robert Picardo with a terrific opportunity to display the full breadth of his acting skills, while providing the Doctor with the opportunity to earn the respect and gratitude of his shipmates. At Kes's urging, the Doctor (torn between one of three names for himself) chooses the name Schweitzer, only to abandon it at the end of his journey*

because of the sad memories it would always recall. Meanwhile, Janeway and Torres, who share a passion for scientific discovery, continue the bonding initiated in "Parallax." Kim is returned from the dead again, marking his second Lazarus experience, and for the second time, Voyager harms an unknown alien life form, killing one being and imprisoning another before correcting the mistake.
BEST SCENE: *Invited to share the tale of his glorious deeds at his host's banquet table, the Doctor savours a tasty leg of elk and shares the story of his epic battle against...an outbreak of the measles!*
BEST DIALOGUE: *Freya to the Doctor: "You are truly a man of many talents, Lord Schweitzer. Your people must value you greatly." Replies the Doctor, "You would think so."*

CATHEXIS

Week of 1 May 1995, No. 113
Directed by: Kim Friedman
Written by: Brannon Braga
Story by: Brannon Braga and Joe Menoksy
STARDATE: 48734.2
Paranoia grips the crew when an unseen alien presence invades *Voyager* and takes possession of crew members' minds. **Durst:** Brian Markinson. **Lord Burleigh:** Michael Cumpsty. **Mrs. Templeton:** Carolyn Seymour.
✦ *Where disease-ridden Vidiians harvest the organs of other life forms in their unending quest to survive as a species, the aliens encountered by Voyager in this episode harvest neural energy from the brain. The entire episode, in fact, is an exploration of the mind, its power and mystery. Using her fledgling telepathic abilities, Kes helps the crew detect the alien presence while Torres and the Doctor compare their knowledge of "the medicine wheel," a talisman (sacred to Chakotay's tribe) by which Chakotay's wandering soul can find its way home.*
BEST DIALOGUE: *Prior to moving a stone placed on the medicine wheel by Torres, the Doctor points out that the stone – a signpost for Chakotay's soul to follow – would have led Chakotay "into the Mountains of the Antelope Women." Moving the stone, the Doctor adds, "According to [Chakotay's] tradition, an extremely attractive locale. He might not want to leave."*

FACES

Week of 8 May 1995, No. 114
Directed by: Winrich Kolbe
Written by: Kenneth Biller
Story by: Jonathan Glassner
and Kenneth Biller
STARDATE: 48784.2

The Vidiians capture Torres (Roxann Biggs-Dawson) and subject her to DNA tests, eventually separating her into two beings: one human, the other Klingon. **Sulan/Durst:** Brian Markinson. **Talaxian:** Rob LaBelle. **Guard No. 1:** Barton Tinapp.

✦ *Roxann Biggs-Dawson, who captured Torres's tempestuous mood swings earlier in the season, goes the distance as B'Elanna's fierce Klingon warrior comes face to face with her meek human "half." Terrific performance and a marvellous opportunity for Torres to appreciate the Klingon half she has always tried to hide. Second encounter with the Vidiians introduced in "Phage," whose leper-like condition leads them to enslave other beings and kill them for their body parts. Truly one of the most vile races yet encountered in the entire Star Trek universe, witnessed when a Vidiian scientist, enamoured by the full Klingon Torres, strips the face from Voyager captive Durst and wears it in an attempt to woo the Klingon Torres, who only feigns attraction to the Vidiian in order to escape with her human counterpart.*

SHOW WATCH: *B'Elanna, who has always rejected her Klingon heritage, learns that both halves are necessary if she wishes to be whole, reminiscent of the lesson Kirk and crew learned in "The Enemy Within."*

🖝 JETREL

Week of 15 May 1995, No. 115
Directed by: Kim Friedman
Written by: Jack Klein,
Karen Klein and Kenneth Biller
Story by: James Thornton
and Scott Nimerfro
STARDATE: 48832.1

Neelix (Ethan Phillips) faces painful memories of his former home on Rinax, the destroyed moon of his Talaxian homeworld, when he confronts the mastermind (James Sloyan) responsible for the moon's destruction. **Gaunt Gary:** Larry Hankin.

✦ *In the year marking the 50th anniversary of the dropping of the atomic bomb on Hiroshima, Star Trek delivers a powerful treatise on the horrors of war and its weaponry of mass destruction. Ethan Phillips takes a break from comedy to delve into Neelix's loss and secret shame as the Talaxian first confronts, then forgives, the man responsible for the horrifying death of his entire family more than 15 years earlier.*

BEST DIALOGUE: *Jetrel: "If I had not discovered the cascade, it would have been someone else, don't you see? It was a scientific*

inevitability, one discovery flowing naturally to the next. Something so enormous as science will not stop for something as small as man, Mr. Neelix." Neelix: "So you did it for science?" Jetrel: "For my planet and yes, for science. To know whether or not it could be done. It's good to know how the world works."

STAR WATCH: *Always outstanding, James Sloyan had earlier, equally powerful roles: the Romulan defector Jarok in ST:TNG's "The Defector," the Klingon K'Mtar in "Firstborn" and Dr. Mora Pol in DS9's "The Alternate."*

FEDERATION FACTOID: *The character K'Mtar in ST:TNG's "Firstborn" was Worf's son, Alexander, who had returned from the future and assumed a false name.*

LEARNING CURVE

Week of 22 May 1995, No. 116
Directed by: David Livingston
Written by: Ronald Wilkerson
and Jean Louise Matthias
Story by: Hilary Bader
STARDATE: 48846.5

Tuvok (Tim Russ) tries to introduce Starfleet discipline to Maquis personnel, while Torres (Roxann Biggs-Dawson) and the Doctor (Robert Picardo) work to expunge a highly contagious virus from Voyager's life-support systems. **Chell:** Derek McGrath. **Beatrice:** Lindsey Haun. **Dalby:** Armand Schultz.

✦ *This fitting first-season wrap-up highlights two of Voyager's most critical concerns: its constant vulnerability and the need to unite its patchwork Maquis-Federation crew. Tim Russ has some fine moments as the perplexed Tuvok, a longtime teacher at Starfleet Academy, who fails to instil in his recruits the logic or discipline he believes so necessary – until he too learns to bend.*

BEST SCENES: *The Doctor, who has been told he must show greater sensitivity to his patients' needs, tells a sickly gel-pack, "Don't worry, my little friend." And Chakotay, who's determined to bring his Maquis crew into line, decks crewman Dalby in a display of Maquis discipline.*

FEDERATION FACTOID: *Bolians (represented in the episode by Derek McGrath, who plays a Bolian crew member, Chell) were named after Cliff Bole, a veteran Star Trek director. The Cliffs of Bole, mentioned in DS9's "Invasive Procedures," were another tribute to the man.* ✧

JETREL: GUEST STAR JAMES SLOYAN (FAR RIGHT) MAKES THE MOST OF HIS APPEARANCE AS DR. JETREL, WHO CLAIMS NEELIX (ETHAN PHILLIPS) SUFFERS FROM A DEADLY DISEASE CAUSED BY THE WEAPON OF MASS DESTRUCTION JETREL INVENTED.

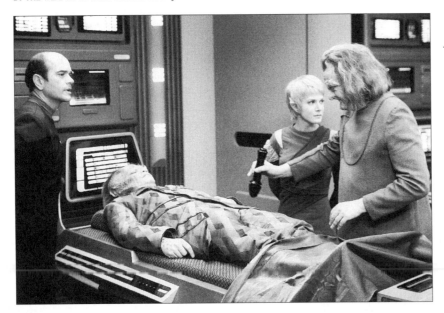

SECOND SEASON

THE *U.S.S. VOYAGER* WOULD RARELY ENJOY PEACE WITH THE KAZONS, WHO CONTINUED THEIR relentless quest to commandeer the ship for its technological secrets, testing the strength of *Voyager*'s shields and the mettle of its crew as *Star Trek: Voyager* glided into its second season. The Vidiians, too, would attempt to clap the crew in a dark medical grip for the purposes of organ harvest, while some of *Voyager*'s greatest dangers would erupt from within its own crew. Kes's burgeoning telekinetic ability would on one occasion escalate out of control (similar to the dark influence of Gary Mitchell when he acquired telekinetic power in the classic *Star Trek* episode "Where No Man Has Gone Before") and Tuvok would become a raging Vulcan – and a threat to the crew – through a dangerous mind-meld. Yet, despite all the space battles and inner strife, there would grow bonds of trust and friendship. Emotional ties would spring forth, strong and enduring, between *Voyager*'s captain and crew.

THE 37's: *GUEST STAR SHARON LAWRENCE AS AMELIA EARHART RESOLVES THE MYSTERY SURROUNDING THE DISAPPEARANCE OF THE FAMOUS 20TH-CENTURY AIR PILOT.*

THE 37's
Week of 28 Aug. 1995, No. 120
Directed by: James L. Conway
Written by: Jeri Taylor
and Brannon Braga
STARDATE: 48975.1
Finding a 20th-century pickup truck floating in space, *Voyager* tracks a distress signal to a class-M planet where the crew stumbles upon the legendary air pilot Amelia Earhart (Sharon Lawrence) in a cryogenic sleep. **Fred Noonan:** David Graf. **Japanese Soldier:** James Saito. **Jack Hayes:** Mel Winkler.

✦ *Star Trek history is made when* Voyager *lowers its landing gear to become the first starship to safely touch down on a planet's surface. The show was originally intended for the first season, but scheduling demands held the episode back. It's a tense show as Capt. Janeway realizes she has discovered a world whose inhabitants may have the technology to send* Voyager *home (given that aviator Amelia Earhart and her contemporaries had been plucked from planet Earth). Upon learning that the technology is no longer accessible, the captain is then faced with losing her starship crew, who are offered permanent residence on the Earth-like planet.*

SHOW WATCH: *In an earlier close encounter,* ST:TNG's *crew met another legendary real-life figure, Samuel Clemens (who wrote under the pseudonym Mark Twain), in the two-part "Time's Arrow."*

INITIATIONS
Week of 4 Sept. 1995, No. 121
Directed by: Winrich Kolbe
Written by: Kenneth Biller
STARDATE: 49005.3
While alone on a shuttle in space, Chakotay (Robert Beltran) is attacked by a young Kazon who must kill an enemy in battle to prove himself as a warrior. **Kar:** Aron Eisenberg. **Razik:** Patrick Kilpatrick. **Haliz:** Tim de Zarn.

✦ *The Kazon culture offers a glimpse of what the Klingons may have been like before they united under Kahless the Unforgettable. Like the Klingons, the Kazons relish battle and conquest, training to be warriors from an early age. And while dissension sometimes erupts within the Klingon world, it is constant amongst the various Kazon sects – they're far from being a cohesive superpower.*

SHOW WATCH: *Aron Eisenberg, Nog on* Star Trek: Deep Space Nine, *displays his full range of talent as Kar, the Kazon boy anxious to kill Chakotay in order to earn his Ogla name in battle.*

PROJECTIONS
Week of 11 Sept. 1995, No. 117
Directed by: Jonathan Frakes
Written by: Brannon Braga
STARDATE: 48892.1
A computer malfunction enables the Doctor (Robert Picardo) to leave Sickbay, and suddenly he doesn't know whether he's human or holographic after a Kazon attack leaves him bleeding. **Lieut. Barclay:** Dwight Schultz.

✦ Voyager's *Doctor wrestles with the universal questions: Who am I and where do I come from? He takes his place alongside Spock, Data and Odo, all of whom provide a unique perspective on what it means to be human. Reminiscent of Picard's defence of Data's rights as a sentient being in ST:TNG's "The Measure of a Man," Chakotay tries to convince the holographic Doctor that he is real: "Just because you're made of projected light and energy doesn't mean you're any less real than someone made of flesh and blood…What matters is who you are."*

STAR WATCH: *Dwight Schultz reprises his role as Barclay.*

FEDERATION FACTOID: *The Doctor was first activated on stardate 48308.*

ELOGIUM
Week of 18 Sept. 1995, No. 118
Directed by: Winrich Kolbe
Written by: Kenneth Biller
and Jeri Taylor
Story by: Jimmy Diggs
and Steve J. Kay
STARDATE: 48921.3
The ship's passing through a swarm of

unknown space creatures causes Kes (Jennifer Lien) to begin her "elogium," the one time in her Ocampan life she's able to conceive a child. **Ensign Wildman:** Nancy Hower. **Male crew member:** Gary O'Brien.

✦ *A lifetime away from Earth, Janeway faces the inevitable – children aboard Voyager – when Ensign Wildman announces her pregnancy and Kes experiences "elogium," an Ocampa's one time to become pregnant. It's a difficult moment for Kes, who doesn't wish to miss her one chance at motherhood, and the relationship between Kes and Neelix is reinforced as Neelix struggles with his own feelings of fatherhood after Kes asks him to consider fathering her baby.*

SHOW WATCH: *Chakotay will become a father after Seska cunningly impregnates herself with some of his DNA in "Maneuvers."*

BEST LINE: *Tuvok to Janeway after the space creatures break their attack on Voyager, "It appears we have lost our sex appeal, Captain."*

FEDERATION FACTOID: *Tuvok has four children.*

NON SEQUITUR

Week of 25 Sept. 1995, No.122
Directed by: David Livingston
Written by: Brannon Braga
STARDATE: 49011

When his shuttlecraft enters a time stream anomaly, Ensign Kim (Garrett Wang) finds himself living an alternative life back on Earth – where he becomes a *Starfleet* engineer rather than joining *Voyager*'s crew. **Cosimo:** Louis Giambalvo. **Admiral Strickler:** Jack Shearer. **Lasca:** Mark Kiely. **Libby:** Jennifer Gatti.

✦ *An interesting alternate-reality episode providing lots of background information on Ensign Harry Kim, who graduated from Starfleet Academy on Stardate 47918 and lived in San Francisco with his girlfriend, Libby, before his assignment to Voyager.*

SHOW WATCH: *Actor Jack Shearer first appeared as Ambassador Vadosia on Deep Space Nine's "The Forsaken." Another what-life-might-have-been-like episode was Star Trek: The Next Generation's "Tapestry," in which Q gives Capt. Jean-Luc Picard the chance to live part of his life all over again.*

TWISTED

Week of 2 Oct. 1995, No. 119
Directed by: Kim Friedman
Teleplay by: Kenneth Biller
Story by: Arnold Rudnick and Rick Hosek
STARDATE: Unknown

The ship's passageways become an ever-changing labyrinth when *Voyager* encounters a distortion in space. **Gaunt Gary:** Larry A. Hankin. **Sandrine:** Judy Geeson. **Crew Member:** Terry Correll. **Baxter:** Tom Virtue.

✦ *Voyager's computer is enriched with information when communications from an unknown source download 20 million gigaquads of data.*

BEST LINE: *Neelix to Kes during her birthday celebrations: "Imagine, two years old today. If you ask me, you don't look a day over one."*

PARTURITION

Week of 9 Oct. 1995, No. 123
Directed by: Jonathan Frakes
Written by: Tom Szollosi
STARDATE: Unknown

After coming to blows over Kes's affections, Neelix (Ethan Phillips) and Paris (Robert Duncan McNeill) are stranded on a planet where they must work together to save the life of a new-born alien. **Computer Voice:** Majel Barrett.

✦ *Neelix's caring nature shines when he and Paris encounter an abandoned alien hatchling, and Neelix refuses to leave the creature, despite Paris's warnings about what could happen when the creature's mother comes looking for the baby. Working together is clearly not something Neelix and Paris were meant for, but they do share a rewarding moment together when the alien is reunited with its parent.*

BEST LINES: *After Kes explains that the Ocampa mate for life, the Doctor replies, "Your world must have very dry literature." When Janeway asks how long he's been eavesdropping on her, the Doctor replies, "I am a doctor, not a voyeur."*

PERSISTANCE OF VISION

Week of 30 Oct. 1995, No. 124
Directed by: James L. Conway
Written by: Jeri Taylor
STARDATE: Unknown

In a strange region of space, the crew enters a hallucinatory state where dreams

and fears become real. **Lord Burleigh:** Michael Cumpsty. **Mrs. Templeton:** Carolyn Seymour. **Beatrice:** Lindsey Haun. **Henry:** Thomas Alexander Dekker. **Admiral Paris:** Warren Munson. **Mark:** Stan Ivar. **Bothan:** Patrick Kerr. **T'Pel:** Marva Hicks. **Computer Voice:** Majel Barrett.

✦ *Definite sense of déjà vu in this episode: In the classic series' "Shore Leave," Capt. James Kirk and a landing party were chased and challenged by creations from their own dreams and fears; and Cmdr. Sisko and party met all sorts of odd characters when an alien intelligence tried to communicate with them in Star Trek: Deep Space Nine's first season episode "If Wishes Were Horses."*

TATTOO

Week of 6 Nov. 1995, No. 125
Directed by: Alexander Singer
Written by: Michael Piller
Story by: Larry Brody
STARDATE: Unknown

While surveying a moon, Chakotay (Robert Beltran) discovers evidence that its inhabitants may have visited Earth. **Young Chakotay:** Douglas Spain. **Antonio:** Joseph Palmas. **Ensign Wildman:** Nancy Hower. **Alien:** Richard Fancy. **Chief:** Richard Chaves. **Kolopak:** Henry Darrow. **Computer Voice:** Majel Barrett.

✦ *The origin of Chakotay's facial tattoo comes to light in this episode which also offers insight into the rainforest expedition he made with his father as a teenager, searching for the origins of their tribe – and the differences he and his father never settled. This Deep Space Nine show also delivers a few doses of humour, with the Doctor infecting himself with a flu-like virus after Kes points out that he lacks proper bedside manner.*

COLD FIRE

Week of 13 Nov. 1995, No. 126
Directed by: Cliff Bole
Teleplay by: Brannon Braga
Story by: Anthony Williams
STARDATE: Unknown

The *Voyager* crew locates a space station similar to the Caretaker's *Array* and their hopes are raised when evidence suggests they've found the Caretaker's lover, who may have the power to send *Voyager* home. **Tanis:** Gary Graham. **Ocampa:**

Norman Large. **Suspiria:** Lindsay Ridgeway.

✦ *The Caretaker's lover, by every example in the episode, does possess the ability to send* Voyager *home, but she's only interested in one thing: revenge. Manifesting herself in the guise of a little girl, she blames Janeway for the death of her lover, the Caretaker, and tries to destroy the ship. Yet Kes uses her growing telekinetic ability to drive away the Caretaker's beloved, Suspiria. Still learning to control her new power, Kes almost kills Tuvok by making his body boil. It's a terrifying scene as his Vulcan eyes bulge and bleed green Vulcan blood.*

MANEUVERS

Week of 20 Nov. 1995, No. 127
Directed by: David Livingston
Written by: Kenneth Biller
STARDATE: 49208.5
When Kazons attack *Voyager* and steal transporter technology, Chakotay (Robert Beltran) risks his life by heading alone into Kazon space to retrieve the *Federation*'s property – and confronts his former-lover-turned-traitor, Seska. **Culluh:** Anthony DeLongis. **Haron:** Terry Lester. **Kelat:** John Gegenhuber.

✦ *Martha Hackett returns as Seska, who is fast becoming a formidable opponent for the Starship Voyager, given her Maquis, Cardassian and Starfleet tactical experience. Seductive and thirsty for power, she's the dark muse whispering in the ear of the Kazon Culluh, who is equally thirsty for power but impulsive where Seska is calculating. She has a definite knack for inflicting deep and lingering pain. Chakotay recovered from the physical pain wrought by his interrogation at the brutal hands of Culluh, but is left feeling very hurt, exploited and empty at the episode close when Seska informs him that she has injected herself with some of Chakotay's DNA and is pregnant with his child. The act of retaliation transports the character to a new level of viciousness.*

RESISTANCE

Week of 27 Nov. 1995, No. 128
Directed by: Winrich Kolbe
Written by: Lisa Klink
STARDATE: Unknown
Janeway reluctantly plays daughter to a grief-stricken resistance fighter (Joel Grey) after an away mission to a class-M planet pits her against the oppressive Mokrans. **Augris:** Alan Scarfe. **Darod:** Tom Todoroff. **Caylem:** Joel Grey.

✦ *Grief is universal. Few Star Trek performers have delivered this truth with the same quiet power as Joel Grey (remembered for his 1972 Oscar-winning performance in "Cabaret"). Cast as the Alsaurian Caylem, he borders on madness in the belief that his wife and true daughter are still alive – though they were in fact killed by the Mokrans. He won't give up, just as Janeway refuses to give up the hope of getting home, and it's this common thread that enables Janeway to bond with Caylem as a father figure in one of* Voyager*'s most heart-wrenching finales. Winrich Kolbe does a fine job directing his real-life partner, Kate Mulgrew, in this sensitive Kathryn Janeway story line.*

SHOW WATCH: *Like Janeway, Ensign Ro found a father figure in ST:TNG's "Preemptive Strike." Similarly, Major Kira would find a father figure in a Bajoran farmer in DS9's "Progress."*

PROTOTYPE

Week of 15 Jan. 1996, No. 129
Directed by: Jonathan Frakes
Written by: Nicholas Corea
STARDATE: Unknown
B'Elanna Torres (Roxann Biggs-Dawson) re-activates a humanoid robot (Rick Worthy) found floating in space, only to be taken hostage by the robot, who demands she make more of his kind to fight a war with another android race. **6263:** Hugh Hodgin.

✦ *Working tirelessly to revive the android, Torres feels betrayed when the recovered robot steals her away to a ship of androids where Torres agrees to assemble and activate more androids for them in order to save* Voyager.

SHOW WATCH: *The android Lore from ST:TNG also had a lethal survival instinct, as did the android Ruk from the classic episode "What Are Little Girls Made Of?"*

ALLIANCES

Week of 22 Jan. 1995, No. 131
Directed by: Les Landau
Written by: Jeri Taylor
STARDATE: 49337.4
Janeway learns that friendship can be deceiving when *Voyager* and an alien race known as the Trabe form an alliance against the Kazons. **Culluh:** Anthony DeLongis. **Seska:** Martha Hackett. **Hogan:** Simon Billig. **Jonas:** Raphael Sbarge. **Mabus:** Charles O. Lucia. **Rettik:** Mirron E. Willis. **Tersa:** Larry Cedar.

✦ *The Trabe, we learn, are the cause of the Kazon quest to conquer. Janeway, until this point, hasn't had reason to feel sympathy for the Kazons, and finds no tears for them in the future, but for a fleeting moment she displays here a touch of compassion for the race who were once treated as slaves while under Trabe domination.*

THRESHOLD

Week of 29 Jan. 1996, No. 132
Directed by: Alexander Singer
Written by: Brannon Braga
Story by: Michael De Luca
STARDATE: 49373.4
Paris (Robert Duncan McNeill) makes history by breaking the warp 10 barrier aboard a shuttle, but his experience causes him to undergo some bizarre physical changes. **Rettik:** Mirron E. Willis. **Michael Jonas:** Raphael Sbarge. **Lizard No. 1:** Susie Rossitto. **Lizard No. 2:** Cindy Sorenson.

✦ *Paris's feelings of insecurity are amplified by the after-effects of his warp 10 flight, causing him to lash out uncharacteristically toward Janeway – whom he kidnaps and takes to warp 10 aboard a shuttle. He then super-evolves into a lizard-like being and has baby lizards with the captain, who also super-evolves.*

MELD

Week of 5 Feb. 1996, No. 133
Directed by: Cliff Bole
Written by: Michael Piller
Story by: Michael Sussman
STARDATE: Unknown
Unable to understand a crew member's seemingly senseless motive for murder, Tuvok (Tim Russ) becomes a danger to the crew when he mind-melds with the murderer and acquires his violent emotions. **Suder:** Brad Dourif. **Hogan:** Simon Billig. **Ricky:** Angela Dohrmann.

✦ *An episode for anyone who ever wondered what Vulcans may have been like before Surak helped his people purge themselves of their violent instincts about 2,000 years earlier. Beaten in his struggle* to contain the violent influence of Suder's emotions, Tuvok revels in his feelings of superiority over humans and, by his display, demonstrates the ancestral link between Vulcans and Romulans.

SHOW WATCH: *Brad Dourif returns in "Basics, Part I," the cliff-hanger that closes the season.*

DREADNOUGHT

Week of 12 Feb. 1996, No. 134
Directed by: LeVar Burton
Written by: Gary Holland and Lisa Klink
Story by: Gary Holland
STARDATE: 49447

To prevent the destruction of a planet, Torres must outwit her own programming brilliance when *Voyager* encounters a Cardassian-built missile whose programming the former Maquis resistance fighter tampered with several years earlier in the Alpha Quadrant. **Ensign Wildman:** Nancy Hower. **Lorrum:** Michael Spound. **Kellan:** Dan Kern. **Jonas:** Raphael Sbarge.

✦ *Touches of "2001: A Space Odyssey" come through in this tale of woman against machine. Torres calls the missile Dreadnought, but the missile could just as easily be called Hal as it slowly and politely speaks to Torres (supplying the missile's voice) while keeping itself from being disabled.*

DEATH WISH

Week of 19 Feb. 1996, No. 130
Directed by: James L. Conway
Written by: Michael Piller
Story by: Shawn Piller
STARDATE: 49301.2

When the *Voyager* crew discovers a member of the Q Continuum (Gerrit Graham) imprisoned inside a comet for trying to commit suicide, another Q (John de Lancie) shows up to contest the first Q's request for asylum. **Riker:** Jonathan Frakes.

✦ *Capt. Janeway has her first encounter with Q (John de Lancie), who toyed with the crews of ST:TNG and DS9, but it's not the same irrepressible character whom fans had come to know over the years. This time it's a rather serious Q who comes aboard the ship in an effort to convince the other Q that his request to die would tear apart the very fabric of the Continuum order. But by the very nature of that*

appeal, Q rediscovers something he'd lost prior to his visit: a zest for living and the knowledge that his rebellious character inspired other members of the Continuum.

STAR WATCH: *Gerrit Graham played an alien hunter in DS9's "Captive Pursuit."*

LIFESIGNS

Week of 26 Feb. 1996, No. 136
Directed by: Cliff Bole
Written by: Kenneth Biller
STARDATE: 49504.3

In an attempt to save a Vidiian (Susan Diol) from the decaying effects of the Phage, the Doctor transfers her Vidiian brain waves into a holographic image – and finds himself falling in love with her. **Jonas:** Raphael Sbarge. **Lorrum:** Michael Spound. **Seska:** Martha Hackett. **Gigolo:** Rick Gianasi.

✦ *Beauty extends beyond the surface. The Doctor learns an important lesson in love when he must return the brain waves of his Vidiian patient, Dr. Danara Pel (Susan Diol), to her disease-ridden body and discovers that, despite her disfigurement as a victim of the Phage, he loves her nonetheless. The closing moments between the Doctor and Pel, who has learned to appreciate her own inner beauty, casts the holographic medical wonder in a different light as viewers observe his growing air of chivalry.*

SHOW WATCH: *Susan Diol would return later in the season as Dr. Danara Pel in "Resolutions."*

INVESTIGATIONS

Week of 11 March 1996, No. 135
Directed by: Les Landau
Written by: Jeri Taylor
Story by: Jeff Schnaufer and Ed Bond
STARDATE: 49485.2

After Paris is kidnapped by Kazons upon joining a Talaxian convoy, Neelix discovers that Paris is

actually part of a plan to uncover the on-board spy who has been in contact with the Kazons. **Michael Jonas:** Raphael Sbarge. **Hogan:** Simon Billig. **Laxeth:** Jerry Sroka.

✦ *Paris's unruly behaviour, which has been building throughout the past several episodes, is finally explained. His open criticism of command, his blind eye to Starfleet protocol – and even the punch which he dealt Chakotay – were all under the orders of Janeway, who, by this episode, proves to be a somewhat unconventional captain. Given her unique problems in the Delta Quadrant, it's not surprising that her methods are not to be found within any Starfleet handbook.*

STAR WATCH: *Jordanian crown prince*

DEATH WISH: *IN A TERRIFIC RETURN APPEARANCE AS Q, GUEST STAR JOHN DE LANCIE RESURFACES – ON BEHALF OF THE Q CONTINUUM – TO PRESENT CAPT. KATHRYN JANEWAY (KATE MULGREW) WITH A TOUGH, MORAL DECISION.*

Abdullah Bin Hussein has a cameo as a Starfleet crew member in the opening.

DEADLOCK

Week of 18 March 1996, No. 137
Directed by: David Livingston
Written by: Brannon Braga
STARDATE: 49548.7
To escape the Vidiians, *Voyager* enters a plasma cloud only to encounter a duplicate *Voyager*, and there's just enough anti-matter to sustain only one of the two ships. **Ensign Wildman:** Nancy Hower. **Hogan:** Simon Billig. **Vidiian Surgeon:** Bob Clendenin. **Vidiian Commander:** Ray Proscia. **Vidiian No. 1:** Chris Johnston. **Vidiian No. 2:** Keythe Farley.

✦ *Ensign Kim is sucked out into space through a hull breach (a rare accident in Star Trek), Ensign Wildman's baby dies, then most of the ship systems go off-line – and that's a partial plot summary. This episode challenges many of the hard-and-fast notions about what can and cannot happen in Star Trek. The subsequent uncertainty makes for a rivetting show.*

BEST LINE: *Janeway captures the essence of Star Trek when she says: "Mr. Kim, we're Starfleet officers. Weird is part of the job."*

SHOW WATCH: *Kirk, in "Star Trek Generations" was also sucked through a hull breach on the Enterprise-B.*

INNOCENCE

Week of 8 April 1996, No. 138
Directed by: James L. Conway
Written by: Lisa Klink
Story by: Anthony Williams
STARDATE: Unknown
Surviving a shuttle crash on an unknown planet, Tuvok (Tim Russ) discovers three children who've been left to die by their people. **Alicia:** Marnie McPhail. **Tressa:** Tiffany Taubman. **Elani:** Sarah Rayne. **Corin:** Tahj D. Mowry. **Bennet:** Richard Garon.

✦ *Even as a true Vulcan – supposedly unencumbered by emotions – Tuvok cannot repress a hint of compassion for the abandoned children. In one of the episode's most unforgettable scenes, Tuvok comforts the little ones as they're huddled around a campfire at night. Then the normally aloof Vulcan lulls them to sleep with a Vulcan song. Emotions peak in the final scene where Tuvok says goodbye to one of the children he tried so hard to save.*

THE THAW

Week of 29 April 1996, No. 139
Directed by: Marvin V. Rush
Written by: Joe Menosky
Story by: Richard Gadas
STARDATE: Unknown
Torres (Roxann Biggs-Dawson) and Kim (Garrett Wang) are trapped by a maniacal clown (Michael McKean) while attempting to free alien humanoids held in a state of hibernation. **Viorsa:** Thomas Kopache. **Spectre:** Carel Struycken. **Little Woman:** Patty Maloney. **The Physician:** Tony Carlin. **The Programmer:** Shannon O'Hurley.

✦ *It's no day at the circus for the crew of Voyager. Not since Tim Curry donned clown make-up and terrorized a town in the Stephen King nail-biter "IT" has television experienced such a nightmarish clown. Michael McKean draws from the quirkiness of the Lenny Kosnowski character he played in* Laverne & Shirley, *and the resulting edge of unpredictability to the clown character introduces a dark element of dementia rarely seen in Star Trek antagonists.*

SHOW WATCH: *Carel Struycken (Lurch of the 1991 "The Addams Family" movie), who appears as Spectre, first turned up in Star Trek: The Next Generation as Mr. Homn, manservant to Lwaxana Troi in several episodes ("Haven" and "Ménage à Troi," among them).*

TUVIX

Week of 6 May 1996, No. 140
Directed by: Cliff Bole
Written by: Kenneth Biller
Story by: Andrew Price
and Mark Gaberman
STARDATE: 49655.2
A bizarre transporter malfunction causes Tuvok and Neelix to rematerialize aboard ship as a single joined being named Tuvix (Tom Wright). **Hogan:** Simon Billing. **Swinn:** Bahni Turpin.

✦ *The merging of two beings into one was inevitable. The transporter has long been an unpredictable piece of Starfleet hardware, and has certainly caused some intriguing mishaps through Star Trek's 30-year history. In the original Star Trek series, the device split Capt. James T. Kirk into two different captains ("The Enemy Within"). Then it wreaked havoc by tossing Kirk and a landing party into a mirror universe in "Mirror, Mirror." The list of*

malfunctions has grown throughout The Next Generation *and* Deep Space Nine. *It was only a matter of time before the transporter threw a new malfunction into the works, and this one is a stand-out, with the resulting character, Tuvix – a curious blend of the stoic Tuvok and the oddly charming Neelix – being one of the most engaging creations of the second season. (The show was shot under the working title "Symbiogenesis.")*

RESOLUTIONS

Week of 13 May 1996, No. 141
Directed by: Alexander Singer
Written by: Jeff Taylor
STARDATE: 49690.1
After contracting a deadly virus, Capt. Janeway and Chakotay (Robert Beltran) leave *Voyager* to take refuge on a planet which may shield them from the effects of their fatal disease. **Dr. Danara Pel:** Susan Diol. **Hogan:** Simon Billig.

✦ *The constraints of Starfleet protocol are cast aside when Capt. Janeway and Chakotay, alone and seemingly destined to die, begin to explore the full scope of their relationship.*

SHOW WATCH: *Similarly, Picard and Dr. Beverly Crusher explored long-simmering feelings when caught alone on a hostile planet in ST:TNG's "Attached."*

BASICS, PART I

Week of 20 May 1996, No. 142
Directed by: Winrich Kolbe
Written by: Michael Piller
STARDATE: Unknown
A distress signal from a Kazon shuttle brings the disturbing news that Seska (Martha Hackett) has been killed at the hands of Culluh (Anthony DeLongis), which prompts Chakotay (Robert Beltran) to embark on a mission to rescue his newborn son. Part one of two. **Suder:** Brad Dourif. **Teirna:** John Gegenhuber. **Kolopak:** Henry Darrow. **Seska:** Martha Hackett.

✦ *Janeway's hope of ever getting home appears permanently lost when the Kazons – relentless throughout the entire season in their quest to capture Voyager – finally claim victory. Falling into a trap set by Seska, Voyager's crew members are marooned on a hostile planet where, as the title suggests, it's back to basics in order to survive – with their starship now carrying the Kazon banner.* ✧

Flashback

This is where the voyage began: the turbulent, creative, antic-filled early days of *Star Trek*, driven by Gene Roddenberry's vision – a dream that led to four TV series and eight movies. And the voyage has no end in sight. As they say in television: To Be Continued.

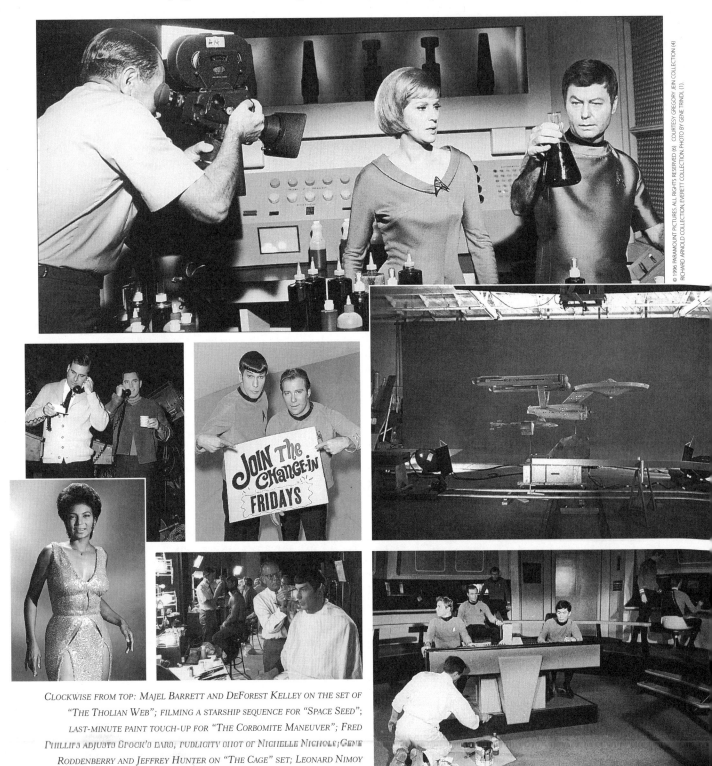

CLOCKWISE FROM TOP: MAJEL BARRETT AND DEFOREST KELLEY ON THE SET OF "THE THOLIAN WEB"; FILMING A STARSHIP SEQUENCE FOR "SPACE SEED"; LAST-MINUTE PAINT TOUCH-UP FOR "THE CORBOMITE MANEUVER"; FRED PHILLIPS ADJUSTS SPOCK'S EARS, PUBLICITY SHOT OF NICHELLE NICHOLS, GENE RODDENBERRY AND JEFFREY HUNTER ON "THE CAGE" SET; LEONARD NIMOY AND WILLIAM SHATNER PROMOTING THE NEW FRIDAY-NIGHT TIME SLOT IN 1967